C000133604

MAPPING TERRORISM RESEARCH

Although an enormous volume of research on terrorism has been undertaken before and especially after 9/11, surprisingly few books have been published taking an inventory as to the state-of-the-art of knowledge in the field.

This book provides an overall assessment of research achievements and gaps in scholarly efforts towards understanding terrorism as a complex behavioural and social phenomenon. It aims to indentify strengths and weaknesses in scholarly output and thereby define an intellectual basis for the next wave of research.

Magnus Ranstorp has adopted a thematic approach, disaggregating specific approaches with a critique as to their individual and collective contribution. Ultimately, this book provides a pathway for future research agendas into terrorism and counterterrorism. This is further enhanced by the provision of a unique list containing 490 indentified research topics developed by the United Nations Terrorism Prevention Branch.

Written by contributors from the older and younger cutting-edge research community, this volume constitutes essential reading for students of terrorism and international security, as well as counterterrorism professionals.

Magnus Ranstorp is the Research Director of the Centre for Asymmetric Threat Studies at the Swedish National Defence College, directing a large project on Strategic Terrorist Threats to Europe. He is internationally recognised as a leading expert on Hizballah, Hamas, al-Qaeda and other militant Islamic movements. In 2003 he testified before the 9/11 Commission. He is the author of *Hizb's Allah in Lebanon: The Politics of the Western Hostage Crisis* (1996), and numerous journal articles.

CASS SERIES: POLITICAL VIOLENCE
Series Editors: Paul Wilkinson and David Rapoport

TERRORISM VERSUS DEMOCRACY: THE LIBERAL STATE
RESPONSE
Paul Wilkinson

AVIATION TERRORISM AND SECURITY
Paul Wilkinson and Brian M. Jenkins (eds)

COUNTER-TERRORIST LAW AND EMERGENCY POWERS IN THE
UNITED KINGDOM, 1922–2000
Laura K. Donohue

THE DEMOCRATIC EXPERIENCE AND POLITICAL VIOLENCE
David C. Rapoport and Leonard Weinberg (eds)

INSIDE TERRORIST ORGANIZATIONS
David C. Rapoport (ed.)

THE FUTURE OF TERRORISM
Max Taylor and John Horgan (eds)

THE IRA, 1968–2000: AN ANALYSIS OF A SECRET ARMY
J. Bowyer Bell

MILLENNIAL VIOLENCE: PAST, PRESENT AND FUTURE
Jeffrey Kaplan (ed.)

RIGHT-WING EXTREMISM IN THE TWENTY-FIRST CENTURY
Peter H. Merkl and Leonard Weinberg (eds)

TERRORISM TODAY
Christopher C. Harmon

THE PSYCHOLOGY OF TERRORISM
John Horgon

RESEARCH ON TERRORISM: TRENDS, ACHIEVEMENTS AND
FAILURES
Andrew Silke (ed.)

A WAR OF WORDS: POLITICAL VIOLENCE AND PUBLIC
DEBATE IN ISRAEL
Gerald Cromer

ROOT CAUSES OF SUICIDE TERRORISM: THE GLOBALIZATION
OF MARTYRDOM
Ami Pedahzur (ed.)

TERRORISM VERSUS DEMORCRACY: THE LIBERAL STATE
RESPONSE, 2ND EDITION
Paul Wilkinson

COUNTERING TERRORISM AND WMD: CREATING A GLOBAL
COUNTER-TERRORISM NETWORK
Peter Katona, Michael Intriligator and John Sullivan (eds)

MAPPING TERRORISM RESEARCH: STATE OF THE ART, GAPS
AND FUTURE DIRECTION
Magnus Ranstorp (ed.)

MAPPING TERRORISM RESEARCH

State of the art, gaps and future direction

Edited by Magnus Ranstorp

Routledge
Taylor & Francis Group

LONDON AND NEW YORK

First published 2007
by Routledge
2 Park Square, Milton Park, Abingdon, Oxon, OX14 4RN

Simultaneously published in the USA and Canada
by Routledge
270 Madison Ave, New York NY 10016

*Routledge is an imprint of the Taylor & Francis Group,
an informa business*

Transferred to Digital Printing 2007

© 2007 Magnus Ranstorp

Typeset in Times New Roman by Keyword Group, Wallington

British Library Cataloguing in Publication Data
A catalogue record for this book is available from the British Library

Library of Congress Cataloging in Publication Data
Mapping terrorism research: state of the art, gaps and future
direction/edited by Magnus Ranstorp.
p.cm – (Political violence)
Includes bibliographical references and index.
1. Terrorism–Research. I. Ranstorp, Magnus. II. Series.
HV6431.M3625 2006
363.325072–dc22   2006-011250

ISBN10: 0-415-39991-2 (hbk)
ISBN10: 0-415-45778-5 (pbk)
ISBN10: 0-203-96900-6 (ebk)

ISBN13: 978-0-415-39991-3 (hbk)
ISBN13: 978-0-415-45778-1 (pbk)
ISBN13: 978-0-203-96900-7 (ebk)

CONTENTS

CONTENTS

NOTES ON THE EDITOR AND THE CONTRIBUTORS

About the Editor

Dr Magnus Ranstorp is Research Director of the Centre for Asymmetric Threat Studies at the Swedish National Defence College, directing a large funded project on Strategic Terrorist Threats to Europe which focuses on both radicalisation and recruitment of salafist–jihadist terrorists across Europe and the critical issue of the convergence between CBRN and terrorism. Previously he was Director of the Centre for the Study of Terrorism and Political Violence at the University of St Andrews, Scotland. He is the author of 'Hizballah in Lebanon' and other numerous articles and monographs on terrorism and counterterrorism. He is on the International Editorial Advisory Board of the academic journal *Studies in Conflict and Terrorism.*

He is internationally recognised as a leading expert on Hizballah, Hamas, al-Qaeda and other militant Islamic movements. He has conducted extensive fieldwork around the world, interviewing hundreds of terrorists as well as members of militant Islamic movements. His work on the behaviour of the Hizballah movement was recognized by Israeli media in March 2000 as among the contributing factors leading to the decision by the Israeli government to withdraw from southern Lebanon.

Dr Ranstorp has briefed many senior government and security officials from around the world and lectures regularly to most major universities, think tanks and intergovernmental organisations. In 2003, he was invited to testify before the 9/11 Commission at its first hearing. He was also a member of an Advisory Panel on Terrorism in Europe advising the EU counterterrorism coordinator. In 2005, he contributed to the George C. Marshall Center directed project on Ideological War on Terror: Synthesizing Strategies Worldwide (a project funded by the Office of the Secretary of Defense). In 2006 Dr Ranstorp was invited to join the European Commission Expert Group on Violent Radicalisation, a formal advisory body on all matters relating to radicalisation and recruitment of extremists within the EU.

About the contributors

Jeffrey B. Cozzens is a specialist in militant Islamism with AMTI's Intelligence and Terrorism Analysis Group and Research Associate at the Centre for the Study of Terrorism and Political Violence (CSTPV), University of St Andrews (Scotland). A PhD candidate at St Andrews, his research focuses on the nexus of al-Qaeda's ideology and warfare. As CSTPV Research Associate, Jeff has addressed various American and European audiences on trends in Islamist militancy and has contributed to several publications, including Magnus Ranstorp's 2003 statement to the National Commission on Terrorist Attacks upon the United States. In addition to his analytical work for AMTI, Jeff was the primary terrorism analyst for the US, Department of Homeland Security's VNN TV during the 2005 TOPOFF exercise. His recent publications include 'Islamist groups develop new recruiting strategies' (*Jane's Intelligence Review*, February 2005) and a chapter in a forthcoming book *Mapping Terrorism Research* (ed Ranstorp and Nicander), entitled 'Approaching al-Qaida's warfare: function, culture and grand strategy'. Prior to his work at St Andrews and AMTI, Jeff was employed by the US, Department of State, Office of Counterterrorism (S/CT). Jeff holds bachelor's degrees in political science (Wheaton College, Illionis) and religious studies (Michigan State University) and received the Master of Literature degree in international security studies from the University of St Andrews in 2003.

Professor Ronald Crelinsten is a Senior Research Associate at the Center for Global Studies at the University of Victoria, Canada. He has been studying the problem of combating terrorism in liberal democracies for thirty years. His research interests include terrorism and counterterrorism, global security, gross human rights violations, the mass media, policy-making in a multicentric world, and the challenges of global governance, particularly in the area of security. He is one of the founding members of *Terrorism and Political Violence* (Taylor & Francis), the leading academic journal on terrorism studies. His publications include *The Politics of Pain: Torturers and Their Masters* (Westview Press, 1995), *Western Responses to Terrorism* (Frank Cass, 1993), *Hostage-Taking* (Lexington Books, 1979) and *Terrorism and Criminal Justice* (Lexington Books, 1978). His current project is entitled 'The Terrorism–Counterterrorism Nexus: Global Governance in an Age of Global Terror'.

Dr Isabelle Duyvesteyn is a lecturer and researcher at the History of International Relations Department at the Institute of History, Utrecht University in the Netherlands. Her research interests include the study of terrorism and counterterrorism, the nature of war and peace in the developing world, and irregular warfare and strategy. Her work has been published in several journals including, among others, *Civil Wars, Security Studies* and *Studies in Conflict and Terrorism*. She is also the co-editor of *Rethinking the Nature of War* (Frank Cass, 2005) and *Understanding Victory and Defeat in Contemporary War* (Frank Cass, forthcoming).

Dr Nancy K. Hayden is a Senior Member of the Advanced Concepts Group at Sandia National Laboratories in Albuquerque, New Mexico.

Dr Karin von Hippel is the Co-Director of the Post-Conflict Reconstruction Project at the Center for Strategic and International Studies (CSIS) in Washington, DC. Previously she was a Senior Research Fellow at the Centre for Defence Studies, King's College London, and spent several years working for the United Nations and the European Union in Somalia and Kosovo. In 2004 and 2005 she participated in two major studies for the UN – one on the UN Integrated Missions and the second on the UN humanitarian system. Also in 2004, she was part of a small team investigating the development potential of Somali remittances, funded by USAID. In 2002, she advised the OECD on what co-operation on development can do to get at the root causes of terrorism. Since then, she has participated in numerous conferences and working groups on the subject in Africa, Europe and North America. She also directed a project on European counterterrorist reforms, funded by the MacArthur Foundation, edited the volume *Europe Confronts Terrorism* (Palgrave Macmillan, 2005), and was a member of Project Unicorn, a counterterrorism police advisory panel in London. Additional publications include *Democracy by Force* (Cambridge, 2000), which was shortlisted for the Westminster Medal in Military History. She received her Ph,D, in International Relations from the London School of Economics, her MSt from Oxford, and her BA from Yale University.

Dr John Horgan joined the School of International Relations as a Lecturer in 2005, and is also Senior Research Fellow at the Centre for the Study of Terrorism and Political Violence. Prior to his appointment at St Andrews he was Lecturer in Forensic Psychology at the Department of Applied Psychology, University College, Cork, from where he received his PhD in 2000. A Chartered Psychologist, his primary area of research relates to socio-political and psychological aspects of political violence, with a particular focus on understanding radicalisation into terrorism. Some of his previous research has examined political violence in Ireland and the relationship between Irish Republican terrorism and organised crime, especially in the context of the group and organisational dynamics of terrorist movements. He has also conducted extensive research on individual disengagement from terrorism. Dr Horgan's work is widely published: he has authored over two dozen academic articles and book chapters, and his books include *The Future of Terrorism* (2000, co-edited with Max Taylor) and *The Psychology of Terrorism* (2005). He is a member of the Editorial Board of *Terrorism and Political Violence* and is regularly invited to speak to government, police, military, academic and public audiences around the world.

Albert J. Jongman (1955) majored in Western sociology at the University of Groningen in 1981. During his studies he gained practical experience as a research assistant at the Stockholm International Peace Research Institute (SIPRI) in Sweden. From 1982 to 1987 he worked as a researcher at the Polemological Institute of the University of Groningen, where he dealt with several research topics including the quantitative study of war, political violence, armament and disarmament issues and human rights. In 1987 he moved to the University of Leiden where he acted as data manager of the Project on Interdisciplinary Research on the Root Causes of Gross Human Rights Violations (PIOOM). He also worked on several research projects, including the World Conflict and Human Rights Map, 20th Century Genocides, and Monitoring Human Rights Violations. In 2002 he moved from academia to government. Since early 2002 he has worked as a senior terrorism analyst for the Dutch Ministry of Defence. His 'World Directory of Terrorist and other Organizations associated with Guerrilla Warfare, Political Violence and Protest was included in the award-winning *Political Terrorism. A New Guide to Actors, Authors, Concepts, Data Bases, Theories, and Literature* (2nd edition, 1988) edited by Alex P. Schmid and published by North-Holland. During the 1990s he regularly contributed to the Dutch Yearbook on Peace and Security.

Dr Neal A. Pollard is Vice President of Hicks & Associates, Inc., He is also General Counsel and Board Director of the Terrorism Research Center, a corporation he co-founded in 1996. He is Adjunct Professor at Georgetown University, where he teaches undergraduate and graduate courses on science and technology policy, counterterrorism planning and intelligence reform for three faculties: the Edmund A. Walsh School of Foreign Service, the Georgetown School of Medicine Department of Microbiology and Immunology, and the Georgetown Public Policy Institute. He holds degrees in mathematics and political science, a Master of Letters from the University of St Andrews, Scotland, and a Juris Doctor *cum laude* from the Georgetown University Law Center. He is an International Affairs Fellow of the Council on Foreign Relations.

Professor Martin Rudner is a Professor at the Norman Paterson School of International Affairs, Carleton University, Ottawa, and founding Director of the Canadian Centre of Intelligence and Security Studies at Carleton. Professor Rudner was born in Montreal, Quebec, and was educated at McGill University, the University of Oxford and Hebrew University of Jerusalem, where he received his doctorate. He has lived and worked at universities in the United Kingdom, Israel, Malaysia, Singapore and Australia. He is the author of over seventy books and scholarly articles dealing with international affairs, Southeast Asia, and Intelligence and Security studies. His recent publications include 'Hunters and Gatherers: The Intelligence Coalition against Islamic Terrorism', *International Journal of Intelligence and Counterintelligence* (2004); and 'Challenge and Response: Canada's Intelligence Community in the War on Terrorism', *Canadian Foreign Policy* (2004). He is a frequent commentator on Canadian and international media. Martin is a past President of the Canadian Association for Security and Intelligence Studies and a member of the Board of Directors of Ovarian Cancer Canada.

Dr Andrew Silke has a background in forensic psychology and criminology and has worked both in academia and for government. His most recent books are *Terrorists, Victims and Society: Psychological Perspectives on Terrorism and its Consequences* (Wiley, 2003) and *Research on Terrorism: Trends, Achievements* *and Failures* (Frank Cass, 2004). He is the author of over 70 articles and papers on subjects relating to terrorism and has presented numerous talks and given invited lectures on the topic at conferences across the world. His advice has been sought by several governments, as well as by many scientific societies such as the Royal Society in the UK and the National Academies in the USA He is an Honorary Senior Research Associate of the Centre for the Study of Terrorism and Political Violence at the University of St Andrews and is a Fellow of the University of Leicester. His work has taken him to Northern Ireland, the Middle East and Latin America. He is a member of the International Association for Counter-terrorism and Security Professionals and he serves on the United Nations roster of terrorism experts. He is currently the Field Leader for Criminology at the University of East London.

Dr Joshua Sinai is working at The Analysis Corporation (TAC) on terrorism and counterterrorism issues. Previously he was Program Manager for Terrorism and Counter-Terrorism Studies at Logos Technologies in Arlington, Virginia. Prior to joining Logos in mid-August 2005, Dr Sinai worked at ANSER (Analytical Services), which had seconded him, from November 2003 to April 2005, to function as a government official in the Science & Technology Directorate, Department of Homeland Security (DHS), where he managed a project on the social and behavioural components of terrorism and its impact on society. As part of his duties he co-chaired an interagency working group, under the White House Office of Science & Technology Policy, on how the social, behavioural and economic sciences can contribute to counterterrorism, which produced a report on this subject in April 2005. He also contributed to the formulation of the announcement for proposals to create the DHS Center on Terrorism Studies and was part of the team that evaluated the proposals. Dr Sinai's publications include chapters in edited academic volumes and national security journals, and his column on Terrorism Books appears regularly in the *Washington Times*' book review section. He is also a frequent presenter at academic conferences on terrorism.

Michael Taarnby is a Research Fellow in the Department of Globalisation and Governance at the Danish Institute of International Studies (DIIS) in Copenhagen, Denmark. Having a Master's degree in Social Anthropology and Political Science from Aarhus University, he specialises at DIIS in research into terrorist radicalisation and recruitment. His most recent project relates to the development of assessment tools for targeted development aid related to counterterrorism activities. Previously he authored several reports for the Danish Ministry of Justice, the most recent being *Recruitment of Islamist Terrorists in Europe: Trends and Perspectives* (2005).

Paul Wilkinson is Professor of International Relations and Chairman of the Advisory Board of the Centre for the Study of Terrorism and Political Violence (CSTPV) at the University of St Andrews. Prior to his appointment at St Andrews in 1989 he was Professor of International Relations, University of Aberdeen, 1979–1989. He was visiting Fellow at Trinity Hall, Cambridge in 1979 as well as in 1998 and is Honorary Fellow of the University of Wales, Swansea.

His publications include *Political Terrorism* (1974); *Terrorism and the Liberal State* (1977/1986); *The New Fascists* (1981/1983); *Contemporary Research on Terrorism* (as co-editor, 1987); *Aviation Terrorism and Security* (as co-editor, 1999); and *Terrorism versus Democracy: The Liberal State Response* (2001). His latest publication, co-authored with Joseph S. Nye, Jr, and Yukio Satoh, is *Addressing the New International Terrorism; Prevention, Intervention and Multilateral Co-operation, a report to the Trilateral Commission* (May 2003). He is co-editor of the academic journal *Terrorism and Political Violence*, and is currently director of a research project, funded by the ESRC, on the domestic management of terrorist attacks in the UK. He served as Adviser to Lord Lloyd of Berwick's Inquiry into Legislation against Terrorism, and authored Volume. two, the*Research Report for the Inquiry* (1996).

1

INTRODUCTION: MAPPING TERRORISM RESEARCH

Challenges and priorities

Magnus Ranstorp

One of the chief practical obstacles to the development of social inquiry is the existing division of social phenomena into a number of compartmentalised and supposedly independent non-interacting fields.[1]

Are we academic nationalists? We have been trained since graduate school to defend our turf against assaults from Deans, dilettantes, and adjacent disciplines. We organize our journals, scholarly organizations, and university departments within precisely demarcated boundaries. We gesture vaguely in the direction of interdisciplinary cooperation, rather in the way sovereign states put in polite appearances at the United Nations; reality, however, falls short of what we routinely promised. And we have been known, from time to time, to construct the intellectual equivalent of fortified trenches from which we fire artillery back and forth, dodging shrapnel even as we sink ever deeply into mutual incomprehension.[2]

On reflection, my own involvement in the terrorism studies field spans almost twenty years when terrorism seemed more predictable, the motivations more understandable and the logic of violence more clear and restrained. Three separate, and all to a degree inseparable, personal events etched an inedible impression in my early academic career. Collectively they also serve to reveal the broader complex character of terrorism as a subject or field of inquiry. Firstly, attendance at a 1987 Wilton Park conference on the symbiosis between the media and terrorism (coming in the wake of the infamous TWA 847 affair) sharply exposed the complexities of the dilemmas posed by the role media played in exacerbating the effects of terrorism. In particular, it became evident that media coverage of terrorism greatly complicated and compressed the time for decision-makers to respond to often choreographed spectacles. The role of the media as the oxygen of terrorism would take on a new added meaning, urgency and complexity with globalisation and the instruments of cyberspace. From the 9/11 planes flying into the twin towers to beheadings in Iraq, terrorist events reverberate in seconds around the globe, uniting extremists and shocking public audiences. These events are impressively choreographed and designed to greatly amplify the effect of the violence. The constantly mutating networks and cells that transformed al-Qaeda into a global 'salafist-jihadist' movement thrive in this globalisation-affected media milieu. It allows it, like a 'ghost', to be everywhere but physically nowhere and provides it with a self-generating momentum to replicate, replenish losses and shift direction globally at a moment's notice.[3] It defies simplistic or one-dimensional solutions. Countering a constantly mutating ideology attached to the dark underside of globalisation will probably remain among the most illusive challenges in the next century. For the West, this task is complicated by the role of different cultural norms and the inner logic of tribalism governing behaviour and outlook.[4] In many ways, argues David Ronfeldt, al-Qaeda and its affiliates represent a global tribe waging segmental warfare.[5]

Secondly, participation in the West European–Soviet Dialogue on Countering Terrorism with senior counterterrorism officials in meetings held in Moscow, St Andrews and Paris in 1990 revealed urgency in that the changing complexity of terrorism needed new partnerships and multilateral solutions. These unique meetings during the last days of the Cold War generated policy advice that was distributed to the penultimate leaderships in Moscow, London, Paris and Bonn and ominously warned of the growing 'Lebanonisation' of the Balkan conflict. Shortly after these meetings, the Balkans descended into a self-destructive spiral of ethnic and religious violence. This conflict fault line joined Afghanistan as a training ground for a generation of foreign jihadists which would later be interchangeable with those conflicts in Kashmir and Chechnya where Muslims were 'besieged'. Those of us interested in this dimension were early introduced to the ideological tracts of Abdallah Azzam (Bin-Laden's ideologue) whose content urged the Muslim youths everywhere to literally 'Join the caravan' (of martyrs) and act in defence of Muslim lands. These ideological tracts were detected within the Bosnian civil war among the foreign fighters. No one could fathom that this embryo would later develop into the multi-headed hydra that plague and dominate the contemporary international security agenda and discourse. It also powerfully demonstrated the enduring lesson to always expect the unexpected.[6]

A third event that changed my outlook occurred in the autumn of 1990 when a Provisional Irish Republican Army (PIRA) sleeper unit infiltrated an international terrorism conference organised by my centre at the Royal Overseas League in the heart of London. Amidst tight security procedures by New Scotland Yard's Anti-Terrorism Branch, the PIRA sleeper operative managed to conceal, underneath the speaker's podium, 2 lb of Semtex plastic explosives that accidentally but fortuitously was discovered by a sound technician. For those of us present at this event and who narrowly averted tragedy (the meeting went ahead without the British Defence Minister and without drama the following day) it provided a stark reminder that the research arena itself concerned real people and real events and was not without a degree of personal risk. The exact level of risk was naturally commensurate for those of us who substituted the comforts of the ivory tower for field interviews with an assortment of guerrilla leaders and terrorists in hostile and complex conflict environments. The pioneering spirit of the academic-adventurer Gerard Chaliand,[7] who spent time with the Algerian FLN, Palestinian factions in Amman before Black September, the North Vietnamese Viet Cong and the Kurdish PKK, paved the way how to really push the envelope in our understanding of guerrilla and terrorist movements worldwide (and innovatively parting with culinary expertise gathered during the same process).[8] Of course, the dilemma of working in this area is also that the researcher may eventually attract adverse attention from the terrorists themselves, as I most recently discovered when receiving a personal letter from the infamous 1974 Alphabet bomber. The terrorism academic speciality provided an exotic research environment but also unique challenges in data collection as the clandestine and underground existence of the subject studied remained for many inaccessibly remote and dangerous.

Prior to 9/11, the size of the academic community interested and committed to building a sustained body of knowledge remained resiliently very small but academically diverse. It attracted a handful of political scientists, sociologists and military strategic experts. Literally overnight with 9/11 the field of terrorism studies catapulted from the relative periphery into the absolute vortex of academic interest and policy concern worldwide. Retrained academic cold warriors and war correspondents competed to translate anything on al-Qaeda into a commercial success often without regard for quality, sources or other sound academic praxis. Within the United States, journalists entered the academic world without formal qualifications and good academics left for government vacancies or were inserted into the intelligence architectures in new burgeoning bureaucracies that were trying to readjust to the post-al-Qaeda world. More traditionally oriented academics struggled to readjust the explanatory power of international relations theory to the dominance and challenge of sub-state actors.[9] Some like John Gray[10], Keohane[11] and Richmond[12], partially succeeded while many other theory specialists are still lost in the wilderness of a hostile, alien and new intellectual non-state-centric environment.

Among the most remarkable features amidst the explosion of academic interest in terrorism and political violence is the relative absence of any reflective state-of-the-art reviews of what the field has achieved, identification of where major gaps and weaknesses in research are, and recommendations for future areas of research. A noteworthy exception is David Leheny, who constructively recommended that symbolism, strategic signalling and social movement theory could offer a useful vehicle to more closely connect the sphere of international relations scholarship with terrorism studies.[13] This extremely valuable contribution underscored that these fields rarely connect and exist largely independently from each other. However, many critics of terrorism studies seem largely ignorant that two specialised and refereed academic journals, *Terrorism & Political Violence* and *Studies in Conflict and Terrorism*, exist and have made sustained research contributions for almost two decades.

The critical processes of taking stock of the field are an ambitious and challenging undertaking. It is necessary to build new avenues of knowledge and identify new directions in research which are basic and usually sound praxis within most academic disciplines. However, the terrorism studies field has largely failed in this respect from within the old and relatively new academic research communities. Remarkably few academic analyses are devoted to critiquing levels of where research and knowledge are at on the many different levels.

There are always a few exceptions to this norm. No comparable monographs or books are devoted to the merits of research or provide a cogent future pathway except for the pioneering efforts authored by Alex Schmidt[14], Peter Merkl[15] and Paul Wilkinson[16] in the mid- to late 1980s and more recently by Andrew Silke, specifically addressing research achievements and merits of various social science methodologies.[17] The lacunae in developing a basic inventory or more advanced critiques of research and identification of future avenues remain one of the most critically missing ingredients which undermine the broader credibility of the field. This process of challenging assumptions, critiquing arguments and reflecting on research occurs normally in many different social science disciplines. It is normal and sound social scientific practice to reflect on research achievements as a base for the next wave of research and its likely direction. Unquestionably, few established scholars would deny that this is now an urgent necessity.

This paucity of critiques of terrorism studies literature is worryingly evident in the limited number of relevant articles focusing on methodology or other research methods. Less than a dozen serious scholarly articles are exclusively devoted to critiquing the terrorism studies field – not just in the last few years following 9/11 but cumulatively over the last thirty years. Of course, the evolution of knowledge within the field is accumulated through progressive results based on past analyses. However, few actually address directly the methodological aspects. The problem with the research agenda, according to terrorism doyen Martha Crenshaw, is that the field is probably still plagued by the enduring challenges posed by a lack of definition (what terrorism constitutes), the inability to build a cohesive integrated and cumulative theory (built around larger data-sets and over longer time periods) and 'the event-driven character of much research.'[18] It is, therefore, an essential and valuable task to periodically take inventory of the aggregate achievements made alongside any weaknesses and to identify a set of priorities for future direction of research. In a nutshell, it is this task that this edited book is about: to contribute to the larger and necessarily continuous mapping process of terrorism research in order to assess what contributions have been made from different social and behavioural disciplines and from different themes, research questions and methodologies. More importantly, this research collection brings together different strands of academic perspectives, cross-fertilising veteran insights with the emerging new academic talents within so-called 'terrorism studies'. It is not meant to be considered a definitive guide to terrorism research but rather is designed, hopefully, to generate new questions across specific thematic areas. It is generally meant to stimulate interest in and provide guidance for those serious new and old academics who are interested in pushing the intellectual boundaries of the field and in questioning the methodologies and assumptions underpinning a field in order to generate new knowledge and research agendas.

Understanding the research landscape and the research challenge

Over the last thirty-odd years, the field of terrorism studies has been largely confined to a small nucleus of scholars that were largely ensconced in the ivory tower. A few of these academics had a sustained research engagement; some with periodic field experience from conflict zones; some with direct contact with underground movements and access to the clandestine inner sanctum of terrorists whom they interviewed in captivity or freedom. Other academic trailblazers had very real practical on-the-ground counterterrorism or counterinsurgency experience to draw from, most notably an effort spearheaded by Maj.Gen. Richard Clutterbuck.[19] However diverse and atomized in scope, all these individual efforts inadvertently contributed to the process of building a collective body of knowledge of terrorism as a complex and interdisciplinary social and behavioural phenomenon. These parallel academic efforts were undertaken largely by a small core group of scholars defiantly swimming against the mainstream current (or prevailing wisdom) within their respective scholarly disciplines. Schmidt and Jongman identified in 1988 only 32 leading main terrorism researchers.[20]

This pioneering core research was complemented by a sea of one-time contributions reacting spasmodically to the evolution of terrorism, the specificity of problems or cases, changing actors and methods as well as its impact on statecraft and the international system. Edna O.F. Reid reveals through a comprehensive bibliometric study that 1166 publications on terrorism were produced and identified for the period 1960–1990.[21] However, Reid showed also that the specific growth of terrorism as a research speciality had not evolved in a steady trajectory but instead had gone through four different periods of expansion and contraction. The real 'take-off' stage occurred between 1970 and 1978 and was reflective of the contemporary waves of terrorism and its commensurate media coverage. It did, however, decline between 1986 and 1990 in terms of volume of publications, number of involved academics and collaboration. This decline across the board could be explained by the lack of financial support for research, a reduction in volume of terrorism incidents, or maybe even a reflection of the general demotion of terrorism as a major foreign policy or international security concern. Reid's inventory did highlight that the terrorism research community remained a small and closed group as only 24 scholars were classified as high and moderate producers, having contributed during this collective period at least ten to 34 or more articles or books. This key productive pool of scholars played a critical role in expanding interdisciplinary engagement and creating a close-knit network of academics.[22] These key scholars were instrumental in the establishment and growth of the speciality of the field and in the development of the contours of the specific conceptual and methodological boundaries.

The downside to this dominance was that it reflected the primary interests of a few key knowledge-producing academics. Reid has correctly identified a few specific problems with these so-called 'invisible colleges of terrorism researchers'. A scarcity of primary data on terrorism meant a large over-reliance on media coverage of terrorism and other forms of political violence as primary sources. This does not need to be necessarily a problematic issue dealing with largely incident-driven research. However, many have questioned the reliability of media coverage and in particularly the tendency to reproduce and collate from diverse sources at times in a duplicating and regenerative fashion, making the identification of original sources very difficult. Conflicting reports about actual events themselves were difficult to resolve and extremely time-consuming to find and crosscheck (for those of us who actually remember carrying out research before the computer era with its data bases and other knowledge management systems). This criticism does not extend to the entirety of the academic community, who used a mixture of types of sources including invaluable terrorist ideological tracts or manifestos and unique interviews with terrorist prisoners. Nor did this criticism reflect the frequent and often valuable role played by the media by providing insight into clandestine and underground groups, individuals and environments. It did, however, contribute to circular reporting and recycling of the same media material in different formats and contexts. As such, the exact source of the information is critical to originate in order to determine its veracity and credibility. In today's world there is an ocean of signals and information about terrorism globally. It has, however, not changed the basic problem. As highlighted in Andrew Silke's exhaustive survey of research methodologies, most terrorism research in the pre-9/11 period relied exclusively on secondary sources, some with questionable credibility and precision.[23]

A related methodological problem, pointed out by Reid, Gordon as well as Schmidt and Jongman, was the strong tendency of researchers to create an often closed and circular research system as they relied on each other's work, government publications and media reporting, functioning in a constantly reinforcing feedback loop.[24] This relatively closed system, argued Reid, 'indicates a static environment; the same hypotheses, definitions and theories continued to be analysed, assimilated, published, cited, and eventually retrieved.'[25] A problematic issue illustrative of this criticism was the often publicly repeated assumptions or theories that had become conventional wisdom within the field without ever being based on any serious or tested quantitative or qualitative field research or survey results. Relatively meaningless generalisations and statements, as exemplified by Brian Jenkins' 'terrorists like a lot of people watching rather than a lot of people dead', do underscore the strong communicative element in terrorist violence and may demonstrate a trend in its broadest sense. It is, however, difficult to extract any real scientific meaning. As highlighted by Martha Crenshaw, 'the study of terrorism, which is widely recognized as theoretically impoverished, stands to gain in theoretical scope, precision, and cumulativeness of findings.'[26]

Others have appreciated the necessity to understand terrorism in its specific context as 'it erupts and flourishes in different places at different times due to an often idiosyncratic combination of factors.'[27] As a rule, however, this context-specificity became an almost overlooked dimension as terrorism was too often described generically and with a 'one-size-fits-all' formula. It has also been pointed out that the small size of the academic community largely devoting itself to terrorism studies stymied the receptivity for challenging conventional wisdom or assumptions and that efforts to explore new ideas and hypotheses were largely absorbed within existing established paradigms. In addition, there is only a small fraction of this community that innovatively explores the merits and possibilities of moving beyond the existing literature into other social science disciplines to explore the merits of different approaches, concepts and paradigms in unlocking new and truly innovative dimensions. How is it possible to ignore cultural anthropology and sociology in understanding today's salafist-jihadist challenge?

A major difficulty for the terrorism studies field is that as a complex social and behavioural phenomenon 'it is characterised by contradictory assumptions' underpinning different levels or units of analysis and across the various disciplines within social sciences. As Schorkopf aptly observed, terrorism studies 'cannot be considered a distinct academic discipline'[28] and are situated awkwardly between the often clashing ontologies and epistemologies used by different subjects and disciplines. Moreover, this complexity is further compounded by the fact that terrorism continues to be a deeply contested concept requiring a subjective evaluation. The decades of countless UN political debates without consensus and sharp disagreement, even within the academic community, have failed to yield a universally agreed definition of terrorism. Most illustrative of this difficulty has been Schmidt and Jongman's collation of 109 different definitions that isolated common specific characteristics. Bruce Hoffman and others have underscored terrorism as a specific methodology with identifiable characteristics directed primarily at inflicting or threatening to inflict violence against an innocent civilian population. While it led Walter Laquer to criticise the usefulness of trying to resolve the definitional dilemma, Alex Schmidt put it succinctly: 'terrorism is the peacetime equivalent of a war crime.'[29]

The absence of any universal agreement on the concept of terrorism has its obvious academic consequences in developing and applying appropriate research methods at different levels of analysis. A further contested issue is whether the terrorism studies field should solely concern terrorism from below (by sub-state actors) or above.[30] Some criticise the focus on terrorism from below rather than above. To some extent this has resulted in the failure to comprehensively understand a range of issues related to the relationship between terrorism from above and below. At the heart of this issue is the understanding of the efficacy of terrorism and the processes as well as the consequences of counterterrorism policies. It is also the case that the diverse categorisation of different types

7

of terrorism as a methodology by diverse actors 'poses obvious problems for theory-building.'[31] Often the field was criticised for using findings derived from too small samples or because the inferences were made often erroneously and hastily drawn from too divergent examples across non-comparable cases in order to conveniently fit generalisations and broad theories. As cautioned by Crenshaw, researchers should be careful in 'constructing general categories of terrorist actors that lump together dissimilar motivations, organisations, resources and contexts.'[32]

Another area of contention is the rivalry between the preferred emphasis on either policy-driven research or more theory-driven intellectual contributions. It has been recognised that international relations theory has had difficulty in adjusting to, dealing with, and developing theories responding to the dominance of adversaries other than with a state-centric focus.[33] A major failure has been the development of a body of knowledge that tries to explain the underlying root causes of terrorism. Again, the diverse types and complex forms of terrorism have greatly complicated this task alongside the context-specificity of terrorism in being driven by the interrelationship between diverse causes at the individual, group, environmental or international levels. These different levels of causation are unevenly studied and their interrelationship poorly understood. There are some recent seminal studies that provide insight and constructive pathways to our collective understanding of causes at different levels. Perhaps the best under-stood levels are at the individual and group levels where Martha Crenshaw, Jerrold Post and more recently John Horgan and Andrew Silke, among the most notable academics, have provided groundbreaking analytical frameworks in advancing our understanding of what causes engagement in terrorism on the individual psychological level. Although they unanimously acknowledge the futility of developing taxonomies or typologies of terrorist personalities or profiles, their research has opened up new vistas for exploring how and why terrorists join, how group dynamics work and what necessary factors influence disengagement from terrorism.[34] Similarly, Jerrold Post skilfully unpacked the multi-faceted and multi-level generic factors influencing the behaviour of terrorist groups, while Gordon H. McCormick provides probably the most enduring analytical *tour d'horizon* of terrorist decision making with an impressive and ambitious inventory of literature and research on the subject.[35] Another notable contribution has been made by Bruce Hoffman and Gordon McCormick in advancing our understanding of the communicative aspects of terrorism as a complex form of strategic signalling.[36] Equally, Tore Bjorgo has made a noteworthy effort in unpacking the kaleidoscope of factors behind root causes at the systemic and international level from a series of case studies, isolating a range of systemic pre-conditions (that do not produce terrorism themselves) and providing a list of over a dozen precipitant causes alongside triggering factors and others that motivate and sustain terrorism campaigns and individual involvement.[37] Collectively these factors provide a useful multi-causal framework for further research and signifi-cantly enhance our understanding of the root causes debate. At another level,

Brynjar Lia has usefully examined the impact of globalisation on terrorism and its likely future evolution.[38]

Identifying and understanding the causes of terrorism and political violence and their organic and dynamic processes require the development of context-specific and relational analysis within and between cases. An alternative useful level of analysis to make sense of how these *processes* work in practice and theory can be found through sociological theories, most notably Charles Tilly's resource mobilisation theory[39] and Donnatella Della Porta's social movement theory.[40] As underscored by Crenshaw, Della Porta provided 'a more complex framework that links individual life histories to political and social environments.'[41] In the post-9/11 context, Quintan Wiktorowitcz singularly stands out as having broken new ground by fusing a social movement theory approach to the context of adaptive and sophisticated radical Islamist movements.[42] This approach provides an extremely useful vehicle to explore constructivist issues such as 'violence and contention, network and alliances, and culture and framing'[43] – the ingredients towards understanding the processes and radicalisation and recruitment strategies of violent salafist-jihadist networks and other broad-based Islamist activist movements. A major advantage of this approach is that it provides the continuum to explain the process of moving from non-violent radicalism into violence itself. Another seemingly important element is to understand the role and function of trust in networks as underscored by Charles Tilly and others.[44] This notion of trust in networks should be explored in combination with studies on small-group dynamics.[45]

In the wake of 9/11, terrorism research has intensely focused on the phenomenon of the inner logic and dynamics of why suicide bombings occur. Some veteran scholars, most notably Mark Juergensmeyer and Scott Appleby, have pioneered the identification of the critical role of religious themes in the justification of violence and the role of charismatic leadership across extremism within the three monotheistic faiths as well as for sects and cults. These analytical interpretations have shown that sacred violence is often perceived and pursued for self-defensive purposes in a cosmic war in order to create or restore 'a true moral order.'[46] Others have more controversially argued that suicide operations are largely pursued for strategic rather than religious reasons.[47] In addition, Quintan Wiktorowitcz has posited the rational actor models against the merits of arguments of those advancing belief systems as the primary motoring forces for why suicide bombings occur.[48] Another scholar pushing the intellectual envelope is David Cook, unpacking radical Islam and martyrology.[49] Whatever the driving factor(s) identified around so-called martyrdom operations, a major weakness in the terrorism literature is the failure to incorporate Occidental or non-Western sources and interpretations. Collectively, Feijsal Devji,[50] Montasser al-Zayyat,[51] Fouad Hussein[52] and other interesting native approaches have provided a useful start in this direction in offering an alternative discourse and interpretation for our understanding of the al-Qaeda phenomenon and beyond. Much more collaborative efforts are necessary to more genuinely challenge prevailing Western assumptions and perspectives. At the same time, the Anglo-Saxon dominance of the discourse and research on terrorism would greatly benefit by taking into account parallel research efforts in other European languages and other academic centres.

There are also major challenges in the expectations of the predictive qualities of terrorism research, especially of networked asymmetric adversaries. As forcefully argued by Colin Gray, 'we cannot predict specific asymmetric threats ... and we tend to lock onto yesterday's event and project it forward as the menace of the era.'[53] It is the case that today's complex global asymmetric milieu necessitates increasingly to expect the unexpected. Some scholars, most notably Bruce Hoffman, have admitted that 'on 9/11, of course, bin Laden wiped the slate clean of the conventional wisdom on terrorists and terrorism.'[54] However, a failure to predict 9/11 by the academic community does not negate all previous assumptions or research findings but naturally may alter the primary focus. It may stimulate the necessary knowledge growth from cognate disciplines for the terrorism studies field towards becoming a mature speciality. This work, however, should build on, or at least be cognisant of, the often fragmentary but select and seminal analytical foundations made in the past. While the 9/11 attacks brought about a profound urgency about the scale of potential future violence and the scale of the problem as a strategic threat, it has also ushered in a growing need and even pressure on the academic community to produce timely and policy-relevant advice on a range of different issues. This push for policy-relevant focus can adversely affect and divert attention away from the critical task of theory building and theory formation. The net effect is often misplaced priorities. In turn, this problem is compounded by the fact that most terrorism research has traditionally been funded by the government. As astutely observed by Gaetano Joe Ilardi, 'the result has been a spiralling of the literature that in the end adds little to our overall understanding of terrorism.'[55]

Terrorism research and public policy occupy an uncomfortable position as they have been the primary cause for the often event-driven nature of the research focus.[56] While terrorism research has generally been recognised as having failed in its capacity to predict terrorist events, it has played a critical function in educating the broader public, politicians and the counterterrorism communities about terrorism in its broader strategic context. Occupying a unique educational and independent platform, terrorism researchers have provided important policy advice to parliamentary committees, military and law enforcement communities and diplomatic audiences worldwide, taking advantage of their impartiality to place immediate issues in a broader horizontal and more long-term perspective. This select academic community has also acted, when deemed necessary, as a critical advocate of normative principles as exemplified by the precarious debates and balance between civil liberties and security. The ability of terrorism researchers to be ensconced in the ivory tower, contemplating for long periods about terrorism in context rather than the immediacy of the threat itself, is a major natural advantage over the strictly operational intelligence domain. Conferences, workshops and other forums serve an invaluable role for acclimatising the practitioner to the strategic domains and in grounding the academic to the practical realities of opportunities and constraints from the field operator's perspective in fighting the terrorism phenomenon. This exposure or cross-fertilisation is absolutely critical in bridging the tactical and strategic domains and in achieving a better and healthy equilibrium between theory and practice. In these exercises it is critical that the terrorism researcher is cognisant of the necessity to remain independent and academically authoritative rather than becoming closely embedded with the intelligence community to the extent that one's credibility is in danger or may become undermined. Any academic work purporting to be based in part on classified CIA briefings of captured detainees who have not been given the opportunity to hear a case in a court of law is not only unverifiable according to any scholarly criteria.[57] This masquerade of evidence must also be considered severely unethical according to most obvious professional or personal standards, even if the academic can produce evidence to underpin assertions. The relative 'silence' of the rest of the terrorism research community is simply scientifically and morally indefensible.

A major unresolved debate today within the research community is whether terrorism is dramatically 'new' or just an evolution of past tactics and strategies fused with a technological revolution through globalisation.[58] This so-called 'network of networks'[59] seemingly defies precision of vocabulary or sufficient explanations of its mutating qualities to a degree that academics and media pundits regularly compete with each other in offering relatively meaningless adjectives or analogies. Perhaps winning the prize of banality are the descriptions by Rohan Gunaratna of both al-Qaeda training camps in Afghanistan and the Iraqi insurgency as a terrorist 'Disneyland.'[60] As pointed out correctly by Mohamedou, 'the multiplicity of analogies betrays the organisation's novelty and masks its teleology.'[61] The more rigorous academics have advanced a divergent range of paradigms to explore the modalities of various networked designs: from social network models,[62] corporate management and organisational theory[63] to synthesis of complexity theory (focusing on the dynamics of networks)[64], 'dune' typology,[65] to the 'cultural autonomy' paradigm[66] and to 'neomedievalism'[67] among a few. Xavier Raufer has also underscored the difficulty in exactly diagnosing the phenomenon of al-Qaeda.[68] This diverse range of analytical lenses is invaluable in providing new and innovative avenues towards our understanding of the nature of asymmetric adversaries. They are particularly valuable in providing a series of durable and contrasting analytical frameworks from different perspectives. Collectively, they challenge our past conceptions and bring clarity towards the processes that underpin this complex adaptive system.

It is unclear whether the role of history can provide an instructive guide on what to expect for the future. David Rapoport have shown through his 'four waves' theory, beginning with the anarchists, anti-colonialist, New Left and religious waves, each wave having a projected life cycle of 45 years,[69] that the al-Qaeda phenomenon may disappear and be replaced by something else around 2025. Some would argue the wave theory is probably an underestimation of the likely projected longevity and power of a global wave of terrorism lasting over several generations as it thrives on the underside of an increasingly complex coming anarchy.[70] It does, however, underscore the role and relevance of history in understanding contemporary or so-called 'new' terrorism. Albert Bergesen and Yi Han argue for the value of more comparative historical approaches and suggest that 'terrorism not only bunches but may cycle.'[71] Extracting the lessons of the history of terrorism will be invariably a valuable exercise in unlocking a new dimension within social scientific disciplines and new potential research avenues. Historical longitudinal studies across comparable contexts and cases are unfortunately only a rarity.[72] Andrew Silke catalogued the 490 articles published during the entire 1990s in the two major specialised terrorism journals and found that only 13 articles focused on 'non-contemporary terrorism and only seven of these look at terrorism prior to 1960.'[73] This paucity of research may not be reflective of groundbreaking and authoritative studies in other journals or in other languages but it clearly illustrates where the majority of the current research effort is prioritised and focused.

Although research focusing on history's role and its connection to terrorism may be relatively poorly developed, other social scientific disciplines are, through individual academic efforts, developing research questions and agendas to explore new interdisciplinary pathways and innovative approaches from different and often divergent perspectives. Introspective research inventories are being developed by geographers, exploring spatial dimensions of complex networks and the role of political geography within the context of counterterrorism policies,[74] while sociologists are debating understanding terrorism in terms of social construction[75] and political scientists debate the notion and concept of risks in society.[76] In all these social scientific explorations an emphasis is naturally placed on surveying the current state of knowledge, the literature and various methodological approaches before exploring their applicability to terrorism specifically. Another question will remain whether these are isolated pioneering efforts or whether this will receive any research traction, allowing others to follow, explore and perhaps sustain a longer term engagement with terrorism studies within each discipline. Among the well-researched areas of terrorism studies are the communicative aspects of violence for political effect and as a sophisticated form of psychological warfare.[77] In a rapidly changing global era, this theme may prove to be a fruitful avenue to connect to the terrorism studies field from outside the speciality. Providing new or continuous research inventories will be essential to move the field forward. In essence, interdisciplinary focus and innovation will remain absolutely vital in efforts to develop a critical knowledge base in future terrorism research.

Thomas Mockaitis has astutely observed that a major dilemma for terrorism research is fragmentation of effort both in understanding the phenomena of terrorism itself and in devising a strategy against it.[78] This dilemma is perhaps most acutely felt in the strategically important area of research on weapons of mass destruction (WMD) or chemical, biological, radiological and nuclear (CBRN) weapons, devoted to understanding the convergence of when two extremes meet to produce either mass disruption or, in a worst-case scenario, 'catastrophic societal destruction.'[79] Some excellent past work has been done in this area.[80] However, as pointed out by Gary Ackerman, a recent survey of all WMD terrorism publications indicated that the field has 'reached something of an "interpretative impasse"' that is reminiscent of the problems associated with early terrorism studies research, with a small closed community and the recycling of the same material and assumptions. He further suggests that the research community move to make policy-relevant threat assessments, to analyse collaboration within complex milieus between extremist elements and to advocate second-order analysis to predict the likely time scales of terrorist transition to WMD and by what mechanisms.[81] Equally, Gavin Cameron poignantly reminds us that terrorism research must be considered beyond technical issues and group dynamics in its wider social and political context and the WMD dimension may also include areas beyond strictly CBRN agents such as agriculture and cyber targets.[82] The issue of the potential convergence between terrorist groups and cyber terrorism presents similar methodological challenges to predicting when terrorist groups are likely to acquire and employ WMD.[83] It is widely recognised that this shift may not appear in a linear and progressive trajectory but may occur with dramatic and sudden quantum leaps, especially as there are few categorisations still valid in a world driven by globalisation and as the pattern of horizontal and vertical interaction is a constantly changing and shifting constellation of actors and factors. These 'wild cards' have focused attention towards applicability of complex adaptive systems and the role of complexity theory in understanding, managing and predicting complex networks, asymmetric adversaries and guarding against really large systemic surprises.[84]

Mastering the sheer complexity of multidimensional factors in constant flux inhibits accurate and consistent predictions of any future terrorism events. There are, however, mechanisms that can be employed that provide insight into the interplay between the individual, group and environmental levels. Already in 1985, Crenshaw used innovatively Albert O. Hirschman's *Exit, Voice, and Loyalty* as a framework to map out the multiplicity of different choices that confronts terrorist leaders and their followers.[85] A relatively underexplored critical area of terrorism research is the understanding of the processes of innovation within groups and cells. Hoffman provides a fascinating glimpse of the technological synergy of innovation in the detonation mechanisms developed by PIRA in Northern Ireland and its effects on British military countermeasures.[86] However, few academic research works focus at length and in depth on the role and processes of how groups precisely innovate, absorb new ideas and integrate different types of technologies towards these ends.[87] This applies particularly towards mapping out processes and types of these innovations and trajectories and how these may differ from case to case and across divergent geographical and cultural contexts.

A truly innovative exercise towards understanding terrorist innovation was spearheaded in 1999 at a conference organised in Paris in a joint collaboration between the Center on Terrorism and Irregular Warfare of the Naval Postgraduate School and Centre de Recherche sur les Menaces Criminelles Contemporaines of the University of Paris (II). This conference examined variables influencing terrorist decision making in relation to cyber terrorism and involved a unique collection of past and active terrorist members as well as hackers.[88] Other scholars, most notably Crenshaw, have drawn attention to this research area as a valuable line of inquiry, employing psychological theories towards the processes of innovation with a special emphasis on understanding the multiplicity of factors producing and influencing so-called 'mental leaps' alongside other factors such as revenge, leadership, and personal knowledge and experiences.[89] However, this specialisation is urgently in need of further expansion in collaborative and parallel interdisciplinary efforts. A major reason for this weakness is the analytical level and the absence of available and necessary fine-grained information. Another reason is the absence of knowledgeable social scientists with hard science backgrounds and requisite military field experience.[90] One potential unexplored research area is the role of innovation in relation to old and new technologies, especially tracing the evolution and application of so-called IEDs or improvised explosive devices within a particular group capability and specific context.[91] Others have argued that the research priorities should focus on understanding violence with the greatest potential 'to achieve catastrophic social destruction.'[92]

Understanding the kaleidoscope of various forms of terrorism is a complex academic exercise and various aspects of the field are in many ways still embryonic in its development. It would be a gross mischaracterisation and an injustice to fail to recognise the enduring and invaluable academic foundation made by a handful of pioneering scholars over the last three decades pre-9/11. Without their assistance in the development of conceptual roadmaps and empirical case studies of terrorist groups and their behaviour as well as methodologies, the academic communities across disciplines and policymakers would largely still be in relative darkness in crafting a cohesive and measured response to the intellectual and practical challenges posed by 9/11. An impressive multitude of case studies across different contexts on terrorist groups and movements exists in abundance, especially in helping us to understand the changing contours of the so-called 'old terrorism'. Much of this rich literature does not classify itself as belonging to the terrorism studies field *per se*. There are also major research achievements in the area of counterterrorism crafted from a rich history, tradition and experience from counterinsurgency and in understanding guerrilla warfare.[93] Similarly, more normative aspects of terrorism within the confines of legal norms and the balance between security and civil liberties have collectively been extensively and thoroughly examined by key scholars within the terrorism studies field as well as outside in the political philosophy domain.[94] Among the foremost and widely recognised contributions is Paul Wilkinson's *Terrorism and the Liberal State*, which provides a *tour d'horizon* of the challenges of this normative balancing act with an enduring contemporary relevance.[95]

In contrast to the efforts to understand terrorism as a complex social and human phenomenon, the critique of the counterterrorism research landscape is relatively limited or even muted. This can possibly be explained by either the range of qualitative studies conducted according to context-specificity (Northern Ireland, Basque region and other more enduring ethnic or nationalist/separatist conflicts), the historical lessons from confronting past terrorist campaigns, or even perhaps by the relative paucity of research in understanding the totality of relationships between the complex facets of counterterrorism regionally or even globally. Few scholars have ventured to provide comparative studies of counterterrorism policies and practices.[96] Even fewer have focused on addressing the 'effectiveness' of counterterrorism policies more generically away from specific contexts.[97] Although 9/11 has refocused the issue of pre-emption and even introduced the notion of preventive war, some research focuses interestingly on the notion of deterrence and its applicability within the context of counterterrorism.[98] Others have focused on the dichotomy between the criminal justice and the war models in countering terrorism.[99] A wealth of academic studies has provided useful autopsies on specific strands of counterterrorism, from the micro and macro levels. It is also in this arena that the non-specialist scholar may usually find comfort to connect to the terrorism studies field, given its state-centric nature. Unresolved, however, is the larger questionable value in divorcing an analysis of counterterrorism from its specific context and its causative dynamic interaction which in turn changes the terrorists' behaviour and choice of tactics. The lack of academic focus on this cyclical environmental complexity is illustrative of the priority given by certain well-established terrorism scholars on future research efforts in understanding how and why terrorism ends; decision making in counter terrorism;[100] effective crisis management procedures;[101] and public reactions to terrorism.[102] More research is simply needed that captures the dynamics of the relationship between terrorism and counterterrorism. A few academic contributions have begun to examine political pathways out of violence that capture this two-way process.[103]

A similar set of prioritised research areas was identified by the expert panel group of the US-based National Research Council of the National Academies, stressing the need for comparative research knowledge about the processes of terrorism and the communicative aspects.[104] This latter point emphasises the rapidly changing role of the media and technology in today's global information age with corresponding indirect and direct effects on terrorism. As such, the role of information operation studies as a vehicle to understand the total spectrum of effects is only likely to increase in attractiveness in the future, especially as the US may intensify its efforts in the so-called 'war of ideas'. This focus needs to integrate and prioritise a non-Western approach to provide cultural traction within targeted societies and against extremist mindsets. It is clear we operate only on the rudimentary and superficial level today in this complex sphere.

Unpacking the complexities of counterterrorism is an academically challenging task. It is complex not only given its context-dependency but also in efforts to calibrate the various instruments of counterterrorism in simultaneous horizontal and vertical harmony. In this multifaceted task, Alex Schmid has provided an extremely useful conceptual toolbox in unpacking the various elements of counterterrorism policies including: politics and governance; economic and social; psychological–communicational–educational; military; judicial and legal; police and prison system; intelligence and secret service and other instruments.[105] This toolbox can be a useful checklist and a pathway towards understanding the complexities in the necessity of constantly evaluating which instruments to apply, to what degree and in what direction according to the context. These instruments may be strategically directed but operate on the tactical level in constant flux.

Among the many strands within the counterterrorism toolbox is the intelligence sphere that can itself provide new interesting avenues to unlock new dimensions. Few academic studies successfully connect the terrorism and intelligence studies fields as it demands mastery of two relatively inaccessible information and analytical domains. Beyond the contested arena of bureaucratic politics and new institutional architectures, intelligence studies offer not only a useful but an ideal vehicle to develop new and innovative methodologies that account for, and can better deal with, today's increasing complexity and uncertainty in the world. A series of 'think pieces' by the CIA's Sherman Kent Center exemplifies the value of challenging prevailing assumptions and preconceptions in methodologies while handling uncertainty and the complex volume of contradictory pieces of information and analysis through collaborative exercises.[106] As such, the intelligence field may constitute a useful auxiliary social science field with a high degree of synergy with terrorism studies as it deals with processing analysis through different methodologies. Despite this potential in synthesising the two fields, few academic crossovers occur as the intelligence studies field is a small and marginal speciality with few established scholars and relatively esoteric specialised journals.[107] Both fields, however, underscore that history and case studies are essential and that a wealth of primary source material exists in national archives, from policy documents and public testimonies as well as from a multiplicity of court records from terrorist trials worldwide. A recent extraordinary document is the *9/11 Commission Report* which provides a unique first-hand insight into the event itself, the operational art of the perpetrators and the difficulty of decision making and organisational flaws within the US counterterrorism bureaucracy and even decision making at the highest political levels.[108] Based on exhaustive interviews and 2.5 million documents, the *9/11 Commission Report* is already confined to the annals of history and is surprisingly and relatively unused as a reference within the scholarly terrorism studies literature. The report's footnotes themselves reveal a remarkable degree of useful information about the operational art and behaviour of the asymmetric adversary. Similarly, the explosion of over 7000 salafist-jihadist and other extremist websites provides a treasure trove for the Arabic-speaking researcher and instantaneous access to ideological tracts and documents similar to those analysed by the academic communities in the 1970s and 1980s.[109] On the flipside, a main difficulty remains to actually verify the reliability and more critically the authenticity of the ocean of documents available. This contemporary research milieu stands in stark contrast to the relative inaccessibility of the field during its earlier days and may alleviate against the dangers of a closed research community. However, as in the past, today the primary challenge remains to struggle to avoid the event-driven nature of research efforts and avoid the technically driven and overly funded research on purely mechanistic processes of critical infrastructure protection at the expense of soft social science research.

Illustrative of the complex and interdisciplinary nature of research into 'terrorism' was the effort made by the United Nations Terrorism Prevention Branch (TPB) in April 2000 when it designed a research *desiderata,* a matrix of 24 research headings with over 180 subtopics represented as key priority areas of research for the academic and governmental research communities. A year and a half later, the events of 9/11 seemingly eclipsed the urgency and relevance of the UNTPB list as the policymaking and scholarly communities rapidly sought to readjust their research priorities and policy postures. In the post-9/11 world, the terrorism studies field finds itself at the absolute vortex of national security concerns and the focus of intense interest by the international community. Past analytical perspicacity is essential as a conceptual foundation to move the field forward. However, the academic field also finds itself at a critical juncture in terms of its prioritised direction. The menu of choices to choose from may be complex and large but priority must certainly remain on fostering collaborative avenues and on innovative interdisciplinary focus to allow the terrorism studies field to consolidate its growth of durable knowledge.

Whatever path it takes, it remains an important task to critically take stock of past research achievements, gaps and possible directions for future research. It is what this book strives to achieve. A principal aim is to slow down the velocity of largely event-driven research around al-Qaeda, the war on terrorism and other unfolding extremist groups and terrorist events. As forcefully argued by John Steinbruner, 'very few would continue to argue that either analytical comprehension or practical mastery are likely to emerge from a simple continuation of past efforts. It is evident that some productive innovation is needed; but far from evident, of course, is what innovation would be productive.'[110]

A roadmap for a future research agenda?

This book is the cumulative result of an international conference held at the Swedish National Defence College in Stockholm on 21–23 March 2005. It was generously sponsored by the Swedish Emergency Management Board (SEMA) and greatly benefited from the wise academic counsel by Professor Bengt Sundelius and Johan Hjelm alongside the continuous critical quality guidance provided by both Professors Wilhelm Agrell and John Eriksson.[111] This conference brought together a vibrant and eclectic but thoughtful research community distinguished by one principal characteristic: they were representative of a small body of researchers who had critically and intelligently reflected in their past writings on the merits of research within their specialised areas in the terrorism studies field. It would be a mistake to think that the contributions in this book provide all the answers to what exactly the research community has achieved and what is still missing and where efforts should be prioritised. Nevertheless, it provides a partial answer or at least fragments to a process of reflecting more broadly and deeply on the absence of a grand theory and multiple methodologies available and the diversity of contending interdisciplinary approaches in the elusive quest towards better understanding terrorism as a complex social and behavioural phenomenon. Far too few efforts are made questioning assumptions behind research and assertions and arguments. In some way one could liken the current research efforts after 9/11 to a football match where all the players are rushing after the ball without a strategy rather than marking different players or utilising different areas of the pitch. Some are of course doing it for funding reasons. Apart from Andrew Silke (and the ongoing efforts of Alex P. Schmid of the United Nations Terrorism Prevention Branch), no books have been published that adopt a research inventory approach since the late 1980s. And, perhaps more worryingly, only a handful of refereed academic articles that reflectively and critically focus on this subject have been published over the last three decades. Of course, many academic articles exist that progressively build on an evolving body of scientific knowledge. This book will hopefully stimulate more explicitly critical introspection and efforts towards interdisciplinary collaboration. For the next generation of academics and students it provides a useful vehicle through which to evaluate past and present work while, hopefully, giving rise to new ideas or avenues for research efforts into the 'known unknown'.

This book is divided into different thematic parts beyond the larger conceptual (and perhaps artificial) division between terrorism and counterterrorism. In the first part, devoted to diverse efforts to understand terrorism as a complex social and behavioural phenomenon, Joshua Sinai takes the lead, focusing on the overarching strengths and weaknesses in the various approaches to our social science and behavioural understanding on terrorism. With almost surgical precision and clarity, his analysis provides a balance sheet across the spectrum of ten thematic areas. In several areas Sinai emphasises the necessity to understand multifaceted causal factors and their relationship with the social, political and individual contexts. Interestingly, he also stresses that research needs to be conducted on how ideas are translated into action and how these influence everyday choices and decision making for terrorists and their followers. He concludes by underscoring the necessity to understand how and why terrorism ends and perhaps hints at further research on political pathways out of terrorism.

Next Isabelle Duyvesten provides a critical and incisive historical perspective about the continuity of terrorism research. Providing interesting reflections on the different meanings of the epochs of terrorism and its history, she concludes insightfully that it is critical to avoid thematic labelling and that understanding terrorism in context is absolutely crucial. Additionally, she encourages more non-Western perspectives from the global South in relation to the evolution of terrorism alongside more interdisciplinary research and the necessity for a closer understanding of the dynamics between terrorism and counterterrorism. Finally, she cautions the academic and policymaking community against expecting too much of academics in making, or being able to make, predictions about the future direction of terrorism.

The third contributor, Andrew Silke, provides another calm and collected analytical reflection on the impact of 9/11 on research on terrorism. An updated survey, based on his previous review of methodology of journal articles (1990–1999),[112] reveals a number of interesting patterns within the terrorism studies field since 9/11: limited statistical or historical analysis; limited original field work or sources; excessive focus on al-Qaeda and a dramatic increase in focus on WMD as well as suicide tactics. However, Silke notes some reasons for optimism in research terms as more work is being conducted collaboratively among researchers that are much greater in number and from different disciplines. He concludes by arguing that terrorism studies are far from becoming an own discipline and that may not be entirely a bad thing.

A fourth contribution is authored by Karin von Hippel who bravely tackles the contentious issue of responding to root causes of terrorism. She provides a survey of the different arguments advanced within the public domain as to the causal and facilitating factors of terrorism. In particular, von Hippel underscores the problems of collapsed or weak states alongside regional conflicts. Additionally, she illustrates the multi-dimensional levels of causes that complicate the efforts of response to religious extremism.

The final contribution in this section is provided by psychologist John Horgan who provides an incisive pathway towards understanding terrorist motivation from a socio-psychological perspective. In this comprehensive analysis, Horgan provides an applicable toolbox in unpacking the arguments and complex factors as to why individuals involve themselves with terrorism, remain involved and dis-engage from the group and violence. He emphasises the necessity to understand the psychology of terrorists as process-based and always occurring in context as he offers a valuable model for these processes. He concludes by arguing for a greater synergy of learning between government analysis and academic work and admits that the state of the art of psychological literature on terrorism is still embryonic and lacks the necessary primary data.

The next section of this book is devoted to exploring various understandings of terrorism post-9/11 that both explicitly and implicitly may contribute to new pathways in understanding the al-Qaeda phenomenon and beyond as well as in the challenges of responding to it. In a groundbreaking analysis, Jeffrey B. Cozzens moves us away from simplistic and uni-dimensional organogramme approach to al-Qaeda and instead examines the role of function, culture and grand strategy. This complex analysis unlocks new dimensions of different themes, from fourth generation warfare to culturalist factors, which is urgently needed to enrich our knowledge about the behaviour of future asymmetric adversaries following the ideology and narrative of al-Qaeda and beyond.

Michael Taarnby provides an auxiliary analysis in the next contribution that examines the contours of recruitment of Islamist terrorists in Europe. He provides a broad survey of recruitment patterns across Europe with a typology of different processes before raising the issue and role of potential non-violent gateway organisations. Taarnby concludes that the research on this strategically important issue is often fragmentary, quickly outdated and lacking in analytical sophistication due to the simple fact that this issue has been neglected within research and is admittedly difficult to handle and confront.

The next section of this book deals with research contributions within the field of counterterrorism. Martin Rudner skilfully provides an interesting assessment of the strengths and weaknesses of the various Western intelligence architectures and their analytical methodologies in dealing with contemporary terrorism threats. In addition he provides a conceptual toolbox in understanding the complex challenges for intelligence analysis as they adjust themselves to deal with terrorism through various institutional reforms. In conclusion he argues the essential need for recognition of the value of the intelligence analyst within the profession itself as an enduring career path.

Ronald D. Crelinsten examines the global geopolitical context where terrorism and counterterrorism interact before proceeding to argue for global governance as an approach to identify new potential avenues for research. This ambitious and thought-provoking analysis underscores the complexities involved in understanding the different types of knowledge necessary in an era of globalisation and increased asymmetry.

Finally, Neal Pollard contributes with a forward-looking analysis of the consequences of globalisation and advances in technology on terrorism and efforts to deal with it effectively. Not only does he succeed in showing that asymmetric adversaries are more adroit at exploiting these information architectures but he also points towards substantive legal and policy challenges that undermine cooperation. All these vistas require changes in our approach and not only open up policy problems and a host of legal dilemmas but also highlight the need for new research agendas to incorporate rapid technological changes that are increasingly creating new vulnerabilities.

The final section of this book is devoted to the future landscape of terrorism research. Berto Jongman provides not only a personal reflection on the research challenge but also, uniquely, an annotated analysis of the expanded list of research topics developed by him and Alex P. Schmid at the UNTPB. This list of research topics or *desiderata* originally contained 24 research headings with 180 subtopics but has now expanded to over 444 different subtopics for prioritised research for the established scholar and prospective students. This annotated analytical commentary is a tribute to the longstanding contributions made by Alex P. Schmid to the field but is also a unique foundation and vehicle for further research in the future.

Nancy Hayden of Sandia National Laboratories introduces us to the complexity of analysing asymmetric threats and terrorism and asserts that the problem of al-Qaeda and the new networked structures represent so-called 'wicked problems' that are resistant to simple one-dimensional solutions or even understanding. In some instances these problems have no solution. She maps out the implications of wicked problems that require the terrorist analyst to be the master of a complex spectrum of analytical skills.

Finally, Paul Wilkinson, regarded by many as one of the founding fathers of the discipline of terrorism studies, provides a broad reflection of achievement in research over the last three decades. He concludes with some reflections brought about by the so-called new terrorism for the international system generally and the balance between civil liberties and security specifically. Judging by his impressive scholarship and record in highlighting what will be the future issues and challenges, there could hardly be a better guide to calmly navigate us through a minefield of issues. This enduring security and normative challenge require us to counsel wisdom and experience. Undoubtedly, sustained research knowledge of terrorism will continue be in critical demand.

Already in 1978 terrorism doyen Stephen Sloan made the case for 'the urgent need for crucial programs based on scholarly research, operational expertise and incisive policymaking and execution is absolutely vital in view of the sobering degree of coordination and cooperation among terrorist groups who are now acting together in a global assault on the civil order.'[113] Furthermore, as prophetically argued back in 1986, Walter Laquer identified that future historians would probably 'draw the conclusion that those living in this "age of terrorism" perhaps never quite understood the exact nature of the threat.'[114] If only more people would then have counselled their wisdom about the future of terrorism and made the necessary intellectual and practical investments.

Notes

1 John Dewey, *Logic: The Theory of Inquiry* (New York, NY: Holt, 1938): p. 509. For further analysis on the merits of interdisciplinary research, see: John Gerring, *Social Science Methodology: A Critical Framework* (Cambridge: Cambridge University Press, 2001).

2 John Lewis Gaddis, 'History, Theory and Common Ground', *International Security*, Vol. 22, No. 1 (1997): p. 75.

3 See: Abu Ubeid al-Qurashi, 'Fourth Generation Wars', *Al-Ansar: For the Struggle Against the Crusader War*, February 2003.

4 For example, see: Reed W. Wadley, 'Treachery and Deceit: Parallels in Tribal and Terrorist Warfare', *Studies in Conflict and Terrorism*, Vol. 26, No. 5 (September–October 2003): pp. 331–345.

5 David Ronfeldt, 'Al-Qaeda and Its Affiliates: A Global Tribe Waging Segmental Warfare', *First Monday*, Vol. 10, No. 3 (March 2005).

6 For an early and excellent analysis on this, see: Charles F. Parker and Eric Stern, 'Blindsided? September 11 and the Origins of Strategic Surprise', *Political Psychology*, Vol. 23, Issue 3 (September 2002).
7 Gerard Chaliand, *Guerilla Strategies* (University of California Press, 1982) and a host of other incisive historical books.
8 The author is the proud owner of a personally signed copy of Gerard Chaliand, *Food Without Frontiers* (London: Longwood Publishers, 1982) which is based on recipes from guerrillas around the world and revolves around the cultural principle that food and cooking underpin the most intimate trust and friendship in many societies around the world. The lesson for the researcher is to not neglect this valuable tool in field interviews.
9 David Leheny, 'Terrorism, Social Movements, and International Security: How Al Qaeda Affects Southeast Asia', *Japanese Journal of Political Science*, Vol. 6, No. 1 (2005): pp. 87–109.
10 John Gray, *Al-Qaeda and What It Means to Be Modern*.
11 Robert O. Keohane, 'The Globalization of Informal Violence, Theories of World Politics, and the "Liberalism of Fear"', *International Organisation* (Spring 2002): pp. 29–43.
12 Oliver Richmond, 'Realizing Hegemony? Symbolic Terrorism and the Roots of Conflict', *Studies in Conflict and Terrorism*, Vol. 26 (2003): pp. 289–309.
13 David Leheny, 'Symbols, Strategies, and Choices for International Relations Scholarship after September 11', *International Organisation* (Spring 2002): pp. 57–70.
14 Alex Schmidt and Berto Jongmann, *Political Terrorism* (1988).
15 Peter Merkl (ed.), *Political Violence and Terror: Motifs and Motivations* (University of California Press, 1986).
16 Paul Wilkinson and Alasdair Stewart (eds), *Contemporary Research in Terrorism* (University of Aberdeen Press, 1989).
17 Andrew Silke, *Research on Terrorism: Trends, Achievements and Failures* (London: Frank Cass, 2004).
18 Martha Crenshaw, 'The Psychology of Terrorism: An Agenda for the 21st Century', *Political Psychology*, Vol. 21, No. 2 (2000): p. 405.
19 Richard Clutterbuck, *Kidnap and Ransom: The Response* (London: Faber & Faber, 1978).
20 Alex Schmidt and Berto Jongman (1988), *Political Terrorism* (1988).
21 Edna O.F. Reid, 'Evolution of a Body of Knowledge: An Analysis of Terrorism Research', *Information Processing & Management*, Vol. 33, No. 1 (1997): pp. 91–106.
22 See: Jonny Burnett and Dave Whyte, 'Embedded Expertise and the New Terrorism', *Journal for Crime, Conflict and the Media,* Vol. 1, No. 4 (2005): pp. 1–18.
23 Andrew Silke, 'The Devil You Know: Continued Problems with Research on Terrorism', *Terrorism and Political Violence*, Vol. 13, No. 4 (2001): pp. 1–14.
24 For example, see: Avishag Gordon, 'Terrorism and the Scholarly Communication System', *Terrorism and Political Violence*, Vol. 13, No. 4 (Winter 2001): pp. 116–124.
25 Edna O.F. Reid, 'Evolution of a Body of Knowledge: An Analysis of Terrorism Research', *Information Processing and Management*, Vol. 33, No. 1 (1997).
26 Martha Crenshaw, 'Current Research on Terorrism: The Academic Perspective', *Studies in Conflict and Terrorism*, Vol. 15 (1992): p. 1.
27 Bruce Hoffman, 'Current Research on Terrorism and Low-Intensity Conflict', *Studies in Conflict and Terrorism*, Vol. 15 (1992): p. 26.

28 Frank Schorkopf, 'Behavioural and Social Science Perspectives on Political Vio-lence', in: Schorkopf (ed.) *et al.*, *Terrorism as a Challenge for National and International Law: Security versus Liberty?* (Berlin/Heidelberg: Springer, 2003).

29 Alex Schmid, 'The Response Problem as a Definition Problem', in: Alex Schmid and Ron Crelinsten (eds), *Western Responses to Terrorism* (London: Frank Cass, 1993). Also see: Alex Schmid, 'Frameworks for Conceptualising Terrorism', *Terrorism and Political Violence*, Vol. 16, No. 2 (Summer 2004): pp. 197–221.

30 Martha Crenshaw, 'Current Research on Terrorism: The Academic Perspective', *Studies in Conflict and Terrorism*, Vol. 15 (1992): p. 2.

31 Martha Crenshaw, 'Current Research on Terrorism: The Academic Perspective', *Studies in Conflict and Terrorism*, Vol. 15 (1992).

32 Martha Crenshaw, 'The Psychology of Terrorism: An Agenda for the 21st Century', *Political Psychology*, Vol. 21, No. 2 (2000): p. 417.

33 Anton du Plessis, 'International relations theory and the discourse on terrorism: Preliminary reflections on context and limits', *Strategic Review for South Africa*, Vol. 23, Issue 2 (November 2001): p. 134.

34 For example, see: John Horgan, *The Psychology of Terrorism* (London: Routledge, 2005).

35 Gordon H. McCormick, 'Terrorist Decision Making', *Annual Review of Political Science*, Vol. 6 (2003): pp. 473–507.

36 Bruce Hoffman and Gordon McCormick, 'Terrorism, Signalling, and Suicide Attack', *Studies in Conflict and Terrorism*, Vol. 27 (2004): pp. 243–281.

37 Tore Bjorgo (ed.), *Root Causes of Terrorism* (London: Routledge, 2005).

38 Brynjar Lia, *Globalisation and the Future of Terrorism: Patterns and Predictions* (London: Routledge, 2005).

39 Charles Tilly, 'Collective Violence in European Perspective', in: T.R. Gurr (ed.), *Violence in America*, Vol. 2 of *Protest, Rebellion, Reform* (Beverly Hills, CA: Sage Publications, 1989).

40 Donnatella dela Porta (ed.), *Social Movements and Violence: Participation in Under-ground Organizations*, (Greenwich: JAI Press, 1992). Also see: Donatella della Porta and Sidney Tarrow (eds), *Transnational Movements and Global Activism* (Rowman and Littlefield, 2004).

41 Martha Crenshaw, 'The Psychology of Terrorism: An Agenda for the 21st Century', *Political Psychology*, Vol. 21, No. 2 (2000): p. 409.

42 Quintan Wiktorowitcz (ed.), *Islamic Activism: A Social Movement Theory Approach* (Bloomington, IN: Indiana University Press, 2004). Also see: Aldon D. Morris and Carol McClurg Mueller (eds), *Frontiers in Social Movement Theory* (New Haven: Yale University Press, 1992).

43 David Leheny, 'Terrorism, Social Movements, and International Security: How Al Qaeda Affects Southeast Asia', *Japanese Journal of Political Science*, Vol. 6, No. 1 (2005).

44 Charles Tilly, *Trust and Rule* (Cambridge: Cambridge University Press, 2005).

45 Manuel Castells (ed.), *The Network Society: A Cross-Cultural Perspective* (Edward Elgar, 2005).

46 Austin T. Turk, 'Sociology of Terrorism', *Annual Review of Sociology*, Vol. 30 (2004): pp. 271–286.

47 Robert Pape, *Dying to Win: The Strategic Logic of Suicide Terrorism* (New York, NY: Random House, 2005).

48 Quintan Wiktorowitcz, 'Suicide Bombings – Do Beliefs Matter?', unpublished manuscript, September 2004.

49 David Cook, *Understanding Jihad* (Berkeley, CA: University of California Press, 2005).

50 Fejsal Devji, *Landscapes of Jihad* (Cornell University Press, 2005).
51 Montasser Al-Zayyat, *The Road to Al-Qaeda* (London: Pluto Press, 2004).
52 Fouad Hussein, *Al-Zarqawi – The Second Generation* (Amman, 2005).
53 Colin S. Gray, 'Thinking Asymmetrically in Times of Terror', *Parameters* (Spring 2002): pp. 5–14.
54 Andrew Silke, *Research on Terrorism: Trends, Achievements and Failures* (London: Frank Cass, 2004): p. xviii.
55 Gaetano Joe Ilardi, 'Redefining the Issues: The Future of Terrorism Research and the Search for Empathy', in: Andrew Silke, *Research on Terrorism: Trends, Achievements and Failures* (London: Frank Cass, 2004).
56 See for example, Raphael S. Ezekiel and Jerrold M. Post, 'Worlds in Collision, Worlds in Collusion: The Uneasy Relationship Between the Policy Community and the Academic Community', *Terrorism and Political Violence*, Vol. 11 (1988).
57 This is best exemplified by the work of Rohan Gunaratna. For example, see footnotes 36, 37, 59, 60, 61 in: Rohan Gunaratna, 'Ideology in Terrorism & Counter-Terrorism: Lessons from Combating Al Qaeda an Al Jemaah Al Islamiyah in Southeast Asia', *CSRC Discussion Paper*, 05/42, September 2005.
58 Thomas Copeland, 'Is the "new terrorism" really new? An analysis of the new paradigm for terrorism', *Journal of Conflict Studies*, Vol. 11, No. 2 (Fall 2001): pp. 2–27.
59 See: Paul Wilkinson, 'International Terrorism: the Changing Threat and the EU's Response', *Challiot Paper*, No. 84 (October 2005).
60 For example, see his address to Hawaii National Chamber of Commerce, September 2005, and many other interviews to the media.
61 Mohammad-Mahmoud Ould Mohamedou, *Non-Linearity of Engagement: Transnational Armed Groups, International Law, and the Conflict between al Qaeda and the United States* (Cambridge, MA: Program on Humanitarian Policy and Conflict Research, Harvard University, July 2005): p. 9.
62 John Arquilla and David Ronfeldt, *The Advent of Netwar* (Santa Monica, CA: RAND, 1996); Jörg Raab and H. Brinton Milward, 'Dark Networks as Problems', *Journal of Public Administration Research and Theory*, Vol. 13, No. 4 (2003): pp. 413–439; Manuel Castells, *The Rise of Network Society* (Oxford: Blackwell, 1996, 2000).
63 Brad Macallister, 'Al Qaeda and the Innovative Firm: Demythologizing the Network', *Studies in Conflict and Terrorism*, Vol. 27, No. 4 (July/August 2004): pp. 217–239; Renate Mayntz, 'Organisational Forms of Terrorism: Hierarchy, Network or a Type sui generis', *MPIfG Discussion Paper* 04/4 (Max-Planck-Institut für Gesellschaftsforschung, May 2004); Lee G. Bolman and Terrence E. Deal, *Reframing Organizations: Artistry, Choice, and Leadership* (San Fransisco, CA: Jossey-Bass, 1997).
64 Russ Marion and Mary Uhl-Bien, 'Complexity Theory and al-Qaeda: Examining Complex Leadership', *Emergence*, Vol. 5, No. 1 (2003): pp. 54–76.
65 Shaul Mishal and Maoz Rosenthal, 'Al Qaeda as a Dune Organization: Toward a Typology of Islamic Terrorist Organizations', *Studies in Conflict and Terrorism*, Vol. 28, No. 4 (2005): pp. 275–294.
66 Michael Vlahos, *Terror's Mask: Insurgency Within Islam*, Occasional Paper of the Joint Warfare Analysis Department of the Applied Physics Laboratory, John Hopkins University (May 2002).
67 Philip G. Cerny, 'Terrorism and the New Security Dilemma', *Naval War College Review,* Vol. 58, No. 1 (Winter 2005): pp. 11–33.
68 Xavier Raufer, 'Al Qaeda: A Different Diagnosis', *Studies in Conflict and Terrorism*, Vol. 26 (2003): pp. 391–398.

69 David C. Rapoport, 'The Four Waves of Rebel Terror and September 11', *Anthropoetics*, Vol. 8, No. 1 (Spring/Summer 2002).

70 Mary Kaldor, *New and Old Wars Organised Violence in a Global Era* (London: Polity Press, 2003). For the so-called 'new barbarism' thesis see: Robert D. Kaplan, The Coming Anarchy (Vintage, 2001). For a rejoinder, see: Dag Tuastad, 'Neo-Orientalism and the new barbarism thesis: aspects of symbolic violence in the Middle East conflict(s)', *Third World Quarterly*, Vol. 24, No. 4 (2003): pp. 591–599.

71 Albert J. Bergesen and Yi Han, 'New Directions for Terrorism Research', *International Journal of Comparative Sociology*, Vol. 46, Nos. 1–2 (2005): pp. 133–151.

72 A valuable contribution is: Lindsay Clutterbuck, 'The Progenitors of Terrorism: Russian Revolutionaries or Extreme Irish Republicans?', *Terrorism and Political Violence*, Vol. 16, No. 1 (2004): pp. 154–181.

73 Andrew Silke, 'The Road Less Travelled: Recent Trends in Terrorism Research', in Andrew Silke, *Research on Terrorism: Trends, Achievements and Failures* (London: Frank Cass, 2004).

74 Colin Flint, 'Terrorism and Counterterrorism: Geographic Research Questions and Agendas', *The Professional Geographer*, Vol. 55, No. 2 (2003): pp. 161–169.

75 Austin T. Turk, 'Sociology of Terrorism', *Annual Review of Sociology*, Vol. 30 (1994). Also see: William D. Casebeer and James A. Russell, 'Storytelling and Terrorism: Towards a Comprehensive "Counter-Narrative Strategy"', *Strategic Insights*, Vol. 4, Issue 3 (March 2005).

76 Ulrick Beck, *Risk Society: Towards a New Modernity* (London: Sage, 1992).

77 See: A.P. Schmid and J. de Graaf, *Violence as Communication: Insurgent Terrorism and the Western Media* (London: Sage Publications, 1982).

78 Thomas R. Mockaitis, 'Conclusion: The Future of Terrorism Studies', *Small Wars & Insurgencies*, Vol. 14, No. 1 (March 2003): pp. 207–212.

79 John Steinbruner, 'Terrorism: Practical Distinctions and Research Priorities', *International Studies Review*, Vol. 7, No. 1 (March 2005): p. 137.

80 Jonathan B. Tucker (ed.), *Toxic Terror: Assessing Terrorist Use of Chemical and Biological Weapons* (Cambridge, MA: MIT Press, 2000); and John Parachini (ed.), *Motives, Means, and Mayhem: Terrorist Acquisition and Use of Unconventional Weapons* (Santa Monica, CA: RAND, 2005). Also see: Robin Frost, 'Nuclear Terrorism Post-9/11: Assessing the Risks', *Global Society*, Vol. 18, No. 4 (October 2004): pp. 397–422.

81 Gary Ackerman, 'WMD Terrorism Research: Whereto from Here', *International Studies Review*, Vol. 7, No. 1 (March 2005): p. 137.

82 Gavin Cameron, 'Weapons of Mass Destruction Terrorism Research', in Andrew Silke, *Research on Terrorism: Trends, Achievements and Failures* (London: Frank Cass, 2004): p. 86.

83 For example, see: Lars Nicander and Magnus Ranstorp (eds), *Terrorism in the Information Age – New Frontiers* (Stockholm: Swedish National Defence College, ACTA B29, 2004).

84 See: Russ Marion and Mary Uhl-Bien, 'Complexity Theory and al-Qaeda: Examining Complex Leadership', *Emergence*, Vol. 5, No. 1 (2003); and John L. Petersen, *Out of the Blue: How to Anticipate Big Future Surprises* (Oxford: Madison Books, 1999). Also see: Mark Duffield, 'War as a Network Enterprise: the New Security Terrain and Its Implications', *Cultural Values*, Vol. 6, Nos. 1–2 (2002): pp. 153–165.

85 Martha Crenshaw, 'An Organizational Approach to the Analysis of Political Terrorism', *Orbis*, Vol. 29, No. 3 (Autumn 1985): pp. 473–487. Also see the authoritative overview of research on terrorist decision-making: Gordon H. McCormick, 'Terrorist Decision Making', *Annual Review of Political Science*, Vol. 6 (2003).

86 Bruce Hoffman, *Inside Terrorism* (New York, NY: Columbia University Press, 1999).
87 A valuable exception is: C.J.M. Drake, *Terrorists' Target Selection* (London: Palgrave, 1998).
88 'Future of Armed Resistance: Cyberterror? Mass Casualties?' Final Report on a Conference held May 15–17 2000 at the University Pantheon-Assas (Paris-II), available on: http://www.nps.navy.mil/ctiw/files/substate_conflict_dynamics.pdf
89 See: Martha Crenshaw, 'The Psychology of Terrorism: An Agenda for the 21st Century', *Political Psychology*, Vol. 21, No. 2 (2000): p. 416.
90 It should therefore not come as a surprise that RAND is leading this scholarly inquiry. See: Brian A. Jackson *et al.*, *Aptitude for Destruction: Organizational Learning in Terrorist Groups and Its Implications for Combating Terrorism*, Vol. 1 (Santa Monica, CA: RAND, 2005).
91 An exception is: Brian A. Jackson, 'Technology Acquisition by Terrorist Groups: Threat Assessment Informed by Lessons from Private Sector Technology Adoption', *Studies in Conflict and Terrorism*, Vol. 24 (2001): pp. 183–213.
92 John Steinbruner, 'Terrorism: Practical Distinctions and Research Priorities', *International Studies Review*, Vol. 7, Issue 1 (March 2005): p. 137.
93 For example, see: Ian F.W. Beckett, *Modern Insurgencies and Counter-Insurgencies: Guerillas and their Opponents since 1750* (London: Routledge, 2001) and Bard E. O'Neill, *Insurgency & Terrorism: From Revolution to Apocalypse* (2nd edition) (Dulles, VA: Potomac Books, 2005). For an exceptionally useful study on the contribution of low-intensity conflict literature, see: Bruce Hoffman, 'Current Research on Terrorism and Low-Intensity Conflict', *Studies in Conflict and Terrorism*, Vol. 15 (1992): pp. 25–37.
94 See: Kenneth Waltz, *Man, The State and War* (Columbia University Press, 1959); and Conor Gearty, 'Terrorism and Morality', *RUSI Journal* (October 2002).
95 Paul Wilkinson, *Terrorism and the Liberal State* (London: Macmillan, 1977). In addition, see: Magnus Ranstorp and Paul Wilkinson (eds), *Terrorism and Human Rights* – A Special Issue of Terrorism and Political Violence, Vol. 17, Nos. 1–2 (Winter 2005).
96 See: Peter Chalk, *West European Terrorism and Counter-Terrorism: The Evolving Dynamic* (Macmillan, 1997); Peter Chalk and William Rosenau, *Confronting 'The Enemy Within': Security Intelligence, the Police, and Counterterrorism in Four Democracies* (Santa Monica, CA: RAND, 2004).
97 See: Raphael Perl, *Combating Terrorism: The Challenge of Measuring Effectiveness*, CRS Report for Congress (23 November 2005).
98 See: Paul K. Davis and Brian Jenkins, *Deterrence and Influence in Counterterrorism: A Component in the War on al Qaeda* (Santa Monica, CA: RAND, 2002). Also see: Doron Almog, 'Cumulative Deterrence and the War on Terrorism', *Parameters*, (Winter 2004/5): pp. 4–19, and Jonathan Stevenson, 'Terrorism and Deterrence', *Survival*, Vol. 46, No. 4 (2004): pp. 179–185.
99 See: Alex Schmid, 'Frameworks for Conceptualising Terrorism', *Terrorism and Political Violence*, Vol. 16, No. 2 (Summer 2004); Peter Chalk, 'The Response to Terrorism as a Threat to Liberal Democracy', *Australian Journal of Politics and History*, Vol. 44, No. 3 (September 1998): pp. 373–388; Ami Pedazhur and Magnus Ranstorp, 'A Tertiary Model for Countering Terrorism in Liberal Democracies: The Case of Israel', *Terrorism and Political Violence*, Vol. 13, No. 2 (Summer 2001): pp. 1–26.
100 See: Martha Crenshaw 'The Psychology of Terrorism: An Agenda for the 21st Century', *Political Psychology*, Vol. 21, No. 2 (2000): pp. 416–417; Dennis Pluchinsky, 'Academic Research on European Terrorist Developments: Pleas from a

Government Terrorism Analyst', *Studies in Conflict and Terrorism*, Vol. 15 (1992): pp. 13–23.

101 Charles F. Parker and Eric Stern, 'Blindsided? September 11 and the Origins of Strategic Surprise', *Political Psychology*, Vol. 33, Issue 3 (September 2002).

102 For a unique list of research questions, see: Martha Crenshaw, 'Current Research on Terrorism: The Academic Perspective', *Studies in Conflict and Terrorism*, Vol. 15 (1992): pp. 1–11.

103 See: Leonard Weinberg and Ami Pedazhur, *Political Parties and Terrorist Groups* (London: Frank Cass, 2003). Also see: Robert Ricigliano (ed.), *Choosing to Engage: Armed Groups and Peace Processes* (London: Accord, 2005).

104 For a list of prioritized research areas, see: *Terrorism: Perspectives from the Behavioral and Social Sciences*, Panel on Behavioral, Social, and Institutional Issues, Committee on Science and Technology for Countering Terrorism, National Research Council (Washington, D.C.: National Academy Press, 2002): pp. 50–56.

105 These categories contain further sub-categories, see: Alex P. Schmid, 'Towards Joint Political Strategies for De-legitimising the Use of Terrorism', in: Alex P. Schmid (ed.), *Countering Terrorism through International Cooperation* (Milan: ISPAC, 2001): pp. 266–273.

106 For example, see: 'Making Sense of Transnational Threats', *Occasional Papers*, Vol. 3, No. 1 (October 2004); and 'Rethinking "Alternative Analysis" to Address Transnational Threats', *Occasional Papers*, Vol. 3, No. 2 (October 2004). Both studies are available publicly on CIA's official website.

107 Michael Hermann, Christopher Andrew and Martin Rudner represent a small but extremely authoritative scholarly community in this field and some with past professional experience in the intelligence community. For example, see: Michael Herman, *Intelligence Power in Peace and War* (Cambridge: Cambridge University Press, 1996). The most prominent journals are: *International Journal of Intelligence and CounterIntelligence* (Routledge); *Defence Intelligence Journal* (Joint Military Intelligence College); *Intelligence and National Security* (Routledge).

108 *9/11 Commission Report: Final Report of the National Commission on Terrorist Attacks upon the United States* (New York, NY: W.W. Norton & Company, 2004).

109 For example, see the work of Allison Jamieson in: *The Heart Attacked: Terrorism and Conflict in the Italian State* (London: Marion Boyers, 1989); and Joanne Wright, *Terrorist Propaganda: The Red Army Faction and the Provisional IRA, 1968–86* (London: Macmillan, 1991).

110 Steinbruner's comments focus on civil conflicts and efforts to resolve them and connections to terrorism but they equally imply the state of knowledge; see: John Steinbruner, 'Terrorism: Practical Distinctions and Research Priorities', *International Studies Review*, Vol. 7, Issue 1 (March 2005).

111 Additionally, my gratitude extends to Anne Louise Eksborg, the Director General of SEMA, and Under-Secretary of State Dan Eliasson, Ministry of Justice Department, for their presence at the conference and their willingness to contribute with incisive keynote addresses. Equally my gratitude goes to conference moderator Ulf Wickbom for his extraordinarily skilful stewardship during the conference and to Professor Dennis Töllborg for providing, as always, stimulating and provocative analysis of the balance between civil liberties and security from a local Swedish perspective. Last but not least I would like to thank the Swedish National Defence College and principally the President Henrik Landerholm, Christina Weglert, Lars Nicander and his entire wonderful CATS team for their continuous support on the day and subsequently in bringing this project to a successful conclusion. I am particularly grateful to Anders Stävberg for his administrative skills and magnificent support.

112 Andrew Silke, 'The Devil You Know Continued Problems with Research on Terrorism', *Terrorism and Political Violence*, Vol. 13, No. 4 (2001).
113 Stephen Sloan, 'International Terrorism: Academic Quest, Operational Art and Policy Implications', *Journal of International Affairs*, Vol. 32, No. 1 (1978).
114 Walter Laqueur, 'Reflections on Terrorism', *Foreign Affairs* (Fall 1986).

Part I

ADVANCES TOWARDS OUR UNDERSTANDING OF TERRORISM AS A COMPLEX BEHAVIOURAL AND SOCIAL PHENOMENON

2

NEW TRENDS IN TERRORISM STUDIES: STRENGTHS AND WEAKNESSES

Joshua Sinai

Terrorist insurgencies, in all their configurations and local conflicts, constitute the primary warfare threat facing the international community. This is especially the case after September 2001, with al-Qaeda and its affiliates demonstrating their world-class ambitions to inflict catastrophic damage on their adversaries. In other conflicts, such as the rebellions by the LTTE in Sri Lanka and ETA in Spain, such insurgencies are largely localized. However, in the Palestinian–Israeli arena, although the Palestinian component is localized, other transnational groups are also involved, such as the Lebanese Hizballah and al-Qaeda and its affiliates, which also target Israel and its overseas interests. Because of the worldwide reach of al-Qaeda and its affiliates, including the spontaneous emergence of al-Qaeda-inspired groupings around the world, many nations have been upgrading their homeland security defenses and calling on their academic communities to provide analytical understanding of the nature and magnitude of the threat and how to counteract and resolve it. As a result, terrorism courses, research institutes and certificate programs have been proliferating at universities and other academic institutions around the world, although the quality of their instructors' expertise, curriculum and textbooks is mixed.

On the positive side, since its early stages as an academic discipline in the 1960s, although modern terrorism actually began in the 1880s,[1] terrorism studies have greatly benefited from the accumulated knowledge, concepts and methodologies produced by the social sciences. Several recent academic[2] and government[3] reports attest to the contribution by the social sciences to our understanding of terrorism, its origins and nature, and the types of counteractions that enable us to prevent, contain and resolve such threats. On the negative side, however, there is still insufficient theory development in this study field, as exemplified by several problem areas, which are discussed in this chapter.

The objective of this chapter is to highlight some of the strengths and weaknesses in the academic study of terrorism and to recommend ways in which improvements will enable analysts to better understand how to study terrorism, especially in assessing, modeling, forecasting and preemptively countering current and future terrorist threats. As a preliminary effort, the chapter is not intended to comprehensively and exhaustively assess the state of the discipline, but rather to discuss some areas of concern requiring further analytical and R&D efforts.

To examine the strengths and weaknesses in terrorism studies, this chapter is divided into eleven sections that span the spectrum of research on these issues. These are: (1) terrorism studies as an academic discipline; (2) defining terrorism; (3) mapping group typologies and taxonomies; (4) investigating the origins of terrorism; (5) uncovering the psychology of terrorists; (6) exploring how individuals become radicalized and recruited into terrorist groups; (7) diagramming the organizational dynamics that terrorists construct to maintain and sustain themselves; (8) understanding the modus operandi characterizing how terrorists conduct their warfare; (9) creating incident chronology databases to capture the magnitude of terrorist warfare; (10) forecasting future terrorist warfare trends; and (11) formulating measures to counter terrorism to terminate such insurgencies.

(1) Can terrorism studies constitute a scientific academic discipline?

Terrorism is a tactic of warfare, distinguished from guerrilla, conventional and "high intensity" warfare. As a form of warfare, it is part of military science. Terrorist warfare employs weapons and devices that are part of the "hard" sciences, making this subject part of the disciplines of biology, chemistry, physics, engineering, medicine and other sciences. Terrorism's violence against civilian noncombatants and illicit financial activities by its practitioners make it a criminal activity, so this topic is also part of criminology and criminal justice. However, terrorist rebellions are also directed at the larger society and government, and are a product of a spectrum of root causes resulting from societal disequilibria. Terrorist operations are part of an insurgent group's psychological warfare, with terrorist incidents intended to damage the targeted population's psychological resiliency. As such, terrorism studies are by nature interdisciplinary, encompassing the social sciences. The interdisciplinary nature of terrorism studies, however, also presents a problem because there are very few interdisciplinary research efforts worldwide that study terrorism in an integrated manner.[4]

Although the terrorism discipline encompasses the components of the qualitative and quantitative sciences, it can never achieve the capability of a true "science" because of the clandestine and warfare nature of terrorist activities. First, unlike the scientific method, where experiments can be conducted in a controlled laboratory environment, it is difficult, although not impossible, for terrorism researchers to conduct field investigations or interview terrorists engaging in ongoing operations. It is possible to interview incarcerated terrorists, although most academic researchers lack access to such prisoners. Second, the clandestine nature of terrorism makes it difficult to collect accurate and authoritative data (which are available, although with limitation, to government agencies, but not academic researchers) about terrorist groups' modus operandi and activities, such as plots and operations that are aborted, thwarted, or successfully accomplished. Third, unlike the natural and physical sciences, in terrorism research, due to the difficulty of collecting primary data and because of the "rare" and random event nature of terrorist activities, as well as the constant shifting by terrorist groups of their modes of operation, unlike the controlled environment of a scientific laboratory, the past is not always the best predictor of future operations; this makes it difficult, although not impossible, to predict and forecast future incidents. Fourth, because terrorists are not "viruses" that can be controlled and "cured" through epidemiological intervention, there are no medical antidotes to resolve terrorist rebellions, although it is possible to conceptualize the spectrum of measures that are necessary to counteract and resolve such threats, including hypothesizing the likely impact of such measures on the terrorist adversary.

As a result of these factors (with many more requiring further extrapolation), the discipline of terrorism studies has not yet, and may never, become a "hard" science, but will always remain somewhere in between.

(2) Defining terrorism

Defining terrorism is one of the weakest components in terrorism studies, with no consensual definition of terrorism that encompasses attacks, whether against civilian noncombatants or armed military. One of the most widely used definitions of terrorism is provided by the US Department of State. According to this definition, terrorism is "premeditated, politically motivated violence perpetrated against noncombatant targets by subnational groups or clandestine agents, usually intended to influence an audience."[5] As part of this definition, the term "noncombatant" includes civilians and military personnel who are unarmed or not on duty.[6] The term "international terrorism" refers to terrorism "involving citizens or the territory of more than one country,"[7] while the term "terrorist group" refers to "any group practicing, or that has significant subgroups that practice, international terrorism."[8]

The Department of State's definition is operationally useful for legal reasons, because it provides a legal basis to arrest and indict the perpetrators of such acts. However, at the analytical level, as mentioned above, there are no consensual definitions in the social and behavioural sciences on what constitutes terrorism. As found in a literature survey by a National Research Council (NRC) panel, there are no "precise general definitions of terrorism," but rather "a multiplicity of overlapping efforts, some more satisfactory than others, but none analytically sufficient."[9] The term is considered an "'ressentially contested concept,' debatable at its core, indistinct around its edges, and simultaneously descriptive and pejorative."[10] To remedy this deficiency, the NRC formulated its own working definition, which includes the components of "(a) illegal use or threatened use of force or violence (b) with an intent to coerce societies or governments by inducing fear in their populations (c) typically with political and/or ideological motives and justifications and (d) an 'extra-societal' element, either 'outside' society in the case of domestic terrorism or 'foreign' in the case of international terrorism."[11] This definition, however, is still of limited utility because other critical variables need to be included. For example, the NSTC Subcommittee on the Social, Behavioral and Economic Sciences in its February 2005 report on *Combating Terrorism* argues that using the term "terrorism" "may over-simplify different types of actors, warfare and motivations, encapsulating them in a single group or act so that critical variables are overlooked."[12] Here, the "overlooked critical variables" would include activities that fall below the threshold of violence, such as mobilizing support among a group's radical subculture, providing social welfare services, and even maintaining internet-based web sites.

Definitions of terrorism used in the social sciences also vary as to whether terrorism includes attacks against only "noncombatant" targets (as is specified in the Department of State's definition) or whether terrorism is also a tactic of warfare used by sub-national groups against all citizens of a state, whether civilian or military, including attacks against an "armed" military. This has analytical, statistical, and legal implications that need to be addressed and resolved. If terrorism is defined as attacks against only noncombatant targets, then attacks by groups that engage in terrorism against "armed" military targets should not be counted, as they are, in many cases, in terrorist incident chronology databases,[13] and the perpetrators of these attacks should be tried in military courts as guerrillas or armed combatants. Or, alternatively, terrorist attacks against armed targets might be counted separately as "guerrilla" incidents, as they are in the ICT's terrorist incident chronology database.[14]

Two solutions have been offered to remedy the problem of counting as terrorism either attacks against noncombatant or combatant targets. The first, by Alex Schmid, advocates using as a point of departure the consensus of what constitutes a "war crime."[15] Thus, "if the core of war crimes – deliberate attacks on civilians, hostage taking and the killing of prisoners – is extended to peacetime, we could simply define acts of terrorism as 'peacetime equivalents of war crimes.'"[16] The second solution, by Boaz Ganor, defines terrorism as "a form of violent struggle in which violence is deliberately used against civilians in order to achieve political goals (nationalistic, socioeconomic, ideological, religious, etc.)."[17] He asserts that the use of "deliberate" targeting of civilians in order to achieve political objectives is what distinguishes a terrorist act from guerrilla warfare, where military units are targeted.[18]

Ganor's formulation is important because it facilitates the outlawing of terrorism by the international community since all nations can agree that the deliberate targeting of civilians is illegitimate and should be universally legislated against as a crime, whereas attacks against military personnel would be considered as part of regular warfare, including the right to retaliate by a country's armed forces against those perpetrators. Ganor concludes that if acts of terrorism were universally outlawed as a form of warfare by the international community, then terrorist groups would have no choice but to "abandon terrorism and focus on guerrilla activity to achieve their political aims."[19]

Third, most definitions of terrorism used in the social sciences focus on the use of terrorism to "influence" or "coerce" the targeted audience by spreading fear beyond the localized incident throughout the wider society.[20] However, as demonstrated by the attacks of 9/11 in New York and Washington, and 3/11 in Madrid, groups such as al-Qaeda (and its affiliates) also intend to cause their adversaries massive human casualties and physical destruction. Thus, a new component in the definition might include the mass destruction component of terrorism, which is a manifestation of the latest trends in terrorist warfare.

Finally, another definitional problem concerns counterterrorism and homeland security. These terms are usually placed under the overall umbrella of combating terrorism, with anti-terrorism considered as largely defensive and "homeland security" oriented (e.g., involving law enforcement and judicial measures as well as critical infrastructure protection), while counterterrorism is viewed as the offensive (e.g., involving military and other "foreign" measures). However, the transnational nature of contemporary terrorism is leading to blurring of the distinctions between defending national interests overseas and the "homeland," thereby necessitating a new conceptualization of counterterrorism and homeland security.

(3) Group and warfare typologies

To enable us to understand the nature of terrorist groups, including similarities and differences among them, terrorist groups and their warfare can be classified according to general typologies. Different typologies used in the social sciences focus on different characteristics: whether groups espouse single or multiple issues, whether they are nationalist, nationalist-separatist, social revolutionaries or religious fundamentalists, whether they are urban or rural, whether they are state sponsored or operate independently, whether they are local, regional or transnational, and whether their organizational style is hierarchical to networked. Groups of each type are also characterized by particular origins, goals, and modus operandi that are shaped by their sociological, cultural and historical contexts.

Further, a group's particular origin, character and organizational type will also influence its choice of warfare. There are three basic types of warfare carried out by terrorist groups, ranging from conventional low impact (CLI), where conventional means are used to cause relatively few casualties; conventional high impact (CHI), where conventional means are used to cause catastrophic damage, such as crashing airliners into the World Trade Towers; and chemical, biological, radiological or nuclear (CBRN) warfare, where "unconventional" means are used to inflict mass casualties (although chemical and radiological devices may also cause a relatively low number of casualties). This is not intended to be a rigid trichotomy, and it is possible for groups to use a combination of these types of weapons and devices in their warfare.

Placing a group in one of these or other typologies enables an analyst to understand the context in which the group is operating, and assists in forecasting its likely future directions.

(4) Origins of terrorism

Terrorism does not emerge in a vacuum. It generally is not the product of a single causal factor but a confluence or convergence of a multitude of interrelated factors and causes, with such causes varying from one conflict to another. It is important to analyze these underlying factors because, at least by definition, addressing such factors would solve problems that have identifiable root causes. Uproot the cause and the problem is solved. By contrast, leave the roots intact and the problem will persist. Using theories and methodologies developed by the social sciences, researchers have systematically identified, itemized and correlated root causes ranging from the general to the specific, including those at the individual, group, societal and governmental levels.[21]

Root causes are not static, but dynamic and constantly changing. In fact, even when a government begins to address a root cause, it is always possible for the terrorist group to claim that another, yet unresolved, root cause needs to be resolved; so, to attain a complete picture of the underlying causes driving an insurgency it is crucial to examine them from the points of view of the insurgents, the targeted governments, and academic researchers.

Various theories, whether general or specific, developed by social science are especially relevant to understanding the origins of terrorism. Structural theories, for example, "focus on social conditions ('structures') that affect group access to services, equal rights, civil protections, freedom, or other quality-of-life measures."[22] Examples of structural factors include government policies and bureaucracies, the geographic location of the insurgent group, the actions of security forces, and access by a local population to social institutions.[23] The state or government is the key focus in structural theories of terrorism because of its role in serving as the precipitating factor for a terrorist uprising. According to this theory, societal injustice, popular discontent, the alienation of elites and a sense of societal crisis are key ingredients for a terrorist eruption in society.[24]

Unlike structural theories which focus on the central role of the state and its instruments of power in causing terrorist rebellions, relative deprivation (RD) theory, which was developed by Ted Robert Gurr, focuses on the relationship between frustration and aggression.[25] As applied to the terrorism milieu, according to Gurr, feelings of frustration and anger underlie individual decisions to engage in collective action against the perceived source of their frustration and constitute one of the necessary conditions for joining a terrorist group. Their motive for engaging in political violence is their perception that they are *relatively* deprived, *vis-à-vis* other groups, in an unjust social order. When rising expectations are met by governmental resistance in the form of sustained political repression, low ranking socio-economic or political status, or lack of educational opportunities, a group is likely to turn to political violence.

As a corollary to relative deprivation, absolute deprivation theory holds that when a group has been deprived of the basic necessities for survival by a government or social order, such as physical abuse, poverty or starvation, it turns to political violence.[26] Thus, the difference between relative and absolute deprivation is based on the degree of discrepancy experienced by an individual or group between what people have and what they need for daily sustenance, as opposed to what they have and what they believe they deserve *vis-à-vis* others in society. Both types of deprivation are capable of driving those believing themselves to be aggrieved into carrying out acts of political violence.

Moving from these general theories to more specific indicators of terrorist outbreaks, the social sciences have also studied factors at the societal, group and individual levels. At the societal level, countries experiencing economic and social inequality, poverty, low levels of social services, a lack of political or civil rights, low literacy rates and a lack of education, and ethnic conflict are likely to serve as springboards for terrorism, or at least some manifestation of active discontent that may fall below the threshold of violence. The group level of analysis intervenes between the societal and individual levels. Thus, at the group level, agents of mobilization, such as charismatic leaders, radical movements and their political and religious ideologies, serve as causal factors for terrorist outbreaks. At the individual level, susceptibility to radicalization and actual recruitment into terrorist organizations are additional causal factors. According to Arie Kruglanski, extremist ideology is appealing to individuals experiencing psychological uncertainty because such ideologies are "formulated in clear-cut, definitive terms" and provide "cognitive closure."[27] The ecological framework or springboard for terrorist insurgencies is therefore composed of at least three levels – individual, group and societal, with additional explanatory value provided by theories at more general levels.

As demonstrated by these approaches, no single theory or factor provides a sufficient explanation for terrorism. Links between poverty, lack of education and other socio-economic variables, including the clash between tradition and modernity, and terrorism are complex, as are the links between state repression, lack of political opportunities and terrorism. Other political factors may also contribute to terrorism, such as the ability of terrorist groups to exploit political disorder or a lack of political order in weak or failed states. At other times, however, groups may actually receive political support from governments (such as support by the Iranian government of the Lebanese Hizballah). Theories or models for understanding terrorism therefore need to focus on the causal mechanisms or processes in which multiple factors, working together in specific social and other contexts, influence and drive terrorist uprisings.

Employing these conceptual frameworks, once a terrorist insurgency is selected for research, one would begin the process of investigating the underlying conditions, or root causes, why such warfare is being waged against a specific adversary (or adversaries). The underlying causes would then be hierarchically decomposed, itemized, categorized (e.g., poverty, political inequality, foreign subjugation, religious extremism, nihilism, etc.) and codified (e.g., short-, medium- or long-term, 1st order root cause, 2nd order root cause, etc.). One of the shortfalls in such mapping of root causes is that no software-based tools are available to enable a researcher to populate templates with such data, which could then be replicated, updated and revised by others.

As demonstrated in this discussion, however, we still lack comprehensive theories and computation tools to explain, hierarchically decompose and map terrorism's root causes and generate hypotheses to resolve them, with only a single edited volume published through 2005 on this subject, and the methodologies presented in the volume still in their preliminary phases.[28]

(5) Terrorist psychologies

The social science literature has found few common psychological characteristics among terrorists, whether at the levels of leaders, operatives or followers. At the leadership level, it is important to examine the characteristics and traits of leaders who effectively recruit and persuade individuals to join their groups and sacrifice their lives for the cause. John Horgan, for example, has found that there are no specific personality traits that predict effective leadership, but that successful leadership qualities are contextually dependent.[29] There are, however, certain management traits that are necessary for an effective terrorist leader, such as the ability to attract a coterie of dedicated and capable associates to help manage and sustain the group, as well as an ability to impose strict discipline over the rest of the group.

Researchers have also developed profiles of terrorist operatives based on structured and unstructured interviews with them and/or their friends and associates. Some studies have shown that those who join a terrorist group are driven by a variety of different psychological factors, such as individual aggressiveness, narcissism (even pathological narcissism), antisocial personality disorder or paranoid personality disorder. Other researchers, however, argue that those who engage in terrorist violence, and even suicide bombings, are essentially "normal" people, although inclined to altruistic and fatalistic behavior.[30]

Understanding terrorists' psychological makeup and motivations is crucial in formulating measures to dissuade individuals from joining terrorist groups, carrying out operations and, in general, persisting in carrying out terrorist activities. It is here, moreover, that the social sciences can also contribute to helping detect and prevent attacks at the tactical level. For example, research in the social sciences can aid in detecting behaviors and patterns (what is termed in the literature as "determination of intent"), such as certain gait, facial expressions and speech patterns, that are characteristic of individuals about to carry out terrorist attacks; e.g., traits exhibited by suicide bombers as they approach a target. Detecting such psychological and behavioral indicators and observables could provide security forces at the intended site of attack with a warning and interdiction capability.

(6) Radicalization and recruitment

Studying how individuals become radicalized and recruited into terrorist groups provides insight into how terrorism originates and how it is sustained by a continuous influx of new operatives. The relationship between terrorist groups and their sympathizer and support communities can be viewed as a pyramid, with the terrorist groups at the apex and the sympathizers and supporters at the base. The higher levels of the pyramid are characterized by increasing levels of mobilization, commitment and engagement in terrorist activities, with the lower levels marked by activities that fall below the threshold of violence, such as establishing infrastructures to expand a group's support circles, for instance, at religious and educational institutions. For a terrorist group to sustain itself and grow over time, it requires a continuous and ever expanding connection to the larger pyramidal base for general support and a pool of new recruits not only to expand its operational ranks, but also to replace operatives who are arrested or killed in action. Terrorist groups cannot survive without support from a constituent community which, as in the case of groups such as al-Qaeda or Hamas, is based on religious and ethnic ties. The constituent communities can also be termed as radical subcultures in society, and they vary in size, whether as immigrant communities in societies with different majority religions, or in prisons, where the radical subcultures are minority populations in these institutions. Overall, however, such radical subcultures serve as the "susceptible" or "feeder" communities for terrorism because of the ease with which they can be infiltrated by terrorist movements for potential recruits and supporters.

Problems facing individuals whose societies are transitioning from traditional to modern ways of life while coping with the challenges ushered in by modernization are another important determinant and engine of radicalization and recruitment into terrorism. The drive towards modernization produces socioeconomic and political dislocations in society. This change ushers in new elites representing democratization, secularization, industrialization and technocracy that emerge to positions of influence, replacing traditional counterparts, which often results in a series of conflicts between advocates and opponents of the benefits of modernity. Among those who cling to traditional religious values and ways of life, some will respond by espousing revivalist ideologies that promote resentment and even xenophobia towards those who espouse the benefits of modernity, including foreigners (especially as represented by Western Europe and the United States). Revivalist ideologies, such as the Saudi Wahhabism and the Global Salafi Jihadism espoused by al-Qaeda, promote the restoration of their own societies to a state of religious "purity" that supposedly had existed in previous centuries. It is such revivalist ideologies and the movements that espouse them that provide the fertile ground for support of, and recruitment into, terrorist organizations.

Social network analysis (SNA) is a methodology that is particularly relevant to understanding the processes of radicalization and recruitment into terrorism because it maps the types and frequencies of interactions among individuals in order to discern who among them are acting as groups in pursuit of common goals, such as terrorism. It utilizes methodologies and visualization tools that provide analysis and mapping of terrorism at the level of networks by incorporating, correlating and visualizing biographical, psychological, demographic, geographic and other relevant data. For example, using social network analysis, Marc Sageman found that a significant proportion of terrorists who join the Global Salafi Jihadist movement are drawn into such groups by social bonds – some linked through marriage and family connections and others through friendships acquired at a local mosque. He argues that such social interactions are a crucial factor in explaining why, for example, upwardly mobile, middle class and yet lonely and disaffected men turn to certain mosques where they become radicalized and recruited into terrorism. For other individuals, such as Muhammad Atta (one of the 9/11 operatives), after leaving their home country in the Middle East to be educated in the West, religion provides them with a means to find friends, gain a sense of spiritual fulfillment and restore their sense of self.[31]

Understanding how individuals become radicalized and terrorist groups recruit potential operatives – or how individuals in general choose to join terrorist groups – provides the basis for understanding the magnitude of the terrorist threat faced by the targeted country. Because of its ability to map how terrorist groups recruit new members and how these members interact once they have joined these groups (including the location of their activities), social network analysis, whether as an analytical methodology or software-based tool, is a particularly valuable method in mapping how terrorist groups recruit new members (and whether such recruitment is top down or bottom up), and how these members interact and are linked once they have joined these groups (including the locations of their activities), as well as indicating their organizational networks, whether as clusters, hubs or nodes.[32]

Ideas, and, in the contemporary period, especially radical religious ideologies, are among the major drivers that mobilize individuals and groups into committing acts of terrorism and provide them with a cultural and religious underpinning and guide for action. However, there are problems in the terrorism discipline in understanding why individuals and groups turn to religious fundamentalism for their ideological solutions, especially when progress in so many areas is made possible through the modern, secular, pluralistic and democratic paths. Because this process is not clearly understood, the analytical literature does not place religiously fundamentalist radicalization within the context of modernization theory, which is necessary to understand such phenomena.

Additional social sciences research is needed to study how the ideas that shape the objectives of terrorist groups are capable of influencing the thinking and daily activities of new recruits and veteran operatives alike. In another area requiring new research efforts, there is a tendency among researchers, especially in the United States, to regard Islamic radicalization and the proliferation of such radical subcultures as only an "overseas" as opposed to a "domestic" problem affecting one's own society.[33] As a result, such domestic problems are often overlooked, resulting in attack "surprises" (e.g., the suicide bombings by British Jihadists of London's transport system in July 2005).

(7) Organizational dynamics

Organizational theory helps to explain the dynamics underlying the organizational patterns adopted by terrorist groups to manage their personnel and activities. The types of organizational patterns chosen by groups are also intended to ensure loyalty, devotion and cohesiveness of their members because of the high premium placed by these groups on sacrificing one's life for the cause. Factors such as the characteristics and appeal of a group's leader, ideology, mode of operation in a hostile security environment, and availability of recruits, funding and logistical apparatus, contribute to shaping the type of organizational formation that groups adopt.

Over the years, effective organizational structures by terrorist groups have adapted to changing circumstances. Such adaptations have included expanding an organization's logistical infrastructure to conduct sophisticated operations regionally and transnationally, upgrading the security capability to evade monitoring and penetration by counterintelligence/counterterrorist agencies, and the acquisition of new communications technologies, such as satellite telephones and Internet encryption devices, that allow operatives at all levels to communicate efficiently with one another without detection. As a result, terrorist organizational patterns have evolved from the more "traditional" hierarchical types of organization, such as the Provisional Irish Republican Army (PIRA), to increasingly cellular and network-based structures that are part of a "solar" network of linked groupings, such as al-Qaeda and its affiliates. In addition, an increasing number of terrorist groups have adopted the "leaderless resistance" organizational model, in which operational cells deny that they are part of larger units with identifiable leaders.

Finally, some of the larger and more established terrorist groups, such as the Palestinian Hamas and the Lebanese Hizballah, also maintain parallel 'legal' organizational structures, such as political, economic and social welfare front organizations, which enable them to expand their bases of support by providing services to their constituents. This was one of the strengths of PIRA, whose political front, Sinn Fein, succeeded in gaining seats to the British Parliament.

In analyzing new trends in the organizational framework of terrorist groups, four critical inter-related components need to be considered. The first component is the different ways in which rural and urban terrorists construct and organize their insurgent movements, with geography and terrain influencing the types of structures that are required to conduct covert operations. The second component is whether terrorist groups are organized according to hierarchical, cellular or networked formations, or a variation of these three organizational frameworks. Here the role of leadership, especially command and control, plays a crucial role, with marked differences between the traditional groups, such as the PIRA, which tend to be hierarchical, and religiously fundamentalist and epochal groups, such as al-Qaeda, where cells are loosely affiliated and ad hoc. The third component is the role of communications, not only in terms of internal and external communications, but the way in which the Internet is being exploited to serve as a virtual command and control mechanism between leaders, operatives and followers, with traditional organizational patterns becoming increasingly irrelevant. The fourth component is the role of funding, particularly the relationship between terrorist groups and their economic and social welfare fronts, which generate income for the groups and provide them with long-term sustainability and wider support.

Social network analysis is also useful in analyzing a group's organizational formation because of its ability to diagram how such networks are formed, where cells are located, and the relationships within and among terrorist operatives, including linkages formed among terrorist groups.

(8) Modus operandi

To understand a group's internal operating procedures, it is necessary to acquire qualitative and quantitative data about its modus operandi. The term "modus operandi" refers to a particular way or manner of operating, generally of an unvarying, routine or habitual method of procedure, in order to achieve particular objectives. Like other organizations, terrorist groups also engage in some form of decision making to plan and conduct operations. They decide on target selection, tactics, personnel, and the division of tasks within operational cells. They also conduct surveillance, allocate resources for operations, arrange for administrative and logistical assistance for their operatives, and execute the plan of attack.

Terrorist groups are inclined to use a blend of old and new tactics to achieve their objectives. One could even argue that for terrorists the conventional definition of modus operandi does not apply because they attempt to learn lessons from their – and others' – previous terrorist campaigns in order not to repeat them, so the past may not always be the best predictor for future terrorist actions. Therefore, to avoid getting blindsided by a new modus operandi, those involved in countering terrorism must always anticipate new and innovative tactics, organizational procedures and weaponry by a terrorist adversary. Nevertheless, counterterrorism planners still need to examine a group's modus operandi in conducting their previous attacks in order to gain an understanding of what it is capable of achieving, while at the same time trying to anticipate new procedures of warfare.

Here the social sciences can be utilized to study questions such as whether decision making processes in religiously fundamentalist organizations are different from their secular counterparts and the extent to which terrorist groups consistently follow or adhere in their operations to their ideological or religious guidance and agendas.

(9) Incident chronology databases

The development of terrorist incident chronology databases has greatly benefited from statistical methodologies and software tools produced by the social sciences. Databases, which by their nature are continuously updated, can be populated with information about the details of incidents, and longitudinal and other types of analyses can be conducted to generate trends and other insights into terrorism (such as geographical areas where incidents tend to take place, the types of groups that carry out attacks, links between groups, the demographic characteristics of operatives, social networked relations among operatives, their modus operandi, types of weapons used, target selection, and escalation or de-escalation in warfare), the effectiveness of counterterrorism measures (in terms of influencing the increase or decrease of attacks in certain geographical locations), as well as the impact of terrorism on society (such as patterns of political, socio-economic or psychological consequences for the inhabitants in the affected areas).

To reach this scientific level of analysis, however, one has to create objective criteria by which to determine whether an event qualifies as a terrorist act. Current criteria used to create databases may result in seriously underestimating the magnitude of a terrorist threat because virtually all incident chronology databases focus only on successful incidents, but not on the spectrum of operations carried out by groups that fall short of the "success" threshold. Thus, aborted operations, in which operatives give up on their attempts due to a variety of internal factors, or thwarted operations, where government security forces succeed in preventing an attack, are generally not included in most databases. Because aborted and thwarted operations may, in certain cases, constitute the majority of terrorist activities against their government adversaries, the failure to count them results in a statistically misleading quantification of the magnitude of the actual threat.

Further, as discussed above, if terrorism is defined as acts committed only against noncombatant targets, then only those incidents will be entered; whereas acts against "armed" military targets will be included in other types of incident databases. Since different incident databases utilize different coding rules and definitions, it is not possible to produce comparable statistical analyses.

Data collection constitutes another problem area. Governments possess the resources to gather data through classified intelligence and unclassified open sources. At the academic level, however, social science researchers can only rely on data acquisition from open sources, such as media reports, Internet sites (including those created by the government or terrorist groups) and other unclassified sources, some of which may be inaccurate.

Thus, one of the limitations of academic level data gathering to populate terrorist incident chronology databases is that is can never approximate the authoritativeness and exhaustiveness of government databases. On the other hand, it is the social science that produces the theories and methodologies and computational tools – e.g., the statistical procedures required to generalize from infrequent events – that enable researchers to generate insights and hypotheses from the accumulated data. Once databases are appropriately populated, they can be used to assess the magnitude of the threat, including identifying and anticipating potential threats.

(10) Forecasting and predicting terrorism

Forecasting is not the same as predicting. Prediction entails anticipating and, in the case of a government, acquiring tactical intelligence about an imminent terrorist attack in terms of identifying the likely group and the attack's timing, location, targeting, type of weapon and tactics. Forecasting involves determining at a more general level whether a group is likely to conduct "conventional" versus "suicide" attacks (whether or not operatives will seek to stay alive or blow themselves up at an operation), to be conservative or innovative in its tactics, or to resort to conventional low impact (CLI), conventional high impact (CHI) or chemical, biological, radiological or nuclear (CBRN) warfare, also known as weapons of mass destruction (WMD).

Forecasting or predicting terrorism, which is a "human-made" disaster, is vastly different from anticipating naturally caused disasters, such as extreme weather, hurricanes and earthquakes. Meteorologists, for example, using sophisticated tools, have attained a relatively high degree of accuracy in monitoring weather conditions to predict the likelihood of rain or snow over a short-range period. Similarly, scientists can forecast months in advance the likelihood of hurricanes in a specific geographic region. This is due to the capability of "hindsight" projections based on previous historical data or predictive projections based on the relatively constant nature of tropical weather and the ability of satellite and radar technologies to track hurricanes at the earliest phases of their development and paths. Similarly, early prediction of potentially damaging earthquakes is made possible by studying previous historical frequency patterns in a specific area, where a fault system is located, or the rate at which strain accumulates in the rock.[34] However, while it is possible to estimate where earthquakes are likely to occur, "there is currently no reliable way to predict the days or months when an event will occur in any specific location."[35]

Although not yet attaining the reliability level of forecasting and predicting natural disasters, the social sciences have developed methods to anticipate terrorism. For example, computer-based analyses of incident chronology databases can generate knowledge about terrorist incidents – whether aborted, thwarted or successful – in order to map the likely geographical location and distribution of attacks and identify regions of greatest risk. Thus, for each terrorist group, the data produced by details and characteristics of previous attacks and "unsuccessful" operations can generate warning signals to predict the likelihood, frequency and geographical locations of future attacks.

It is still unknown, however, whether such data-driven trend analyses can attain the predictive validity of comparable analyses in the natural sciences. For example, can mathematical algorithms be incorporated into such tools, with appropriate weighting properties, to generate predictions of the magnitude of likely terrorist attacks? At the very least, the social sciences can provide a rigorous framework to forecast such data in more general terms, for example, by assigning the components of a group's modus operandi as independent variables and the level or magnitude of terrorism as the dependent variable in order to project likely future trends, as opposed to the likelihood and magnitude of imminent attacks. Thus, forecasting methodologies can help us understand the evolution, patterns and trajectory of terrorism by an individual group or multiple groups, including changes in the profiles and characteristics of their operatives, and warfare trends such as "conventional" versus suicide attacks, or low impact versus high impact operations.

(11) Countering terrorism

To be effective, a government's campaign to combat terrorism[36] must employ an appropriate mix of coercive (e.g., military or law enforcement) and conciliatory (e.g., political, diplomatic or socio-economic) measures that either will militarily defeat the insurgents on the battlefield or peacefully terminate the insurgency by resolving the root causes and conditions that may prolong the conflict. The social sciences provide the methods that enable analysts and government practitioners to understand how to resolve terrorist insurgencies, as well as to measure the effectiveness of such countermeasures. Root cause analysis, for example, provides a methodology to research and systematically map the spectrum of root causes underlying a rebellion's origins, grievances and demands. In ideal cases, it is hoped that such mapping of root causes will then produce the knowledge to formulate appropriate governmental responses.

Understanding a conflict's underlying root causes can provide a government with the capability to effectively calibrate its response strategies and tactics to specific challenges and threats. For the underlying factors to be resolved, however, it is also up to the insurgents to incorporate into their demands grievances and other objectives that are amenable to the "give and take" of compromise and negotiations because otherwise even addressing a conflict's root causes may not succeed in terminating the insurgency. Some insurgent movements are inherently extremist and not interested in compromising their demands, such as militant religious fundamentalists who are intent on establishing highly authoritarian theocratic states (e.g., in Algeria, Egypt, Jordan and Lebanon[37]) or are filled with unrelenting rage against a superpower and Western nations (e.g., al-Qaeda's group and its network of affiliates). Thus, in such cases no peaceful accommodation may be possible between governments and insurgents even when governments are willing to resolve a conflict's "root causes," such as socio-economic and political inequalities, because of the insurgents' uncompromising agenda.

One way to determine whether it is possible for governments and insurgents to arrive at a negotiated compromise is by distinguishing between insurgents' legitimate and illegitimate grievances. Legitimate grievances may be defined as those that are anchored in international law, particularly in the areas of constitutionalism and human rights, and are politically, legally, economically and geographically equitable to all relevant parties affected by the conflict. Illegitimate grievances, on the other hand, generally are based on anti-democratic, theocratic, religiously exclusionary or criminal principles and objectives, as well as desiring the destruction or annihilation of the adversary.

The social sciences help us understand how to counter terrorism at a more tactical level. For example, one of the advantages of terrorist groups against their state adversaries is their capability to conduct their operations covertly while revealing as little information as possible about their operatives and imminent attack intentions, although more general pronouncements about their intentions are usually posted on their Internet web sites. Social network analysis, however, can be used to reduce the terrorist adversary's advantages by enabling counterterrorist practitioners to map how terrorist groups, beginning at the cellular level, are organized, how they recruit and organize themselves, whether in their home countries or overseas, to carry out operations. In another window of opportunity for counter terrorism practitioners, while simple operations require a relatively few operatives, complex operations require a more elaborate planning process involving a longer time frame, larger numbers of operatives with multiple and specialized taskings, ranging from administrative, logistical, intelligence, to combat, and wider geographical areas of operation. Such elaborate planning and preparation during the pre-incident process may turn out to be a vulnerability for terrorists and an opportunity for security organizations to track their activities. It is here that geospatial and social network methodologies can be used to assist in mapping geographical patterns associated with the locations and movements of terrorist adversaries, how they may be planning future attacks, and characteristics of their operatives, all of which can enable counterterrorist organizations to formulate appropriate response measures.

One of the main deficiencies in the academic study of counterterrorism is the lack of methodologies and templates to assess the effectiveness of governmental measures to counter terrorism. With few analytical exceptions that are primarily methodology based,[38] there are no tools that can be populated with indices and metrics to assess the effectiveness of measures to counter terrorism. Mission area analysis (MAA), a methodology that is employed in the military milieu but is not widely used in counterterrorism studies, could be adapted into a software tool to formulate a roadmap for how strategic objectives can be implemented by appropriate tactical measures on the ground, including milestone and performance metrics. Once such a tool is operationalized, it could be used to outline and formulate a computerized template to populate the specific step-by-step tasks required to achieve the objectives in a government's campaign to combat terrorism, as well as assessing the effectiveness in achieving these objectives. Measures of effectiveness in countering terrorism might include data on indices such as internal group dissension (whether at the leadership or leadership-follower level), defections, difficulties in recruiting new operatives, funding problems, loss of support among a group's constituency, loss of a state sponsor, a decline in a group's military effectiveness, and an increase in a group's marginalization among potential supporters.

A final area in countering terrorism in need of further methodological tool development is in mapping how operatives end their participation in terrorism. Studies have been conducted on disengagement from terrorism by examining how some terrorists have left their groups because of dissatisfaction with their former groups or in response to a promise of immunity.[39] Once such vulnerabilities in terrorist groups are identified they can be exploited by counterterrorist organizations to increase dissatisfaction and dissension within groups, thereby weakening these groups and influencing members to leave. It would be useful to be able to populate databases with information about former terrorist operatives in order to generate trends and other insights about their disengagement, including data on why other operatives choose to continue to engage in terrorism.

Conclusion

As discussed in this chapter, the social sciences have made great contributions to the terrorism academic discipline. Terrorism studies, however, have yet to achieve the level of a "hard" science and there remain a number of problem areas, particularly in formulating a consensual definition of terrorism, especially whether it involves attacks against civilians and the military, because without consensual coding or counting rules (including counting aborted and thwarted incidents) terrorist incident chronology databases will remain incapable of providing analytically relevant data on the magnitude of a threat facing a country. It is hoped that future social science academic research efforts, including the development of software-based tools, in these and other areas will upgrade our capabilities to better understand and respond with the most effective countermeasures against the magnitude of the terrorist challenges facing us.

Notes

1 See David C. Rapoport, "The Four Waves of Modern Terrorism," pp. 46–73 in Audrey Kurth Cronin and James M. Ludes (eds), *Attacking Terrorism: Elements of a Grand Strategy* (Washington, DC: Georgetown University Press, 2004).

2 See Scott L. Plous and Philip G. Zimbardo, "How Social Science Can Reduce Terrorism," *Chronicles of Higher Education,* September 10, 2004, p. B9; and Neil J. Smelser and Faith Mitchell (eds), *Terrorism: Perspectives from the Behavioral and Social Sciences* (Washington, DC: National Academies Press, 2001); and Andrew Silke (ed.), *Research on Terrorism: Trends, Achievements and Failures* (Portland, OR: Frank Cass, 2004).

3 See White House, *National Strategy for Combating Terrorism* (Washington, DC: White House, February 2003); and NSTC, *Combating Terrorism: Research Priorities in the Social, Behavioral and Economic Sciences* (Washington, DC: White House Office of Science and Technology Policy, NSTC Subcommittee on Social, Behavioral and Economic Sciences, February 2005). The author of this chapter served on the panel that contributed to the report.

4 RAND's Terrorism and Homeland Security Program, the International Policy Institute for Counterterrorism (ICT) at the Interdisciplinary Center, Herzliya, Israel, and the University of Maryland's National Consortium for the Study of Terrorism and Responses to Terrorism (START), represent some of the few integrated, multidisciplinary research efforts in terrorism studies around the world, although even among these efforts some are better at analyzing the terrorism problem than in developing methodologies and tools to advance the state of the discipline.

5 United States Department of State, *Patterns of Global Terrorism 2003* (Washington, DC: Office of the Secretary of State, Office of the Coordinator for Counterterrorism, April 2004), p. xii.

6 United States Department of State, *Patterns of Global Terrorism 2003* (Washington, DC: Office of the Secretary of State, Office of the Coordinator for Counterterrorism, April 2004).

7 United States Department of State, *Patterns of Global Terrorism 2003* (Washington, DC: Office of the Secretary of State, Office of the Coordinator for Counterterrorism, April 2004).

8 United States Department of State, *Patterns of Global Terrorism 2003* (Washington, DC: Office of the Secretary of State, Office of the Coordinator for Counterterrorism, April 2004).

9 Neil J. Smelser and Faith Mitchell (eds), *Terrorism: Perspectives from the Behavioral and Social Sciences*, p. 2.

10 Neil J. Smelser and Faith Mitchell (eds), *Terrorism: Perspectives from the Behavioral and Social Sciences*.

11 Neil J. Smelser and Faith Mitchell (eds), *Terrorism: Perspectives from the Behavioral and Social Sciences*.

12 NSTC, *Combating Terrorism: Research Priorities in the Social, Behavioral and Economic Sciences*, p. 7.

13 This argument is also made by the United Nations Office on Drugs and Crime: "If terrorism is defined strictly in terms of attacks on non-military targets, a number of attacks on military installations and soldiers' residences could not be included in the statistics" [http://www.unodc.org/unodc/terrorism_definitions.html]. Interestingly, the MIPT Knowledge Base includes in its statistical data terrorist incidents against military targets, whereas the incident database compiled by the International Policy Institute for Counterterrorism (ICT) in Herzliya, Israel, differentiates between attacks against civilians, which it considers as "terrorist incidents," and attacks by terrorists against military targets, which it considers as "guerrilla incidents."

14 See http://www.ict.org.il.

15 United Nations Office on Drugs and Crime, "Definitions of Terrorism," http://www.undocs.org/unodc/terrorism_definitions.html

16 United Nations Office on Drugs and Crime, "Definitions of Terrorism," http://www.undocs.org/unodc/terrorism_definitions.html

17 Boaz Ganor, *The Counter-Terrorism Puzzle: A Guide for Decision Makers* (New Brunswick, NJ: Transaction Publishers, 2005), p. 17.

18 Boaz Ganor, *The Counter-Terrorism Puzzle: A Guide for Decision Makers* (New Brunswick, NJ: Transaction Publishers, 2005), p. 20.

19 Boaz Ganor, *The Counter-Terrorism Puzzle: A Guide for Decision Makers* (New Brunswick, NJ: Transaction Publishers, 2005), p. 24.

20 Bruce Hoffman, "Terrorism," Microsoft® Encarta® Online Encyclopedia 2005, http://encarta.msn.com © 1997–2005.

21 See Walter Reich (ed.), *Origins of Terrorism: Psychologies, Ideologies, Theologies, States of Mind* (Washington, DC: Woodrow Wilson Center Press, 1998); and Tore Bjorgo, (ed.), *Root Causes of Terrorism* (New York: Routledge, 2005).

22 Gus Martin, *Understanding Terrorism: Challenges, Perspectives, and Issues* (Thousand Oaks, CA: SAGE Publications, 2003), p. 67. Martin based his analysis on the works of Steven E. Barkan and Lynne L. Snowden, *Collective Violence* (Boston, MA: Allyn & Bacon, 2001) and Jack A. Goldstone, "Introduction: The Comparative and Historical Study of Revolutions," in Jack A. Goldstone, (ed.), *Revolutions: Theoretical, Comparative, and Historical Studies* (San Diego, CA: Harcourt Brace Jovanovich, 1986).

23 Gus Martin, *Understanding Terrorism: Challenges, Perspectives, and Issues* (Thousand Oaks, CA: SAGE Publications, 2003), p. 67.

24 Gus Martin, *Understanding Terrorism: Challenges, Perspectives, and Issues* (Thousand Oaks, CA: SAGE Publications, 2003), p. 68.

25 Ted Robert Gurr, *Why Men Rebel* (Princeton, NJ: Princeton University Press, 1970).

26 See Charles Y. Glock, "The Role of Deprivation in the Origin and Evolution of Religious Groups," in R. Lee and M. E. Marty (eds), *Religion and Social Conflict*, (New York: Oxford University Press, 1964), pp. 24–36.

27 Arie Kruglianski, "Inside the Terrorist Mind," paper presented to the National Academy of Science annual meeting, Washington, DC, April 29, 2002.

28 See Tore Bjorgo (ed.), *Root Causes of Terrorism* (New York: Routledge, 2005).

29 John Horgan, "The Search for the Terrorist Personality," pp. 3–27 in Andrew Silke (ed.), *Terrorists, Victims and Society: Psychological Perspectives on Terrorism and its Consequences* (New York: John Wiley & Sons, 2003).

30 Arie Perliger and Leonard Weinberg, "Altruism and Fatalism: Characteristics of Palestinian Suicide Terrorists," *TerrorismExperts.Org*.

31 Marc Sageman, *Understanding Terror Networks* (Philadelphia, PA: University of Pennsylvania Press, 2004).

32 See Marc Sageman, *Understanding Terror Networks* (Philadelphia, PA: University of Pennsylvania Press, 2004), whose profiles of operatives in the Global Salafi Jihad have been operationalized by computational tools.

33 In Israel, for example, there is a similar tendency by terrorism experts to focus primarily on the Palestinian threat while at the same time ignoring the threats posed by the proliferation of religiously fundamentalist, right-wing Jewish individuals and groupings that have the potential to carry out their own version of suicide bombings, assassinations of the country's political leaders, and attacks against Palestinian holy places in order to sabotage any progress in the peace process between Israel and the Palestinians.

34 US Geological Survey, "Predicting Earthquakes," http://pubs.usgs.gov/gip/earthq1/predict.html

35 Ruth Ludwin, "Earthquake Prediction," http://www.geophys.washsington.edu/seis/pnsn/info_general/eq_prediction.html

36 Combating terrorism is used as an umbrella concept incorporating the defensively-based anti-terrorism and offensively-based counter-terrorism.

37 In the case of Lebanon, Hizballah's political party is part of the country's confessional democratic political system, but a major intangible element is whether at some point it will seek to overthrow the political system and impose an Iranian-based theocracy over the country.

38 See, for example, Boaz Ganor, *The Counterterrorism Puzzle: A Guide for Decision Makers* (New Brunswick, NJ: Transaction Publishers, 2005).

39 Studies on disengagement from terrorism include Tore Bjorgo, "Recruitment and Disengagement from Extreme Groups: The Case of Racist Youth Subcultures," paper presented at the 7th International Seminar on Environmental Criminology and Crime Analysis, Barcelona, Spain, 21–24 June 1998; Tore Bjorgo, "Exit Neo-Nazism: Reducing Recruitment and Promoting Disengagement from Racist Groups," Paper #627 (Oslo, Norway: Norwegian Institute of International Affairs, June 2002); and John Horgan, "Psychological Issues on Disengaging from Terrorism: Some Preliminary Issues and Considerations," paper prepared for the Madrid Summit Working Group, March 8–11, 2005.

3

THE ROLE OF HISTORY AND CONTINUITY IN TERRORISM RESEARCH

Isabelle Duyvesteyn

Introduction

Until recently, a running joke among terrorism experts was that the number of scholars studying terrorism far exceeded the actual number of terrorists. This was certainly true in the cases of the North American Weathermen and the German Rote Armee Fraktion. Today, with the prevalence of terrorism inspired by political Islam, the number of terrorists has risen substantially compared to the 1970s. Concomitantly, and not surprisingly since 9/11, the number of experts has also increased. In the current climate, the fear is such that we are now led to believe that the situation is reversed and that the terrorists outnumber the experts.

The existing fear caused by terrorist threats has striking similarities with the late nineteenth century, when anarchist violence held sway in the Western world. Not only were anarchists similarly organised in a shadowy network that seemed to encompass all European states, but they also created an all-pervasive fear that gripped whole societies; 'Among the general public, small incidents led to panic. In separate incidents in Paris, faulty electrical wiring on a streetcar and the collapse of some scenery at a theatre sent people rushing out, screaming hysterically because they were fearful of impending explosions'.[1] With the benefit of hindsight, we can now conclude that this situation was rather exaggerated. The anarchists who were held responsible for the terrorist acts had the habit of applauding any use of violence that was aimed at conservative bastions of power. They even applauded violence that they had nothing to do with, such as criminal acts, which they claimed questioned the existing conventions of property ownership. Furthermore, the advent in the nineteenth century of the popular press and its coverage of attacks substantially contributed to this climate; 'The myth of anarchist terrorism and the power of dynamite as created by sensationalistic newspapers, a fearful populace and the anarchists themselves was as important in the development (and containment) of anarchist terrorism as the heterogeneous acts of violence themselves'.[2]

This historical analogy is not presented here to suggest that we are over-reacting when dealing with current terrorist threats. Instead, it is intended to illustrate that what we are experiencing today might not be as new as we think (with the exception, perhaps of the increase in the number of experts). The problem this contribution will address is the fact that there exist to date very few studies on the development, past trends and patterns of terrorism in the modern period. We know little about the history of terrorism, and what we think we know is not really the subject of debate.[3] This is the starting point of this contribution.

In one of the many terrorism handbooks that has recently appeared a striking chapter was included: 'How to Research Terrorism?'[4] The author provides the reader with many suggestions, including internet resources, library catalogues, newspapers and legal papers. At no point in this extended description is a mention made of historical and archival resources relating to terrorism. This book unfortunately is not the only example. Terrorism seems to be a subject with almost no history.[5]

This state of affairs, however, does not seem to have been an impediment for many experts to make claims about the characteristics and historical development of the phenomenon. For example, there has existed a strong tendency to focus on so-called new features of terrorism without properly consulting history.[6] In particular, religiously inspired terrorism has recently and unjustifiably been called completely new.[7] Historians, while often aiming to stress continuity where necessary, do not discount innovation *a priori*. The concept "new" can be defined in the following way: '"New" can signify that a phenomenon has not been witnessed before, such as the discovery of a new star in a far-away galaxy. Alternatively, the label "new" can rightly be applied when it concerns seen before phenomena but an unknown perspective or interpretation is developed, such as the theory of relativity or the idea that the earth is round'.[8] The expressions of terrorism that most likely could be seen as new are eco-terrorism, narco-terrorism and cyber-terrorism, three phenomena not seen before, which are inextricably linked to developments in the last half of the twentieth century. However, they have rarely been described as new in the existing debate about new terrorism.

The aim of this contribution is not to make a case for history and historians as producing the only valuable knowledge on terrorism. Rather, the aim is to argue that history should be incorporated more strongly into the study of terrorism. To date, terrorism studies have been dominated by political and social sciences, which have produced insightful findings into terrorism and terrorist behaviour. However, the paradigm most dominant in current research activity, the multi-disciplinary approach, has percolated into terrorism studies but not included historical studies to a sufficient degree. How the historian and the historical approach have made and can make a contribution to develop our understanding of terrorism is the subject of this contribution.

The history at the centre of discussion in this contribution is not the history and mythology that is prevalent in and around terrorist groups. In particular, terrorist groups fighting within the context of national liberation struggles have thrived by the existence of national myths about historical greatness and independence. Northern Ireland is a case in point; 'The uses of history as memory, not only keep the past alive but sustain a sense of deprivation, marginalization, not to speak of the affronts, discrimination, prejudice, and the like has sustained the tensed boundaries of the Irish working class community extremely well'.[9] Sri Lanka and the struggle of the Tamil Tigers and the Basque ETA movement are other examples.[10]

The history that will be the centre of discussion in this contribution is the history of the phenomenon of terrorism itself. The approach will follow the point of view of E.H. Carr of history being concerned with social relevance rather than the explanation and understanding of historical events *an sich*.[11] Carr defined it as follows: 'the dual and reciprocal function of history [is] to promote our understanding of the past in light of the present and of the present in light of the past'.[12]

In the remainder of this contribution, first, the characteristics of the study of history will be discussed. Second, a more detailed discussion will be presented, looking at the development of terrorism in the nineteenth and twentieth centuries. This discussion is based on present claims and insights regarding the history of terrorism. It includes a series of questions and suggestions for a possible future debate on the history of terrorism.

The role of history in the study of terrorism

History is the study of the past, and, in that sense, an interpretative science. The way in which we look at the past can be influenced by many factors. The questions that we ask are influenced, among others, by personal, social, political, ideological and economic factors. The same questions can be asked and answered in completely different ways and new questions can arise that find familiar answers; 'when we attempt to answer the question "what is history?" our answer, consciously or unconsciously, reflects our own position in time, and forms part of our answer to the broader question what view we take of the society in which we live'.[13] This makes clear that historical studies are not value-free.[14]

Working by time periods and geographical location are the most important characteristics of historical studies. Furthermore, historical research can also focus on an entity, organisations or a problem. The material for historical research is both primary and secondary source material from which facts is selected. This selection process of both the framework and the facts is influenced by the aforementioned factors or context; '[t]he facts of history cannot be purely objective, since they become facts of history only in virtue of the significance attached to them by the historian'.[15] With these facts the historian will build his or her narrative and set the scene for interpretation. This process of inductive reasoning is very common in historical studies, but by no means all historians work in this fashion. On top of the collection of facts and the interpretation, the historian aims to understand the historical occurrences in their own context.

What is the status of knowledge today in historical studies? The majority of historians will argue that there is a certain body of historical knowledge that is irrefutable, and on which the discipline continues to build, so-called basic knowledge. On top of this basic knowledge is the so-called applied knowledge or constructions of ordered facts that are open for (re-)interpretation and discussion. As opposed to those supporting the existence of basic knowledge, there are also those, a minority, who are more sceptical. All the historian can present his or her readers is a 'personal vision of the past, and the materials out of which they in turn can fashion a personal vision which corresponds to their own aspirations and sympathies'.[16] History, in this perspective, can only be a personal story.

History concentrates fundamentally on the study of humans and their environment. Historical studies generally form part of the Humanities; 'history is essentially a *hybrid* discipline, combining the technical and analytical procedures of a science with the imaginative and stylistic qualities of an art'.[17] However, the question whether historical studies should be more properly placed among the social sciences offers a *mer à boire*. Suffice it to say here that social sciences have been aspiring to be closer to the natural sciences in their quest to uncover general laws about human behaviour. At the same time they are often compared to historical studies, where developments towards generalising and theorising have been taking place to a lesser extent. Where social scientists are satisfied with rough descriptions of time periods and typologies, historians deem the understanding of time periods and uniqueness of events essential.

The social scientist in the past has displayed little interest in historical studies, desiring instead to concentrate on what distinguishes this science from the historical art. The concentration on natural science methodologies in the field of social science has led to a situation in which the social sciences have focused on present subject matter. The sociologist uses a wide variety of organising principles, frameworks and systems in order to develop models. Most of these models are not only based on Western experiences in the modern period; they are also teleological or predetermined instead of allowing for change, and have therefore been criticised by historians.

Instead of building fences between the social scientist and the historian, the commonalities could be more emphasised. Both studies share a common interest in developing an understanding of all aspects of men and women and their behaviour in their environment. In order to do this the historian has an important tool, namely chronology. This contributes to, but does not solve, the important question of understanding. On top of chronology the historian has narrative and interpretation.

The dominant paradigm in the field of humanities and social sciences is interdisciplinary or multi-disciplinary. The grey areas between disciplines that used to be dividing walls have now become promising new areas for research.

Exciting new fields of research such as conflict and environmental studies but also anthropology of the Middle Ages and the economics of international relations are but a few examples. In many of these fields, disagreements on fundamentals and methods not withstanding, new and encouraging findings have been produced. Looking at the main works that have, until recently, appeared in the field of terrorism studies, this multi-disciplinary reality has only slowly started to find its way here.[18] However, what is striking in this respect is the absence of clear historical approaches to terrorism.

Not only is the paradigm characterised as multi-disciplinary, eclecticism is also an important feature. The latter seems to be more strongly represented than the former. A clear example forms the work of Bruce Hoffman, who states in one of his studies that his aim is to investigate

> why terrorist do what they do as well as to shed light on likely future patterns and potentialities. This somewhat selective – and thus perhaps idiosyncratic – approach deliberately emphasizes key historical themes over abstract theory and relies on empirical evidence rather than explanatory models to illustrate and support its main arguments.[19]

The historical themes do not seem to be grounded in pure historical studies, but are chosen more on what are perhaps preconceived ideas about important developments in terrorism. The fact that the dominant research paradigm of multi-disciplinary approaches has had only limited application, and that history is (ab)-used to suit the predetermined needs of experts, both lead to a problematic state of affairs in terrorism studies.

Another problem in the field is the issue of definition, which has significantly scarred the debate. In the social sciences it is deemed essential to agree on the basic outline of what the subject entails, to be able to compare across cases and draw conclusions. It is unlikely that any form of agreement on the definition of terrorism will be reached in the foreseeable future. The often-quoted 109 definitions of Alex Schmid found in the 1980s continue to be representative of the field.[20] Even in the hypothetical case of agreement being reached on defining the term, the application will provide a second set of pitfalls. In historical studies this problem is important but less pressing because of the approach of the historian towards his or her subject. Temporal designs and historical significance form more important cut-off points for historical research than issues of definition.

A final set of problems important for this discussion concerns the fact that there exist some persistent categorical claims about terrorism with only a limited empirical foundation. As Walter Laqueur noted: 'Generalizations with regard to terrorism are almost always misleading'.[21] This has not prevented him and a few other scholars from coming to some striking points of view regarding the historical development of terrorism. In the second part of this contribution an overview incorporating these claims will be presented. This can be seen as a macro-perspective on terrorism but also, or more so, as a set of questions that deserve more thorough historical investigation. This description will illustrate the widespread habit of compartmentalisation. Broad time periods (decades) are linked to schematic typologies of terrorism; e.g. the 1960s were characterised by left-wing terrorism. It is questionable whether such broad labels contribute to getting to the bottom of the historical development of terrorism and to an understanding of what the phenomenon is really about.

The reader is asked to keep in mind, while reading the rest of this contribution, that the limitation of historical studies as being bound by time and place is here even more applicable than ever. By describing the findings and claims of other experts, I have not tried to attain a comprehensive picture of modern history. Rather I have attempted to do justice to the existing state of knowledge and points of view, to ask critical questions and to pinpoint lacunae.[22] The main sources for this treatise are books and articles devoted to general historical treatments of terrorism. Some case study material and findings have been incorporated as well.

An overview of historical knowledge on terrorism

In the following paragraphs, the nineteenth and twentieth centuries will be dealt with chronologically.

The nineteenth century[23]

In the nineteenth century, it is claimed, the use of the instrument of terror shifted from regicide, or the targeting of heads of state, to a wider form of terror aimed at close associates or other representatives of power.[24] Political murder, another word for regicide (or tyrannicide), formed the foundation for the development of modern terrorism. However, the last decade of the nineteenth century, for example, is often called the decade of political murder, when between 1892 and 1901 more heads of state were killed than in any other period in history.[25] Furthermore, political murder has continued to occur up to the twenty-first century. There are thus strong indications of continuity.[26] The question is where did the roads between political murder and terrorism diverge? When was a political murder just that, and when did it become terrorism? Or is political murder always a terrorist act? These questions have not been answered satisfactorily.

Several specific factors have been emphasised that have contributed to the development of terrorism in the nineteenth century: organisational, theoretical and technological.[27] First, the organisational development that occurred, and which is deemed important, focuses on the establishment of secret societies of like-minded individuals with the specific aim of using violence to realise political goals. The most influential of these were the Carbonari sects in what is today Italy. They strove from 1807 onwards for the establishment of an independent, unified and republican state.[28] Whereas this development was important in itself, the question is to what extent did it form a sea change in the practice of terrorist activity? Conspiracy has always been a common way of planning to eliminate opponents, who continue to be powerful individuals representing established power.[29]

Second, it is argued that an essential theoretical leap was taken in the development of modern terrorism in the formulation of murder as necessary to realise political goals. In other words, murder was justified as the most effective means to bring about change. The writings of Karl Heinzen and Johann Most are argued to have been groundbreaking in this respect.[30] Two questions are in order here. The secularisation of the nineteenth century was important, but how significant was it for the justification of murder? To what extent is this different from the practice of murder that was justified by religious thinking, aimed as well at unjust rulers and political change? Furthermore, in earlier periods secular justifications of murder also existed, e.g. the thinking of Machiavelli; how different is this nineteenth century idea from these earlier expressions?

In terms of theory, the idea of 'propaganda by deed' was also significant. The term was coined in 1878 by a French anarchist, Paul Brousse, who described the practice of recruiting new activists by shaking them into action through violent examples.[31] Recruitment, both passive and active, was thought to occur after people witnessed not only the terrorist attack but also government repression that almost always followed. The repression became a strong recruitment mechanism. By 1881, at the International Anarchists Congress, propaganda by deed was adopted, which was clearly outside the law.

Third, technological developments, such as the development of the printing press which allowed for mass production of cheap newspapers, and the invention of dynamite, were, according to many experts, instrumental in widening the impact of terrorist acts and increasing their lethality. The technological developments that occurred in this era were adopted by the terrorists. They are argued to have made the difference between regicide and terrorism.[32] The invention of dynamite truly formed a revolutionary development, but it was revolutionary for the whole of society even in its peaceful applications, e.g. the construction of railroads. Is it fair to ascribe to it a revolutionary effect only on the phenomenon of terrorism? To what extent can societal developments and changes in the practice of terrorism be separated?

The anarchist organisations that were active in the late nineteenth century have, to many observers, epitomised these developments.[33] However, it should be emphasised that terrorist activity existed before the advent of anarchism and it is therefore not accurate to equate terrorism with anarchism.[34] Furthermore, anarchists had the habit of applauding other violent anti-state activity. Many terrorist acts, therefore, were ascribed to anarchists, which might not have been accurate. Not only the anarchist but two other identifiable strands of terrorism existed in this period. The Russian Revolutionaries and the radical nationalists were active, but all three are deemed to have been highly 'individualistic' and without 'great political significance'.[35]

While, at the start of the nineteenth century, the *regime de la terreur* – according to most experts the etymological source of terrorism – had a positive ring, and even many anarchists wore the name *terrorist* as a badge of honour, at the end of the century terrorism started to gain a negative connotation.[36] Why was the nineteenth century first the 'heroic period of terrorism' and why did terrorists subsequently come to be seen as villains?[37] 'Using the term terrorism came not only to imply that an adversary employed a particular strategy or style of violence but it could also be argued that the "true nature" of the opponent was thereby revealed'.[38] Why and how did this shift in meaning and connotation occur?

The nineteenth century witnessed the rise of the middle class in Western societies. The middle class produced many terrorists.[39] These men and women from the bourgeoisie, according to experts, were responsible for most cases of terrorism in the modern period, with an important exception of nationalist terror campaigns.[40] It can be questioned whether this finding does not contradict the often-heard claim that poverty forms the main breeding ground for terrorism.[41] The middle class will expectedly suffer less than the working classes in economic dire straits. There is evidence that poverty might not be an important cause as is claimed.[42] Nevertheless, poverty can be a motivation for terrorist acts.

A last important fundament of terrorism that the nineteenth century brings forward is the link with periods of general upheaval. In particular, anarchism has been found to appear together with rapid social and economic change, industrialisation and demographic explosion.[43] This finding seems to be consistent for the whole of the modern period: 'post-revolutionary, post-colonial, and post-war situations often have provided the most material for students of civil strife', including terrorism.[44] This is also an argument made in regard to the rise of religious terrorism in the 1990s, which will be discussed in more detail below.[45]

The nineteenth century is indeed important for understanding the roots of modern terrorism. The question, however, is whether the right emphasis is being placed on phenomena that constituted continuity (political murder) or that were so influential that they affected the whole of civilised society (dynamite). The rise of the middle class, secularisation, the rising level of education, the role of the popular press but also urbanisation and unbridled capitalism have all put a stamp on the form that terrorism adopted. Equally important or even more important was perhaps the rise of 'liberation' ideologies from the ideas of the French Revolution such as democracy, Marxism and nationalism, which were to have such a large effect on twentieth century history, including terrorist activity. In none of the sources these factors seem to receive the attention they can be argued to deserve.[46] This is surprising in the light of the almost omnipresent tendency to label terrorism movements in the twentieth century, using the above terms.

Furthermore, this representation of terrorism in the nineteenth century largely bypasses activities in the non-Western world.[47] Especially since this period is strongly marked by imperialism, it would be very interesting to find out if and how terrorism occurred during the 'scramble for Africa', for example. Decolonisation was to put a strong mark on the subsequent development of terrorism.[48] This and the other questions raised above would provide interesting avenues for further research.

The twentieth century

The first half of the century

Until the First World War, terrorism was often regarded as an activity engaged in by mainly left-wing political ideological activists.[49] Not only anarchism, but also the Social Revolutionary Party in Russia, are the cases to which this claim is linked. However, some experts have pointed out that this kind of terrorism had, by the turn of the century, in most parts of Europe, substantially declined because of the rise of non-violent channels for social opposition, such as labour unions.[50] The notable exception was Russia.

Nationalism, at the start of the twentieth century, came to be seen as another motor for terrorist violence.[51] This was exemplified by the murder of the Habsburg heir in Sarajevo in 1914 by Serb nationalist Gavrilo Princip. This political murder – a continuing trend from the nineteenth century – might be seen in the context of a campaign of violence to realise frustrated nationalist dreams against the Habsburg Empire. Not only Serbs but many other minorities in multi-ethnic states, such as Macedonians, Armenians and the Irish, used terrorism to seek attention for their claims. However, this nationalist terrorism was really not very new. The roots of this type of terrorism can clearly be found in the nineteenth century. For example, it can be argued that the Carbonari sects, mentioned above, were also nationalist – striving for Italian unity – and their activities started in the early 1800s. Not only did it start earlier, it lasted much longer than some experts argue. It is claimed that nationalist terrorism subsided at the end of the First World War after the breakdown of the Habsburg and Ottoman empires.[52] However, there is also evidence that, exactly at this point, a new period started which was to last into the 1960s, and which was characterised by struggles for national self-determination.[53]

While an impression might exist that terrorism was a force of political emancipation or frustrated nationalism, the precursors to the autocratic right-wing regimes taking centre stage in the *inter bellum* also used terrorist measures to make their presence felt. Both left-wing and right-wing terrorism in this period shared hatred against the existing order, and both often found overlap with patriotism and sometimes religion.[54] State terrorism reached its apex with the atrocities committed by the Hitler and Stalin regimes. This form of collective violence is often excluded in treatises of terrorism. State terrorism as a category generally stands apart from what is considered terrorist activity.[55] It can be questioned whether the distinction is really that clear when state terrorism, as carried out by such regimes as Hitler's Germany and Stalinist Russia, was also aimed at political change through the threat or use of violence. The difference might be simply one of scale. It might be the case that these regimes formed precursors for other ideologically motivated terrorism linked to limitless murder.

Not only in the shape of terror exerted by the state machinery, the impact of the Second World War can also be gauged in the development of new mind-sets in the non-Western world. The Atlantic Charter, agreed to by Roosevelt and Churchill in August 1941, stated that both territorial and political changes should be decided only by the desires of the people concerned.[56] Furthermore, the fall of Singapore, in early 1942, has been marked as starting the decline of Western colonial influence around the world, leading to violent decolonisation struggles.[57] These two events are argued to have been important catalysts for the struggles for independence that were to follow and for the shape that terrorism was to adopt in the post-war world: 'the anti-colonial terrorist campaigns are critical to understanding the evolution and development of modern, contemporary terrorism'.[58]

It can be questioned whether it is correct to speak of anti-colonial terrorist campaigns or whether we should more properly speak of wars of independence, knowing that so many colonial powers found it difficult to part with their colonial possessions. Many of the decolonisation struggles were fought out violently, in guerrilla-style wars. Guerrilla war is often separated from terrorism: 'The strategy of guerrilla warfare is to liberate territory' but '[i]t is virtually impossible to establish free zones in a city'.[59] The role of territory is thus argued to be the factor distinguishing terrorism from guerrilla war.[60] However, it can be questioned whether guerrilla forces do not use terrorist acts in order to wage or support their struggle. For example, the Algerian men and women fighting for independence from France in the 1950s could be seen as terrorists because they carried out bomb attacks against civilians. At the same time they were in control of parts of the sparsely inhabited countryside and, one could argue, of the Algiers Kasbah. Where they guerrilla fighters or terrorists? When asked 'what are you?', Yacef, one of the instigators of the Battle for Algiers, answered 'we are assassins ... [i]t is the only way in which we can express ourselves'.[61] The roles of murderer, terrorist and guerrilla fighter are difficult, if not impossible, to separate.

Furthermore, using the concept of war does justice to the aspect of interaction between the terrorists and the government against whom the violence was directed; there was reciprocal influence on the courses of action that were selected. The government, by instituting repressive measures after terrorist attacks, confirmed the terrorists in their struggle. This mechanism was an important part of the revolutionary war concept, including Che Guevara's 'focoismo', but was also present in the teachings of the populist People's Will organisation in Russia in the nineteenth century.[62]

Returning to the Algerian example, there is an important significance attached to the ultimate success of the *Front de Libération Nationale* in Algeria as the 'last of the immediate post-war anti-colonial struggles. For that reason, perhaps, it had the most direct and discernible impact on many later ethno-nationalist terrorist campaigns'.[63] It is argued to have influenced not only the Palestine Liberation Organisation but also the African National Congress.

The shadow of these independency struggles was thus projected long into the future as examples for others to emulate. This terrorism is also claimed to have been innovative in terms of involvement of the (international) press. The terrorist movements fighting colonialism 'were the first to recognize the publicity value inherent in terrorism'.[64] To stay with the Algerian example, some members of the FLN were specifically charged with attracting international press attention, in France and the United States, with quite some success.[65] While it might be clear that state terrorism did not fare well with prying press eyes, earlier terrorist movements had in fact used the channels that the media offered. The nascent international press in the nineteenth century did report on terrorist acts to such an extent that the strengths of some terror movements were extremely overestimated, as noted in the introduction.

Nationalist terrorism campaigns stand out in comparison with other expressions of terrorism, due to the success they are said to have achieved. Terrorists on the whole are regarded as not very successful, with the notable exception of those fighting for nationalist aims, e.g. Israel and Algeria.[66] In terms of outcomes, an important distinction should be made between being successful and being effective:

> To be effective, terrorism need merely produce a decided or decisive effect, which may not reflect the original intent of the actor. ... to claim that terrorism is successful implies that it is effectual, in the sense of producing the effects its users sought and anticipated. ... Terrorism can be effective without being successful.[67]

This is a consistent finding, also, in studies of political murder:

> The history of countless assassinations, examined with an eye to comparing apparent motives with actual outcomes, contains almost none that produced results consonant with the aims of the doer, assuming those aims to have extended at all beyond the miserable taking of a life.[68]

While terrorism inspired by nationalist goals can be successful, terrorism inspired by other aims can be effective. When terrorist organisations change into political parties and participate in parliamentary elections, in general, they have not fared too well. The cases of Northern Ireland, the Basque country and Irgun in Israel supposedly prove this point.[69] The notable exceptions to this rule seem to be the PLO and the ANC.

The immediate post-Second World War terrorist campaigns are argued to have innovated terrorism through the development of a blueprint for the organisation and operation of terrorist movements, the use of the international media and the fact that they showed that terrorism could be successful, i.e. the realisation of independence. Even more substantial changes were in store during the following decades.

The 1960s

The 1960s are widely regarded as a watershed in the development of terrorism: 'the "terrorist problem" had no significance until the 1960s, when the full impact of modern technology was felt, endowing most individuals as individuals or as members of small groups, with capacities they never had before'.[70] For some, the war in Vietnam became the catalyst for this new wave of terrorism.[71] The groups that started their campaigns in this period, e.g. the Brigate Rosse and the Rote Armee Fraktion, saw themselves as *porte-parole* for the Third World. For others, there is an exact time and place for the birth of modern terrorism: 22 July 1968, on board an Israeli El Al aircraft from Rome to Tel Aviv.[72] The aircraft was hijacked and the hijackers not only let it be known that they aimed for an exchange of the hostages for Palestinian prisoners but also forced direct contacts with the Israeli government. This proved a very effective strategy; it made the attack into a widely reported media event and the group gained implicit recognition by the Israeli government, which had hitherto escaped them.

Several features were new or became more pronounced in this period, according to received opinion. First, many terrorist organisations started to operate internationally. The PLO is credited as the 'first truly "international" terrorist organization, it also consistently embraced a far more internationalist orientation than most other terrorist groups'.[73] However, international contacts and support have been features of terrorism predating the 1960s.[74] The origins can be found after the First World War and the trend continued, notably, in independence struggles after the Second World War.[75] This state sponsorship shifted, it is claimed, to a higher gear in the 1980s and 1990s.[76] The international contacts of the PLO included recruiting foreign nationals to carry out attacks on their behalf.[77] Apart from the claim that terrorist groups started to operate internationally, a new feature was also the fact that governments used terrorist organisations as tools of foreign policy, i.e. state-sponsored terrorism.[78] Examples were not only Libya but also Iraq and Syria. According to some, this is interpreted as proxy warfare in the context of the Cold War.[79]

Second, not only is the PLO seen as the first organisation to operate internationally, it is also credited with being the first organisation to purposely seek to increase its finances.[80] However, there is evidence that structured financial organisation of terrorism already occurred in the 1930s.[81] While anarchists were almost by definition poor, nationalist groups became striking exceptions. Financing was secured both covertly and overtly. Criminal activity is generally separated from terrorist activity.[82] Criminal behaviour, in theory, is supposed to be aimed at personal gain, whereas terrorism is supposed to seek larger goals. However, in many instances a link between terrorism and criminal activity seems to exist.

Criminal activity enables terrorist groups to finance their activities. Bank robbery and extortion, for example, are means for the terrorist to gain financially and to make the terrorist group operational. This aspect can therefore not be so easily discarded in investigations into terrorism. There are some recent claims that the links between terrorism and crime have become tighter.[83] However, there is more convincing evidence of long historical links: 'The idea of the alliance between the revolutionary avant-garde and the criminal underworld was to reappear from time to time in the history of nineteenth-century terrorist movements (pace Narodnaya Volya) and again among the American and West German New Left militants of the 1960s'.[84]

Third, the 1960s form a new chapter in the development of terrorism for another reason, namely ideologically. The 1960s are generally regarded as dominated by a wave of left-wing terrorism.[85] However, not only was this terrorism based on thinking derived from Marxism, dating from the nineteenth century. It was also clearly inspired by the philosophy of 'propaganda by deed' developed in the nineteenth century.[86] The left-wing terrorism was heavily constrained in order not to alienate potential supporters. Terrorists shied away from extreme violence to attract an audience, which had to be made aware of the 'truth' through violence.

Fourth, methods and technology changed substantially in this decade. In the 1960s a trend developed of urban terrorism, carried out mostly by left-wing groups.[87] Urban campaigns, however, do have a longer pedigree, as described above. Technological developments in this era, such as TV coverage of terrorist activity, international airline travel, were also deemed to be a defining feature of this decade.[88] They offered opportunities for terrorism to reach further and deepen its impact unheard of in earlier years. In particular, hijacking of international airliners enjoyed great popularity, reaching around 100 cases each year in the 1970s.[89]

Fifth, the development of an indigenous form of Latin American terrorism in this period is also regarded as new. After many of the rural guerrilla campaigns in the developing world did not achieve the desired effect, a refocus on urban centres occurred. The Red Army Faction (RAF) acknowledged drawing inspiration from the Tupamaros campaign in Uruguay.[90] There seems to be more than a slight contradiction when guerrilla wars are separated from the phenomenon of terrorism, as claimed above. These urban guerrilla campaigns, such as the RAF activities, were linked to and part of revolutionary guerrilla wars, both in the Third World and in the West.

Sixth, the 1960s are also important in the discussion of the history of terrorism because specific aspects of terrorism were starting to receive scientific attention.[91] Terrorist psychologies became a subject of investigation. While the use of violence by individuals suffering from psychological abnormality or even derangement was generally separated from terrorism, the question was asked whether terrorists displayed deviant psychological behaviour. Even though there is no convincing general evidence for mental derangement in terrorists, there are indications that certain mental states are linked to terrorist behaviour.[92] Furthermore, on a more general level, phenomena such as 'group think' and a general detachment from society have been found.

Apart from attention from a psychological approach, the role of women started to receive attention. Women were prominent already in Russian populist organisations, such as the People's Will, where educated women played important roles in the leadership.[93] It is claimed that this formed an exception until the advent of the 1960s.[94] The role played by women, for example, in the Algerian independence struggle seems to be overlooked. The high percentage of female activists participating in American and German terrorist organisations in the 1970s was striking and became a further source for scientific study.[95]

The 1960s are thus represented as a sea change in the phenomenon of terrorism because of international, financial, ideological and technological reasons, as well as the scientific study of terrorism. The internationalisation of terrorism, the professionalism of financial structures, the advent of a powerful force of left-wing ideology and the new methods and technologies should, however, be subject to closer investigation, as suggested above.

The 1970s and beyond

It is argued that the 1970s witnessed a major resurgence of terrorism that was characterised by nationalist separatist tendencies.[96] This resurgence is mainly exemplified by the activities of ETA and the IRA. However, to what extent were these activities different from the earlier phases of nationalist terrorism, or were they a continuation of nationalist separatist struggles dating from the nineteenth century? Furthermore, not only did both these organisations have long roots, they also became inspired in this period by left-wing activism. Nationalism seems to be too narrow a term to describe the broad agenda of both ETA and IRA in this era. Finally, some see reason to question the ideological content of these organisations: '[a] decline [occurred] in the importance of ideology and intellectual debate in all societal circles in favour of the simplistic sloganeering and cynical techniques of manipulation that terrorists had learned to master'.[97] This seems to be a clear contradiction that warrants further investigation.

A significant turning point in the 1970s is said to have occurred in the form of a dehumanisation of the enemy and an increasing brutality of terrorist attacks.[98] The attack of the Black September group against the Israeli athletes during the Olympic Games in 1972 is supposed to be the illustration of this point.[99] This example begs several questions. Is 1972 a starting point? Even in earlier phases of terrorist activity were attacks seen as without bounds, e.g. the bombing of the King David Hotel in 1946, which killed 92 Britons.[100] The example, furthermore, begs the question whether the brutality cannot simply be explained by the inherent logic of terrorism for the next attack to be harder in order to create the same impact, particularly since the 1960s witnessed quite a lot of terrorist activity.

Finally, is the example appropriate for the claim of indiscriminate killing? To this day there is controversy over who killed the nine athletes during the raid at Fürstenfeldbruck military airport.

The 1980s and early 1990s witnessed terrorism that has been categorised as right-wing in inspiration.[101] It focused on anti-immigration and foreigner issues and was regarded as less discriminating in its targeting than left-wing terrorism. Little attention is being paid in the literature to the fact that the ETA and IRA continued their activities in the 1980s. Another surprising aspect is the fact that the end of the Cold War has not been qualified as a major event for terrorism. This is surprising in the light of the Soviet support that many terrorist organisations received. Several contradictory claims are made about the impact of the end of Soviet sponsorship of terrorist organisations. Not only has it been found that '[d]uring the 1980s and early 1990s there was a worldwide decline in terrorist action. The left-wing groups with a very few exceptions had disappeared'.[102] It has also been argued that 'notwithstanding the end of the Cold War ... the number of groups espousing Marxist–Leninist–Maoist dogma ... remained unchanged'.[103] This is a puzzle that deserves further investigation.

According to most experts the 1990s formed another sea change with the emergence of religiously inspired terrorism.[104] The advent of this kind of terrorism was deemed to be so significant that the label 'new terrorism' has been used to indicate a break with all previous terrorist expressions.[105] The cases on which these claims are based are not only the al-Qaeda activities but also the Aum Shinrikyo sect's sarin gas attack on the Tokyo subway in 1995 and Timothy McVeigh's bombing of the Oklahoma Federal Building, also in 1995.

First, the terrorism is called new because the terrorists are said to act internationally.[106] However, many traditional terrorist groups also had international ties, starting allegedly with the PLO. Not only nationalist groups but also those inspired by left-wing ideology operated worldwide. Marxism clearly had universal aspirations.

Second, this terrorism is supposed to be new because it is inspired by religion instead of nationalism or left-wing politics. Religion has been a feature of terrorism even before the nineteenth century. This does not negate the fact that both the old and the new terrorists have multiple and overlapping aims.

Third, the new terrorists supposedly seek to kill a maximum number of people in their attacks, if possible, with the use of weapons of mass destruction. However, an increase in the number of victims of terrorist attacks has been taking place since the early 1980s and does not overlap with the rise of the new terrorism since the mid-1990s.[107] It does, more or less, coincide with the aftermath of the Iranian revolution of 1979. Many previous attacks have been perceived as being without bounds.

Fourth, the victims of the new terrorists are picked at random. This type of terrorism is said to be indiscriminate. The use of weapons of mass destruction, although extremely threatening, cannot be really argued to form a trend. There are only two examples; the Aum Shinrikyo sarin gas attack in 1995 and the anthrax letters scare in the United States after the 11 September attacks. Both old and new terrorists continue to use conventional weaponry in their attacks.

After the 1960s, the decade between 1991 and 2001 is, according to the literature, the most significant for understanding the nature and essence of terrorism. In the following section, several observations regarding the development and description of terrorism will be discussed.

Observations

There are several striking aspects to the existing history of terrorism. First, thematic labels, such as nationalist, left-wing and religious, are very popular to distinguish historical periods in terrorism. However, their explanatory power is very limited in helping us to understand what terrorism was really about. On top of that, the labels do not do justice to the complex reality. Most terrorist organisations in the 1960s might be characterised as left-wing in political orientation. This did not prohibit these same organisations from holding religious and nationalist agendas at the same time. Mono-causality is rather limited and a very unproductive approach to research.

Second, technological developments seem to be very important in defining new episodes in terrorism. They are awarded large explanatory powers for understanding expressions of terrorism. While changes in technology might be important as driving changes in terrorism, the question remains why dynamite, airplane hijacking and WMD receive a lot of attention but not the parcel or the car bomb. These developments do seem to have been looked into: 'The first ... parcel bombs ... were used on the eve of the First World War. At the same time, Russian and some of the French terrorists played with the idea of using motorcars'.[108] However, they are not judged as significant events, because they do not seem to overlap with a high incidence of terrorist activity. Furthermore, it can be questioned whether the mass printing press, dynamite, the launch of the first television satellite and the invention of weapons of mass destruction are not awarded too much importance, since they impacted on most aspects of modern life.

Third, terrorism should be explained only in its own context, which has often been disregarded. The *Zeitgeist* of the 1960s can be judged to be more important than the single fact of increases in international air travel that made the hijacking of airliners interesting. Similarly, the growing role of the media in modern society was a development that started in the nineteenth century, but became more significant with the television set conquering a place in every Western household. As Christopher Harmon has argued: 'The most successful groups calibrate their use of terrorism to suit their political and social environs, and they use multiple means, altering their approach to suit changes caused by the environment, governmental interference, [and] good or bad fortune'.[109] Therefore, a history of terrorism should preferably be written in a context of modern social and military history.[110]

Fourth, terrorism seems to comply with a law of 'diminishing returns'[111], which has not received a lot of attention. The conclusion that targets and weaponry have become unlimited can be questioned by the logic of terrorist activity. Is this not inherent in terrorism to become more extreme for people to take note? Hurting or annihilating an opponent is paramount but attention from an audience is not far behind. To attract this attention, more and harder, are too crucial requirements of subsequent attacks.

Fifth, Eurocentric is perhaps too strong a term to describe the history of terrorism as sketched above.[112] Attention has been paid to terrorist activity in other parts of the world such as Latin America, Asia and Africa but very often related to European activity (decolonisation struggles and the spread of Marxist ideology) or compared to Western experiences (state terrorism in Latin America). What did happen in other parts of the world? Are there overlapping trends with the above description, or do different issues and developments play a role?

Sixth, terrorism has, in a historical perspective, not been studied in conjunction with counterterrorism.[113] This is difficult to comprehend, especially when the countermeasures that are instituted can be argued to have played a role in the recruitment and the strengthening of resolve of terrorists. Some claims about the development of counterterrorism have been made. Counterterrorism has been found to be increasingly less successful.[114] Technological advances are said to benefit the terrorist more than the terrorist fighter, bound by bureaucracy and judiciary.[115] What has best proven its usefulness is infiltration, which has become more and more difficult to carry out.[116] However, several questions can be asked. First, what is the measure for success in this regard, the eradication of the terrorist movement? Second, a thwarted terrorist attempt does not make it into the news and would be very hard to prove in a scientific way. Third, it is not completely convincing that our increases in technology and international communication are of no benefit to the security services in contributing to terrorism prevention. These questions and problems could provide opportunities for further historical research.

Conclusion

As Immanuel Kant noted over two hundred years ago, 'history without sociology is blind and sociology without history is void'. In order to avoid further pitfalls ending in blindness or vacuity in research, historians and social scientists should work together more closely in the field of terrorism studies. This contribution has argued for an inclusion of historians and historical studies in the debate. The foundations of terrorism studies in historical research are not very deep. Without wanting to preclude a necessary debate between those advocating the point of view that all instances of terrorism are so unique that they are beyond comparison or that there is only continuity between the terrorism of the French Revolution and what we witness today,[117] debate is necessary and essential to increase our understanding. What this contribution has argued for is that a proper debate should take place, arguments should be exchanged, and a shift of focus towards the historical roots of pressing problems of today should take place.

What should the parameters be for this historical investigation? The development of a proper historical context for the phenomenon forms a minimum requirement in order to escape the tendency to call everything new. Terrorism and counterterrorism should be studied integrally. There is a process of interaction and reciprocal influence. More room should be made for inductive reasoning but also for proper cross-case comparison. Labels and typologies should not be emphasised in order to limit framing, preoccupations and a reduction of the material.

Many terrorism experts, whose work has been discussed above, have close ties to the world of policy-making and the media. They are not only requested to advise government but are also regular performers on television and are sought for their comments in the written press. There is no problem in itself with this state of affairs, were it not that both policy makers and the media often seek to tempt the experts to predict the future. As Mike Smith has noted before:

> While not denying the right of scholars ... to have their say on how to tackle such [counterterrorism] matters, academics do have to tread carefully if they start to advocate detailed policy and if they are to remain true to their vocation. Part of the problem has been that much of the literature on terrorism published over the years has betrayed an over-emphasis on, and sometimes even an obsessive concern for tactical countermeasures which leaves the analyst poorly placed to undertake the more considered long-term diagnosis of the crisis.[118]

The preoccupation with the present strongly influences the questions posed and problems tackled in terrorism studies. This contribution has also argued for the present guiding the formulation of research questions. Historians are generally hesitant to take the next step and predict. They would therefore recommend restraint in this area. Projection into the future of historical trends is very tempting. In this respect the value of historical studies lies in the fact that it has been able to point out the enduring features of the *condition humaine* and those that have been ephemeral. The phenomenon of terrorism should be subjected to this treatment.

Acknowledgements

The author wishes to thank the following people for their input in this article: Mark Tawil, Bob de Graaff, Elsbeth Locher-Scholten, all the participants at the Conference on Terrorism and Counter-Terrorism in Stockholm, 21 March 2005, in particular Magnus Ranstorp, Wilhelm Agrell and Johan Eriksson, and all the participants at the session 'Terrorism and Political Science' at the Flemish–Dutch Political Science Conference, Antwerp, 19–20 May 2005.

Notes

1 Richard Bach Jensen, 'Daggers, Rifles and Dynamite: Anarchist Terrorism in Nineteenth Century Europe', *Terrorism and Political Violence*, Vol. 16, No. 1 (2004), 116–153, 140. See also: Paul Avrich, *The Anarchists* (London: Thames and Hudson, 1973); James Joll, *The Anarchists* (London: Methuen, 1969).

2 Richard Bach Jensen, 'Daggers, Rifles and Dynamite: Anarchist Terrorism in Nineteenth Century Europe', *Terrorism and Political Violence*, Vol. 16, No. 1 (2004), 142–143.

3 Isabelle Duyvesteyn, 'How New is the New Terrorism?', *Studies in Conflict and Terrorism*, Vol. 27, No. 5 (2004), 439–454.

4 Harry Henderson, *Global Terrorism; The Complete Reference Guide* (New York: Checkmark, 2001), 147–160. In another more or less authoritative handbook, the history of terrorism is described in two pages on a total of over 400; Gus Martin, *Understanding Terrorism; Challenges, Perspectives and Issues* (Thousand Oaks, CA: Sage, 2003), 4–5.

5 One expert claims that this state of affairs has been brought about by the fact that terrorism used to be an 'untouchable' subject and mostly journalists were involved in its investigation: Michel Wieviorka, 'Terrorism in the Context of Academic Research', in: Martha Crenshaw (ed.), *Terrorism in Context* (University Park, PA: Pennsylvania State University Press, 1995), 597–606, 597.

6 Isabelle Duyvesteyn, 'How New is the New Terrorism?', *Studies in Conflict and Terrorism*, Vol. 27, No. 5 (2004), 439.

7 See more on this issue below.

8 Isabelle Duyvesteyn, 'How New is the New Terrorism?', *Studies in Conflict and Terrorism*, Vol. 27, No. 5 (2004), 439.

9 David J. Whittaker (ed.), *The Terrorism Reader* (London: Routledge, 2004), 106. Paul Apter, 'Reading Violence', in: David Apter (ed.), *The Legitimization of Violence* (New York:New York University Press, 1997).

10 David J. Whittaker (ed.), *The Terrorism Reader* (London: Routledge, 2004), 93. Bruce Kapferer, 'Remythologizing Discourses: State and Insurrectionary Violence in Sri Lanka', in: David Apter (ed.), *The Legitimization of Violence* (New York: New York University Press, 1997).

11 John Tosh, *The Pursuit of History: Aims, Methods, and New Directions in the Study of Modern History* (London: Longman, 1991), 24.

12 E.H. Carr, *What is History?* (Harmondsworth: Penguin, 1978), 107–108.

13 E.H. Carr, *What is History?* (Harmondsworth: Penguin, 1978), 8.

14 Most other scientific approaches cannot claim anything different.

15 E.H. Carr, *What is History?* (Harmondsworth: Penguin, 1978), 120.

16 John Tosh, *The Pursuit of History: Aims, Methods, and New Directions in the Study of Modern History* (London: Longman, 1991), 130.

17 John Tosh, *The Pursuit of History: Aims, Methods, and New Directions in the Study of Modern History* (London: Longman, 1991), 129 (italics in orginal).

18 An excellent example is: Martha crenshaw (ed.), *Terrorism in Context* (University Park, PA: Pennsylvania State University Press, 1995). Based on the background of the authors, mention should be made of: Walter Reich, *Origins of Terrorism, Psychologies, Ideologies, Theologies, States of Mind* (Washington, DC: Woodrow Wilson Center Press, 1998), even though this book focuses on psychological explanations of terrorism.

19 Bruce Hoffman, *Inside Terrorism* (New York: Columbia University Press, 1998), Preface.

20 Alex P. Schmid, Albert J. Jongman *et al.*, *Political Terrorism; A New Guide to Actors, Authors, Concepts, Data Bases, Theories and Literature* (New Brunswick, NJ: Transaction, 1988), 5–6.

21 Walter Laqueur, *The New Terrorism: Fanatics and the Arms of Mass Destruction*: (London: Phoenix, 2001), 21. He has furthermore claimed that labels are useless: Walter Laqueur, *A History of Terrorism* (New Brunswick, NJ: Transaction, 2001]).

22 The fact that Walter Laqueur, as the Nestor of the historical approach to terrorism, has claimed that 'To write a "world history" ... of political terrorism is a hopeless undertaking' has not deterred the author from undertaking this effort. Walter Laqueur, *A History of Terrorism* (New Brunswick, NJ: Transaction, 2001), 6.

23 I have divided the modern period broadly into a treatment of the nineteenth and the twentieth century. Other authors have made several different suggestions for timeframes: Isaac Cronin argues that there are two 'pre-histories of terrorism, one starting in the first century a.d. and the second in 1870 continuing till today'. Isaac Cronin (ed.), *Confronting Fear: A History of Terrorism* (New York: Thunder's Mouth, 2002), 2–3. Rapoport identifies four waves of terrorism: 1880–1920, 1920–1960, 1960–1979, 1979–2001. David C. Rapoport, 'The Fourth Wave: September 11 in the History of Terrorism', *Current History* (December 2001). Walter Laqueur in his *History of Terrorism* distinguishes between a first period of approx. 1860 till 1945 and 1945 till the end of the 1970s. Their arguments for these cut-off points will be incorporated in the following narrative.

24 Martin A. Miller, 'The Intellectual Origins of Modern Terrorism in Europe', in: Martha Crenshaw (ed.), *Terrorism in Context* (University Park, PA: Pennsylvania State University Press, 1995), 27–62.

25 Richard Bach Jensen, 'Daggers, Rifles and Dynamite: Anarchist Terrorism in Nineteenth Century Europe', *Terrorism and Political Violence*, Vol. 16, No. 1 (2004), 134.

26 In chronological order: French president Carnot (1894), Spanish prime minister Canovas (1897), Empress Elizabeth of Austria (1898), King Umberto of Italy (1900) and American president McKinlay (1901).

27 Martin A. Miller, 'The Intellectual Origins of Modern Terrorism in Europe', in: Martha Crenshaw (ed.), *Terrorism in Context* (University Park, PA: Pennsylvania State University Press, 1995).

28 Laqueur finds that 'the terrorist element in Carbonari activities was grossly exaggerated'. Walter Laqueur, *A History of Terrorism* (New Brunswick, NJ: Transaction, 2001), 24.

29 Franklin L. Ford, *Political Murder: From Tyrannicide to Terrorism* (Cambridge, MA: Harvard University Press, 1985). Laqueur has found that, particularly in the decade of regicide, all perpetrators acted alone. Walter Laqueur, *A History of Terrorism* (New Brunswick, NJ: Transaction, 2001), 14.

30 Isaac Cronin (ed.), *Confronting Fear: A History of Terrorism* (New York: Thunder's Mouth, 2002), 17–21. Walter Laqueur, *The New Terrorism: Fanatics and the Arms of Mass Destruction* (London: Phoenix, 2001), 13–14. In an earlier book Laqueur emphasises that it was also the Russian social revolutionaries who had a profound influence on the theoretical development of terrorism. Walter Laqueur, *A History of Terrorism* (New Brunswick, NJ: Transaction, 2001), 30–43.

31 Walter Laqueur, *A History of Terrorism* (New Brunswick, NJ: Transaction, 2001), 49.

32 Walter Laqueur, *A History of Terrorism* (New Brunswick, NJ: Transaction, 2001), 105.

33 Martin A. Miller, 'The Intellectual Origins of Modern Terrorism in Europe', in: Martha Crenshaw (ed.), *Terrorism in Context* (University Park, PA: Pennsylvania State University Press, 1995).

34 Richard Bach Jensen, 'Daggers, Rifles and Dynamite: Anarchist Terrorism in Nineteenth Century Europe', *Terrorism and Political Violence*, Vol. 16, No. 1 (2004).

35 Walter Laqueur, *A History of Terrorism* (New Brunswick, NJ: Transaction, 2001), 15–16.

36 Laqueur claims that the negative connotation already appeared in 1795. Walter Laqueur, *A History of Terrorism* (New Brunswick, NJ: Transaction, 2001), 6. Rapoport has found that Lehi, a Zionist terrorist organisation operating in Palestine, was the last to call itself terrorist. David C. Rapoport, 'The Fourth Wave: September 11 in the History of Terrorism', *Current History* (December 2001), 419–424, 420. He sees journalism as the source for the change in language and meaning.

37 Walter Laqueur, *No End to War: Terrorism in the Twenty-First Century* (New York: Continuum, 2003), 13.

38 Martha Crenshaw, 'The Effectiveness of Terrorism in the Algerian War', in: Martha Crenshaw (ed.), *Terrorism in Context* (University Park, PA: Pennsylvania State University Press, 1995), 473–513.

39 David J. Whittaker (ed.), *The Terrorism Reader* (London: Routledge, 2004), 46.

40 Walter Laqueur, *A History of Terrorism* (New Brunswick, NJ: Transaction, 2001), 123.

41 Walter Laqueur, *No End to War: Terrorism in the Twenty-First Century* (New York: Continuum, 2001), 15.

42 Walter Laqueur, *No End to War: Terrorism in the Twenty-First Century* (New York: Continuum, 2001), 18–19.

43 James Joll, *The Anarchists* (London: Methuen, 1969), 21, 57.

44 Franklin L. Ford, *Political Murder: From Tyrannicide to Terrorism* (Cambridge, MA: Harvard University Press, 1985), 383.

45 David C. Rapoport, 'The Fourth Wave: September 11 in the History of Terrorism', *Current History* (December 2001), 420.

46 The only reference to these ideas I could find was in the context of Russian revolutionary terrorism. Walter Laqueur, *A History of Terrorism* (New Brunswick, NJ: Transaction, 2001), 63–69.

47 In the most extensive treatment of the history of terrorism, only brief mention is made of India and the Ottoman empire in this period. Walter Laqueur, *A History of Terrorism* (New Brunswick, NJ: Transaction, 2001), 13–14, 43–49.

48 These two main questions form a consequentialist argument, which would be abhorrent to many a historian. Since we have to start somewhere with asking questions, I hope historians will overlook this shortcoming.

49 Walter Laqueur, *The New Terrorism: Fanatics and the Arms of Mass Destruction* (London: Phoenix, 2001), 21.

50 Martin A. Miller, 'The Intellectual Origins of Modern Terrorism in Europe', in: Martha Crenshaw, (ed.), *Terrorism in Context* (University Park, PA: Pennsylvania State University Press, 1995), 55–56.

51 Laqueur is the only one who clearly locates the roots and earliest expressions of this terrorism in the nineteenth century. Walter Laqueur, *A History of Terrorism* (New Brunswick, NJ: Transaction, 2001), 69–70.

52 Walter Laqueur, *The New Terrorism: Fanatics and the Arms of Mass Destruction* (London: Phoenix, 2001), 21.

53 David C. Rapoport, 'The Fourth Wave: September 11 in the History of Terrorism', *Current History* (December 2001), 420. Even today there are important terrorist organisations with nationalist aims.

54 Walter Laqueur, *A History of Terrorism* (New Brunswick, NJ: Transaction, 2001), 74. Laqueur also notes that ideology was important but not all-pervasive in order to understand this terrorism. Some of it was simply inspired by a desire for action, 76.

55 Both Hoffmann and Laqueur exclude state terrorism in their approaches. Cronin includes state terrorism. The reason to exclude state terrorism can be, of course, the fact that much of the state terror occurred within the confines of the (revised) law, as the state has the legal monopoly on violence. Nikolaus Wachsmann, *Hitler's Prisons; Legal Terror in Nazi Germany* (New Haven, CT: Yale University Press, 2004). State-sponsored terrorism is more widely included in analyses of terrorism; see more on this below.

56 Bruce Hoffman, *Inside Terrorism* (New York: Columbia University Press, 1998), 45.

57 Bruce Hoffman, *Inside Terrorism* (New York: Columbia University Press, 1998), 45.

58 Bruce Hoffman, *Inside Terrorism* (New York: Columbia University Press, 1998), 65.

59 Walter Laqueur, *The New Terrorism: Fanatics and the Arms of Mass Destruction* (London: Phoenix, 2001), 8–9. See also: Walter Laqueur, *A History of Terrorism* (New Brunswick, NJ: Transaction, 2001), 18–19.

60 See also: Isabelle Duyvesteyn, 'The Concept of Conventional War and Armed Conflict in Collapsed States', in: Isabelle Duyvesteyn and Jan Angstrom (eds), *Rethinking the Nature of War* (London: Frank Cass, 2005), 65–87.

61 Alistair Horne, *A Savage War of Peace, Algeria 1954–1962* (London: Pan, 2002), 214.

62 John Shy and Thomas Collier, 'Revolutionary War', in: Peter Paret (ed.), *Makers of Modern Strategy: From Machiavelli to the Nuclear Age* (Oxford: Clarendon, 1991), 815–862. Franz Fanon, *The Wretched of the Earth* (London: Penguin, 2001), 67.

63 Bruce Hoffman, *Inside Terrorism* (New York: Columbia University Press, 1998), 60.

64 Bruce Hoffman, *Inside Terrorism* (New York: Columbia University Press, 1998), 65.

65 Alistair Horne, *A Savage War of Peace, Algeria 1954–1962* (London: Pan, 2002).

66 Walter Laqueur, *A History of Terrorism* (New Brunswick, NJ: Transaction, 2001), 119. Bruce Hoffman, *Inside Terrorism* (New York: Columbia University Press, 1998), 64. Robert A. Pape, 'The Strategic Logic of Suicide Terrorism', *American Political Science Review*, Vol. 97, No. 3 (2003), 343–361, 344.

67 Martha Crenshaw, 'The Effectiveness of Terrorism in the Algerian War', in: Martha Crenshaw (ed.), *Terrorism in Context* (University Park, PA: Pennsylvania State University Press, 1995), 475. Walter Laqueur, *A History of Terrorism* (New Brunswick, NJ: Transaction, 2001), 116–119, 221.

68 Franklin L. Ford, *Political Murder: From Tyrannicide to Terrorism* (Cambridge, MA: Harvard University Press, 1985), 387.

69 Walter Laqueur, *The New Terrorism: Fanatics and the Arms of Mass Destruction* (London: Phoenix, 2001), 43.

70 David C. Rapoport, 'Introduction', in: David C. Rapoport and Yonah Alexander (eds), *The Morality of Terrorism: Religious and Secular Justifications* (New York: Columbia University Press, 1989), xii. See also: Isabelle Duyvesteyn, 'How New is the New Terrorism?', *Studies in Conflict and Terrorism*, Vol. 27, No. 5 (2004), 442.

71 David C. Rapoport, 'The Fourth Wave: September 11 in the History of Terrorism', *Current History* (December 2001), 420.

72 Bruce Hoffman, *Inside Terrorism* (New York: Columbia University Press, 1998).

73 Bruce Hoffman, *Inside Terrorism* (New York: Columbia University Press, 1998), 84. David C. Rapoport, 'The Fourth Wave: September 11 in the History of Terrorism', *Current History* (December 2001), 421. The PLO is also the only terrorist organisation that was awarded formal representation in the United Nations General Assembly.

74 For antiquity see: David C. Rapoport, 'Fear and Trembling: Terrorism in Three Religious Traditions', *American Political Science Review*, Vol. 78, No. 3 (1984), 658.

75 Walter Laqueur, *A History of Terrorism* (New Brunswick, NJ: Transaction, 2001), 87, 112–116.

76 Walter Laqueur, *A History of Terrorism* (New Brunswick, NJ: Transaction, 2001), xi.

77 Walter Laqueur, *A History of Terrorism* (New Brunswick, NJ: Transaction, 2001), 194.

78 David C. Rapoport, 'The Fourth Wave: September 11 in the History of Terrorism', *Current History* (December 2001), 421.

79 Striking is the fact that many of these sponsors of terrorism in this period still appear on the current list of President Bush's axis of evil, e.g. Syria.

80 Bruce Hoffman, *Inside Terrorism* (New York: Columbia University Press, 1998), 84.

81 Walter Laqueur, *A History of Terrorism* (New Brunswick, NJ: Transaction, 2001), 88, 90.

82 Donna M. Schlagheck, *International Terrorism; An Introduction to the Concepts and Actors* (Lexington, MA: D.C. Heath, 1988), 5.

83 See also: E.R. Muller, R.F.J. Spaay, A.G.W. Ruitenberg, *Trends in Terrorisme* (Trends in Terrrorism) (Alphen aan den Rijn: Kluwer, 2003), 44–57; C. Dishman, 'Terrorism, Crime and Transformation', *Studies in Conflict and Terrorism*, Vol. 24 (2001), 43–58; Michael Radu, 'Terrorism After the Cold War; Trends and Challenges', *Orbis*, Vol. 46, No. 2 (2002), 275–287, 278.

84 Walter Laqueur, *A History of Terrorism* (New Brunswick, NJ: Transaction, 2001), 27, also 102–103.

85 Walter Laqueur, *The New Terrorism: Fanatics and the Arms of Mass Destruction* (London: Phoenix, 2001), 27.

86 To be fair, this left-wing fervour was often adopted by groups oriented towards nationalism. David C. Rapoport, 'The Fourth Wave: September 11 in the History of Terrorism', *Current History* (December 2001), 421. This issue will be further dealt with below.

87 Walter Laqueur, *A History of Terrorism* (New Brunswick, NJ: Transaction, 2001), 175.

88 According to Walter Laqueur, the first known hijacking of an airplane occurred in Peru in the 1930s. Walter Laqueur, *The New Terrorism: Fanatics and the Arms of Mass Destruction* (London: Phoenix, 2001), 43.

89 David C. Rapoport, 'The Fourth Wave: September 11 in the History of Terrorism', *Current History* (December 2001), 421.

90 Walter Laqueur, *A History of Terrorism* (New Brunswick, NJ: Transaction, 2001), 176.

91 Walter Laqueur, *A History of Terrorism* (New Brunswick, NJ: Transaction, 2001), 136–148.

92 Jerrold Post, 'Terrorist Psycho-logic: Terrorist Behavior as a Product of Psychological Forces', in: Walter Reich, *Origins of Terrorism, Psychologies, Ideologies, Theologies, States of Mind* (Washington DC: Woodrow Wilson Center Press, 1998), 25–40.

93 Philip Pomper, 'Russian Revolutionary Terrorism', in: Martha Crenshaw (ed.), *Terrorism in Context* (University Park, PA: Pennsylvania State University Press, 1995), 63–101, 76.

94 Walter Laqueur, *A History of Terrorism* (New Brunswick, NJ: Transaction, 2001), 121.

95 Walter Laqueur, *The New Terrorism: Fanatics and the Arms of Mass Destruction* (London: Phoenix, 2001), 38–39.

96 Walter Laqueur, *The New Terrorism: Fanatics and the Arms of Mass Destruction* (London: Phoenix, 2001), 32.

97 Isaac Cronin, (ed.), *Confronting Fear: A History of Terrorism* (New York: Thunder's Mouth, 2002), 45.

98 Walter Laqueur, *A History of Terrorism* (New Brunswick, NJ: Transaction, 2001), 234. Walter Laqueur, *No End to War: Terrorism in the Twenty-First Century* (New York: Continuum, 2001), 24.

99 Walter Laqueur, *No End to War: Terrorism in the Twenty-First Century* (New York: Continuum, 2001), 25.

100 Thurston Clarke, *By Blood and Fire: The Attack on the King David Hotel* (London: Hutchinson, 1981).

101 Walter Laqueur, *The New Terrorism: Fanatics and the Arms of Mass Destruction* (London: Phoenix, 2001), 9.

102 Walter Laqueur, *No End to War: Terrorism in the Twenty-First Century* (New York: Continuum, 2001), 28.

103 Bruce Hoffman, *Inside Terrorism* (New York: Columbia University Press, 1998), 91.

104 Rapoport argues that this last new period, the fourth wave, started in the 1980s after the 1979 revolution in Iran. David C. Rapoport, 'The Fourth Wave: September 11 in the History of Terrorism', *Current History* (December 2001), 421.

105 Walter Laqueur, *No End to War: Terrorism in the Twenty-First Century* (New York: Continuum, 2001), 8–9. Bruce Hoffman, 'Change and Continuity in Terrorism', *Studies in Conflict and Terrorism*, Vol. 24 (2001). Steven Simon and Daniel Benjamin, 'America and the New Terrorism', *Survival*, Vol. 42, No. 1 (Spring 2000), 66.

106 See also: Isabelle Duyvesteyn, 'How New is the New Terrorism?', *Studies in Conflict and Terrorism*, Vol. 27, No. 5 (2004).

107 Bruce Hoffman, *Inside Terrorism* (New York: Columbia University Press, 1998), 94, 201.

108 Walter Laqueur, *The New Terrorism: Fanatics and the Arms of Mass Destruction* (London: Phoenix, 2001), 42. Even in the nineteenth century ideas about bombs hidden in letters and dropped from 'airships' were developed. Walter Laqueur, *A History of Terrorism* (New Brunswick, NJ: Transaction, 2001), 59–60, 95.

109 Christopher C. Harmon, 'Five Strategies of Terrorism', *Small Wars and Insurgencies*, Vol. 12, No. 3 (2001), 39–66. See also: Robert Jervis, 'An Interim Assessment of September 11: What Has Changed and What Has Not?', in: Demetrios James Caraley (ed.), *September 11, Terrorist Attacks, and U.S. Foreign Policy* (New York: Academy of Political Science, 2002), 37–54, 38.

110 For historical terrorism research it deserves investigation whether terrorism should not be approached in an instrumental way. Caleb Carr argues that terrorism needs to be studied within the context of military history as it is an instrument of power used to break the political will of the enemy, which is the essence of warfare. Caleb Carr, *The Lessons of Terror: A History of Warfare Against Civilians: Why it Has Always Failed, and Why it Will Fail Again* (London: Little Brown, 2002), 6. Walter Laqueur has noted that '[t]he term terrorism has come to encompass such wide

varieties of violent activities' that this can perhaps also be read to underline the above suggestion. Walter Laqueur, *A History of Terrorism* (New Brunswick, NJ: Transaction, 2001), xiii.

111 Walter Laqueur, *A History of Terrorism* (New Brunswick, NJ: Transaction, 2001), 108.

112 See also: Adrian Guelke, *The Age of Terrorism and the International Political System* (London: I.B. Tauris, 1998), 31–33.

113 A history of counterterrorism does not seem to exist either. This is rather surprising in the light of the present race to institute the most effective countermeasures.

114 Walter Laqueur, *The New Terrorism: Fanatics and the Arms of Mass Destruction* (London: Phoenix, 2001), 45–46.

115 Walter Laqueur, *The New Terrorism: Fanatics and the Arms of Mass Destruction* (London: Phoenix, 2001), 45.

116 Walter Laqueur, *The New Terrorism: Fanatics and the Arms of Mass Destruction* (London: Phoenix, 2001), 45.

117 Michel Wieviorka, 'Terrorism in the Context of Academic Research', in: Martha Crenshaw (ed.), *Terrorism in Context* (University Park, PA: Pennsylvania State University Press, 1995), 605.

118 M.R.L. Smith, 'Holding Fire', in: Alan O'Day (ed.), *Terrorism's Laboratory: The Case of Northern Ireland* (Aldershot: Dartmouth, 1995), 23.

4

THE IMPACT OF 9/11 ON RESEARCH ON TERRORISM

Andrew Silke

Constructing government policy without evidence is building on sand. If the result does not fail and collapse it is only because of luck and good fortune. For a very long time, governments across the globe have developed counter-terrorism policy in the absence of good evidence to guide decisions, resourcing and legalisation. One may think that this is because terrorism is a new problem and, as a result, evidence is lacking in many areas. Consequently, one could argue that hunches, assumptions, anecdotes and personal fears and expectations are acceptable foundations for policy (in the absence of anything better).

Yet, terrorism is not a new problem. While the attacks of 11 September 2001 and the ensuing global war on terror have galvanised world attention on the issue, states have been grappling with low-intensity conflicts throughout recorded history. Indeed, it is rare to find any century in the past two thousand years which cannot supply at least one example of what today would be described as a terrorist conflict.[1] Nevertheless, while terrorism has been around for a very long time, our understanding of it has remained relatively poor. The lack of evidence on which to build policy is not to do with the problem being an unfamiliar one, but rather with a long-running lack of research and analysis on the issue. In contrast to the science and energy poured into the preparation and fighting of conventional warfare, effectively responding to terrorist campaigns has for decades lagged far behind.

'9/11' however highlighted that terrorism can have a profoundly negative impact on even the most powerful states. Terrorism, generally a very peripheral issue for Western governments, has achieved a much higher profile in the wake of the Washington and New York attacks (with added nudges such as the Bali and Madrid bombings). Effective policy and responses to terrorism are under-mined, however, by the level of knowledge and understanding that we have developed to understand the phenomenon. While appearances can sometimes suggest the contrary, governments usually are genuinely interested in finding and using the most effective policies. They are in a constant search for the approaches that will have the most positive impact at the least negative cost. The calculations on which governments make these assessments, however, can often be deeply flawed. The evidence needed for good decisions is often lacking and incomplete and this certainly has been the case when one is trying to deal with terrorism.

A large research literature has built up on terrorism over the past three decades. Despite its quantity, several reviews have found that the quality of this literature is generally very poor.[2] The review described in this chapter explores and assesses the impact 9/11 has had on research on terrorism. This current survey follows in the footsteps of a review carried out by this author prior to 9/11.[3] That previous review examined the published output of the primary journals in the area for the years 1990–1999. Research on terrorism has had a troubled history and studies in the area have tended to suffer from many flaws. The past surveys have found that there has always been a shortage of experienced researchers in the subject. Indeed, most of what is written about terrorism is written by people who have never met a terrorist and who never actually spent time on the ground in the areas most affected by these conflicts. Terrorism research is very top-heavy with desk accounts of the phenomenon, where second-hand conclusions are reached based on media reports, magazine articles and other published accounts. Even then, the authors are often unfamiliar with the existing literature and lack the experience needed to tell the good studies apart from the bad.

Indeed, a great proportion of research in this area is produced by transient researchers: individuals who rarely carry out research on terrorism and who quickly move on to other subjects. The pre-9/11 survey found that over 80% of research articles published on terrorism in the 1990s were from one-timers (i.e., writers who wrote only one article in the mainstream terrorism journals during the entire ten-year period).[4] Sometimes a fresh perspective on a research question can be extremely valuable, but many commentators have expressed deep concern that the transient researchers are frequently very poorly aware of past research on terrorism and their work can be inadequately linked with existing theory and knowledge.

This earlier review also found that terrorism research in the 1990s was very heavily dependent on easily accessible sources of data and only a small minority of articles provided substantially new knowledge which was previously unavailable to the field.[5] Taken as a whole, the review conducted in 2000 concluded that terrorism research was in a very unhealthy state. It relied heavily on the cheapest and fastest research methods and approaches. Analysis of available data was generally of the most fleeting nature. Indeed, the review found that the field was relying on the same limited methodologies and levels of analysis of previous decades and that, while the field could often appear to be relatively active and energetic, growth in our actual understanding of several key issues remained stunted and halting.

In order to properly understand terrorist conflicts – to properly assess root causes and what policies and responses will and will not work – one needs reliable evidence, and this can only be supplied by good researchers using good methods and approaches for gathering information. The reality is that such work has been much rarer than we could hope for. A limited range of methodologies in data gathering, combined with a reluctance to use more rigorous analysis and a shortage of experienced researchers, has left the field with serious deficiencies in many respects. Ultimately, the methods used by most terrorism researchers are essentially exploratory and, as a result, the field struggles in its efforts to explain terrorism or to provide findings of genuine predictive value. It has been argued that 'the ability to make correct predictions [is] ... the outstanding characteristic of science. If knowledge is deficient, prediction is impossible'.[6] Yet when it comes to terrorism our ability to predict what will happen next has been lamentable.

Such was the state of affairs in the years running up to 9/11. The purpose of this chapter is to consider what impact 9/11 and the following Global War on Terror have had on research in this area. Replicating the approach taken for the 1990s review, this survey focuses on the two major academic journals that are concerned with research on terrorism: *Terrorism and Political Violence* (TPV) and *Studies in Conflict & Terrorism* (SICAT). Taken together, these two journals can be regarded as providing a reasonably balanced impression of the research activity and interests in the field. This chapter presents the results of a review of the published output of the primary journals in the area in the three years since the 9/11 attacks (2002–2004). The research output from this period is compared with the research output from 1990 to 2001, and the aim of this chapter is to assess what changes, if any, can be seen in terrorism research post-9/11.

Issues to consider

Academic journals have a surprisingly diverse range of content. For the two journals under consideration here, this range includes articles, research notes, editorials, book reviews, conference reports, review essays, database reports, and official documents and reports. The most immediate question facing a surveyor is: how much of this material should be considered? In deciding this, the main criterion has to be: which items are consistently the best indicators of significant research activity and effort? This review replicates the approach used in the pre-9/11 study and focuses solely on *articles* published in the journals during the time period. The judgement is made that peer-reviewed journal articles provide a good measure of the broad quality of research work.[7]

The literature of terrorism is very young but is growing enormously. In their famous review of the existing literature in 1988, Schmid and Jongman judged that more than 95 per cent of all books and articles on the topic had been written in the period from 1968 to 1988.[8] Probably almost as much again was written between 1988 and 2001. Since 2001, however, the growth has escalated even further, and one recent review of electronic databases suggested that over

60 per cent more research was being carried out post-9/11 compared to what was taking place in the late 1990s (though even this may be too conservative an estimate).[9]

In examining the quality of research on terrorism, however, Schmid and Jongman noted that 'there are probably few areas in the social science literature on which so much is written on the basis of so little research'. They estimated that 'as much as 80 per cent of the literature is not research-based in any rigorous sense; instead, it is too often narrative, condemnatory, and prescriptive'.[10] Further, while the backgrounds of researchers may be relatively diverse, there has in general been a consistent lack of researchers to carry out investigative work in the area. This bleak assessment was entirely supported by the later survey of research conducted in the 1990s.

How then has terrorism research reacted to the aftermath of 9/11? Have the problems and limitations which have plagued this field of study for nearly forty years shown any signs of improvement? The remainder of this chapter attempts to provide some answers to these questions.

The research community

A traditional problem in the field has already been highlighted, namely that there has been a long-term shortage of experienced terrorism researchers. Very few academics and researchers have been willing (or able) to devote considerable parts of their career to work on terrorism, and one consequence of this shortage is that most terrorism research has been carried out by single individuals working on lone projects. In the 1990s, only 9.4% of published research articles were the result of collaborative efforts. This also stresses the reality that the vast majority of research was being conducted with very limited resources. Research teams and partnerships were rare and the field was extremely dependent on the efforts of individuals who conducted research on terrorism in an independent and relatively isolated manner.

Figure 4.1, however, suggests that the situation has improved in the years immediately after 9/11. Collaborative studies now account for 20 per cent of the articles in the major terrorism journals. This represents a moderate but still significant increase in the size of the research community, and also offers the potential for more ambitious, difficult and rigorous research projects to be taken on by the field.

Methods of data collection

The lack of researchers in the area has also traditionally been cited as an explanation for the use of a relatively limited range of data gathering methods. Schmid and Jongman found that only 46% of researchers used methods that could generate new data.[11] The 1990s review found that this state of affairs had persisted, with a very small range of methodologies dominating the approaches taken by

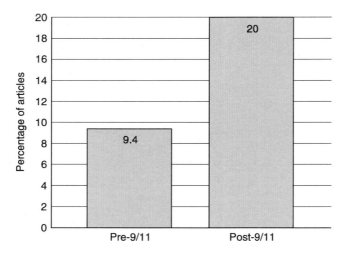

Figure 4.1 Collaborative research on terrorism.

investigators. Again, most research was based on secondary data analysis and more specifically on analysis based on archival records. Over 80 per cent of all research on terrorism prior to 9/11 was based either solely or primarily on data gathered from books, journals, the media (or media-derived databases) or other published documents. Researchers remained very heavily dependent on easily accessible sources of data and only about 20 per cent of articles provided substantially new knowledge that was previously unavailable to the field. Sixty-eight per cent of the published articles were essentially literature reviews of knowledge and findings published elsewhere.

While the amount of collaborative work since 9/11 has increased, this has not transferred into a meaningful improvement in terms of the data collection methods being used by the research community. Figure 4.2 shows that literature reviews still account for most of the work. Sixty-six per cent of the articles published since 9/11 took this form, only fractionally less than before the attacks. The finding indicates that the field is still generally very limited in the methods being used to gather data.

Statistical analysis in terrorism research

Since the 1950s, all of the social sciences have turned increasingly to statistical analysis as a way to improve the reliability and trustworthiness of research. Statistics are not seen as suitable for every situation or question, but the major disciplines have all come to accord them a significant and substantial place in any healthy research area. Descriptive statistics enable the researcher to summarise and organise data in an effective and meaningful way. Inferential statistics

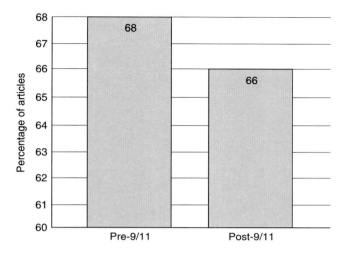

Figure 4.2 Literature review research.

allow the researcher to make decisions or inferences by interpreting data patterns. Inferential statistics are regarded as particularly valuable as they introduce an element of control into research which can help to compensate if relatively weak data collection methods were used.[12]

As shown in Figure 4.3, prior to 9/11 just 19 per cent of research papers in the major terrorism journals involved the use of descriptive and/or inferential analysis. This situation has improved somewhat in the years after 2001, and currently nearly 26 per cent of articles now make use of some statistical analysis. The increase can partly be explained by the growth in collaborative research (though the area still lags seriously behind research in other areas). For example, Figure 4.4 compares terrorism research post-9/11 with the use of statistics in research in criminology and forensic psychology (research areas which face many similar demands to those faced by those working on terrorism). Eighty-six per cent of research papers in forensic psychology and 60 per cent of papers in criminology contain at least some form of statistical analysis. In both cases, inferential statistics account for the majority of this analysis. In contrast, inferential statistics are used in just over one study in twenty in the terrorism journals.

In other areas of scientific analysis, the use of statistics is seen as an important and accepted way in which to ensure that the claims made by researchers meet recognised quality controls. Ultimately, research on terrorism has improved in this area since 9/11, and the quality and reliability of the conclusions being reached by researchers are probably somewhat stronger now. However, the change has been a relatively modest one – significant compared to the situation in the 1990s but still very far behind the practices commonly seen in other areas. Terrorism research clearly still suffers from a substantial imbalance in this

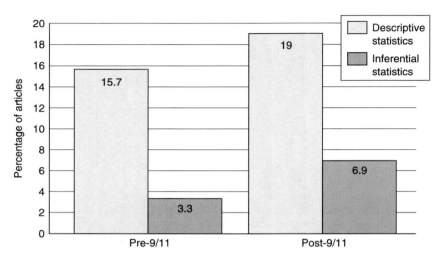

Figure 4.3 Statistics in terrorism research.

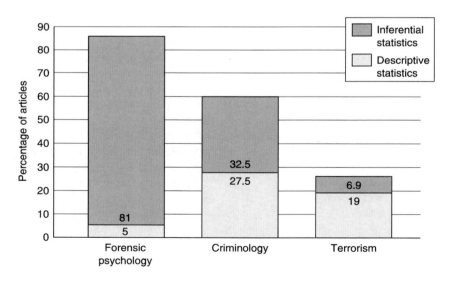

Figure 4.4 The use of statistics in different disciplines.

regard and even more effort is needed to address this deficiency. Reiterating the conclusion of the earlier review, statistics alone are not the way forward, but neither is avoiding their use to the degree that the terrorism research community still currently does.

The group focus of research

In any contest between a state and a terrorist group, the terrorist group will usually lose. One report in the early 1990s suggested that 90 per cent of terrorist organisations were entirely defeated within the first year of the conflict.[13] Of the remaining 10 per cent of groups, many could endure for long periods, in a very few cases stretching over centuries, but in most conflicts the state would, eventually, endure and persevere. It is interesting then to consider the groups that have been the focus of research.

In judging whether a research paper is focused on a particular group or not, this survey required that the article had to be primarily about one or at most two groups. It was not sufficient that a group was briefly mentioned or received discussion of a page or two. The group had to be clearly the major focus of the article. This follows the rationale used in the previous survey.

Figure 4.5 illustrates which groups received the most research attention. It is not surprising that, in the post-9/11 period, 20 per cent of all research with a group focus centred on al-Qaeda. As the perpetrators of the 9/11 attacks and the primary target of the subsequent Global War on Terror, it is only natural that al-Qaeda should receive such concentrated attention. Indeed, no terrorist group

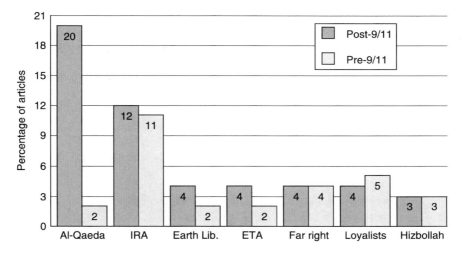

Figure 4.5 Research on terrorist groups.

over (at least) the past 16 years has received such concentrated research attention. However, the heavy attention paid to al-Qaeda in the three years after 9/11 is in stark contrast to the very limited research attention the group received prior to 9/11. Only 2 per cent of articles with a group focus prior to 9/11 examined al-Qaeda. As a result, al-Qaeda did not even manage to make the 'top twenty' list of terrorist groups which received the most research attention.

Such a low level of attention has been held up as perhaps the most significant research failing in the field of the past twenty years. Prior to 9/11, al-Qaeda was not a trivial organisation. As far back as 1992, the group was believed to have been behind three bombings that targeted US troops in Yemen. It was also believed to have been involved in the 1996 attack against the Khobar Towers facility in Saudi Arabia, which killed 19 American citizens and wounded another 500. In August 1998, al-Qaeda killed some 301 people and injured over 5000 in attacks against US embassies in Kenya and Tanzania. Then, in October 2000, there was another high profile attack, this time against the USS *Cole* off the coast of Yemen, which killed 17 US Navy personnel and injured 39 more. The group was also involved in plans to simultaneously bomb the US and Israeli embassies in Manila and other Asian capitals in 1994. In 1995 it planned to use bombs to destroy a dozen US trans-Pacific flights and also aimed to kill President Clinton during a visit to the Philippines. Behind the scenes al-Qaeda was known to be funding, supporting and training militants from a wide range of Islamist groups. It had links to fighting in Bosnia, Chechnya and Kashmir, and was building a network of extremists that went across Africa, Europe, the Middle East, Central Asia, South East Asia and stretched even into North America. The organisation's profound hostility to the US was never a secret. In August 1996, Osama bin Laden issued a declaration of Jihad against the US from his base in Afghanistan. This was followed by similarly aggressive fatahs in following years which explicitly encouraged Muslims to kill Americans – *any* Americans – anywhere in the world where they could be found. Throughout the 1990s, al-Qaeda grew dramatically in strength and influence and the threat it posed increased alarmingly.

Yet the growth in the threat posed by the group was not matched by a growth in research on the movement. Instead, Osama bin Laden's organisation languished in the basement levels of the research world, while organisations such as the Branch Davidians, US militias and the Italian Red Brigades were among the top six most studied groups.[14] Prior to 9/11, the terrorist group which *did* attract most research interest was the Provisional Irish Republican Army (PIRA). Far more articles focused on the activities and structure of this organisation than on any other terrorist group. Incredibly, Figure 4.5 shows that the proportion of articles looking at the IRA has actually *increased* even further since 9/11 (moving from 11 to 12 per cent). The IRA is unquestionably the most heavily studied terrorist organisation of the past forty years and it is interesting (though strange) that the field's fascination with the movement seems to have actually increased after 9/11.

While al-Qaeda certainly seemed to slip through the cracks prior to 9/11, research trends were more astute in other respects. In the survey, some articles considered several different groups which shared similar ideologies, backgrounds, activities etc. However, if the article was examining more than two groups it was not considered for Figure 4.5. As a result, the survey added an additional level for considering articles and assessed whether articles were focused on discussing a particular broad type of group or a particular set of groups (e.g., an article on the IRA could also be regarded as an article on a nationalist/separatist terrorist group).[15] Examined in this way, the survey found that research was showing an increasing recognition of the growing threat posed by the broader category of extremist Islamic groups.

As Figure 4.6 shows, studies on these types of organisation had been increasing significantly well before 9/11. In the early 1990s, roughly 14 per cent of studies were looking at Islamist terrorist organisations such as Hamas, Hizbollah, Islamic Jihad and al-Qaeda. By the late 1990s, this category had risen to nearly a quarter of all research and was matched only by research on nationalist/separatist terrorist groups such as the IRA and ETA. Thus, in this trend at least, research was showing a justified awareness of an increasing threat and significance. Since 9/11, Islamist groups now utterly dominate research attention, with nearly 60 per cent of articles with such foci being directed on Islamist groups. It is likely that in the history of terrorism research no single category of terrorist group type has enjoyed so much attention in this way (certainly in the past 16 years no other category of terrorist group has ever received even half as much research attention as is being currently lavished on the extreme Islamist organisations). This is an understandable state of affairs, but one must wonder how healthy it is in research terms if it endures for too long.

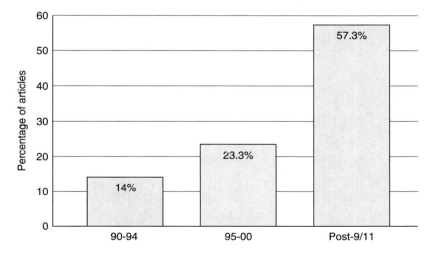

Figure 4.6 Research on extreme Islamic groups.

Research on terrorist tactics

Suicide terrorism is not a new phenomenon, but prior to 9/11 it was certainly relatively ignored by terrorism researchers, being considered more of a curiosity than a major subject for analysis. Figure 4.7 shows that only a tiny proportion of articles – 0.7 per cent, a bare handful – looked at this issue. That however changed in the aftermath of 9/11, the most devastating terrorist attacks of all time, accomplished through the use of suicide tactics. Since 9/11, the amount of research work being focused on this phenomenon has increased enormously. For every one study carried out prior to 9/11, 23 are being carried out now. Nearly one article in nine published on terrorism since 9/11 has been focused particularly on suicide terrorism. So intense has been the growth of research on this one aspect of terrorism, that some researchers are now pushing for the creation of a sub-discipline of suicide terrorism studies. How realistic (or necessary) such ambitions are is questionable, but the debate does at least emphasise the enormous growth of activity in an aspect of terrorism that traditionally was grossly under-explored.

The increased work being focused on suicide terrorism is arguably both overdue and useful. However, increased research is also being focused on other aspects of terrorism that are less obviously of growing importance. Of particular concern is the growing amount of research investigating the (potential) use of weapons of mass destruction (WMD) by terrorists. Figure 4.8 shows that the amount of research focused on WMD terrorism has more than doubled since 9/11. This is a disappointing trend: 9/11 was not a WMD attack. Three thousand people may have been killed, but the hijackers did not use a nuclear bomb to

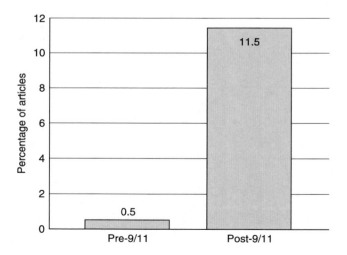

Figure 4.7 Research on suicide terrorism.

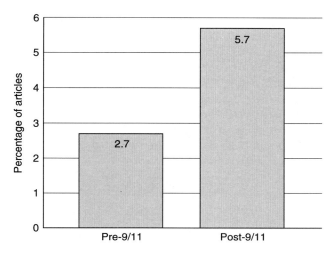

Figure 4.8 WMD terrorism.

cause the carnage, they did not spray poisonous chemicals into the atmosphere or release deadly viruses. They used box-cutters. Nevertheless, WMD research has more than doubled. Is this increase justified?

The short answer is probably not, but then WMD terrorism has always probably been over-subscribed. Prior to 9/11, nearly six times more research was being conducted on WMD terrorist tactics than on suicide tactics. Indeed, no other terrorist tactic (car bombs, hijacking, kidnapping, assassinations etc.) received anywhere near as much research attention in the run-up to 9/11 as WMD. If the relatively low amount of research attention that was given to al-Qaeda is judged to be the most serious failing of terrorism research in the years prior to 9/11, the relatively high amount of research focused on the terrorist use of WMD must inevitably be seen as the next biggest blunder.

To date, in the few cases where terrorists have attempted to develop WMDs they have almost always failed. In the handful of instances where they have actually managed to develop and use such weapons, they have only once been able to kill as many as 12 people. In the list of the 200 most destructive terrorist attacks of the past twenty years, not a single one involved WMDs. Yet somehow one impact of the 9/11 attacks is that WMD research – already the most studied form of terrorist tactic during the 1990s – has actually managed to attract even more research attention and funding, more than doubling the proportion of articles focused on WMD in the journals.

If the articles were focused on mass casualty terrorism this would be more understandable. 9/11 was certainly a *mass casualty* terrorist attack, and indeed there have been a few studies which have looked at mass casualty terrorism since 2001.[16] However, the WMD research is not taking such an approach and instead is very much focused on terrorist use of chemical, biological, radiological or nuclear weapons (CBRN). This relative (but increasing) obsession with WMD is disturbing for a number of reasons. First, it detracts attention from more lethal tactics which terrorists frequently and routinely use. Consider the lack of attention given to suicide tactics in the 1990s. Well over 1000 people were killed by suicide terrorism in the 1990s. In the same period, attacks using so-called weapons of mass destruction killed just 19 people. Yet it was WMD which attracted six times more research energy than suicide terrorism.

This was a serious mistake and one which is arguably being compounded after 9/11, as research on WMD more than doubles. A degree of research looking at WMD terrorism is justified. Instances such as the 1995 Tokyo subway attack and the post-9/11 anthrax letters show that CBRN attacks *can* happen (albeit very rarely). Such attacks have never caused mass fatalities, however, and the popular acronym of WMD is desperately misleading. Despite the rarity – and the extreme unlikelihood of terrorists being able to accomplish a truly devastating attack using these weapons – WMD remains a popular topic for government and funding bodies. They will award research grants for work on this topic when other far more common and consistently far more deadly terrorist tactics are ignored.

Those who had hoped that 9/11 – a stunning example of how non-CBRN weapons can be used to kill thousands of people – might then have heralded at least a modest shift away from CBRN research will be disappointed. Ultimately, the central lesson of 9/11 in this regard has been profoundly missed.

The lessons of history

A further cause for concern can be seen with regard to the level of research that focuses on non-contemporary terrorism. It is natural and reasonable that, in the years immediately after the most destructive terrorist attacks in recorded history, the research field should focus on current issues, actors and events. Figure 4.9 certainly shows that this is happening. Currently nearly 99% of all articles are looking at current events and current terrorist campaigns. Older terrorist campaigns feature very little in the journals. Such a strong focus on contemporary issues, however, runs the real risk of losing an understanding of the broader context of terrorist conflicts, patterns and trends, and without such awareness important lessons can be missed.

For example, many observers treat the US military involvement in Iraq as a strictly modern issue linked only to the previous Iraq war and the more recent Global War on Terror. There is no awareness that this is not the first time that the US military has faced an insurgency in an occupied country where the insurgents frequently use suicide tactics to attack technologically superior American forces. Yet, this was exactly the circumstances faced by US forces at the start of the 20th century as they fought insurgents in the Philippines. Beginning in 1900, US control of the Southern islands of the Philippines was contested by native

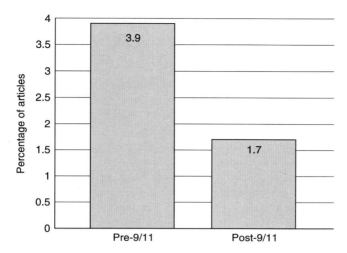

Figure 4.9 Research with a historical focus.

Moro tribes. The US forces typically won overwhelming victories in all their conventional battles with the Moros, but then faced increasing attacks from individual *amoks* and *juramentados*, Moro warriors who attacked US positions and personnel in suicidal efforts, armed often only with swords and spears.[17] It took nearly 13 years of fighting before Moro resistance to the US presence finally receded. Yet the lessons from this bitter and painful conflict are being ignored. A closer inspection of such historical cases may help prevent the current conflict in Iraq enduring 13 years. Ignoring such experiences, however, seems unlikely to improve the odds of a more successful campaign.

Yet terrorism research has never been good at exploring the past. Prior to 9/11, only 3.9 per cent of articles examined non-contemporary terrorism and less than half of these looked at terrorism prior to 1960. We know that terrorism is not a recent phenomenon and that it has been occurring in some form or another for over two thousand years. Yet this wider context is almost entirely ignored as terrorism research is increasingly driven by a need to provide a short-term, immediate assessment of current groups and threats. Efforts to establish more contextualised and stable guiding principles have been almost entirely sidelined. This is a serious cause for concern, and the deteriorating appreciation of historical research since 9/11 is deeply troubling.

Conclusions

Prior to 9/11, the study of terrorism was carried out on the periphery of academia. The funding available for researchers was extremely limited and the number of researchers prepared to focus a substantial element of their careers on the subject was paltry. In most cases it was harmful to an academic or research career to follow such interests, and most of those who were genuinely interested in the subject found that they had to incorporate other issues into their work in order to remain professionally viable. 9/11 has brought much greater interest in the subject of terrorism and, for the first time, the possibility of an expanded core of dedicated researchers exists. It is likely that the field and the amount of research being conducted will continue to grow over the coming years. It is not certain, however, whether this growth will be sustained or even if the gains made in the first years since the New York and Washington attacks will not be eroded over the coming decade. Those who believed, in 2002 and 2003, that a new academic discipline of terrorism studies was in the process of being born are coming now to realise that this is not happening.[18] There may be more courses on terrorism and more research, but there are still no academic departments of terrorism studies and the work remains firmly split among the existing disciplines.

In considering the focus of research on terrorism since 9/11, there are some worrying trends. The greatly increased attention to CBRN threats is unjustified and it is disturbing that even more research activity is being devoted to this area. The relatively heavy focus on CBRN prior to 9/11 was misplaced and produced research which was worthless with regard to what al-Qaeda did then and subsequently. The concern with CBRN is ultimately built on the premise of the fears and nightmares of politicians and policy-makers. The link to reality is often tenacious at best. To date, chemical weapons have by far proved the most deadly in the terrorist's CBRN arsenal, killing 19 people in the past fifteen years. Yet, a more objective assessment shows that, of all the people who have been killed by chemical weapons in terrorist incidents, more than 90% of the victims died because it was the government who had used such weapons (and not the terrorists). For example, in October 2002, 125 hostages were killed in Moscow when the Russian authorities pumped gas into a building to incapacitate the terrorists inside.[19] Similarly, in April 1993, 74 people died when the Branch Davidian compound in Waco, Texas, burned to the ground after federal forces pumped the compound full of a highly flammable CS gas.[20] These two instances alone were responsible for nearly 200 deaths. Based on such metrics alone, when terrorism research does turn to the subject of CBRN one could argue that it should more often be focused on the use of CBRN in *counter*-terrorism rather than on what the terrorists might be doing. But, of course, this is not the case and indeed not a single CBRN-related article in the key journals has taken such a focus in recent decades.

The diminishing place for historical analysis in terrorism research is also a cause for concern, but it is probably wise not to place excessive emphasis on this trend at this stage. The 9/11 attacks were the most destructive terrorist attacks in recorded history and many of the key factors relating to the event were notoriously under-studied (e.g. al-Qaeda, suicide terrorism etc.). It is only natural that the field should now devote serious and substantial effort to improving our knowledge base and understanding of these subjects. Terrorism research, however, does have a legacy of missing important trends. The research of the 1990s would not have flagged to an interested reader that al-Qaeda would be universally regarded as the most important and prominent terrorist group of the 2000s. One wonders what other significant trends are now being dangerously overlooked.

Yet, this survey of research has not reached entirely negative conclusions and it is important to highlight a number of positive trends which can be seen in this initial period after 9/11. To begin with, it is clear that more researchers are working on the subject than before and there has been an increase in collaborative studies. This allows studies to be more ambitious in both data collection and data analysis and, while there has been only a very small shift away from literature review-based research, there has been a much more promising increase in the use of descriptive and inferential statistical analysis. The use of inferential statistics on terrorism data in particular has more than doubled since 9/11, a trend that can only help improve the reliability and validity of the conclusions being reached by researchers. Admittedly, this is an increase that starts from an extremely low level indeed (and still compares very poorly to core journals in other areas), but it is unquestionably a step in the right direction.

Ultimately, it is still very early to judge what overall impact 9/11 and the new world order will have on terrorism research. This review was based on the research studies published in the first three years after the attacks. Within research timeframes this is a very short period of time. Many of the major studies commissioned within the first twelve months of 9/11 are only now being published. It will be another three or four years before a fuller and more reliable assessment of the impact of 9/11 on terrorism research will be possible. To date, we have seen that the field has become even more concerned with contemporary issues than before. This is probably unhealthy if it lasts, but is understandable given the issues that were missed prior to 9/11. There have been small (but welcome) improvements in data collection and analysis, but there have also been some disheartening trends such as the increased obsession on CBRN.

While the field of study of terrorism ultimately does not look as though it is crystallising into a distinct academic discipline, this is not necessarily a bad thing. Good science does not need a ring-fenced academic entity. The multi-disciplinary richness of research on terrorism has always been one of the subject's strengths. Of more concern are some of the other trends highlighted in this review. Whether they persist beyond the wake of 9/11 is now the real issue.

Notes

1 Robert Asprey, *War in the Shadows* (London: Little, Brown & Company, 1994).

2 Most notably see: Alex Schmid and Albert Jongman, *Political Terrorism* (2nd edition) (Oxford: North-Holland, 1988); and, Edna Reid, *An Analysis of Terrorism Literature: A Bibliometric and Content Analysis Study*, PhD dissertation, University of Southern California, Los Angeles, 1983.

3 The results of this review were published in two papers: Andrew Silke, 'The devil you know: Continuing problems with research on terrorism', *Terrorism and*

Political Violence, 13/4 (2001), pp. 1–14; and Andrew Silke, 'The road less travelled: Recent trends in terrorism research', in Andrew Silke (ed.), *Research on Terrorism: Trends, Achievements and Failures* (London: Frank Cass, 2004), pp. 186–213.

4 See Andrew Silke, 'The road less traveled: Recent trends in terrorism research', in Andrew Silke (ed.), *Research on Terrorism: Trends, Achievements and Failures* (London: Frank Cass, 2004), pp. 186–213.

5 See Andrew Silke, 'The devil you know: Continuing problems with research on terrorism', *Terrorism and Political Violence*, 13/4 (2001), pp. 1–14.

6 Quote taken from: C. Frankfort-Nachimas and D. Nachimas, *Research Methods in the Social Sciences* (5th edition) (London: Arnold, 1996), p. 10.

7 These are relatively stringent criteria, and other reviewers may be willing to be more inclusive. See Andrew Silke, 'The road less traveled: Recent trends in terrorism research', in Andrew Silke (ed.), *Research on Terrorism: Trends, Achievements and Failures* (London: Frank Cass, 2004), pp. 186–213, for a fuller discussion of the rationale for this approach.

8 Alex Schmid and Albert Jongman, *Political Terrorism* (2nd edition) (Oxford: North-Holland, 1988).

9 See Avishag Gordon, 'The effect of database and website inconstancy on the terrorism field's delineation', *Studies in Conflict & Terrorism*, 27/2 (2004), pp. 79–88.

10 Alex Schmid and Albert Jongman, *Political Terrorism* (2nd edition) (Oxford: North-Holland, 1988), p. 179.

11 Alex Schmid and Albert Jongman, *Political Terrorism* (2nd edition) (Oxford: North-Holland, 1988), p. 137.

12 In experimental designs control is normally achieved by randomly assigning research subjects to experimental and control groups. However, this can often be very difficult to achieve in real-world research and consequently the lack of control throws doubt on any association between variables that the research claims to find. Inferential statistics, though, can help to introduce a recognised element of control, so that there is less doubt and more confidence over the veracity of any findings.

13 David Rapoport, 'Terrorism', in M. Hawkesworth and M. Kogan (eds), *Routledge Encyclopedia of Government and Politics, Volume 2* (London: Routledge, 1992).

14 For a table listing the twenty most studied terrorist groups in the 1990s see Andrew Silke, 'The road less traveled: Recent trends in terrorism research', in Andrew Silke (ed.), *Research on Terrorism: Trends, Achievements and Failures* (London: Frank Cass, 2004), p. 204.

15 Nine broad categories were used in this regard:
   1. Nationalist/Separatists (e.g. PIRA, ETA)
   2. Islamic extremists (e.g. al-Qaeda, Hizbollah)
   3. Marxist/communist (e.g. Red Brigades, Red Army Faction)
   4. Right-wing extremists (e.g. US militias, neo-Nazis)
   5. Religious cults (e.g. Aum, Branch Davidians)
   6. Environmentalists (e.g. Earth First, Animal Liberation Front)
   7. Criminal (e.g. mafia, drug cartels)
   8. State terrorism (e.g. Apartheid in South Africa)
   9. Other (e.g. Jewish Defence League, Ulster Defence Association)

16 For example the valuable contributions made by Chris Quillen: Chris Quillen, 'A historical analysis of mass casualty bombers', *Studies in Conflict and Terrorism*, 25/5 (2002), pp. 279–292; and Chris Quillen, 'Mass casualty bombings chronology', *Studies in Conflict and Terrorism*, 25/5 (2002), pp. 293–302.

17 For more on this campaign see D. Woolman, 'Fighting Islam's fierce Moro warriors', *Military History*, 9/1 (2002), pp. 34–40.

18 See for example Avishag Gordon, 'Terrorism as an academic subject after 9/11: Searching the internet reveals a Stockholm Syndrome trend', *Studies in Conflict and Terrorism*, 28/1 (2005), pp. 45–60.
19 See Anne Speckhard, Nadejda Tarabrina, Valery Krasnov and Khapta Akhmedova, 'Research note: Observations of suicidal terrorists in action', *Terrorism and Political Violence*, 16/2 (2004), pp. 305–327.
20 See Stuart Wright, 'Anatomy of a government massacre: Abuses of hostage-barricade protocols during the Waco standoff', *Terrorism and Political Violence*, 11/2 (1999), pp. 39–68.

5

RESPONDING TO THE ROOTS OF TERROR[1]

Karin von Hippel

Al-Qaeda's spectacular on 11 September 2001, along with the tragically lethal attacks in places such as Nairobi, Bali and Madrid, attest to its determination, reach and capabilities. The indoctrination strategy is equally long term; the extremist *madrasas* epitomise the patient nurturing of potential recruits. Beyond the military, police, intelligence, legal and financial activities that have been undertaken to confront this threat, a number of longer term preventive measures also need to be adopted by governments and international organisations to thwart this movement, network and organisation.[2] At the risk of stating the obvious, the threat posed by transnational terrorism can be defeated only by a coordinated, robust, long-term, transnational response.

Publicly, all states and international organisations have been committed to tackling root causes since 11 September, though some were quicker than others in articulating their policies. For example, just after the attacks, the European Union outlined a comprehensive counterterrorist strategy that incorporated a major component aimed at root causes through the use of non-violent tools, as did the United Nations and the OECD.[3] At the same time, the United States government had an additional plan to undermine terrorism, that is, war in Iraq. As was patently obvious in the run-up to the war, it was opposed by a number of European (and other) states, and only served to exacerbate a transatlantic rift that had been evident since the end of the Cold War.

In addition to dealing with the alleged weapons of mass destruction, the U.S. was positing that a democratic Iraq would pave the way for more democracy in the Middle East and thereby undermine terrorism, while some European states argued that war in Iraq would in fact do more to enhance the appeal and swell the ranks of al-Qaeda. For Europe and several of the aforementioned multilateral organisations, the focus was not on regime change, but rather on a number of socio-economic reforms in developing states. The U.S. government also officially joined this part of the effort in February 2003, with the publication of the *National Strategy for Combating Terrorism*.[4] This document asserts:

> Ongoing U.S. efforts to resolve regional disputes, foster economic, social, and political development, market-based economies, good governance, and the rule of law, while not necessarily focused on combating terrorism, contribute to the campaign by addressing under-lying conditions that terrorists often seek to manipulate for their own advantage.[5]

The strategy paper goes on to describe how the U.S. government cannot do this alone: 'The United States has neither the resources nor the expertise to be in every place in the world . . . Our friends and allies face many of the same threats. It is essential for America to work with its friends and allies in this campaign.'[6] While much of the language in the *National Strategy* appears bizarrely out of place, and certainly inconsistent with U.S. behaviour since the start of the Bush administration, the U.S. government is, at least publicly, formally committed to dealing with root causes.

However, it transpired that the public strategies of Europe and America con-verged on the issue of tackling root causes (though not on the regime change component), and, however welcome the non-violent aspects of the U.S. approach may be to European policy makers, the question remains as to how well both power blocks actually understand root causes and what their strategies in fact entail for countering them. In the three and a half years since the attacks in America, neither block has implemented significant practical measures, in terms of political and socio-economic reforms, that could fundamentally reduce the appeal and influence of bin Laden and al-Qaeda. Three and a half years on, the progress report has been decidedly mediocre.

Beyond the more radical elements of the al-Qaeda platform which are consid-ered non-negotiable, other underlying causes still need to be tackled, while those that are less well understood, or merely assumptions at this stage, need greater clarification. (This discussion takes it as a given that if President Bush would follow through on his promise to push for peace in the Middle East, this would make an enormous contribution to removing a serious obstacle and perceptions of inequity by many Arabs and Muslims.)

This chapter examines developments in six main areas that have emerged in the public debate as causal and facilitating factors for international terrorism. A closer examination of these factors reveals that, while some energy has been dedicated to understanding and tackling them in the three plus years since the attacks in America, the response has not been adequate. The rhetoric – on both sides of the Atlantic – has not yet been satisfactorily matched by realistic and robust reforms.

Terrorism and poverty: What are the links?

The first area is the complicated link between terrorism and poverty. Since 11 September a number of world leaders, including President Bush, have made a connection between poverty and terrorism. Although conventional wisdom would argue in favour of establishing a direct correlation, the evidence gathered thus far does not fully support this proposition. Indeed, if poverty really were the root cause of terrorism, terrorists would mostly come from the poorest parts of the world, namely sub-Saharan Africa. Thus far, this is not the case.

A Princeton study in 2002 on Israeli and Arab terrorism in the Middle East demonstrated that in this region, terrorists not only enjoyed living standards above the poverty line but also had obtained at the minimum a secondary education.[7] Information gathered thus far regarding the background of al-Qaeda members seems to be consistent with these findings, especially regarding the ability of these terrorists to adapt successfully to foreign environments. In alien cities members of al-Qaeda have had no trouble finding employment, renting apartments, attending graduate schools and enrolling in flying lessons, all of which would have been much more difficult had they been uneducated and indigent. Two additional factors, however, complicate the poverty debate: suicide bombers and education.

Suicide bombers

A more direct link could be established between 'suicide bombers' and poverty in some circumstances, given that the families of suicide bombers are generously compensated by a number of charitable organisations. It could thus be argued that the financial reward can become an attractive incentive for a poor family. In the case of the Palestinians, the sponsors of suicide bombers included, among others, Saddam Hussein. Yet, in her interviews with potential Palestinian suicide bombers, Nasra Hassan found that most came from middle-class and educated families.[8] In contrast, Jessica Stern's research, which focused on the Kashmir dispute, demonstrated that many volunteers did indeed come from poor families, and often because of the financial reward.[9] Further research is needed to shed light on how relevant financial considerations are with respect to such volunteers in many parts of the world.

Education

Education is an additional factor to consider in the poverty debate. In some Islamic countries, such as Somalia or Pakistan, poor parents send their children to *madrasas* and Qur'anic schools because they are heavily subsidised or free of charge. Children also receive food, clothing and books, at no cost to the family. It has become apparent, however, that children who attend certain radicalised *madrasas* are taught to despise 'corrupting Western influences' from an early age, and gain few practical skills to prepare them for working in modern society (for example, some learn no mathematics or science whatsoever).[10] In the late 1990s, it was estimated that more than 10,000 teachers were instructing three million local students plus an additional 10,000 foreign students in *madrasas*. Most of these children came from poor families. Combined spending on this type of education was estimated at over $1 billion per year, with three-fourths of the funds coming from abroad, mostly from Saudi Arabia.

While approximately 30 per cent of the Taliban – the hosts for al-Qaeda – were educated in such *madrasas*, many of the known al-Qaeda terrorists themselves, such as those who committed the 11 September attacks, were not. Interestingly, many of the hijackers had advanced scientific and technical degrees, and were educated in Europe and North America. These discrepancies indicate the need to clarify and categorise educational achievement and standards for different terrorists in order to develop appropriate interventions for these populations.

Support for quality public education could be one way of attacking root causes in some parts of the world. Tentative steps have begun in this direction; for example, the European Union has been exploring innovative approaches to working with the Pakistani *madrasa* system, in an attempt to engage the 'huge untapped source of manpower and funding for educational and development work' in evidence in these communities.[11] The U.S. government has also been applying pressure on Pakistan and other countries to reform the *madrasas* – with minimal success.[12] Yet thus far, the funds dedicated to educational reform, which is sorely needed in all too many parts of the world – such as USAID's commitment in 2002 for $100 million to help reform Pakistan's education system over a five year period – pale in comparison to the amounts spent on defence and indicate that the commitment to educational reform is not as extensive as the Bush administration claims. The Pentagon's missile defence system, now being deployed even though evidence does not exist that it actually works, already has cost U.S. taxpayers over $31 billion, and estimates of the total cost are more than $100 billion.[13]

After the war in Afghanistan, Senator Joe Biden proposed a project to build and supply a thousand schools in Afghanistan in order to counter the influence of the *madrasas*. The idea was soon killed, and not just by the Republican party but also by his own Democratic colleagues.[14] As George Packer explained, 'Spending twenty million dollars on schools in Afghanistan is a harder sell than spending four hundred billion on defense; fear is more compelling than foresight.' According to Biden, 'This is a place where the President's bragging to me, "Mr. Chairman, I don't do nuance"... where he has an advantage.'[15]

It is not only poor children who are being indoctrinated at extremist schools; this applies also to a large number of educational systems in wealthier Middle East countries. In 2002, the Saudis conducted a review of their textbooks and found that 5 per cent of material was 'horrible', 10 per cent 'questionable', while 85 per cent called for 'understanding with other religious faiths.'[16] Thus far Qatar is the only country to completely overhaul its education system, and in this case reform has been attributed to the modernisation package introduced by the ruler, Sheik Hamad Bin Khalifa Thani, rather than as a result of U.S. pressure.

Even if the entire system could be overhauled overnight, there are still millions of children who have already gone through this system, one that began to expand significantly during the 1970s in places such as Pakistan, India and Bangladesh, Indonesia, parts of Africa as well as the Middle East and North Africa (although not all schools have an extremist agenda and not all students will become terrorists).[17] Policy measures focused on these 'graduates' have not even been considered.

Even if many terrorists, and their leaders, are neither poor nor uneducated, they tend to use the plight of the poor as one justification for committing violence, and for broadening their appeal. They often claim to speak on behalf of the poor, just as other middle-class, well-educated ideologues have done in the past. Therefore, it could well be argued that a serious effort to fulfil the Millennium Development Goals, as well as being the right thing to do, is essential in order to remove one of the platforms commonly used by terrorists. As Ambassador David Shinn remarked, 'What is missing is a major, new, long-term program to reduce poverty and social alienation.'[18] Instead of concentrating on the individual terrorist, who is likely to be beyond reach, it may be more important to work on what Louise Richardson of Harvard refers to as 'the enabling environment' or 'complicit society', so that potential sympathisers (who may not espouse violence but may support the arguments of terrorists) can be won over and, hopefully, even oppose terrorism in their communities.

Collapsed and weak states: Breeding grounds or open markets for illegal economic activity?

When discussing the environment in which terrorism flourishes, a further theory links 'failed' states, such as Somalia, to terrorism.[19] The factors that make these places attractive include weak or non-existent government structures, and the inability of the international community to monitor or interfere with trafficking and smuggling pipelines, which are used to move humans, drugs, small arms, natural resources, black money and – potentially – nuclear materials across porous borders. Terrorists in theory can operate with relative impunity, without fear of a government crackdown on operations, or international intervention.

These attractions may be countered by the difficulties facing terrorists when operating in an insecure and foreign environment, where security is itself highly fragmented and infrastructure unreliable. It should be recalled that, when taking refuge in Sudan, bin Laden did not settle in the southern parts of the territory that are considered 'lawless', albeit Christian and Animist, but rather in the Muslim north, in Khartoum, an area where the government is and was firmly in control. Similarly, when he established his base in Afghanistan in 1996, the country was no longer a collapsed state but was instead under the control of the Taliban, except for the northern province of Badakhshan.

While collapsed states may not be the real breeding grounds for terrorists – and there is little hard evidence to support the allegations, particularly in the case of

Somalia[20] – they could, in future, become more attractive territories, especially if the international community tightens its grip over terrorist networks in other states. And currently they are at risk for transhipment activity and for providing sanctuary to some terrorists – the recent Report of the Panel of Experts on Somalia to the Security Council described not only how Somalia harboured some of the terrorists who carried out attacks in Mombassa, but also how the territory was used to smuggle weapons into Kenya. These types of intervention can only serve to undermine nascent state authorities and attempts at democratisation.

While the al-Qaeda network has also penetrated Western societies, at least in Minneapolis, London, Hamburg or Toronto, they leave behind a paper trail, whereas in weak states it is far more difficult to ascertain their movements and activities. All policy papers recognise the need to strengthen governance and security sectors in these places. For example, the U.S. National Strategy likewise declares: 'we will ensure that efforts designed to identify and diminish conditions contributing to state weakness and failure are a central U.S. foreign policy goal. The principal objective ... will be the rebuilding of a state that can look after its own people.'[21] Yet here too, unfortunately, little has been done since 11 September to rebuild weak and collapsed states around the world. For example, funds committed to Somalia by OECD states are not only insignificant in scale, but the totals are also no larger today than prior to 11 September, and most of it is dedicated to humanitarian efforts, not to nation-building. Ideally funds should be used to support local authorities in Somalia until such time as a national government is re-established.[22]

Conflicts hijacked by religious extremists

Wars perceived as threatening Islam have been exacerbated due to the participation of 'foreign volunteers', many of whom have links to al-Qaeda. This occurs in much the same way that past ideological wars, such as the Spanish Civil War, attracted foreign recruits. Bin Laden and other al-Qaeda members – the so-called 'Afghan Arabs' – fought against the Soviet occupation of Afghanistan, which is when al-Qaeda was founded. While researchers and journalists are now revisiting some of the conflicts penetrated by these 'Muslim mercenaries', not enough is known about their participation in places such as Bosnia, Chechnya, Dagestan, Eritrea, Kashmir, the Philippines, Somalia, Sudan and Uzbekistan.

Al-Qaeda involvement can also transform these territories into breeding grounds for terrorists, as occurred in Afghanistan during the late 1990s. Ayman al-Zawahiri, Osama bin Laden's top lieutenant, wrote that he visited Chechnya with the intention of establishing it as a further training base.[23] These conflicts also provide new recruits and expand the network of affiliates. The presence of these 'foreign volunteers' can lead to the improvement of strategies, tactics, quality of equipment, and to the adoption of more violent methods of confrontation – that is, suicide attacks involving massive civilian casualties as opposed to selective attacks against precise military targets.

Attempts should be made to resolve these conflicts through shrewd use of diplomatic and development tools before they are corrupted in this manner. For those conflicts that have already been exacerbated, new tools will have to be utilised, but first, a greater understanding of how these conflicts have been manipulated by the al-Qaeda movement is necessary.

Here again, too little is being done to resolve these conflicts. The recent Beslan school massacre, in Russia's North Caucasus, provides a horrific example of what can happen if these conflicts are left to fester. It only serves Russian Prime Minister Putin's interests to claim foreign involvement, even though it is still unclear if it was purely a domestic terror attack or if 'Muslim mercenaries' played a role.

Fundamentalist charities

Financial support that promotes international terrorism comes from a variety of sources, including wealthy individuals, states, *diasporas*, criminal activities and charitable organisations. Funding from all sources is dedicated, among other things, to planning and executing attacks, assistance for families of suicide bombers, and long-term indoctrination through extremist *madrasas*, religious centres and social support mechanisms. Concerning charitable assistance, a distinction needs to be made between some Islamic charities, such as the Aga Khan Foundation, which provides critical humanitarian and development assistance in neglected rural and urban areas, and others that promote a radical agenda.

Significantly, one of the basic tenets of Islam is charity (*Zakat*), and charity given in a way that does not humiliate the receiver. This discreet method of delivery, however, complicates matters and makes it difficult to discern how certain Islamic charities, along with several governments, such as Iran, propagate their extremist ideology and anti-Western sentiment with their aid in many developing countries. Rohan Gunaratna notes: 'According to the CIA, one-fifth of all Islamic NGOs worldwide have been unwittingly infiltrated by al-Qaeda and other terrorist support groups.'[24] It is important, therefore, to understand how these funding pipelines operate, as well as the extremist advocacy that is channelled through these networks. Incidentally, Western aid agencies may also consider utilising more discreet delivery mechanisms in Islamic countries as an additional means to avoid humiliation.

While international efforts have uncovered information about the financial activities of some of the Saudi-funded charities, and the Financial Action Task Force (FATF) is trying to implement a more stringent regime to make all charitable organisations more transparent and accountable, greater efforts need to be made to understand and improve our response to radical religious funding and advocacy efforts in many parts of the world. The U.S. government also needs to consider alternative ways of 'winning hearts and minds' through its actions, rather than its current policy, which often achieves the opposite effect, for example, by shutting down remittance houses, which are in most cases a lifeline for poor countries.

At the most basic level, it is often simply the dearth of Western international support that makes some developing states vulnerable and susceptible to terrorist ideology. While the religious appeal may not be overwhelming for many families, the lack of alternatives for schooling or health care fuels the growth of the movement. In Somalia, for example, because Western international assistance is not significant in scale, the influence of these Islamic movements has increased. A recent International Crisis Group (ICG) report noted that the fundamentalist movements inside Somalia 'owe their rapid growth since 1990 less to genuine popularity than access to substantial external funding.'[25] Islamic charitable assistance is rarely noted in UN appeals for Somalia (indeed, this is lacking in most UN appeals), and few of these countries or organisations actively participate in the Somalia Aid Coordination Body, established to serve as the permanent coordination body for donors, UN agencies, NGOs and other international organisations.

Every effort should be made to try to include Islamic NGOs in all international coordinating bodies. Currently the work of these NGOs all too often occurs in parallel to those sponsored by OECD states. At the very least, discussion should be promoted and information exchanged with Islamic NGOs in order to prevent overlap and duplication, improve needs assessments and, importantly, enhance the lives of the poor.

Moreover, it appears that over the last decade significant amounts of financing for terrorist activities worldwide has come from Saudi Arabian sources. Saudi money has allegedly funded fundamentalist activity in a wide range of places – from Algeria or Chechnya, in support of insurgent groups, to Europe or Central Asia, where the Saudis have provided the funding for mosques and for free scholarships for students of Islamic studies. The influence of these charities has increased on the quiet, though recently, in the United States, two publications concerning the Saudi connection have received significant attention.[26]

It must also be pointed out here that it is not just the extreme Islamic groups that utilise this method of influence: Christian fundamentalist organisations in the United States, for example, have been supporting certain sides in conflicts that are perceived as threatening to Christianity, with southern Sudan being the most obvious example. President Bush has been openly supporting the southern Sudanese in this long-standing conflict, primarily due to the influence of the Christian fundamentalist lobby.

Transnational mobilisation and recruitment

The fifth area concerns a debate as to whether some economic migrants, asylum seekers and members of certain diaspora communities are joining terrorist groups *after* having spent time in their host country. Mohammed Atta's experience in Hamburg, or Sayyid Qutb's in Colorado, are cited as two examples. It has been suggested that one of the main reasons why immigrants come to support terrorist groups, such as al-Qaeda, is the alienation and prejudice they often experience in the West. This marginalisation is further reinforced by the fact that many remain outside formal state structures because they are not legal residents. Consequently they seek assistance and support from local mosques and Islamic cultural centres – often the first port of call for new arrivals – where they can obtain fake passports and identity cards. It appears that some of these individuals are vulnerable to the aggressive recruitment campaigns being carried out by extremist groups operating across Europe and the United States.

Here too, they often access the extreme Islamist literature that advises them on ways to survive in 'infidel' countries. Such publications, along with al-Qaeda manuals, promote and glorify an isolated existence in Western countries, turning feelings of alienation into a necessary and noble means of survival. Prior to 11 September, many were encouraged by these mosques and centres to attend training camps in Afghanistan. In addition, today, as in the past, they are also recruited in prisons throughout the world, in both North and South.

While this may be happening in some cases, it is also true that many were radicalised at home prior to coming to Europe and North America. It was in fact the liberal laws in Europe that prevented most European countries, for example the United Kingdom and Italy, from returning many wanted radicals to their home countries, for fear they would be tortured or that the government would apply the death penalty. At this stage, too many assumptions are being made on too small a sample size, though it can be said that a fundamental overhaul of Europe's asylum procedures would be a step in the right direction.

The governance factor: The democratic deficit

Strong, authoritarian states that lack democracy and accountability may be the real breeding grounds for international terrorism. The al-Qaeda terrorists who participated in the September 11 attacks, and most of the members of affiliated organisations who have been arrested for other acts of terrorism, come from such states. They oppose what they perceive to be authoritarian, secular rule in their own countries, and view their leaders as corrupted by Western influences. They believe that only through the establishment of Islamic states can these countries be returned to the right path and their former glory.

In these countries, the snowballing anger on the so-called 'Arab Street'[27] hones in on the United States and some other Western countries. Ordinary Saudis or Algerians or Egyptians are resentful of their own governments, but are unable to express that anger in any meaningful way that will bring about change. It is far easier to direct that anger at the United States and other developed states, which anyway are supporting their 'elitist' and non-representative leaders.

This frustration is so strong in some parts of the world that we often hear two entirely different and competing versions of events. Conspiracy theories abound as to who really committed recent terrorist attacks: accusations that the CIA and the FBI were behind the Bali bombing, or destroyed the Twin Towers, are perpetuated by extremist imams. These beliefs are being fed to populations in certain parts of the world that are already disillusioned and distrustful of the intentions of the 'West', or learned to hate the 'West' in school. Moreover, they read and hear about generous financial support for the impoverished, but rarely see evidence that the money reaches the poor. This is not necessarily the fault of developed states, which are often forced to work with corrupt governments in consequence of their own conditionality factors to ensure accountability, or because they are unable to spend funds that have been committed due to lack of accountable partners on the ground.

Nevertheless, the inability of developed states to realise international development goals contributes to this disillusionment and resentment, and allows more and more ordinary citizens to become susceptible to believing these conspiracy theories. This is the 'complicit society' referred to above. Thomas Friedman has argued that every attempt should be made to address the anger on the 'Arab Street,' as once they move into the 'Arab Basement' it is too late to use persuasion and other non-violent measures.[28]

Conclusions

These six areas – poverty, weak and collapsed states, wars hijacked by Islamic extremists, fundamentalist charities, radicalisation in Europe and North America, and the 'democracy deficit' – need deeper analysis to understand how they may facilitate terrorist recruitment and support. They also require a response that goes further than that advocated by current policy in both Europe and America: new, more nuanced tools are required. At the very least, both Europe and America should make more of an effort to implement policies they have committed to since 11 September.

As noted at the beginning of this chapter, the threat posed by transnational terrorism can only be defeated through a dedicated and coordinated transnational response, one that not only focuses on the symptoms but also on the causes, because security and intelligence measures at national, Europe-wide and even Transatlantic levels cannot guarantee that an attack will not take place. All governments have structural weaknesses and vulnerabilities that can be exploited, and no government could be expected to eliminate all vulnerability to terrorist attack. It is simply not possible to prevent attacks in truly globalised, relatively open societies. Thus a complementary campaign that addresses root causes takes on added urgency, and should be spearheaded by the United Nations, as the only neutral and morally legitimate world body, which thus far has been hampered in its own counterterrorism strategy by the Transatlantic rift. As former U.S. President Bill Clinton recently remarked, 'If you come from a wealthy country with open borders, unless you seriously believe you can kill, imprison, or occupy all your enemies, you have to make a world with more friends and fewer enemies.'[29]

Notes

1 Portions of this chapter will also appear in Karin von Hippel, 'Dealing with the Roots of Terror' in James Forrest (ed.), *The Making of a Terrorist: Recruitment, Training and Root Causes* (Westport, CT: Praeger, 2005), and the conclusion in Karin von Hippel (ed.), *Europe Confronts Terrorism* (Palgrave Macmillan, 2005).

2 As defined by Dr Magnus Ranstorp at the University of St Andrew's in Scotland.

3 See http://www.europa.eu.int for more information. The OECD–DAC Secretariat has also been at the forefront in exploring potential root causes and their implications for development cooperation. See the OECD's most recent report, 'A Development Co-operation Lens on Terrorism Prevention: Key Entry Points for Action,' 11 April 2003, DCD/DAC(2003)11/REV1. See also the UN publication 'Annex, Report of the Policy Working Group on the United Nations and Terrorism,' A/57/273, S/2002/875.

4 The White House, *National Strategy for Combating Terrorism* (February 2003). Online at: http://www.whitehouse.gov/news/releases/2003/02/counter_terrorism/counter_terrorism_strategy.pdf.

5 The White House, *National Strategy for Combating Terrorism* (February 2003), p. 23.

6 The White House, *National Strategy for Combating Terrorism* (February 2003).

7 Alan B. Krueger and Jitka Maleckova, 'Education, Poverty, Political Violence and Terrorism: Is there a Causal Connection?' Working Papers, Research Program in Development Studies, Woodrow Wilson School, Princeton University (May 2002).

8 Nasra Hassan, 'An Arsenal of Believers,' *The New Yorker*, 19 November 2001, pp. 36–41.

9 Jessica Stern, 'Pakistan's Jihad Culture,' *Foreign Affairs* (November/December 2000).

10 See Jessica Stern, 'Meeting with the Muj,' *Bulletin of the Atomic Scientists*, Vol. 57, No. 1 (January/February 2001), pp. 42–51.

11 As noted in Brigid Smith, 'Review of Primary Education in Pakistan During Last 10 Years; Madrassah Schooling: Potential for Growth,' Consultancy to European Commission: Pakistan, ARCADIS BMB and EUROCONSULT, Pakistan, April 2002, p. 8, paragraph VI. See also 'Pakistan: Madrasas, Extremism and the Military,' ICG Asia Report 36, International Crisis Group, Brussels, 29 July 2002.

12 See Febe Armanios, 'Islamic Religious Schools, Madrasas: Background,' Report for Congress (Washington, DC: Congressional Research Service, October 2003), p. 6.

13 See Bradley Graham, 'The Bush Record: Missile Defense Interceptor System Set, but Doubts Remain Network Hasn't Undergone Realistic Testing,' *Washington Post* (29 September 2004) p. A01.

14 See George Packer, 'A Democratic World,' *The New Yorker* (16 and 23 February 2004) pp. 100–108.

15 As cited in George Packer, 'A Democratic World,' *The New Yorker* (16 and 23 February 2004), pp. 107–108.

16 Febe Armanios, 'Islamic Religious Schools, Madrasas: Background,' Report for Congress (Washington DC: Congressional Research Service, October 2003), p. 4.

17 Febe Armanios, 'Islamic Religious Schools, Madrasas: Background,' Report for Congress (Washington DC: Congressional Research Service, October 2003). See also Uzma Anzar, 'Islamic Education: A Brief History of Madrassas with Comments on Curricula and Current Pedagogical Practices' (Washington, DC: World Bank, March 2003).

18 David Shinn, 'Fighting Terrorism in East Africa and the Horn,' *Foreign Service Journal* (September 2004), p. 42.

19 See, for example, 'Banks-to-Terror Conglomerate Faces U.S. Wrath,' *The Daily Telegraph* (28 September 2001). This article claimed that 'between 3,000 and 5,000 members of the al Qa'eda and al-Itihad partnership are operating [in Somalia], with 50,000 to 60,000 supporters and reservists.'

20 For more information, see Ken Menkhaus, 'Somalia: Next Up in the War on Terrorism?' *CSIS Africa Notes*, 6 (January 2002); Andre Le Sage, 'Prospects for Al Itihad and Islamist Radicalism in Somalia,' *Review of African Political Economy*, Vol. 27, No. 89 (September 2001); 'Somalia and the "War" on Terrorism,' *Strategic Comments*, Vol. 8, No. 1 (January 2002); and Karin von Hippel, 'Terrorist Space,' *World Today* (February 2002).

21 The White House, *National Strategy for Combating Terrorism* (February 2003), p. 23.

22 For financial contributions to Somalia, see http://www.sacb.info

23 As cited in Lawrence Wright, 'The Man Behind Bin Laden: How an Egyptian Doctor Became a Master of Terror,' *The New Yorker* (16 September 2002), pp. 80–81.

24 Rohan Gunaratna, *Inside Al-Qa'ida: Global Network of Terror* (London: Hurst & Co., 2002), p. 6.

25 'Somalia: Countering Terrorism in a Failed State,' *ICG Africa Report*, 45 (23 May 2002), p. 13.

26 See, for example, 'Terrorist Financing: Report of an Independent Task Force,' sponsored by the Council on Foreign Relations, Maurice R. Greenberg (Chair), William F. Wechsler and Lee S. Wolosky (Project Co-Directors) (Washington DC, 2002).

27 This term is inappropriate because the anger is also felt by many non-Arabs in other parts of the world.

28 Thomas Friedman, *The New York Times* (23 October 2002).

29 *Yale Alumni Magazine* (January/February 2004), p. 13.

6

UNDERSTANDING TERRORIST MOTIVATION: A SOCIO-PSYCHOLOGICAL PERSPECTIVE

John Horgan

Introduction

Despite the increased attention paid to understanding terrorism since the events of 11 September 2001 (or 9/11), psychological perspectives on terrorism remain underdeveloped. In many ways, what might explain this are issues that have hindered conceptual progress in terrorism research more generally. The 9/11 attacks, like many major terrorist incidents before them, revealed significant gaps in our understanding of terrorism, with some of the most basic questions remaining without useful answers. A reason for the persistence of such gaps might relate to unresolved practical issues (e.g. the fact that a paucity of reliable data exists on all but the most well-researched terrorist groups, the fact that the number of dedicated terrorism researchers has shown no discernable increase in the long-term – interest tends to drop significantly in the time following major terrorist events – and problems of access to activists) that have resulted in an unsatisfactory state of affairs which has persisted since 2001: analyses of terrorism continue to mix fact and fiction, and remain short-term, incident driven, politicised and narrowly focused, with little overall sense of conceptual grounding or theoretical continuation.

While the perspective adopted throughout this chapter is one based on psychology, students of terrorism will always be required to be open to considering the diversity and complexity of terrorism from a variety of disciplinary perspectives. Attempts to understand terrorism from one exclusive view, Reich (1990) asserted, may press the power of that explanation beyond its valid limits. There may well be a danger in this, and in any study of terrorism we need to draw on knowledge from a range of areas. I am not certain that a 'socio-psychological' perspective necessarily redresses this issue, but it does at least suggest that we do not limit ourselves to explanations of terrorism that reside at the level of the individual terrorist. It may be, however, that using terms such as 'socio-psychological' might represent an extension of traditional analyses to allow the development of frameworks in which individual accounts and decisions are encompassed within group contexts in more systematic ways.

A related point, and one that we must accept within an empirical study of terrorism, is that any form of behaviour, terrorist or otherwise, exists within a social and political context (and any efforts to 'counter' that behaviour must also derive from and be focused within that context), but terrorist behaviour (like, for example, criminal behaviour) refers to activities that belong to an environmental context which gives rise to, sustains, directs and controls it largely in the same fashion as any other behaviour. We can never separate terrorism from society because it is embedded in it. Given this, the 'appropriateness', or otherwise, of the use of terrorist violence with respect to some political or distant ideological or religious aspiration is not primarily at issue when we try to 'understand' it. This might appear to be common sense to a social scientist, but given the continuing lack of empirical evidence used to inform thinking about terrorist behaviour, it must be emphasized and its implications considered.

With these issues in mind, for the remainder of this chapter I will attempt to present a set of views on: (a) what a psychology of terrorism might mean; (b) individual psychological perspectives and their incompatibility with the reality of terrorism; (c) the benefit of considering integrated and developmental psychological perspectives on terrorism, which enable us to appreciate the diverse factors contributing to (1) decisions related to initial involvement in terrorism, (2) continuing involvement in terrorism and (3) eventual disengagement from terrorism; and finally (d) some conclusions and suggestions for considering how a programme of research might develop.[1]

What does a psychology of terrorism mean?

In a recent book (Horgan, 2005), I have suggested at least four principal areas that we can explore from a psychological perspective.

Firstly, there is the individual terrorist, and the processes that allow the emergence of and sustenance of violent behaviour (along with associated activities) that we identify as 'terrorism'. This is the focus of much of the psychological research to date, and in a sense this reflects a focus on the individual issues that maintain terrorist behaviour, the reinforcers, the lures and other supportive qualities that create both the impetus for involvement in terrorism (in terms of the increased likelihood of involvement) and engagement in terrorist acts (this also necessarily impinges on the role of non-violent political or supportive behaviour in sustaining more violent behaviour).

Secondly, we can explore from psychological perspectives the relationship between the individual and the political, religious or ideological context in which he or she operates. This often involves the organisational aspects of terrorist movements, and particularly the wide variety of ways in which aspects of the organisation impinge upon the behaviour of the individual.

Thirdly, we could consider the effects of terrorist activity. In a way, this is the task inherent in all analyses of terrorism because it remains impossible to separate our reactions to terrorism from our attempts to understand and conceptualise it. All studies of terrorism and terrorists will inevitably stem from concerns about 'effects' as such, but for the most part psychology has attempted to examine the effects of terrorism across two primary areas – at the level of public reactions (in terms of how we can be directly involved in victimisation through, for instance, post-traumatic stress disorder after a terrorist attack, and being involved more generally as an observer) as well as how the political system and those involved in it at higher levels (i.e. above the electorate) are affected and come to make subsequent decisions about responses to terrorism as a function of those effects.

A fourth and final example of an important issue that we can explore from a psychological point of view is the broader issue of methodology, and the aspects of studying terrorism that we may need to consider and develop in ways that perhaps remain unexplored. Within what is becoming known as 'terrorism studies', it is of course dangerous to accept knowledge of terrorism based on authority, dogma or belief. In any endeavour, only transparency and evidence can settle disputes, and if the subject of terrorism studies is to become rigorous, then we must align our analyses closely with the methodological rigour consistent with established academic disciplines. However, a special problem in existing studies of terrorists is a lack of a variety of important empirical datasets to support particular viewpoints. Most of the data available to researchers is made available through secondary sources – books, newspaper reports, terrorist communiqués, statements, speeches, sometimes even autobiographies, and then, for the longer-standing terrorism researchers, information gained directly from the security services or government. Less effort has been put into listening to (and making sense of) what the terrorists themselves have to say. Unpalatable as this may seem, it is inevitable that in order to understand the development and structure of terrorist behaviour we eventually have to meet with and speak to people who have been, or are, involved in terrorist violence (see Silke, 2004). To the academic reader this point may appear moot, but the reality is not so clear, with academic reluctance to enter the violent field now more obvious than ever before. Given that for most of us it is the drama surrounding terrorist incidents that drives our perceptions and understanding of both the process and its instigators, the need for a reliance on research-driven knowledge is all the more important (how we analyse this data is another issue, and one that will not be discussed here).

Individual psychological perspectives and the reality of terrorism

For many, psychological perspectives are synonymous with a focus on the individual terrorist and the presumed personal qualities that would suggest an 'attractiveness' to becoming involved in terrorism. In particular, much of the early research on terrorist behaviour has attempted to portray terrorist motivation as couched in abnormality, individual personality traits or psychopathology (and even blatant abnormality). In general, not only does such research lack empirical support, but much of it is based on unsteady theoretical and conceptual foundations. The fact that mainstream psychology has largely ignored terrorism, perhaps because of its political connotations, has meant that much psychological theorizing has been of poor quality, of thoroughly inconsistent development, and of much less rigour than that which would be expected in contemporary psychological research. These issues have been explored in detail elsewhere (e.g. Horgan, 2003; Silke, 2003; Taylor, 1988) and will not be repeated here, but perhaps we might usefully summarise critical assertions from analyses of this 'individual-based' research as follows.

- *Any explanation at the level of individual psychology will by default be insufficient in trying to understand why people become involved in terrorism.* The concepts of abnormality or individual psychopathology are not useful in understanding terrorism. A defining feature of terrorism is that it is a group process, and terrorist operations are primarily bound within an inherently rational group and organisational context with identifiable ideological or political dimensions. Qualities of these dimensions will become apparent to the individual terrorist at whatever stage of radicalisation he or she is at.
- *Attempts to arrive at meaningful profiles of terrorists **within the same group** based on personality have failed to reveal discernible commonalities or trends that are static over time.* This has not only been the case because of confusion around who or what a terrorist is (even within a movement designated as 'terrorist') but because of a failure to recognize that the same movement can attract diverse people from a variety of backgrounds and for a variety of reasons, through a variety of pathways. A related fundamental error that relates to this is that such efforts essentially try to compress a very complex process (and the individual's engagement with it) into something linear, static and uniform. Any within-group profile might have some attraction for policy in terms of attempts to capture demographic attributes, but these essentially reflect short-term issues, often pivoting around strategic and tactical considerations and limitations.
- *Attempts to derive similarities in profiles of terrorists **across movements** have failed for similar reasons, but furthermore have failed because they do not appreciate the heterogeneity inherent in terrorism.* If terrorism is a strategy attractive to a wide variety of groups, from different backgrounds and espousing different aims and objectives, it should not necessarily follow

that those who engage in these movements ought necessarily to be 'alike' because of surface similarities (i.e. the use of political violence against non-combatants or other symbolically blurry targets).

Profiling efforts typically assume the existence of homogeneous, invariant qualities that not only match members of a specific terrorist organisation but also serve to distinguish them from non-members. Profiling efforts have looked at trying to develop within-group profiles (e.g. what is a typical 'IRA member' like? what is a typical 'Al Qaeda suicide bomber' like?) and across terrorist groups (e.g. what is a typical 'jihadist' like? or, more broadly, what is a typical 'terrorist' like?).

The main problem here is that the assumptions that drive such questions are not based on the reality of terrorism and what it involves. What some psychological approaches tend to be unaware of is that, rather than being some discrete, static phenomenon, terrorism is a fast moving, complex and diverse phenomenon the very nature of which defies easy description let alone naïve categorisation and wholly inappropriate profiling. Terrorist movements, although in themselves varied in terms of network style, structure and direction, typically entail operating via a variety of roles and functions each of which must be fulfilled to ensure the successful execution of the end result – terrorist attacks – in serving some broader agenda (let alone the survival of the movement itself). A problem for psychological analysis that stems from this complex picture is that we can mislead ourselves into believing that there is such a thing as the 'typical' terrorist, just like there may be a typical 'sadistic rapist' or 'predatory paedophile'. In the context of terrorism, this assumption is frequently based on superficial analyses of those terrorists who have been captured or killed (i.e. those we see or have access to) and not those who engage in the less public (although equally as important) supportive functions (e.g. fundraising, leadership, weapons procurement, technical support, training etc.). For the most part, those who engage in violent activity are few in number relative to the overall movement, and involvement in violent activity (or 'terrorist events') might seem to be the domain of a few 'unusual' or 'special' people within the terrorist organization, but once more the reality is not so straightforward: because so relatively few people in a movement engage in actual 'terrorism' this in itself might lead to the notion that a specific 'profile' explains why there are only a few members engaged in the violence of terrorism (for this is only one feature of a broadly subversive set of interconnected operations). Any terrorist movement is characterized by a variety of roles, with many different kinds of involvement. This diversity of function may be more difficult to appreciate in smaller groups, but it does exist. While notions of profiling may be attractive in an administrative sense, they reflect lazy thinking and weak analysis.

A number of assertions seem relevant at this point:

1 *There is a need to appreciate what **movement** into and through a terrorist group actually involves in behavioural terms.* The reality of what 'becoming' a terrorist involves is a gradual progression into and (sometimes back out of)

certain roles. Involvement in terrorism is best characterised as a dynamic migratory process of incremental change based on initially supportive and attractive (to the recruit) qualities. It is not a state, or a condition that a person 'is in' – rather, terrorism is something that some members of an extremist movement do, among other things.

2   *For the most part, the operational capacity of terrorist movements to engage in violent activity is not determined by the numbers of willing 'volunteers',* but rather is influenced more by (a) internal security and management issues, (b) the external political climate, (c) actions of the state and its agents, among other factors.

3   *In attempting to make 'sense' of the actions of the individual terrorist, observers tend to fall foul of what psychologists term the 'fundamental attribution error'.* Because of the effects' association with terrorist behaviour (death, destruction, general mayhem) we tend to overestimate the dispositional features associated with the terrorist and minimize the situational aspects. In other words, we tend to assume that because someone does something that offends and shocks us it must reflect some inherent personal quality. In such situations we ignore the ideological, leadership, group and organisational context that comes to bear on the activities of an individual terrorist at whatever stage of the process he or she may be.

Successful terrorist attacks represent the public tip of a complex iceberg of activity where the actual 'terrorists' are few in number, and the reality of involvement in terrorism involves the fulfilment of multiple roles and functions into and out of which a wide-ranging, heterogeneous group of people move as a function of time, experience, climate, skills, changes in idiosyncratic, personal circumstances, events etc. Involvement in terrorism implies different things for different people, and the 'tipping points' towards (or out of) different pathways of activity will necessarily vary as a result of individual factors, so neither the terrorist nor terrorism are homogeneous concepts. Unfortunately, typical typologies of terrorism fail to take this into account.

To be able to summarise ways of thinking about the individual's involvement, therefore, we first need to appreciate the complexity of roles (which has increased significantly with the developments of new forms or shades of terrorism, e.g. global Salafi Jihad, single issue, organized crime-related terrorism, and terrorist (or potential terrorist) use of the Internet). We also ought to realize that not all of these roles are necessarily illegal, although since the events of 9/11 we have seen a fundamental shift in the meaning of 'involvement in terrorism' to one of mere association as opposed to having a more firm involvement in the planning, preparation or execution of a terrorist act.

The complexity of roles and functions in terrorist groups might be seen to be a quality solely of the larger groups, but we should realize that this complexity (while less clear) also does exist in small groups where individual functions remain.

And finally, we must appreciate how individual roles are rarely fixed. We have little data on account of migration between roles: individuals clearly move into and out of specific roles and functions, and to appreciate this sense of movement we ought to consider developmental processes as well.

Developmental processes: some important assertions

Let us try to accept an important assumption: a psychological perspective alone will not sufficiently capture the complexity of involvement in terrorism and engagement in terrorist events. We might benefit from a closer consideration of how we might integrate existing psychological notions with criminological concepts, and in particular considering how the Rational Choice framework (as developed in criminological contexts by Cornish and Clarke, 1986) might allow for the development of (a) greater conceptual understanding of the development and sustenance of terrorism, and (b) concomitant increased appreciation of how practical counterterrorism initiatives may develop and become focused as a result of identifying potential intervention points. While it has been commonplace in the criminological literature to attempt to understand crimes such as delinquency in terms of processes (i.e. in terms of identifying 'becoming involved', 'remaining involved' and 'ending involvement' phases), this has largely been ignored in the terrorism literature, with one notable exception (Taylor, 1988).

When we examine accounts of involvement in terrorism, we might benefit from appreciating how terrorism is more accurately understood from the individual's perspective in terms of (a) initially becoming involved in a terrorist organization, (b) continuing that involvement and engaging in terrorist incidents, and (c) ceasing involvement, or disengaging – disengaging does not necessarily mean 'exiting' from a terrorist movement, but might suggest moving from committing terrorist violence to something else, i.e. migrating. Consistent with the Rational Choice perspective is the realization that the factors that relate to each of these 'stages' may not necessarily relate to either or both of the others. In other words, the reasons why people become involved in terrorism in the first place are not necessarily helpful in understanding why the person might remain in, or eventually disengage. Furthermore, the reasons that explain why people become initially involved do not necessarily have a bearing on what they subsequently do as terrorists, or as something else within or connected to the movement.

Overall, while research suggests that individual psychological qualities are neither particularly necessary nor useful in understanding why people become involved in terrorism, talking with terrorists about their own involvement often suggests a gradual process based on initial supportive qualities. The integration of different disciplinary perspectives might offer us some previously unexplored ways of understanding involvement in terrorism. Although a detailed examination of the phases of terrorism has been outlined in

Horgan (2005), it may be useful to present a briefer account of some of the features here.

Why do people engage in terrorism?

The causes of terrorism are complex for a very straightforward reason: there are many different 'terrorisms', both conducted and sustained (and ended) for very different sorts of reasons. In addition, it is not possible to identify a single 'cause' of any individual form of terrorism (e.g. Islamist, global Salafist Jihad, single-issue, right-wing racist, nationalist-separatist etc.), let alone a single cause that explains all of them. The causes are many, interacting, bidirectional, confounded by unknown or misunderstood other variables, and it can be difficult to assert any sense of hierarchy (e.g. which is the 'main' cause, secondary etc.). The following root causes were identified at the Root Causes of Terrorism Conference held in Oslo in 2003 (for the proceedings of this productive meeting, see Björgo, 2005):

- Lack of democracy, civil liberties and the rule of law
- Failed or weak states
- Rapid modernisation
- Extremist ideologies of a secular or religious nature
- Historical antecedents of political violence, civil wars, revolutions, dictatorships or occupation
- Hegemony and inequality of power
- Illegitimate or corrupt governments
- Powerful external actors upholding illegitimate governments
- Repression by foreign occupation or by colonial powers
- The experience of discrimination on the basis of ethnic or religious origin
- Failure or unwillingness by the state to integrate dissident groups or emerging social classes
- The experience of social injustice
- The presence of charismatic ideological leaders
- Triggering events

A popular belief is that by addressing the 'root causes' of terrorism we substantially reduce the threat of terrorism, an apparently plausible effort to contribute towards addressing the problem. This assumes a naïve and simplistic cause and effect relationship, which in reality does not exist. We must not assume that the identification of such root causes allows us to assume terrorists as passive actors. Terrorism, we know, can be, and often is, based on imagined or 'virtual grievances', and whatever perceived grievances are identified as having existed at one time or another, terrorist leaders and their followers can be remarkably adept at changing the identity and nature of such grievances, all the while presenting them in a positive light when frequently attached to other publicized plights. If we were to attempt to produce a representative list of the grievances of terrorist groups we would have a list with thousands of items. Those present at the Oslo conference agreed that we might best view such factors as preconditions that, according to Björgo, 'set the stage for terrorism in the long run ... producing a wide range of social outcomes of which terrorism is only one. Preconditions alone are not sufficient to cause the outbreak of terrorism'.

In attempting to make practical progress here, identifying issues relating to 'how' people become involved may be more valuable than attempting to arrive at answers 'why' people become involved. Essentially, then, we need to shift our expectations about arriving at a simple, and probably naïve, answer about terrorist motivation. This complexity is captured well by Taylor and Quayle (1994), who describe involvement in terrorism as:

> ... in this respect no different from any of the other things that people do. In one sense, embarking on a life of terrorism is like any other life choice ... To ask why an individual occupies a particular social, career or even family role is probably a deceptively easy but essentially unanswerable question. What we can do, however, is to identify factors in any particular situation that helps us understand why particular life choices have been made. This same analysis applies to the development of the terrorist.

The common personal, situational and cultural factors among the various accounts that reveal issues relating to why and how people become involved are usually quite broad and seem unrelated in a practical sense, in that rarely is there a clear, singular, involvement catalyst. When an individual him or herself suggests this catalyst, we ought to interpret its significance with great caution since it often obscures the expected positive features of involvement and generally forms an incomplete picture of the factors seen to influence the decision (even if it is conscious) to become involved. It is clear that when we are in a position to consider accounts from activists around the world different qualities emerge, with different degrees of ideological control, commitment etc. found between members. Sometimes this can reflect simply the degree to which an individual activist is articulate or not, whether he or she has verbalized openly the rationale or morality of his or her activities, or, as is frequently the case, we are able to access accounts from terrorists who have placed their behaviour into such an elaborate, spiritually or ideologically dogmatic framework, that we receive very little (if any) notion of the terrorists having had any apparent conscious role in their movement into terrorism.

In addition, a sense of gradual socialisation into terrorism appears to be a common theme, with an initial sense of involvement seemingly characterised by gradual increases in commitment. Combined with this, group factors are centrally important in attempting to identify supportive qualities of initial engagement, and overall we get a sense of the boundaries between apparent *degrees* of involvement sometimes often appearing more psychological than physical (although actual terrorist operations can bring with them a sense of ritual aimed at ensuring commitment to the group and its activities), with a sense of premium attached not only to membership but moreover to certain, specific roles.

Furthermore, there are frequently overlooked and misinterpreted positive features of increased engagement for the individual terrorist. These include the rapid acquisition of some sort of skill or skills, an increased sense of empowerment, purpose and self-importance, an increased sense of control, which appears to reflect the common effects of ideological control and auto-propaganda, the use of particular involvement steps as currency, as above, mirroring the point made above about distinctions between degrees of involvement, a tangible sense of acceptance within the group, and, in combination with this, the acquisition of real status within the broader community, often expressed subsequently via identification with the broader supportive community. Again, we must note that each and every one of these factors can be brought to influence the individual at any stage of his or her involvement. What we have little or no understanding of currently is at what phase of involvement particular dimensions of ideological control become apparent for the recruit. This would seem to represent a major area for future research.

Although it is not difficult to identify broad preconditions for the development of a climate that supports terrorist activity, it remains the case that very few people will still engage in terrorism altogether, let alone in specific violent terrorist activity. Factors that might help us understand why this sense of *openness to engagement* is more readily found in some people rather than others (even within the same group of people, all of whom may have been clearly exposed to the same assumed generating conditions for terrorism) have been outlined in greater detail in an earlier work (Horgan, 2005, represented in Appendix A), although the predictive ability of these factors remains untested in the absence of more fully developed research. The complex reality of what 'becoming a terrorist' implies justifies an approach to understanding this process by considering it as such. Although the complexity of life histories, the problems associated with relying on the truthfulness of such accounts etc. can be overwhelming, we can identify core psychological themes of what becoming a terrorist appears to involve. Involvement is perhaps best characterised by development based on initial supportive qualities that vary in their significance for the individual, the individual group, and the relationship which both of these have with each other and their surrounding environment (this would also be consistent with Sageman's (2004) analysis). The reality is that there are many factors (often so complex in their combination that it can be difficult to delineate them) that can come to bear on an individual's intentional or unintentional socialisation into involvement with terrorism.

Furthermore, in recognising terrorism as a group process, the consequences of what that recognition implies are obvious: the social and psychological qualities of group membership in terrorism quickly become apparent for the extreme potential both to attract members and to bind them together via sustained commitment and engagement. Extreme conformity and strict obedience are organisational cornerstones that leaders put in place to enhance the effective maintenance of what is already a difficult, secret and, above all, illegal organisation. It follows then that maintaining such conformity is paramount, and having a shared purpose or sense of unity and direction, which in itself is catalysed by having a clearly identifiable enemy, facilitates this. We have also seen that the distinction between where one lies with respect to 'becoming' and 'being' a terrorist is, in one sense, as much a psychological issue as anything else, but thinking of participation in terrorist events as a possible delineation point is useful: any remaining hurdles of finally having one's identity reaffirmed within the terrorist group are often surmounted through engagement in activity considered centrally valuable to the organisation.

Remaining involved, and 'being' a terrorist

The 'being' phase could be considered a crystallisation of what happens to the individual who is becoming increasingly involved in terrorism to the point of engaging in terrorist events. While we identified earlier the specific event factors important to understanding what issues impinge upon the active terrorist, the relevant process factors, we should remember, include: the rapid acquisition of skills, the fitting into a role, the acquisition of special language, an increased acceptance and embracing of that role (and the accompanying integration of personal fantasies), the increased sense of control and personal agency and, furthermore, the use of involvement as currency in acquisition of status. As with the 'becoming' phase, the reality of increased involvement in terrorism reflects a rational, conscious and effortful process.

The nature of the process that impinges upon the individual in remaining a terrorist are specific to that phase, and are neither necessarily related to any of the reasons why people become involved in the first place or, as we shall see, leave. The role of social and group processes is very powerful, with implicit and explicit conformity, compliance and obedience operating as powerful sustaining engagement process factors. The nature of terrorist movements is such that dissent is not tolerated easily, with group conditions frequently becoming stifling as a result, but for the individual terrorist increasing psychological investment, or the process of becoming a more committed member, is shaped most remarkably through engagement in terrorist activities.

The processes engaged by the individual terrorist at this phase can then be identified as possible 'process' points of danger also. For the individual terrorist, these might include, in no particular order:

1 a sense of working towards the acquisition and articulation of a 'special' internal language of both (a) explanation and (b) rationalisation, which is solidly ground in the social and political context in which the violence of the terrorist group emerges;

2   as a result of (1), a sense of growing empowerment, control and defensiveness facilitated by a leader or leadership cadre;

3   as a result of increased engagement in events, a developing sense of engaging in risk-laden behaviours;

4   a probable sense of working through the development and devotion to personal fantasies;

5   specifically in relation to the commission of terrorist activity, a lowering of inhibitions in relation to the expression of violent behaviour (with the group presence and direction from the leadership being two major controlling consequences of this);

6   as an overall consequence of increased involvement and particularly engagement in terrorist activity, an increase in very focused, purposive (i.e. terrorism-related) social activity and, as a result of this,

7   an overall decrease in non-focused, non-purposive (i.e. non-terrorism-related) social activity.

Disengaging

This phase we know very little about. However, preliminary considerations of disengagement would seem to suggest that examining disengagement from terrorism may be potentially as complex a process as that which helps us understand initial involvement in the first place. And again, while models of disengagement can only realistically develop from detailed examinations of individual terrorist group campaigns, we can develop some principles. In a way, it is difficult to treat issues to do with disengaging as separate from issues inherent in reinforcing moves to 'remain involved'. Some of the reasons that might help explain a sense of 'remaining' involved might further be considered as reasons that possibly inhibit or block potential exit routes (be they *psychological* – e.g. through disillusionment with some aspect of the group – or *physical* – e.g. apprehension by the security services). To further complicate matters, we might think of each of these as either *voluntary* in origin (e.g. the decision that continued membership of the group is no longer as important as some overriding personal issue) or *involuntary* (e.g. an individual is forced to leave in the face of some external issue such as the reality of arms decommissioning, or some new legislative initiative, and the implications this has for organisational dissipation, possibly leading to an outright rejection of the group's ideals as a result). We then have two broad possible categories within which we can consider the influences that 'force' or 'attract' a person to leave terrorism behind: voluntary and involuntary disengagement.

We can tentatively identify factors that appear to contribute to a move towards *psychological disengagement*:

1   negative influences as a result of sustained, focused membership (e.g. the influence of unbearable group and organisational psychological pressures) and, as a result,

2   a sense of changing priorities (e.g. the longing for a social/psychological state which (whether real or imaginary) the member feels is lacking, or existed before membership, often a result of self-questioning but mostly following prolonged social/psychological investment as a member from which little return appears evident);
3   a sense of growing disillusionment with the avenues being pursued (e.g. with the political aims, or with the operational tactics and the attitudes underpinning them).

In many ways, reasons for what might be called *'physical'* disengagement are probably easier to identify. Relevant disengagement behaviours and their antecedents might be thought of as physical where there is a change in the role of an individual terrorist away from opportunities to engage in violent behaviour, but where this move may or may not necessarily result in a lessening of commitment to the group. Often there can be physical disengagement from terrorist activity per se, but no change or reduction in support. Indeed, in some cases physical disengagement from terrorism (in terms of being removed from the activity of committing terrorist violence) might involve any of the following, none of which should be considered exclusive:

- apprehension by the security services, perhaps with subsequent imprisonment (or, if not, forced movement by the leadership of the member into a role whereby he or she is less likely to risk arrest);
- forced movement into another role as a result of disobeying orders: at the very least ostracisation may occur, if not outright execution, but if there is some mitigating circumstance the member may instead be pushed into another functional role;
- an increase in 'other role' activity whereby the original role becomes displaced (e.g. an area of specialisation that relates directly to the commission of terrorist offences such as exploiting one's technical acumen by assisting in the preparation of equipment), or increased involvement in political activity (often as a result of imprisonment which, ironically, for some represents a final consolidation of communal identity);
- being ejected from the movement (e.g. for improper use of arms, money, etc. or some disrespectful behaviour that warrants dismissal but not execution);
- as with psychological disengagement, a change in priorities.

The crucial difference between physical and psychological disengagement in this sense, however, is that the terrorist may continue with his or her role in the movement but may later move into another role or function in order to facilitate new personal circumstances (e.g. getting married or having children, and moving into a support or ancillary role as a result): they may still continue to engage in 'terrorism'-related activities, but not 'terrorist events' per se. The other direction from which this role change might emerge is from the leadership, who may place a heavier emphasis on political activity in the months approaching an election. In simple practical terms, this might involve an active terrorist engaging in distributing posters or helping to organise political rallies. Appendix B (adapted from Horgan, 2003) suggests a potential research agenda for further exploration of these issues.

Conclusions

A potential socio-psychological model of terrorism is presented in Appendix C and may be worth considering within this broad 'process-based' framework. Thinking about terrorism as a process of course reflects its complexity, but thinking in this way can also help us to prioritise the questions we need to answer, and better focus policy decisions and resource allocation which, after all, reflect the reality of any response. With some further development, and the necessary data collection, we may be able to ascertain the practical implications of identifying such 'tipping points'.

Again, it is obvious that no one discipline or perspective will exclusively offer tools with which we might claim to 'understand' terrorism. The contribution of psychology to understanding terrorist behaviour, however, has been largely unfocused and impractical to date. It is unfortunate that, even within the discipline of psychology, we continue to speak about terrorism in polarized ways. The problem continues to be viewed as either mysteriously complex or devastatingly clear. Often, what influences which view is taken is access to information, or a particular view of the world which is rooted in our backgrounds, education or training. A single word or phrase in a presentation or document can betray an allegiance, political viewpoint or academic perspective, and, given the overwhelming volume of material being churned out of a veritable terrorism industry, it is easy for us to castigate contributions accordingly or assume irrelevance due to ignorance. Again, at the heart of this issue is a problem of assessing value. One way forward to help us ascertain the quality of academic research and to develop the agendas needed for short- to medium-term future intelligence analyses is for both academia and policymakers to demonstrate their practical applicability and mutual relevance. There is a dual onus of responsibility on academics to show how their analyses are relevant in the real world, and for, in particular, intelligence analysts to recognize the value in the information they collect, classify and file on a routine basis. Indeed, recognising the value of reliable, validated information is probably at the heart of useful collaboration. Often what restricts the sharing of information are issues of mutual mistrust and suspicion and, sometimes, poor past experiences, and naturally, of course, issues of national security. Most of the time however it relates to more basic issues of power and control, but again, the mutually beneficial subject is one of value – how can both communities benefit from some sort of increased involvement with one another? Academia will probably have to produce the vanguard here by demonstrating the relevance of theories and analyses of terrorism, whilst those tasked with responding to the problem of terrorism must consistently voice their needs and concerns accordingly and appropriately. In short, neither side can truly benefit the other, nor in turn the wider community, unless they know what each other wants, needs and is willing to be clear about what each can, in practice, deliver.

Between 8 and 11 March 2005, over 200 terrorism experts and others met at the invitation of the Club de Madrid at an enormously stimulating and productive conference – or more accurately, perhaps, a large series of mini-conferences. One of these consisted of the Working Group on 'Individual Causes of Terrorism'. In terms of attempting to address issues around involvement, the following avenues were suggested as potential intervention focus points:

1 Inhibit potential recruits from joining terrorist organisations in the first place.
2 Produce dissension within existing groups.
3 Facilitate exit from groups.
4 Reduce support for the group and subvert the legitimacy of its leadership.
5 Increase societal resilience and reduce societal vulnerability to the effects of terrorism.

For the moment, we lack the empirical data necessarily to test even the validity of the hypotheses that underpin these questions, although a first step here is to assemble existing knowledge on these areas from experiences with different terrorist groups around the globe.

Finally, it ought to be pointed out that currently not only is there confusion about what a 'psychology of terrorism' implies, but that even in some of the simplest critical analyses of the concept of the terrorist or terrorism, a multiplicity of inconsistent and confusing uses of psychological findings emerge. Because of this confusion, it might appear already that an attempt to develop a psychology of terrorism (let alone a psychology of 'becoming involved' or a psychology of 'disengagement' from terrorism) is an unattainable objective. It might also be the case that perhaps we ought to consider, instead, the exploration of ways in which our knowledge of psychological processes can inform and improve our understanding of terrorism (and all that that implies). At any rate, it would obviously suggest that we attempt to develop a more sophisticated way of understanding involvement in terrorism; perhaps controversially, 'description' might represent a more appropriate objective than 'explanation' given current conceptual and theoretical limitations. This might not be satisfactory to some, but it does represent the reality of where our analyses currently are.

Appendix A: Horgan's (2005) factors of openness to socialization into terrorism: from personality to predisposition

Given the widespread exposure of a group or community of individuals, each of whom is exposed to the presumed generating conditions and triggering factors, and each of whom may be at least tentatively aware of the perceived rewards associated with involvement and subsequent associated lures, why it is that it is only *very few* of those will actually proceed towards increased engagement and subsequently become and remain terrorists by crossing the boundaries between merely being supportive and being engaged in activity as a result of engagement with the group?

One way of answering this question is suggested here: it might be useful for us to identify factors that point to some people having a greater *openness* to *increased* engagement than others. The temptation here of course is to explain the difference in terms of some sort of personality trait, but the reality is more closely related to individual, idiosyncratic (and essentially unpredictable) learning experiences as much as anything else. In the absence of systematic empirical research, these questions are not fully answerable in any reliable or complete sense, and there is the danger of engaging in circular logic in an effort to provide some sort of satisfactory answer. However, we do have ways of developing possible answers from a collective consideration of the following factors. These might be usefully thought of as 'predisposing events' based on individual perceptions and experiences:

1 The individual's experience, degree and nature of some sort of previous relevant engagement (e.g. perhaps through throwing stones at the security services, going out on a protest and experiencing its consequences at an emotional level (via excitement, fear etc.), the extent of prior knowledge and understanding of the group or conflict situation and background, the extent and prior exposure to the accompanying lures of increased engagement, etc.).

2 More specifically, the nature and extent of the individual's relevant *early* experiences (e.g. victimization at the hands of security services, or vicariously experiencing victimization perceived as located against the social grouping with which the individual identifies, be it 'Muslim', 'Palestinian', 'Irish Republican', etc.).

3 The nature of the community context and its significance for the individual, particularly in light of the expected value of involvement (e.g. see especially the accounts elicited by Post *et al.* (2003) in their interviews with militants who appeared to attach significance to the status afforded to militants in their community).

4 The nature and extent of adult socialization, which may affect both the individual's openness to increased involvement and the willingness of the group to accept him or her. For instance, many suicidal terrorists appear to be unmarried males aged in their late teenage years or early twenties – the significance of these demographics at this point might reveal more about the increased range of opportunities for increased engagement open to consideration for those who do not have clear and explicit duties and responsibilities to families, a husband or wife etc. Hamas and Islamic Jihad do not apparently favour married young men as potential martyrs, but rather appear more open to selecting and 'preparing' unmarried men with no families to support – it is

likely that the group is aware of the emotional responsiveness of people at a younger age and the increased susceptibility towards greater involvement this might bring, when combined with the other factors. On the other hand, it does not appear to have been an issue for the PIRA leadership, one of whom, interviewed by White and Falkenberg White (1991), reported: 'I've never found wives a hindrance, you know? I found it a big help. That you have the support of your wife and family, you know? I'd say that being married could be a hindrance in some cases, depending on what type of support you'd get from your wife and family'. The significance or nature of the recruit's personal attachments may be differentially perceived depending on whether or not that attachment exists at recruitment or develops during prolonged membership (while it initially may be a perceived barrier on the part of the leadership, i.e. from the perspective that security and suspicion issues are less problematic for an individual without ties, the leadership may be more amenable to an existing committed member who subsequently engages in a relationship, having at least provided a return on the leadership's initial 'investment'). Naturally too, whether or not the leadership has a particular role in mind for a specific recruit at the time of recruitment will be relevant.

5   A sense of dissatisfaction or disillusionment with the individual's current persona or activity. This may be a factor in helping to understand the reasons that contribute to some peaceful activists progressing to more violent action in the first place, but it also helps us to understand the possible basis for a movement between roles once a member. A sense of dissatisfaction is often interpreted in analyses as a possible personality defect or *vulnerability*, but it might be more appropriate, if not useful, to consider the latter more in terms of how the individual may be more *open to influence*; at any juncture; particularly in terms of recruitment concerns for a terrorist leadership, the role of point 3 above is a real consideration. We saw earlier how terrorist leaders are adept at placing a psychological premium on membership so as to have ostensibly positive features associated with attainment of that role (e.g. status in the community, importance to the group, high regard by a significant influence within the group such as the terrorist leader or a significant religious or political figure).

6   The nature and range of competing alternatives and opportunities. For example, the extent and nature of membership, we must realize, will always be determined by some leadership function, which at any one moment in time functions as a result of internal and external climate factors; on the other hand, and from the perspective of the potential recruit, fear of recrimination from the security services might prevent some from moving into illegal activities and may limit their involvement to a certain point. This might be influenced by any number of factors, including prior experiences and socialization as 1 and 2 above illustrate, which can more obviously translate into fear of losing one's job, given particular family and financial commitments.

Although some or all of these factors might be relevant to any one potential terrorist, we ought to consider their identification as feeding into working hypotheses. These factors may help us understand why given what might appear to be a homogeneous pool of 'potential members' exposed to similar internal and external influences, they may still produce only a relatively small number of people who are open to increased engagement. Indeed, in this sense, they might be perhaps considered as potential 'risk' factors, which might inform individual or group profiling efforts much more appropriately than those currently being extended beyond what they can actually explain (or are intended to).

One clear assertion here however, is that it is again impossible to understand the factors that influence the decision to move into terrorism outside the social and organizational context in which the individual exists and moves. We must remember, however, that these factors can be considered relevant at whatever stage we consider the individual along a possible continuum of junctures for what might be considered 'involvement' (i.e. ranging from the clearly legal, such as expressing support via a public protest, to the illegal).

Appendix B: Research agenda for understanding disengagement from terrorism[2]

What we need to do:

- Assess and understand the nature and extent of the roles played by individual terrorists within their organisations in terms of promoting either momentary or long-term de-escalation of tactical activity, strategic activity or, indeed, of an entire campaign.
- Identify and detail the measures taken (if any) within terrorist organisations in the psychological preparation of organisational de-escalation (with an impending disintegration).
- Identify and analyse what terrorist documentation and training material has to say about individual disengagement.
- Identify what happens to members during temporary cessations of organisational terrorist activity (e.g. during ceasefires) and the steps taken (if any) to attempt to maintain organisational unity.
- Identify what happens in ex-member lives outside the terrorist structure – what are the psychological effects of increased isolation from the group? This might be considered at a variety of levels – personal, family etc. – and explored as a function of varying pressures on the individual depending on the social, political or organisational climate.
- Identify the factors that lead to partial disengagement from role-specific behaviours: for example, voluntary movement away from involvement in actual operations (e.g. shootings, bombings) to voluntary involvement in other activities (e.g. political, organisational, financial etc.).

- Identify how and to what extent former terrorists express remorse, and what actions are taken (if any) to alleviate the associated stress.
- Explore via comparative analyses the experiences of involuntarily disengaged terrorists (e.g. imprisoned terrorists or those who have been moved into other roles, and those affected by organisational disintegration etc.); similarly, comparative analyses between different forms of political extremism.
- Examine the possibility that different roles and functions within terrorist organisations have varying attrition rates with respect to voluntary disengagement (e.g. fundraisers vs gunmen vs bombers vs organisers vs political actors etc.): we might ask what are the psychological implications of performance within specific organisational functions, and are some roles more likely than others to result in voluntary disengagement? This, incidentally, would serve a dual function in moving the nature and direction of other psychological research from the profiling of 'terrorists' per se to the profiling of organisational roles and functions.

Appendix C: A potential socio-psychological model of terrorism

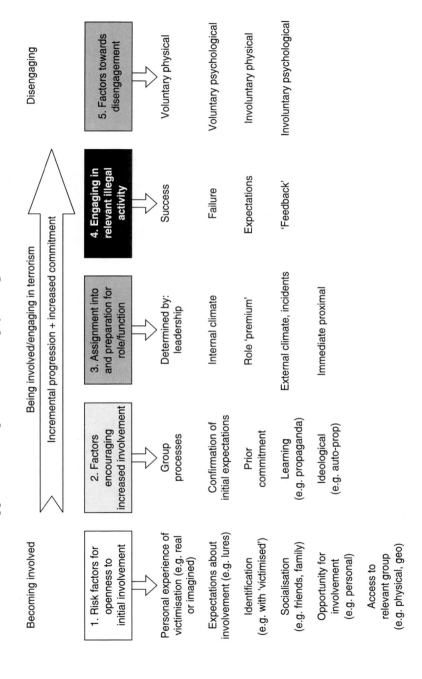

Notes

1 Some of the arguments and issues raised here are taken from Horgan, J. (2005), *The Psychology of Terrorism*. London: Routledge.
2 Adapted from Horgan (2003).

References

Björgo, T. (2005). *Root Causes of Terrorism*. London: Routledge.

Cornish, D.B., and Clarke, R.V.G. (1986). *The Reasoning Criminal: Rational Choice Perspectives on Offending*. New York: Springer-Verlag.

Horgan, J. (2003). 'Leaving terrorism behind: An individual perspective'. In A. Silke (ed.), *Terrorists, Victims and Society: Psychological Perspectives on Terrorism and its Consequences* (pp. 109–130). London: John Wiley.

Horgan, J. (2005). *The Psychology of Terrorism*. London: Routledge.

Post, J.M., Sprinzak, E., and Denny, L.M. (2003). 'The terrorists in their own words: Interviews with 35 incarcerated Middle Eastern terrorists', *Terrorism and Political Violence*, Vol. 15, No. 1, pp. 171–184.

Reich, W. (1990). Understanding terrorist behaviour: The limits and opportunities of psychological inquiry. In W. Reich (ed.), *Origins of Terrorism: Psychologies, Ideologies, Theologies, States of Mind* (pp. 261–279). New York: Cambridge University Press.

Sageman, M. (2004). *Understanding Terror Networks*. Pittsburgh: University of Pennsylvania Press.

Silke, A. (ed.) (2003). *Terrorists, Victims and Society: Psychological Perspectives on Terrorism and its Consequences*. London: John Wiley.

Silke, A. (ed.) (2004). *Researching Terrorism: Trends, Successes, Failures*. London: Frank Cass.

Taylor, M. (1988). *The Terrorist*. London: Brassey's.

Taylor, M., and Quayle, E. (1994). *Terrorist Lives*. London: Brassey's.

White, R.W., and Falkenberg White, T. (1991). 'Revolution in the city: On the resources of urban guerrillas', *Terrorism and Political Violence*, Vol. 3, No. 4, pp. 100–132.

7

APPROACHING AL-QAEDA'S WARFARE: FUNCTION, CULTURE AND GRAND STRATEGY

Jeffrey B. Cozzens

Purify your heart and cleanse it of imperfections. Forget ... that thing which is called the World; the time for amusement is gone and the time of truth is upon us. We have wasted so much time in our life. Should we not use these hours to offer actions that make us closer to God and actions of obedience? ... Sharpen your blade and relieve your sacrifice ... Tighten your clothes as you wear them. This is the way [the righteous predecessors] wore them prior to battle.

–*'The Last Night'* (document of the 11 September hijackers)

Introduction

The above quote and the letter from which it was extracted encapsulate the dual – and analytically problematic – nature of the al-Qaeda and its warfare that is this article's primary concern. Because it was written for the 9/11 hijackers – participants in a plot that took time, patience and extraordinary global coordination to execute – it alludes to a rational al-Qaeda that employs a form of political violence to protest and counterbalance perceived injustices committed by the West against Muslims. Usama bin Laden outlined these in his 1996 'Declaration of War'. Conventional analysis of al-Qaeda's grand strategy – typically regarded as warfare's 'highest' level, where ideology and resultant military objectives coincide – suggests its 'members' are engaged in a roughly three-tiered plan to remedy these grievances through violence in order to: (1) alter US policy in the Middle East, including severing the US–Israeli relationship and expelling Western forces from the region; (2) undermine 'infidel' pro-Western

Arab regimes (the 'near enemy'); and (3) unite the Muslim world under the banner of a new Caliphate.[1] This conception of al-Qaeda's grand strategy reflects Barry Posen's definition: a 'chain' of military means subordinated to furthering tangible political objectives.[2] This 'instrumental' pole of al-Qaeda's warfare is synonymous to Clausewitz's definition of war as 'politics by other means' – violence is instrumental to furthering the affairs of state, or, in this case, the overt objectives of a tangible, calculating al-Qaeda network. In agreement with Mark Sedgwick, at one level, al-Qaeda's warfare can generally be understood – like that of many terrorist organizations throughout history – for its political ambitions.[3]

The instrumental nature of al-Qaeda's warfare was apparent not only on 11 September 2001 but also in many other pre- and post 9/11 operations.[4] Moreover, al-Qaeda's penchant for *Realpolitik* is embodied in the jihadi 'strategic studies' literary genre outlined by Brynjar Lia and Thomas Hegghammer in 'Jihadi Strategic Studies: The Alleged Al-Qaida Policy Study Preceding the Madrid Bombing,'[5] and was poignantly illustrated in the 1 November 2004 bin Laden speech.[6] This view of al-Qaeda as a strategic political entity with a neatly parsed grand strategy persists in much of the current terrorism studies literature and Western policy. Ideology and the 'culture' of al-Qaeda – culture defined in this sense as 'patterns of feeling, thinking, valuing and potential action'[7] – are not typically considered salient operational elements.

However, al-Qaeda and its warfare are dualistic. There is a less apparent 'expressive' and 'existential' quality to al-Qaeda's character and its warfare that is not given due attention in the literature.[8] Expressive-existential war (known hereafter as non-instrumental war), as Christopher Coker argued, is shaped by the 'identity' of combatants and the myriad qualities resident in that term, such as group culture, religion, and the ideology[9] that expresses this culture – in effect, the variables that construct a symbolic world.[10] Non-instrumental warfare directs and shapes violence apart from solely political considerations. The warfare of non-instrumental operatives 'signifies', 'says' and 'expresses' *who they are* – borrowing again from Coker[11] – more so than seeking to advance concrete, utilitarian affairs of state. Violence is perceived as an end as well as a means, and it is often fashioned to represent the symbolic world of the militant – a point reinforced by Bruce Hoffman's recent work on suicide bombing as 'signalling'.[12] This feature was evident even in the 'instrumental' 9/11 operation for which the 'Last Night' document was prepared. Neither political grievances nor strategic planning were mentioned in the letter; instead, graphic tactical counsel infused with religious symbolism dominated its content – a virtual checklist for salvation through death, evoking the qualities of what Colin Campbell has defined as a 'cultic millieu ... a parallel religious tradition of disparaged and deviant interpretations and practices that challenge the authority of prevailing religions with rival claims to truth'.[13] The non-instrumental component of al-Qaeda's warfare has been witnessed in myriad operations, such as the 2004 al-Khobar siege in Saudi Arabia, which was followed by an in-depth account of the role of the supernatural in battlefield, not a political statement.[14]

The non-instrumental component of al-Qaeda's character and combat illuminates a subterranean – albeit no less important – level of its warfare; it portrays an ideology and culture externalised in a non-instrumental strategy transcendent of organizational confines, membership and planning – what Reuven Paz broadly described as a 'culture' (meaning the values, attitudes and beliefs) of global jihad.[15] This ideology is never far from the battlefield. It is a level 'beyond bin Laden', in the words of Magnus Ranstorp, embodied in militants operating 'in the service of al-Qaeda' but without formal affiliation with it.[16] It seems these operatives were influenced by a radical ideology that had not passed through the filter of organized strategic planning – far different from the strategic religo-political terrorism and tangible attributes of membership often attributed to al-Qaeda. This non-instrumental al-Qaeda is more an ideological 'virus' whose tactics often appear to drive strategy, operating without formal remit from 'higher-ups' and quite independent of personalities such as bin Laden or Ayman al-Zawahri. It is a stratum of al-Qaeda where individuals bonded by similar values, attitudes and beliefs conduct operations seemingly as a pious act. This 'culture' is driven by a non-instrumental grand strategy corresponding not to Posen's concept but to John Boyd's: 'a grand ideal, overarching theme or noble philosophy that represents a coherent paradigm within which individuals as well as societies can shape and adapt to unfolding circumstances'. It exists in flagrant contradiction to the organised (if highly networked) strategic al-Qaeda that is apparently extant in both operational domains – the physical and psychological – and still figures prominently in the literature. This duality must be explained if the objective is to develop a more comprehensive understanding of al-Qaeda's warfare, beginning at the grand strategic realm.

Objectives and methodology

The purpose of this chapter is to articulate and apply a theoretical framework called 'Functionalism–Culturalism' that affords a 'character-first' approach to the multi-dimensional warfare of al-Qaeda, beginning with an exposé of arguably problematic 'functionalist' conceptions of al-Qaeda. In order to generate a deeper understanding of how al-Qaeda fights it is necessary to approach it in a manner that looks beyond its structure, function and leadership and past its instrumental warfare to the 'culture' of which it is a product, what Marc Sageman has called the 'global Salafi Jihad' (GSJ), 'a worldwide religious revivalist movement'.[17] This is critical because the grand strategic level of warfare – whether that of state[18] or non-state[19] actors – cannot be fully understood apart from the protagonist's culture, or the ideologies that express them.[20] Moreover, as Coker has argued, warfare possesses both instrumental and non-instrumental layers. While the functionalist conception of al-Qaeda informs a neatly parsed instrumental view of its grand strategy – a problematic concept in itself given the atomization of al-Qaeda over the last four years – the culturalist approach should apply Catherine Wessinger's concept of revolutionary millennialism to divine the non-instrumental grand strategy of the culture of global jihad – a framework sufficient to highlight some long-lived tenets of critical GSJ ideologues but also flexible enough to account for the evolution of its narrative.[21] The application of revolutionary millennialism is important as it approximates the ideology of the GSJ which, drawing from Ann Swidler's work, expresses its culture.[22] Given that the study of grand strategy is crucial to a holistic understanding of warfare, the culturalist approach is imperative as it discerns, through John Boyd, a 'narrative' grand strategy that flows from the GSJ's culture and ideology. This conceptual process divines an elusive grand strategy more existential and expressive than that traditionally attributed to al-Qaeda by Western scholars and reveals a mode of warfare influenced as much by the GSJ's 'catalytic' culture as by al-Qaeda's political agenda. Approaching al-Qaeda through the lens of its function, culture and grand strategy is imperative to contend not only with how it fights but also with what al-Qaeda means at a broad level, as the two are inseparable. In conclusion it will be shown that this theoretical framework could be useful in generating new lines of academic enquiry as well as in directing Western anti- and counterterrorism efforts onto what is arguably a more comprehensive representation of the threat they face.

The logic of effects-based operations

This chapter's methodological approach is informed by the core logic of the 'Effects-Based Operations' (EBO) model for combat planning.[23] Just as Western militaries utilize EBO, which focuses on an enemy's character to model decision-making and plot 'cascading' effects, a discussion of al-Qaeda's warfare should begin by revisiting the innate and essential qualities that comprise al-Qaeda's character and thus inform its operations. Effects-based operations stress critical foreknowledge of an enemy's character – his innate or essential qualities, including ideology. Effect-based operations are 'conceived and planned in a systems framework that considers the full range of direct, indirect, and cascading effects', according to Paul Davis, 'effects that may be achieved by the application of military, diplomatic, psychological, and economic instruments'.[24] Although this study is not concerned with modelling, its structure will follow the inner logic of EBO in that it will focus on the qualitative variable of an enemy's character from which evolve the elements of grand strategy – a premise supported by Smith's and Drake's studies of terrorist organizations as well as numerous studies commissioned by the US military.[25] Although EBO is primarily concerned with 'cognitive modelling' of the decision-making and behaviour of an adversary, and its application focuses on influencing enemy behaviour through kinetic and non-kinetic military operations, this study will implement the logic of EBO by examining the character of al-Qaeda (or the GSJ), initially in recognition of the premise that it is directly related to its grand strategy which, as is implicit in both Posen's and Boyd's arguments, is intertwined with the combat doctrine chosen for its implementation. Therefore, instead of structuring this chapter in a manner that considers the range of 'direct, indirect, and cascading effects' of operations against an adversary, it will implement the logic of EBO *at its outset* by examining alternative conceptions of al-Qaeda's character to distil alternative grand strategies.[26]

Function and 'culture': the duality of networks

The following section will define and assess the 'functionalist' approach to al-Qaeda and its warfare and suggest a better crucible for understanding: the 'culturist' view. Understanding the duality inherent in networks,[27] meaning their functional and cultural properties (a 'network' being the structural form typically ascribed to al-Qaeda), is critical to this process. This will be accomplished through a distillation of the ideas of Manuel Castells, Francis Fukuyama and Paula Uimonen, from whose views two contrasting conceptions of networks emerge. Once this duality is elucidated, the foundation of the functionalist and culturist assessments of al-Qaeda will emerge. Following an overview of the functionalist approach to, and conception of, al-Qaeda – an approach and view necessary to outline as it is commonly expressed in academic and policy circles – it will be critiqued to demonstrate that al-Qaeda's implicit qualities are best analysed through the culturist model, which attributes more importance to the movement behind al-Qaeda, the global Salafi jihad.

Networks are similar to what has been called the 'organic form,' a 'network structure of control, authority, and communication [with] lateral rather than vertical direction of communication,' where 'omniscience [is] no longer imputed to the head of the concern'.[28] Networks are generally the opposite of hierarchies – and superior to them in the 'information age', described by Susan J. Winter and S. Lynne Taylor as 'the third industrial revolution', which is 'widely attributed to the increased importance of information ... and the attendant rise in the use of electronics, computing, and telecommunications'.[29] Because networks function as information exchanges, they have been strengthened more rapidly than hierarchies because of this 'revolution'. 'Great man', 'top heavy' leadership structures of hierarchies are giving way to 'flatter decentralized designs' that encourage individual initiative, timeliness and efficiency over bureaucratic decision-making.[30] This elaboration of the attributes and functions of networks parallels Manuel Castells', who wrote:

> Networks constitute the new social morphologies of our societies ... While the networking form of social organization has existed in other times and spaces, the new information technology paradigm provides the material basis for its pervasive expansion throughout the entire social structure.[31]

While not downplaying entirely the impact of networks' social attributes, Castells highlighted the distinct influence that globalization – according to Mary Kaldor, 'the intensification of global interconnectedness – political, economic, military and cultural'[32] – has had on their function. The marriage of the network form to the information age permits networks to 'thrive like parasites on the advantages of globalisation in creating cross-national networks – enhancing command, control and communication and sources of financial revenues – that enable them to survive, flourish and expand' in ways hierarchies cannot.[33] Castells' view highlights networks' advantages over hierarchies, their marriage to globalization and function in the information age.

Espousing the functionalist perspective of al-Qaeda

Castells considers networks foremost through the attributes of their form and functionality: their marriage of networked structure to globalization. Ideology is arguably less important than form, function and individual 'nodes' of responsibility, whether corporations, individuals, etc. Similar to Castells' view of networks, the functionalist view of al-Qaeda highlights the tactical qualities of its globally networked structure and membership, beholden to time and space, and conceives of al-Qaeda as an entity largely centred on Usama bin Laden, designed to harness the fruit of network design and globalized technology upon which it subsists, whose function is designed to meet concrete political objectives, much as nation states typically wage war. Functionalism stresses al-Qaeda's organizational form and capabilities above its ideology, leading to an explicit, succinct, grand strategy.

Functionalism was reflected in the FBI's investigation of the 1998 African embassy bombings, which generally portrayed al-Qaeda as a monolithic, membership-granting entity. It was after these initial federal investigations that al-Qaeda routinely began to be conceived of as a 'traditionally structured terrorist organization', probably because conspiracy charges required proof of organizational membership.[34] This idea of an al-Qaeda monolith was constructed despite testimony on day nineteen of the bombing trial, which witnessed an FBI agent admit that Khalfan Khamis Muhamed, a suspect in the bombing, told him during interrogation that he had never heard of a group called al-Qaeda, despite confessing involvement with the bombing.[35] Nevertheless, the notion of al-Qaeda as a networked, membership-granting entity took root, evidenced by the literature of that period such as *The Base: In Search of al-Qaeda – The Terror Network That Shook the World*.[36] In fact, at least one alleged al-Qaeda operative under investigation, Jose Padilla, has played to the functionalism conception of membership in an attempt to downplay his commitment to bin Laden.[37]

From the FBI's notion of a monolithic al-Qaeda network emerged a more advanced conception of functionalism centred on discussions of network forms and business analogies. This manifestation of functionalism maintains that al-Qaeda's structure resembles a spider's web consisting of one primary vertical and perhaps three subordinate horizontal strands. The cement connecting the myriad nodes of this network is the impetus to attain al-Qaeda's political objectives through violence against the United States and its allies.[38] The effect of this networked structure is a 'synergy' between al-Qaeda's strands, as Edward Rothstein argued.[39] The relationship between the principle axes and the constellations – the essence of John Arquilla and David Ronfeldt's 'netwar'[40] – yields al-Qaeda creativity, the ability to project power world wide, and great resiliency. Functionalism generally sees al-Qaeda's primary vertical strand, led by bin Laden and subordinates such as al-Zawahiri, providing 'strategic and tactical direction' to principal al-Qaeda operatives, such as Muhammad Atta, for conducting spectacular attacks in the West.[41] Moreover, through this strand, bin Laden functions as a type of 'CEO', providing funding to those proposals he finds 'promising.'[42]

Like Castells' emphasis on a network's function in the globalized age, the functionalist approach highlights the tactical capabilities inherent to a quantifiable al-Qaeda networked design, which can be mapped and dismantled. al-Qaeda's decentralized strands have ensured al-Qaeda's international presence and force projection capabilities. These horizontal strands comprise groups of 'trained amateurs', 'local walk-ins' and 'like-minded insurgents, guerrillas, and terrorists'.[43] The third strand comprises organisations and individuals that have either trained at al-Qaeda's Afghanistan camps or benefited from bin Laden's largesse, such as the signatories to bin Laden's 'Declaration of War' who comprise the 'World Islamic Front'. Functionalism sees a 'deep al-Qaeda bench', allowing it to strike targets around the globe – a concept reinforced by Rohan Gunaratna's speculation that 'between 10,000 to 110,000 recruits graduated from al-Qaeda training camps between 1989 and October 2001', and the International Institute for Strategic Studies' claim that as of 2004 there were '18,000 potential operatives'.[44] This view of al-Qaeda is reinforced in the US government's February 2003 'National Strategy for Combating Terrorism' document, which branded al-Qaeda 'a network' and a 'multi-national enterprise', with 'members' who 'have traveled from continent to continent . . .', forming what amounts to a global terrorist enterprise.[45] This document depicts al-Qaeda's external relations (equivalent to the above-mentioned tiers) by graphs, construing al-Qaeda as the primary 'hub' connected by myriad lines to other hubs like *Jemaah Islamiyya*.[46] This tiered view informs projects designed to map al-Qaeda's structure, such as that being undertaken at the Virginia-based Intel Center, which depicts a web-like organisation revolving around operatives of various standing with bin Laden at its epicentre.[47]

Functionalism sees al-Qaeda's networked form as providing its members with the ability to survive and even thrive in the post-Taliban era as it is being hunted – evidenced by multiple perpetrated or thwarted attacks[48] – owing to the geographic dispersal and network designs for information sharing and operational secrecy adopted by 'sleeper cells' (whether 'hub' or 'all-channel' formations).[49] Moreover, these strands benefit from what Mary Kaldor termed 'wild globalisation', which affords al-Qaeda the ability to initiate and control violence 'from very distant points of the globe', witnessed by the flow of money and personnel to the United States prior to September 11.[50]

Bearing this tiered structure in mind, functionalists typically see the capture of key al-Qaeda personalities – major 'hubs' like bin Laden and Khalid Sheikh Muhammad – as a sure-fire method to dismantle the network, a perspective reflected in the occasional criticism of President Bush for the failure to capture bin Laden. As Yoram Schweitzer suggested, Muhammad's apprehension was significant for symbolic and operational reasons – he was not only a high-ranking member of al-Qaeda but was connected in multiple ways to other, lower-ranking primary operatives.[51] The central importance of personalities to the functionalist paradigm was also captured in Gunaratna's premise that the longevity of al-Qaeda's ideology was linked to bin Laden's.[52] By this logic, functionalism largely views al-Qaeda's ideology as unique to its chief exponents; it has risen and thus will fall with the demise of the al-Qaeda leadership, just as other terrorist organizations have crumbled historically.[53]

Functionalism views personal religious piety, social identity, religion and culture as largely distant from al-Qaeda's warfare. Functionalism gives more attention to the clear-cut motives and objectives of al-Qaeda the political actor, even while recognizing it as an entity with 'religiously formulated' 'ultimate aims'.[54] As Jonathan Spyer suggested, pointing to the 2004 Madrid attacks, '[I]n the matter of political or military strategy, al-Qa'ida ... employs violence for the furtherance of clear political aims'.[55] This perspective resonates with Coker's description of Western, state-centric warfare in that functionalism typically 'divorce[s] violence from its social context', playing to a 'Western bias for the technical', which endeavours to 'understand violence primarily ... in terms of means and ends, [so] that the question of what violence "signifies", "says", or "expresses" seems ... to be of secondary importance'.[56] This approach has focused the attention of many in the West on a 'Clausewitzian' construct of al-Qaeda's grand strategy as outlined in the introduction, in which violence is subordinated to predominantly political objectives. This grand strategy is apparent in the speeches of key al-Qaeda figures like bin Laden, and it is upon this macro level that functionalism chiefly focuses.

Manuel Castells' network theory implicitly considers form and function the virtue of information age networks, more so than the ideas that establish and drive them. This typifies functionalism. The foremost concerns of the functionalist view of al-Qaeda are its structure, capabilities, membership and instrumental political strategy. Functionalists conceive of al-Qaeda as a web, revolving around key personalities and benefiting from globalized technology and organizational forms that afford its multi-tiered affiliates coordination and longevity. However, functionalists believe that al-Qaeda, like other terrorist groups, can be dismantled by law enforcement or military action; as Gunaratna ventured, its Islamism[57] is linked to its icons, especially bin Laden.[58] Functionalism focuses on al-Qaeda's organizational form, tactical methodology and the calculated political interests of its leadership – much as Western military planners would draft succinct 'orders of battle' for combating nation states, thereby conceptualizing its grand strategy as Posen defined it (see Introduction).

Introducing the culturalist approach

The Castellsian perspective – functionalism – is but one way to conceptualize networks. Francis Fukuyama defined a network 'not as a type of formal organization, but as social capital ... By this view, a network is a moral relationship of trust: a network is a group of individual agents who share informal norms or values beyond those necessary for ordinary market transactions'.[59] Fukuyama touches upon the core of Paula Uimonen's concept of the 'culture of networking', where a network is regarded not merely as a practice but also 'the social settings in which they [networks] are embedded ...'.[60] Fukuyama and Uimonen share an implicit understanding that network structure is a secondary component to the real essence of social networks: culture, which creates a bonding ideology. A network's substance, by this perspective, supersedes function and form; network function is merely a means to an end. This view is critical to this study because it reaches beyond the inhibitions of structure and defines a network by its essence: binding commonalities. Apart from the ideological substance of social networks, there is no sound basis for either structure or function, regardless of how important the latter are for facilitating and enhancing a cause. This perspective constitutes the 'culturalist' view of networks.

Applying Fukuyama and Uimonen's culturalist conception of networks to this study is essential as it suggests a 'character first' approach to understanding al-Qaeda and its warfare. The culturalist perspective, coined from Uimonen's description of a 'culture of networking', highlights the relationship between al-Qaeda's culture and its warfare and argues that excavating this nexus forms the basis for a more comprehensive analysis. Sageman's *Understanding Terrorist Networks* stands out as a prominent example of culturalism.

Sageman sees al-Qaeda as an outgrowth of a 'worldwide religious revivalist movement', whose objectives, strategies and tactics are guided by militant Salafi ideology:[61] a proactive worldview that believes Islamic thought and practice have been corrupted by centuries of innovation and must be corrected through violence against the sources of modern infidelity (especially the United States and its 'client' Arab regimes) that promote divergence from the Qur'an's explicit teachings and Muhammad's example, in combination with assiduous individual piety, in order to establish a unified 'transnational community of true believers'.[62] He calls this movement, which subsumes al-Qaeda and the networks and individuals affiliated with it, the 'global Salafi jihad',[63] echoing Quintan Wiktorowicz's definition of the Salafist movement (both its reformist and militant strands) as 'a transnational effort for religious purification, connecting members of an "imagined community" through a common approach to Islam'.[64] The GSJ, Sageman argued in an about-face to functionalism, 'is not simply a political movement'.[65] Likewise, one of the GSJ's primary exponents,

Omar Mahmoud Othman (also known as Abu Qutadah), defines it as 'a movement of Salafi worldview, perceptions, doctrines, and way' that strives to 'eliminate the evil and heretical regimes in the apostate countries' in order to further the
vision of a 'world totally controlled by [the militant Salafist concept of] Islam'.[66]
Following the above rationale, culturalism is both an approach to and a conceptualization of a less apparent and more personally relevant 'al-Qaeda' that is
reflected in nearly every stratum of operative – including al-Qaeda's ideologues –
that embraces its worldview and seeks to implement it through violent jihad. As
much as al-Qaeda 'proper' maintains tangible political goals, its underlying religious framework and intertwined culture of jihad compels its operatives to fight
as 'rational true believers'.[67] In this way culturalism not only places the locus of
analysis on the wider movement of which al-Qaeda serves as the 'vanguard',[68]
the GSJ, but also argues that the GSJ's grand strategy (which parallels the
more obvious instrumental grand strategy of al-Qaeda) is a direct product of its
culture.

Prior to applying the culturalist approach to outline the parameters of the
GSJ's culture, and its relationship to its grand strategy, this chapter will address
the inherent pitfalls of adopting a solely functionalist perspective in analysing
al-Qaeda and its warfare in order to demonstrate the need for an alternative
approach.

The functionalist handicaps

Functionalists view al-Qaeda for its form and function, captured in a convenient, colossal and rather static box, generally ignoring the qualities, impetus
and thus the threat behind its network function and warfare: the ideology and
social dynamics of the GSJ. In many ways, functionalism conforms to Edward
Said's 'orientalism'. It approaches al-Qaeda the way orientalists approach Islam –
a 'heterogeneous, dynamic, and complex human reality' – from 'an uncriti-
cally essentialist standpoint ... suggest[ing] ... an enduring Oriental reality ...
observ[ed] from afar and ... above'.[69] The FBI's conception of al-Qaeda – one
that even until September 2001 'was symptomatic of its focus on short-term
operational priorities [especially convictions], often at the expense of long-term
strategic analysis'[70] – supports the functionalist – orientalist analogy. It substituted an understanding of al-Qaeda's character – the foundation of strategy,
according to Smith and Drake, who advanced 'The foundations of a terrorist group's strategy are often found in the world-view prescribed by their
ideology'[71] – and therefore the threat of al-Qaeda, to facilitate convictions, much
as orientalists study Arab culture as they would 'math'.[72]

However, this study does not suggest that there is no basis for aspects of
the functionalist view. There was, and still likely is, a limited core membership
that could be considered 'al-Qaeda', comprising a select group probably orbit-
ing around, or in communication with, bin Laden and/or al-Zawahiri. It must be
speculated that this core group and its logistical networks are still operational to a

degree, and it likely supports (or orders) some attacks, such as the 2003 Istanbul bombings and the three synchronized May 2003 Riyadh attacks.[73] Moreover, their iconic importance to the GSJ is beyond dispute.[74] However, the functionalist sense of a vast, organized, tangible al-Qaeda network that employs 9/11-calibre operatives and attack modes must be reconsidered in light of, for example, the variegated types of militants currently operating within the GSJ, many of whom show no organizational affiliation to the core al-Qaeda whatsoever. These differentiate between their choices of targets and utilize different attack methodologies in part based upon their degree of attachment to an instrumental terrorist network. For example, the 11 March 2004 Madrid attackers struck a target largely devoid of symbolism using stand-off devices – not the stereo-typical al-Qaeda targeting or attack methodology. The appended depiction of the 'four faces' of post-9/11 operatives and their targets (Appendix 1) supports this premise.

Further, this argument certainly does not suggest that studying the GSJ's capabilities and tactics is less than imperative; the applications are numerous and obvious. Moreover, it does not discount the legacy of Islamism as social and political protest, nor dispute the salience of understanding 'root causes' as catalysts for Islamist contention as they attempt to redefine 'the contours of public and private spheres'.[75] Much stands to be gained, in terms of understanding the many faces of the GSJ and its warfare, from explaining Salafi activism using a social movement theory approach approximating the culturalist paradigm, as Wiktorowicz *et al.* illustrate in *Islamic Activism.*[76] However, this chapter does argue that considerations of structural and political concerns only partially explain how and why the GSJ wages war, yielding a lop-sided view of its grand strategy. Without an alternative, culturalist conception of the less obvious and less instrumental strategic objectives of the GSJ, our quest to understand the character and warfare of al-Qaeda falls short. Determining where al-Qaeda's network begins and ends, who belongs to it, and whose capture will spell its demise is, in the long run, far less important than developing a thorough understanding of the bonding narrative that comprises the heart of the GSJ itself – a narrative that resonates across a spectrum of disparate organisations, reaching even to the individual level.

Mapping

This section alluded earlier to two projects to map the al-Qaeda network. The fruitfulness of these projects appears limited to a retrospective documentation of al-Qaeda's 'hardcore' operatives and the apparent links these have forged with other terrorist groups. These do not necessarily further an understanding of al-Qaeda's character, let alone determine where the movement of global Salafi jihad begins and ends. Form appears to take precedence over substance – a form that will likely result in arrests and could (hopefully) thwart future terrorist plots, but is nevertheless insufficient to gain a better understanding of the ideas behind the decentralizing movement, whether its core strand or 'membership' tiers. Since the end of 2001 and the virtual destruction of their Afghanistan haven, al-Qaeda has splintered considerably. Although a core entity commanded by bin Laden has survived in an obtuse, globally dispersed and unknown structure, the movement now consists of various levels, including al-Qaeda operatives, affiliated al-Qaeda networks, al-Qaeda-inspired networks, and lone individuals inspired by al-Qaeda ideology – all of which share the general precepts of militant Salafism.[77] Furthermore, emerging trends indicate that independent Salafist groups have adopted al-Qaeda tactics, and have no qualms about having their localized activities attributed to a global al-Qaeda agenda. As an al-Qaeda 'interpreter', Salem Almakhi, wrote, 'Since the U.S. assault on al-Qaeda in Afghanistan, [al-Qaeda] has become ... an enterprise of martyrdom spread out all over the world'[78] – and one certainly not limited to the core membership. The previously mentioned network maps of al-Qaeda should – particularly after its ejection from Afghanistan – consider the lines linking the hubs as the graph's most important component, representative of shared ideological themes that form a global bonding narrative linking all components of the movement that undergirds al-Qaeda: the GSJ. As Michael Taarnby wrote, 'The Global Jihad movement does not resemble a traditional organization and there is no point in trying to portray the structure in any kind of organizational diagram. The Global Jihad works on quite a different principle ... a shared ideology and personal interaction'.[79] The locus of analysis should therefore reside on the culture of global jihad. This argument is supported further by consideration of the murky parameters of al-Qaeda's 'membership'.

Membership

Defining al-Qaeda's membership – implicitly necessary to functionalism's claim that al-Qaeda is an organisation or even network – is also an extremely complicated, even ironic undertaking, particularly when considering the '10,000 to 110,000 recruits' that Gunaratna claimed passed through 'al-Qaeda' camps in Afghanistan. If one considers all of these recruits worthy of al-Qaeda membership, as Brian Jenkins did when he labeled them the 'operational utility' of al-Qaeda,[80] then al-Qaeda's core group certainly represents the proverbial tip of the iceberg. However, if all these qualify as members of al-Qaeda, a Pandora's box is potentially opened. Take, for example, the case of an organisation allegedly affiliated with al-Qaeda, Abu Sayyaf.[81] The White House's 'National Strategy for Combating Terrorism' document depicts a graph showing a direct linkage between Abu Sayyaf and al-Qaeda, despite the fact that it 'has largely abandoned Islamic militancy in favour of crime' and maintains only 'tangential, and completely unsubstantiated' links to bin Laden.[82] The few tenuous links that do exist are intertwined with the extremely complicated personal histories of some members of the group who fought in Afghanistan against the Soviets and/or trained at 'mujahideen' camps, not all of which were even run by the al-Qaeda hardcore.[83] However, for a variety of reasons, it has been advantageous for many governments, including that of the Philippines, to make the most of existing or tenuous connections.[84] While the object of this chapter is neither to provide an intelligence brief on al-Qaeda's structure nor to rebuff the idea of a limited, albeit significant international core al-Qaeda cadre, the above demonstrates why al-Qaeda cannot be neatly categorized or, as is crucial to the functionalist endeavour, its membership criteria easily defined. Al-Qaeda's affiliations with 'like-minded groups' are often tenuous, reinforcing the idea that membership claims can be oversimplified. However, this argument can also be taken in a different direction that highlights further shortcomings of an overwhelmingly functionalist approach.

If the notion that al-Qaeda should be viewed increasingly as an ideology is not novel, as suggested by authors like Burke and Hoffman, then why should membership *not* be ascribed to any 'camp' attendee or, for that matter, *anyone* who partakes of its ideology? What of those who 'speak the al-Qaeda language', subscribe to the al-Qaeda 'worldview' and conduct, or attempt to conduct, attacks on the targets al-Zawahiri mentions in *Knights Under the Prophet's Banner*, but never attended Afghan camps, evidenced formal affiliation with the al-Qaeda 'hardcore', or actually understand (or care) about the instrumental political goals of al-Qaeda's ideologues? If American radical Islamic convert Ryan Anderson had succeeded in supplying information to al-Qaeda linked jihadists, despite his absence of an oath to bin Laden or Afghanistan training, does this make him less a 'member'?[85] What of Sarhane Ben Abdelmajid Fakhet, often described as the 'catalyst' behind the Madrid bombings, who apparently never trained in Afghanistan and whose affiliation with al-Qaeda-linked personalities such as Zougam and Ahmed seemed to be necessary only for operational know-how?[86] Or take Muhammad Bouyeri, who gruesomely murdered Dutch filmmaker Theo van Gogh for 'insulting Islam' and was allegedly plotting further attacks with his 'Hofstad group' – and all this despite a lack of Afghanistan training?[87] Little beyond geography and timing separates these individuals, who essentially practised a militant Islamist version of Louis Beam's 'leaderless resistance',[88] from those who trained in the 'al-Qaeda' camps and later took part in terrorist activities directed by the al-Qaeda core. Once again, the qualities of al-Qaeda membership, beyond those of 'hardcore' members like Anas al-Libi, Ayman al-Zawahiri or Saif al-Adel, remain elusive. Defining the parameters of al-Qaeda's membership – particularly after a concerted, four-year-old global offensive against it – is nearly impossible and increasingly meaningless. This calls attention once again to the significance of the ideology behind the global jihadi movement that is the real threat, but not only that: as is apparent above, we must also understand how this ideology manifests itself in multiple strategic currents that do not correspond exclusively to the instrumentality typically ascribed to al-Qaeda, as the appended chart demonstrates. Echoing Sageman, understanding al-Qaeda's warfare means contending with how the culture of global jihad 'determines its mission, sets its goals, and guides its tactics'.[89]

Heroism: A counter to bin Laden centrism

Considering the above arguments, which debate the merit of viewing al-Qaeda exclusively through the functionalist paradigm, it stands to reason, in contravention of Gunaratna's functionalist argument,[90] that depriving the al-Qaeda core of its figurehead, Usama bin Laden, will not spell its demise, particularly if the 'substance' of al-Qaeda – the GSJ – is viewed as more significant than its form. Common grievances and aspirations linked by an underlying body of Islamist ideology legitimised by the 'heroic' paradigms[91] of contemporary militant ideologues and the primary progenitors of the GSJ's militant Salafist ideology – including Qutb, Azzam and al-Zawahiri – propel the global jihad, irrespective of one man's fate.[92] Even bin Laden recognized that the movement of global jihad is dynamic and will carry on without him.[93] New leaders and networks can and have emerged, whether under the al-Qaeda moniker, as they have in Iraq under the inspiration of Abu Musab al-Zarqawi, or as independent jihadi networks that 'reach out' to tap into the legitimacy of al-Qaeda's jihad.[94] As Burke wrote: 'In 1989, scores of men had, like bin Laden, expertise, charisma, access to funds and motivation. This has not changed'.[95] If bin Laden were removed, it is reasonable to suggest not only that another would rise to fill his role as a icon, but his departure would not likely stifle the radical ideology of which he is a product, what theologian Paul Tillich would likely describe as the 'ultimate concern' of many radical Islamists.[96] As a recent supporter of al-Qaeda wrote:

> Let the United States and its allies know that the wombs of the mothers were not sterilized and gave birth to ... people like our Sheik Abdallah Azzam. If Azzam was killed there are thousand Azzams in our nation ... [T]herefore, if Osamah bin Ladin is alive or God forbids he is killed; there are thousand Bin Ladins in this nation. We should not abandon our way ... regardless of the Sheikh or his absence ... I do not need to meet the Sheikh and ask his permission to carry out some operation ... as I do not need his permission to pray, or to think about killing the Jews and the Crusaders ...[97] (errors in original).

Whether our interest is in countering the GSJ or merely endeavouring to better explain its warfare, we should heed the advice of al-Zawahiri, who vigorously resisted any notion that the core al-Qaeda resembled – or should ever approximate – a cult of personality.[98]

Just as the nuances of the Arab world cannot, according to Said, be studied like mathematics, neither can al-Qaeda, as the functionalists attempt. In the pursuit of gaining a deeper understanding of al-Qaeda's (and the GSJ's) character and warfare, however aptly the functionalist paradigm describes its adept harnessing of globalization, it must be recalled that its membership and organizational qualities are of secondary importance to its underpinning ideas, which resonate to the level of the individual Islamist. Without approaching al-Qaeda in a manner that gives foremost importance to the Salafist ideology and culture behind al-Qaeda, the nuances of its warfare will remain obfuscated behind functionalism. After all, how can a militant revivalist movement, bonded together through often 'imagined' ties (as will be elaborated upon) without formal lines of leadership, possess a solely instrumental grand strategy? In keeping with EBO's focus on the nexus of character and warfare, as well as the culturalist approach, this study now turns to address how the ideas and culture underpinning al-Qaeda's jihad impact its warfare.

Applying the culturist approach: revolutionary millennialism and the al-Qaeda idea – a plan for salvation

Unlike functionalism, which focuses on the macro-narrative of al-Qaeda's instrumental objectives and grand strategy, the culturalist approach sees the warfare of the GSJ – the movement of which al-Qaeda is an avatar – as rooted in its culture as an 'imagined community', where a repository of shared Salafist beliefs, supposed by its 'members' to extend back to Muhammad's epoch, links individuals (the lines noted in the myriad network graphs of al-Qaeda) to a 'universal umma' that, whether 'genuine' or 'false', expresses itself in 'the style of which it is imagined'.[99] This expression is an ideology approximating to Catherine Wessinger's revolutionary millennialism.[100] More than a categorical device, Wessinger's revolutionary millennialism encapsulates significant themes of the GSJ's culture and, owing to its catalytic narrative, functions as the GSJ's grand strategy. Defining the GSJ's grand strategy is a seminal platform for conceptualizing other strata of its warfare, for, as B.H. Liddell Hart wrote: '[Strategy and tactics] can never be truly divided into separate compartments because each not only influences but merges into the other'.[101] By relating the GSJ's culture – a 'brotherhood of the persecuted'[102] bonded together through revolutionary millennialism – to its warfare, one is also able to discern the ideational influence of the heroes-cum-ideologues whose teachings were (and remain) legitimized by their sacrificial lives – Qutb, Azzam and al-Zawahiri. By relating the culture of the GSJ to its warfare the non-instrumental grand strategy of al-Qaeda emerges, reflecting the processes upon which EBO is based while simultaneously filling the gap between functionalism's conception of al-Qaeda's grand strategy and Olivier Roy's notion that al-Qaeda has no strategic goals.[103]

Wessinger writes that all radical religious movements stem from one 'genotype, which ... attempts "to construct a more satisfying culture" for a people who have lost control of their destiny'.[104] Central to Wessinger's definition of millennialism is the 'belief in an imminent transition to the millennial kingdom,' tantamount to 'the community's "collective salvation"'.[105] Asserting that millennial groups employ both violent and non-violent tactics to 'liberate' their communities, Wessinger identifies two prominent patterns of millennialism: 'revolutionary millennialism' and 'progressive millennialism'.[106] Jean Rosenfeld, commenting on Wessinger's model, observed that 'Revolutionary millennial movements [the GSJ] "are motivated by a sense that they are persecuted. They believe that revolutionary violence is the means to become liberated from their persecutors and to set up the righteous government and society"'.[107] On the other hand, 'progressive millennialists', such as reformist Salafis like the Palestinian Hamas, adopt a combination of peaceful and violent means to realize the salvation of their communities.[108] A vast amount of rhetoric from GSJ 'interpreters' and sympathizers supports the premise that Wessinger's revolutionary model accurately portrays the ideology and articulates the culture of the GSJ.[109] Moreover, Wessinger's paradigm for classifying the GSJ's ideology is arguably superior to others[110] found in the literature in that it not only showcases the GSJ's activist 'direction' – perpetually moving towards salvation – but is also broad enough to include the relative multiplicity of views that are found within the GSJ.[111] Inherent to Wessinger's model are several characteristics outlined by the Canadian Intelligence Service (whose definition of millennialism parallels Wessinger's) that will provide a framework for crystallizing the primary tenets of the GSJ's ideology and illuminating some key thematic components of the GSJ's culture in a manner that draws attention to its activist 'master plan': communal and individual salvation.[112] The ideological framework includes apocalyptic beliefs, the idea of salvation through conflict, dualism, and the notion of a persecuted chosen – all three of which express key themes of the GSJ's culture.[113]

Apocalyptic beliefs

The Canadian Intelligence Service defines apocalyptic beliefs as doctrines 'similar to [those] of mainstream religions', shaped by 'a theological worldview characterized by an inherent volatility'[114] and a belief that their adherents' violent actions are 'divinely ordained'.[115] Qutb's, Azzam's and al-Zawahiri's militant teachings exemplify these characteristics, thereby supplying 'volatility' to the GSJ's ideology. Further, this pillar of the GSJ's ideology reflects many of the themes found in GSJ culture writ large, among which are: 'God's will', the 'Muhammadan paradigm', and the reinterpretation of history to explain the present.[116] The theme of God's will alludes to a range of issues pertaining to global jihadi culture: defeats in battles or unsuccessful terrorist operations, such as the fall of Fallujah in Iral-Qaeda, are commonly chalked-up to 'God's will',[117] whereas victories are signs of his favour. However, regardless of lost battles, God's will establishes hope as a 'weapon' in that mujahideen (those who struggle in the path of God) are guaranteed victory at the end of time.[118] God's will is a filter through which many GSJ ideologues explain the world. Further, it alludes to the intervention of the supernatural on the battlefield. For example, those terrorists affiliated with al-Qaeda in the Arabian Peninsula who took part in the 2004 al-Khobar housing complex raid in Saudi Arabia recalled 'divine support and benevolence' that allowed them to sleep with unsurpassed 'serenity' during the middle of an engagement with Saudi security forces, similar to the accounts of divine guidance in jihadis' battles in Afghanistan against Soviet and American troops;[119] similarly, jihadi online newsboards covering the battle in Fallujah, Iraq, reported 'angels fighting in the ranks of the mujahideen'.[120]

Malise Ruthven's Muhammadan paradigm (MP) – 'the image of Muhammad as the model hero who successfully wages war against the forces of injustice and oppression' – also accounts for a portion of the GSJ's apocalyptic beliefs.[121] The MP is evidenced in the radical Saudi scholar Abd al-Mun im Halimah Abu Basir's conception of *hijra*, which in its original context refers to Muhammad's flight from Mecca to Medina. Abu Basir wrote. 'One of the goals of immigration is the revival of the duty of Jihad and enforcement of [jihadi culture's] power over the infidels. Immigration and Jihad go together. One is the consequence of the other and dependent upon it'.[122] The 9/11 operatives exemplified this characteristic both while in the United States and during their tenure in Germany after their Afghan training.

Similar to Ruthven's MP, the idea of reinterpreting history also contributes to the GSJ's apocalyptic worldview. At the grand level, this trait is seen in the writing of GSJ figureheads like bin Laden, who apply the battles of early Islamic history to the present to legitimize violence by linking the activities of the militant Salafi 'remnant' to those of the first Muslim community.[123] At lower planes of analyses, this theme was observed in jihadi online banter that speculated about the impending fall of Fallujah, comparing it to the 'Battle of the Trench ... where true believers were burnt to death, but not before having demonstrated a lesson in endurance.'[124] The 'Last Night' document (quoted at the start of the chapter) also illustrates the application of history to the present. Further analysis of the characteristics associated with the apocalyptic beliefs of revolutionary millennialists – salvation through conflict/enemy eradication, dualism, and the idea that they represent a 'persecuted chosen' – will reiterate Azzam's, Qutb's and al-Zawahiri's influence while outlining the principal qualities of the GSJ's ideology and the 'imaginary' culture it expresses.

Liberation by the sword: Jihad and salvation

The idea that the salvation of the umma and individual is achieved through violence is an externalization of three of the most prominent themes around which the GSJ's culture revolves: obligation, martyrdom and selective innovation. Drawing heavily from all three of the aforementioned ideologues (and of course many others), physical jihad is intended not only to 'liberate' Muslim lands but is also an individual obligation to realize the GSJ's messianic objective of the establishment of the 'rightly-guided Caliphate'.[125] Moreover, at the individual level, it is about attaining the forgiveness of sin. Naturally, the obligation to perform jihad goes hand-in-hand with the concept of martyrdom. Abu Hamza al-Masri, another exponent of global jihad, said recently, 'Remember, oh servants of Allah: Why do your brethren want to perform operations of martyrdom? ... Why are there so many martyrs among us? Because we are a nation graced with Allah's mercy.

Because with every *Shahid* [martyr] Allah saves seventy of his family members who were destined to go to the fires of hell'.[126] Even without death, as Saleh al-Oufi, the late al-Qaeda leader in Saudi Arabia, indicated, fighting jihad is a means of purification.[127] Jihad against the perceived enemies of Islam – with or without martyrdom – could therefore be considered an end in itself, as Azzam envisioned it as an act of worship.[128] This was evidenced by the gruesome pseudo-ritualistic violence of the militants during the al-Khobar siege, who portrayed slitting their victims' throats as 'acts of devotion' and correlated their murders to 'bearing witness' and 'preaching'.[129] A quote from bin Laden's 2003 'Sermon for the Feast of Sacrifice' illustrates this point at the macro level: 'The most important religious duty – after belief itself – is to ward off and fight the enemy ... *Jihad* is obligatory now for the Islamic Nation, which is in a state of sin unless it gives of its sons ... to maintain *Jihad*'.[130]

Upholding the themes of obligation and martyrdom is selective innovation, which alludes to the constant reformatting of the Salafi *manhaj* (process) in order to construe violence against 'heretical' Arab regimes as legitimate.[131] Moreover, selective innovation describes the process by which al-Zawahiri amalgamated Azzam's, Qutb's and Faraj's variegated doctrines of jihad – and of course the Islamist discourses of al-Banna and Mawdudi – in order to chart a new course to attacking his international enemies under the guise of 'defensive jihad'.[132] Moreover, at the individual level, selective innovation refers to the indoctrination process of would-be jihadis, particularly in Europe. Many second-generation Islamists living in the West, first-generation Muslims who immigrated as children, and Islamic converts[133] are largely unschooled in the orthodox tenets of the *madhabs* (the four denominations) of Sunni Islam, or even Arabic, and thus open themselves to the indoctrination of Islamists such as Abu Qutadah, al-Masri or Abu Basir (or other Salafist ideologues who post English messages online) who generally preach *jihadi themes* (i.e. obligation, martyrdom etc.) instead of traditional *akeedah* (Islamic ideology).[134] Al-Qaeda also emphasized this type of indoctrination in the training camps to develop solidarity amongst recruits.[135] There is a contemporary concern that selective innovation is manifesting itself in the complex matrix of the Iral-Qaedai conflict, where some (mainly 'foreign') Islamist combatants, initially driven by the premise of Azzam's *In Defence of Muslim Lands*, are developing a penchant for attacking the 'far enemy' on its own soil (whether Western European countries or perhaps the United States); this is likely a product of the visceral, radicalizing experiences of urban combat and interface with militant jihadi Salafi networks such as al-Zarqawi's.[136]

This aspect of revolutionary millennialism, salvation through conflict, reflects Qutb's and Azzam's reliance upon Jihad to effect 'positive' change at every level, whether as a follow-on to Qutb's *takfir* ideology, in Azzam's notion of *ribat* to 'defend Muslim lands', or in al-Zawahiri's emphasis on the 'far enemy', and unites the disparate strands of the GSJ. As evidenced by the story of Abu Thar, who apparently left his family in Yemen at great expense to fight the Americans in Iral-Qaeda in order to 'work for the salvation of [his] soul', viewing the GSJ's jihad solely through the instrumental lens of functionalism is a mistake.[137]

Al-Qaeda's exclusionary ideology

The GSJ's ideology is cast in stark dualistic and cosmic terms – what Ranstorp called its 'exclusionary ideology'[138] – reflecting the culture of global jihad's unequivocal enmity and hunger for parity. Echoing Qutb's philosophy of 'the abode of Islam' in perpetual conflict with 'the abode of war',[139] the GSJ's culture of unequivocal enmity conceives of its minions fighting what David Zeidan called a 'perennial battle' against the forces of evil, embodied by the 'Zionist – Crusader alliance'.[140] This eternal war is part of the timeless cosmic struggle between the 'camps of truth and falsehood', which as 'Saif al-Din al-Ansari' noted serves as the underlying pretext for violence between 'the world jihad movement' and its enemies.[141] As bin Laden wrote, 'Believers are in one tent and . . . infidels are in another. . . . [Believers] should incessantly hate Allah's enemies and curse them, as he should constantly be loyal to the believers'.[142]

Unequivocal enmity facilitates the idea of creating a 'parity of suffering' with the enemies of the jihad movement, one example of which is alleged al-Qaeda spokesman Suleiman Abu Geith's chronology of Muslim suffering at the hands of Jews and Americans. He wrote: 'We have not reached parity with [the Americans]. We have the right to kill 4 million Americans – 2 million of them children – and to exile twice as many'.[143] Unequivocal enmity is supported by what Bruce Hoffman has described as the 'propaganda value of Bin Laden's prescient analysis',[144] which portrays the West at war with Islam. Emile Sahliyeh, echoing the Canadian Intelligence study, characterises this mode of thinking as the 'invocation of millenarian themes'.[145] This component of the GSJ's ideology underscores the belief of many militant Salafists that its warfare is religious before it is political, particularly since Salafism in general finds this distinction heretical.[146]

The persecuted chosen

Inseparable from the notion of 'cosmic war' is the understanding developed by exponents of global jihad that the GSJ represents a *Mustadh'afin* ('brotherhood of the oppressed') – albeit one assured of salvation at the end of time, '*Al Ta'ifa Al Mansoura* [the victorious sect]'.[147] This component of the GSJ's ideology expresses the characteristics of brotherhood and the deep admiration for what could be termed the 'glorified asceticism of the vanguard'. Brotherhood is the promise of entering into the culture of the GSJ and, as accounts of al-Qaeda fighters at Tora Bora and Abdullah Azzam's last book, *The Lofty Mountain*,[148] suggest, reaches its apogee in combat. Taarnby also observes that the GSJ's promise of brotherhood and secure identity are essential components of the recruitment (or 'joining') process, especially in Europe.[149]

The glorified asceticism of the vanguard is related to the GSJ's high regard for heroism and alludes to the premium placed upon the ideals of self-sacrifice, which besides martyrdom involves bearing the hardships of undertaking jihad (whether prison, extended absences away from one's family, financial hardship or physical discomfort) and forsaking 'the love of the world' (*wan*).[150] Bin Laden embodies the glorified GSJ ascetic: he is a wealthy man who, like Azzam, chose the rigors of Afghanistan and an austere lifestyle (so jihadi rhetoric goes) because of his obligation to jihad. As a result of its general self-conception as the 'persecuted chosen', the culture of global jihad legitimizes its radical exclusivity and often-gruesome warfare by what Professor Paul Wilkinson terms the 'absolute justice, or righteousness, of their cause'.[151]

The four benchmarks of revolutionary millennialism articulate the ideology of the GSJ and illuminate critical elements of its culture that cannot be conceptualised through the functionalist approach. Further, through the application of revolutionary millennialism, the culturalist framework demonstrates an ability to highlight relatively long-lived tenets of critical GSJ ideologues while proving flexible enough to account for the evolution of the GSJ's narrative in response to global events. Moreover, owing to the inherent proactivity of the GSJ's revolutionary millenarian ideology – perpetually moving towards the salvation of the individual jihadist and the ummah – the above functions as more than a categorical device: it serves as the GSJ's grand strategy, as John R. Boyd's work demonstrates.

Revolutionary millennialism: the GSJ's grand strategy

Corresponding to the logic of effects-based operations, the success of which is based upon a comprehensive inside-out understanding of the enemy, which allows the protagonist to avoid 'mirror imaging' in order to foment cascading effects[152] – as well as Smith and Drake's premise that strategy flows from ideology – the GSJ's revolutionary millennialism can be conceived as a grand strategy. This premise is backed by Boyd's work.

Boyd offered an expanded understanding of Posen's conception of grand strategy as defined in the introduction. Boyd defined it as:

> A grand ideal, overarching theme, or noble philosophy that represents a coherent paradigm within which individuals as well as societies can shape and adapt to unfolding circumstances – yet offers a way to expose the flaws of competing or adversary systems. Such a unifying vision should be so compelling that it acts as a catalyst or beacon around which to evolve those qualities that permit a collective entity or organic whole to improve its stature in the scheme of things.[153]

Revolutionary millennialism parallels Boyd's definition of grand strategy in that it prescribes the salvation of individuals and communities through violence and consists of several characteristics designed to spark its sympathizers into action, to shape the course of action, and to degrade its enemies. Beyond definitional similarities, the premise to which revolutionary millennialism and Boyd's grand strategy relate conforms to the research of Ann Swidler, who concluded that culture 'provides the materials from which individuals and groups construct strategies of action' and therefore functions as a 'tool kit' (in this case, for warfare).[154] Moreover, paralleling Boyd's definition, Swidler asserted that the attributes or 'contents' of cultures are most evident during periods of social change, expressed through ideologies.[155] In a fusion of Swidler's work to Boyd's and Wessinger's, the GSJ's culture is not only embodied in its ideology but also influences the manner in which the movement shapes its courses of action against enemies, beginning at the grand strategic level. This is because the GSJ is a 'religious revivalist movement' and a culture – genuine or imagined – waging a very real form of warfare that is not wholly subjugated to the Clausewitzian premise of furthering political interests. As social movement theorist Donetella Della Porta argued, '[W]hat is perceived as real produces real consequences'.[156]

Conclusion: the need to re-orient our focus

Developing a deeper understanding of al-Qaeda's warfare necessitates approaching it in a manner that looks beyond form and function and to the culture behind it: the Global Salafi Jihad (GSJ). Al-Qaeda's grand strategy cannot be fully conceptualized apart from looking at this culture and its related ideology. Moreover, as Coker has argued, warfare possesses both instrumental and non-instrumental layers, the latter of which are closely tied to culture. This paper has articulated a theoretical framework for approaching 'al-Qaeda's' multi-dimensional character and warfare that attempted to account for this duality. In so doing it illuminated some of the pitfalls found in the literature that conceive of al-Qaeda *solely* as a quantifiable and instrumental adversary, viewed from a Cold War vantage fixated overwhelmingly on organizational form, function and personalities, which fails to account for the interplay between its culture and warfare. As demonstrated by the culturalist approach, the 'imagined' culture of the GSJ produces a very tangible influence on how it fights, as evidenced by Wessinger's revolutionary millennialism. Revolutionary millennialism approximates the ideology of the GSJ which, drawing from Swidler's work, expresses its culture. It provides a framework sufficient to highlight some long-lived tenets of GSJ ideologues but is also flexible enough to account for the evolution of its narrative. Instead of the functionalist conception of al-Qaeda's neatly-parsed grand strategy – a problematic concept in itself given the atomization of al-Qaeda – the culturalist approach divines the non-instrumental grand strategy of the culture of global jihad. Further, the culturalist approach by default accounts for changes over time in the form of 'al-Qaeda' by highlighting its narrative and cultural – and arguably most dangerous – components. Moreover, culturalism discerns, through Boyd, the 'narrative' grand strategy that flows from the GSJ's non-instrumental culture and ideology, thereby delivering the deeper understanding called for in the intro-duction. Approaching al-Qaeda through the lens of its function, culture and grand strategies is imperative to contend not only with how it fights but also with what al-Qaeda means in the bigger picture, as the two are inseparable. Approaching al-Qaeda and its culture of global jihad through the crucible of the functionalist – culturalist theoretical framework could spark new lines of academic enquiry as well as shape some Western anti- and counter-terrorism efforts – concluding observations this study will now address.

The imperative of an interdisciplinary approach to the GSJ and its warfare

First, the functionalist – culturalist approach reminds academia that the literature on al-Qaeda and the culture of global jihad lacks an interdisciplinary monograph dedicated to its warfare – a gap implicit in this paper that the author's ongoing research hopes to address. This is a critical lapse because the GSJ cannot divorce its Islamist culture from its warfare, nor can 'out of the box' thinking about a complex, multi-faceted adversary emerge without engaging multiple disciplines. We must consider not only the Islamist dimensions of the GSJ's warfare (includ-ing the historical significance of early Islamic military campaigns from which it often draws), along with its status as a religious social movement, but also its place in the transformation of war. The attempt to produce a more holistic picture of how the GSJ fights should begin by juxtaposing literature such as Carole Hillenbrand's *The Crusades: Islamic Perspectives* and Qutb's *Milestones* with Mary Kaldor's *New and Old Wars*, Robert Kaplan's *The Coming Anarchy*, editor Robert J. Bunker's *Non-State Threats and Future Wars* and the previously noted social movement theory approaches of Taarnby, Sageman and Wiktorow-icz that evidence the multidisciplinary approach necessary for understanding the GSJ's warfare. However, to the detriment of the academic, military and pol-icy communities, the GSJ's warfare is typically assessed – however brilliantly – by religious studies scholars who discuss al-Qaeda's Islamism and its evolved understanding of jihad, by military theorists writing on the changing nature of war who contend sparingly with the GSJ's culture as an operational element, or by those focused exclusively on tactics. Given that the nature of GSJ is effec-tively multidisciplinary, the terrorism studies community should adopt a similar approach in order to better grapple with the nature and implications of how it fights.

Culture as an operational element in the warfare of non-state actors

Second, related to the need to utilise a multi-disciplinary approach to conceptu-alise the layers of the GSJ's warfare, functionalism – culturalism calls attention to the imperative of understanding its culture as an operational element. This has implications for academicians and policy-makers alike.

For the academy, functionalism – culturalism challenges us to expand upon Swidler's notion of culture as a 'toolbox' in terms of explaining the GSJ's warfare (and behaviour generally).[157] Even in the West it has been argued that culture 'shapes preference formation by military organizations by telling organizational members who they are and what is possible, and thereby suggesting what they should do'.[158] Further, culture 'explains why military organizations choose the structures and strategies they do'.[159] If culture impacts the instrumental warfare of nation states, it is perhaps even more critical to understand how the GSJ's culture impacts its warfare at levels beyond the grand strategic, particularly given what Lind has described as war's 'fourth generation'[160] (4GW). In 4GW, globalized cultures like the GSJ combat nation states and, because these cultures do not operate at the same level of instrumentality as nation state armies, their culture is closer to the field of battle.

Understanding culture as an operational element also has implications for anti- and counterterrorism policy:

- How does the GSJ's culture impact its choice of targets?
- How does the GSJ's culture impact Western countries' terrorism scenario design and development, such as the UK's 'Atlantic Blue' or the US's Top Officials' Exercise (TOPOFF)?
- Further, how can apprehending the nuances of the GSJ's culture and warfare, such as the disagreement over the brandishing of *takfir* (evidenced by the divergent voices within the culture of global jihad that call for the explicit targeting of Shi'a, or other Sunni Muslims outside the pale of jihadi Salafism), create avenues for exploitation?

Significance of 'the battle of the narrative'

Finally, approaching al-Qaeda from the culturist perspective emphasizes the importance of what Ranstorp has called 'the battle of the narrative'[161] – both 'ours' and the GSJ's – waged in the street, the media and the virtual sphere. Gilles Kepel's recent book discusses this battle at length.[162] Given that the GSJ's ideology seeks the salvation of its sympathizers through violence, while at the same time it functions to augment its solidarity, attract the uncommitted and undermine the West's internal cohesion by fusing psychological operations with kinetic violence, countering this narrative – its root causes, themes and impact – should logically receive priority.[163] While this is perhaps far from novel to suggest, functionalism pays too little attention to this critical element of 'the war against terrorism', despite Hoffman's warnings of the 'propaganda value of bin Laden's prescient analysis'.[164] It was in March 2005 that a high-ranking US Army officer said: '[al-Qaida] can deliver all the videotapes they want, as long as they're not delivering weapons that can kill large numbers of people'.[165] Without diminishing the import of combating the GSJ by military force when necessary, nor detracting from the memory of its victims (including those who have died combating it), this statement reminds us that many have not yet grasped the implications of the narrative battle, where a speech is more than it appears. As Ranstorp said, '[the battle of the narrative] is all about perception management, psychological warfare: deception is everything, amplifying the violence on the ground'.[166]

Appendix 1: The four faces of the Global Salafi Jihad

GSJ level	Hallmarks	Operatives	Strategies/Targets/Operations
Tier 1 – The 'core' al-Qaeda, pre- and post-9/11	• Operations directly support broader strategic objectives (e.g., expelling 'Crusaders' from Arabian Peninsula) • Orders come from leadership, whether from al-Qaeda 'core' *or regional hubs or affiliates* (e.g., Jemaah Islammiyah, al-Zarqawi network) • Violence fused with psychological warfare in attempt to achieve strategic objectives • Strategy generally drives tactics at leadership level	• 1998 bombers of the US embassies in Kenya and Tanzania • Muhammad Atta • Istanbul bombers (who received direct money from al-Qaeda)	• Mass casualty events • Economic assets • Undermine credibility of governments • Isolate the US • Provoke overreaction • Frame attacks as part of a war between 'Crusaders and Jews' and Islam in order to 'awaken' the Muslim 'nation' to its responsibility to physical jihad • Hardened targets remain viable targets
Tier 2A – 'Inspired' individuals	• Attack planning generated from bottom up • These individuals *might* reach out to 'core' al-Qaeda operatives for operational or financial help	• Madrid's Sarhane Ben Abdelmajid Fakhet	• Targets 'softer' than those traditionally selected by core al-Qaeda • Requires lower level of tactical expertise • Less focus on strategic (symbolic) targets

continued

GSJ level	Hallmarks	Operatives	Strategies/Targets/ Operations
	• Motive not strategic, but individual obligation to pursue jihad for the remission of sin, identification with bin Laden's worldview, and other militant 'drivers' • Mix of Afghan training with untrained operatives (motivation critical factor, not capability) • **Operatives of this type are becoming more prevalent**		• Successful execution more important than target selection and attack methodology • Targets are found within areas of familiarity
Tier 2B – 'Inspired' individuals	• Attack planning generated from the bottom up • These individuals *might* reach out to 'core' al-Qaeda operatives for assistance, whether tactical, financial, etc. • Individual obligation to purse physical jihad for the remission of sin merges with bin Laden's worldview, Al-QAIDA's political strategy and other militant 'dirivers'	• Ahmed Ressam of the Millennium Plot	• Same as tier 2A • Hardened targets more viable due to support from core al-Qaeda and personal combat training or direct experience • International and local targets • Symbolic, identifiable targets critical to soliciting 'core' al-Qaeda's support

continued

GSJ level	Hallmarks	Operatives	Strategies/Targets/ Operations
	• Afghan (or other) training present • 'Seed' money provided by al-Qaedia • Impetus comes from personal contact with 'core' al-Qaeda • **This model may become outdated**		
Tier 3 – Radical Islamist version of 'leaderless resistance'	• Operatives driven by al-Qaeda's ideology of global jihad • No contact at all between these operatives and al-Qaeda core • More about individual quest to attain forgiveness of sin through physical jihad, not political strategy • Operatives are sometimes converts or immigrants to the West • Operatives not affiliated with a terrorist organization • **This model may grow as GSJ evolves**	• Mohammed Bouyeri (The Netherlands, 2004) • Attackers in Yanbu, Saudi Arabia • Some ARICs, European converts	• Generally same parameters of target selection as tier 2A • Operatives function based upon the 'intent' of al-Qaeda • Attack generally seen as an end in itself • Martyrdom often regarded as inevitable • Symbolic targets still important, but may give way to targets of opportunity

Notes

1 Similarly, Brigette Nacos wrote that al-Qaeda's objectives include: 'The removal of the U.S. military and thus the reduction or removal of U.S. interest from Saudi Arabia and other countries in the region ... The end of U.S. pressure on and sanctions against Iral-Qaeda ... [and] The destruction of the U.S.–Israeli alliance and the strengthening of the Palestinians' battle against Israel'. (See Brigitte L. Nacos, 'The

Terrorist Calculus behind 9-11: A Model for Future Terrorism?' *Studies in Conflict & Terrorism*, Vol. 26 (January – February 2003), p. 9.)

2 Barry R. Posen, *The Sources of Military Doctrine* (Ithaca and London: Cornell University Press, 1984), p. 25.

3 See Mark Sedgwick, 'Al-Qaeda and the Nature of Religious Terrorism', *Terrorism and Political Violence*, 16:4 (Winter 2004).

4 Al-Qaeda's instrumental warfare is seen, for example, in the 1998 US Embassy attacks in Kenya and Tanzania; the 2000 attack on the USS Cole; and has surfaced in post-11 September al-Qaeda-linked attacks in Indonesia, Kenya, Saudi Arabia, Tunisia, etc. Al-Qaeda's instrumental warfare has also emerged in Iral-Qaeda, where known al-Qaeda operatives directly connected to bin Laden – like Hassan Ghul and the 'emir' of 'al-Qaeda in Iral-Qaeda', Abu Musab al-Zarqawi – have operated against multinational forces and 'apostate' Iraqis to establish a future base for jihad, as well as in the Afghanistan – Pakistan border regions, where central al-Qaeda personalities and their cadres skirmish with coalition forces in attempts to escape capture.

5 See Brynjar Lia and Thomas Hegghammer, 'Jihadi Strategic Studies: The Alleged Al Qaida Policy Study Preceding the Madrid Bombing', *Studies in Conflict & Terrorism*, Vol. 27 (2004), pp. 355–375.

6 See 'Full text of bin Laden's speech' at http://english.aljazeera.net/NR/exeres/ 79C6AF22-98FB-4A1C-B21F-2BC36E87F61F.htm (accessed 1 March 2005). In this speech bin Laden demonstrated a sense of Western political timing and attempted to speak in a manner resembling a statesman delivering a 'State of the Union' address.

7 This description of culture is provided by Esler in his discussion of intercultural communication. See Philip F. Esler, *Galatians* (London: Routledge, 1998), p. 10.

8 See Christopher Coker, *Waging War Without Warriors? The Changing Culture of Military Conflict* (London: Lynne Rienner, 2002), pp. 3–9.

9 Ideology is defined here as the beliefs, values, principles, and objectives by which a group defines itself and justifies its course of action.

10 See Jean E. Rosenfeld, 'The "Religion" of Usamah bin Ladin: Terror as the Hand of God', at http://www.publiceye.org/frontpage/911/Islam/rosenfeld2001.html

11 Christopher Coker, *Waging War Without Warriors? The Changing Culture of Military Conflict* (London: Lynne Rienner, 2002), pp. 3–9.

12 Bruce Hoffman and Gordon H. McCormick, 'Terrorism Signaling and Suicide Attack', *Studies in Conflict and Terrorism*, 27:4 (2004), pp. 243–281.

13 Jean E. Rosenfeld, 'The "Religion" of Usamah bin Laden: Terror as the Hand of God', at http://www.publiceye.org/frontpage/911/Islam/rosenfeld2001.html

14 See 'Commander of the Khobar terrorist squad tells the story of the operation', Middle East Media Research Institute (MEMRI) trans. (Special Dispatch Series no. 731), 15 June 2004, at http://memri.org/bin/articles.cgi?Page=archives&Area=sd& ID=SP73104.

15 Reuven Paz, 'Middle East Islamism in the European Arena', *Middle East Review of International Affairs*, 6:3 (September 2002), at http://meria.idc.ac.il/journal/2002/ issue3/jv6n3a6.html#Dr.%20Reuven%20Paz.

16 The terms of Dr Magnus Ranstorp (conversation with author). For instance, Muhammad Bouyeri, the alleged murderer of Theo van Gogh, evidenced no known connections to al-Qaeda, did not articulate its grand political vision, nor struck the same type of targets. Further, those connected to the alleged plot in Crawley, UK (2004), similarly evidenced no direct connectivity to bin Laden. Moreover, many of

the accused in the Madrid bombings (including Fakhet, one of the leaders) had only ambiguous connections to any strategic, centralized, terrorist organization.

17 Marc Sageman, *Understanding Terrorist Networks* (Pennsylvania: University of Pennsylvania Press, 2004), p. 1.
18 Theo Farrell, 'Culture and Military Power', *Review of International Studies*, Vol. 24 (1998), p. 416; also, Williamson Murray, 'Military Culture Does Matter', Foreign Policy Research Institute (FPRI Wire), 7:2 (January 1999) at http://www.fpri.org/fpriwire/0702.199901.murray.militaryculturedoesmatter.html
19 See William S. Lind, Keith Nightengale, John F. Schmitt, Joseph W. Sutton and Gary I. Wilson, 'The Changing Face of War: Into the Fourth Generation', *Marine Corps Gazette*, 85:11 (October 1989).
20 On the relationship between culture, ideology and action, see Ann Swidler, 'Culture in Action: Symbols and Strategies', *American Sociological Review*, Vol. 51 (April 1986), p. 280.
21 See Catherine Wessinger in Jean E. Rosenfeld, 'The "Religion" of Usamah bin Ladin: Terror as the hand of God', at http://www.publiceye.org/frontpage/911/Islam/rosenfeld2001.html
22 Ann Swidler, 'Culture in Action: Symbols and Strategies', *American Sociological Review*, Vol. 51 (April 1986), p. 280.
23 Paul K. Davis, *Effects-Based Operations: A Grand Challenge for the Analytic Community* (Santa Monica, CA: RAND, 2001); also Christopher Finn (ed.), *Effects Based Warfare* (London: The Stationery Office, 2003).
24 Paul K. Davis, *Effects-Based Operations: A Grand Challenge for the Analytic Community* (Santa Monica, CA: RAND, 2001), p. 79.
25 M.L.R. Smith, *Fighting for Ireland? The Military Strategy of the Irish Republican Movement* (London: Routledge, 1995); C.J.M. Drake, *Terrorists' Target Selection* (New York: St Martin's Press, 1998); also B. Pirnie and S. Gardiner, *An Objectives-Based Approach to Military Campaign Analysis* (Santa Monica, CA: RAND, MR-656-JS, 1996).
26 Paul K. Davis, *Effects-Based Operations: A Grand Challenge for the Analytic Community* (Santa Monica, CA: RAND, 2001), p. 79 .
27 Networks are understood here as structures that pass information to like-minded participants horizontally rather than vertically.
28 T. Burns and G.M. Stalker, *The Management of Innovation* (London: Tavistock, 1961), p. 121.
29 Susan J. Winter and S. Lynne Taylor, 'The Role of Information Technology in the Transformation of Work', in JoAnne Yates and John Van Maanen (eds), *Information Technology and Organizational Transformation: History, Rhetoric, and Practice* (London: Sage Publications, 2001), p. 7.
30 John Arquilla, David Ronfeldt and Michele Zanini, 'Networks, Netwars, and Information Age Terrorism', in Ian O. Lesser *et al. Countering the New Terrorism* (Santa Monica, CA: RAND, 1999), pp. 41 and 49.
31 Manuel Castells, 'The Rise of the Network Society', in *The Information Age* (Oxford: Blackwell, 1996), p. 496.
32 Mary Kaldor, *New & Old Wars: Organized Violence in a Global Era* (Cambridge, UK: Polity, 1999), p. 3.
33 Magnus Ranstorp, testimony to the 9/11 Commission in a panel entitled 'The Attackers, Intelligence, and Counter-terrorism Policy', April 2003.
34 Jason Burke, *Al-Qaeda: The True Story of Radical Islam*, (New York: Penguin Books, 2004), p. 11.
35 Jason Burke, *Al-Qaeda: The True Story of Radical Islam*, (New York: Pinguin Books, 2004), p. 12.

36 Jane Corbin, *The Base: In Search of al-Qaeda – The Terror Network that Shook the World* (London: Simon & Schuster, 2002).

37 US investigators noted in 2004 that Padilla has attempted to 'downplay or deny his commitment to Al Qaeda' by claiming that he never swore an oath of allegiance (*bayat*) to bin Laden. See 'Summary of Jose Padilla's Activities with Al Qaeda' (a de-classified intelligence summary of Padilla's activities released by the US Department of Defence in 2004) at http://www.fas.org/irp/news/2004/06/padilla060104.pdf

38 Rohan Gunaratna, *Inside Al-Qaeda: Global Network of Terror* (London: Hurst, 2002), p. 3; and Steve Emerson, 'Adbullah Assam: The Man Before Osama Bin Laden', at www.iacsp.com/itobli3.html; also Brigitte L. Nacos, 'The Terrorist Calculus behind 9-11: A Model for Future Terrorism?' *Studies in Conflict & Terrorism*, Vol. 26 (January – February 2003), p. 9. According to Nacos, al-Qaeda's objectives include: 'The removal of the U.S. military and thus the reduction or removal of U.S. interest from Saudi Arabia and other countries in the region ... The end of U.S. pressure on and sanctions against Iral-Qaeda ... [and] The destruction of the U.S.–Israeli alliance and the strengthening of the Palestinians' battle against Israel'.

39 See Edward Rothstein, 'A Lethal Web with No Spider', *The New York Times*, 20 October 2001.

40 David Ronfeldt and John Arquilla, 'Networks, Netwars, and the Fight for the Future': http://firstmonday.org/issues/issue6_10/ronfeldt/index.html. Netwar is 'an emerging mode of conflict ... at societal levels, short of traditional military warfare, in which the protagonists use network forms of organization and related doctrines, strategies, and technologies attuned to the information age'.

41 Rohan Gunaratna, *Inside Al-Qaeda: Global Network of Terror* (London: Hurst, 2002), p. 57.

42 See Bruce Hoffman, 'Lessons of 9/11', Congressional Testimony CT-201 (Santa Monica, CA: RAND, 2002), p. 13; also Bruce Hoffman, 'Rethinking Terrorism and Counterterrorism Since 9/11', *Studies in Conflict and Terrorism*, Vol. 25, No. 5 (September/October 2002), p. 309. This was apparently the case in the Millennium plots against the Radisson Hotel in Amman and the Los Angeles Airport.

43 See Bruce Hoffman, 'Lessons of 9/11', Congressional Testimony CT-201 (Santa Monica, CA: RAND, 2002), p. 14; Bruce Hoffman, 'Rethinking Terrorism', p. 310; also Boaz Ganor, 'The Changing Threat of International Terrorism', Lecture delivered August 2002 at the Sydney Institute, Australia, available at http://www.ict.org.il/articles/articledet.cfm?articleid=455; Also, see US Department of State, *Patterns*, pp. 115 and 122–123. 'Trained amateurs', as Hoffman describes them, are represented by Ahmed Ressam. 'Local walk-ins' are composed of members of the Jordanian cell (since linked to Abu Musab al-Zarqawi) who plotted against Jordanian targets in late 1999. The stratum of 'like-minded insurgents, guerrillas, and terrorists' is represented by organizations such as *Abu Sayyaf* in the Philippines, *Jaish-e-Muhammad* in Pakistan, the *jihad* groups in Egypt and the GIA in Algeria (Ganor, 2002).

44 Rohan Gunaratna, *Inside Al-Qaeda: Global Network of Terror* (London: Hurst, 2002), p. 8; also, 'Al-Qaeda "spurred on" by Iral-Qaida war', BBC internet publication, 25 May 2004, at http://news.bbc.co.uk/2/hi/middle_east/3746205.stm; also Brian Michael Jenkins, *Countering al Qaeda: An Appreciation of the Situation and Suggestions for Strategy* (Santa Monica, CA: RAND, 2002), p. 4; Nicholas Lemann, 'What Terrorists Want: Is there a better way to defeat Al Qaeda?', *The New Yorker* (29 October 2001), p. 38; and Eric S. Margolis, 'Afghanistan: The Victory that Wasn't', *The American Conservative*, 2:6 (24 March 2003), pp. 15–18.

45 See http://www.whitehouse.gov/news/releases/2003/02/counter_terrorism/counter_ terrorism_strategy.pdf and Bergen, *Holy War,* p. 215.

46 See US Department of State, *Patterns of Global Terrorism 2003* (Washington, DC: Office of the Coordinator for Counterterrorism, Office of the Secretary, 2003), p. 110; also MJ Gohel and Sajjan M. Gohel, 'Bomb Blast in Jakarta, The Jemmah Islamiyah and the Wider Security Threat', Asia – Pacific Foundation – International Policy Assessment Group Analysis, 4 August 2003, p. 1 (analysis emailed to author 5 August 2003).

47 http://www.intelcenter.com/AL-QAIDA-IOLA-v09.pdf

48 Brian Michael Jenkins, *Countering al Qaeda: An Appreciation of the Situation and Suggestions for strategy* (Santa Monica, CA: RAND, 2002), p. 10.

49 John Arquilla, David Ronfeldt and Michele Zanini, 'Networks, Netwars, and Information Age Terrorism', in Ian O. Lessor *et al., Countering the New Terrorism* (Santa Monica, CA: RAND, 1999), p. 49.

50 Mary Kaldor, quoted in Magnus Ranstorp, testimony to the 9/11 Commission in a panel entitled 'The Attackers, Intelligence, and Counter-terrorism Policy', April 2003, p. 1.

51 Yoram Schweitzer, 'The Capture of Khalid Sheikh Muhammad', *Tel Aviv Notes,* 3 March 2003.

52 Rohan Gunaratna, *Inside Al-Qaeda: Global Network of Terror* (London: Hurst, 2002), p. 235.

53 Anonymous, *Through Our Enemies' Eyes*, p. 17; also Daniel L. Byman and Kennth M. Pollack, 'Bin Laden's Group Will Survive Him', *Newsday*, 25 September 2001.

54 See Mark Sedgwick, 'Al-Qaeda and the Nature of Religious Terrorism', *Terrorism and Political Violence*, 16:4 (Winter 2004).

55 Jonathan Spyer, 'The Al-Qa'ida Network and Weapons of Mass Destruction', *Middle East Review of International Affairs,* 8:3 (September 2004), at http://meria.idc.ac.il/journal/2004/issue3/jv8n3a3.html

56 Christopher Coker, *Waging War Without Warriors? The Changing Culture of Military Conflict* (London: Lynne Rienner, 2002), p. 6.

57 See John L. Esposito, *The Islamic Threat: Myth or Reality?* (Oxford: University Press, 1992), p. 126; also Joel Beinin and Joe Stork, *Political Islam* (California: University of California Press, 1997), p.74. Islamism is defined here as a religio-political theory aimed at revitalizing Islamic societies and/or establishing *Shari'a*-based Islamic states in the place of 'secular' modes of governance. There is a wide range of Islamist thought, some passive and others militant.

58 Rohan Gunaratna, *Inside Al-Qaeda: Global Network of Terror* (London: Hurst, 2002), p. 235.

59 Fukuyama, *The Great Disruption* (New York, N.Y.: The Free Press, 1999), p. 199.

60 Paula Uimonen, 'Networks of Global Interaction', *Cambridge Review of International Affairs*, Vol. 16, No. 2 (July 2003), pp. 273–286.

61 Marc Sageman, *Understanding Terrorist Networks* (Pennsylvania: University of Pennsylvania Press, 2004), p. 1.

62 See Quintan Wiktorowicz, 'The new global threat: transnational Salafis and Jihad', *Middle East Policy Council*, Vol. 8:4 (1 December 2001).

63 Marc Sageman, *Understanding Terrorist Networks* (Pennsylvania: University of Pennsylvania Press, 2004), p. 1. In defining the GSJ, Sageman wrote:

> [The GSJ] is a worldwide religious revivalist movement with the goal of re-establishing past Muslim glory in a great Islamist state stretching from Morocco to the Philippines, eliminating present national boundaries. It preaches [and mandates as a comprehensive template for life, including

politics, society and religion] *salafiyya* (from *salaf*, the Arabic word for 'ancient one' and referring to the companions of the Prophet Mohammed), the restoration of authentic Islam, and advocates a strategy of violent jihad, resulting in an explosion of terror to wipe out what it regards as local political heresy. [The GSJ's global component] advocates the defeat of Western powers that prevent the establishment of a true Islamist state.

Al Qaeda is the vanguard of this movement, which includes many other terrorist groups that collaborate in their operations and share a large support base. Salafi ideology determines its mission, sets its goals and guides its tactics. What sets the global Salafi jihad apart from other terrorist campaigns is its violence against foreign non-Muslim governments and their populations in furtherance of Salafi objectives.

64 Quintan Wiktorowicz, 'The new global threat: transnational Salafis and Jihad', *Middle East Policy Council*, 8:4 (1 December 2001).
65 Marc Sageman, *Understanding Terrorist Networks* (Pennsylvania: University of Pennsylvania Press, 2004), p. 115.
66 See Omar Mahmoud Othman quoted in Paz (as Omar Abu Omar), 'Middle East Islamism in the European Arena,' pp. 68–69, at http://meria.idc.ac.il/journal/2002/issue3/jv6n3a6.html#Dr.%20Reuven%20Paz
67 See Quintan Wiktorowicz, 'Suicide Bombings: Do Beliefs Matter?' (September 2004) at http://www.unc.edu/~kurzman/Soc3264/Wiktorowicz_EXPLAINING_SUICIDE_BOMBINGS.doc
68 Marc Sageman, *Understanding Terrorist Networks* (Pennsylvania: University of Pennsylvania Press, 2004), p. 1.
69 Edward Said, *Orientalism* (New York, N.Y.: Random House, 1978), p. 333.
70 See 'Report of the Joint Inquiry into the Terrorist Attacks of September 11, 2001 – by the House Permanent Select Committee on Intelligence and the Senate Select Committee on Intelligence', p. 336 at http://datacenter.ap.org/wdc/911report.pdf (accessed 8 August 2003).
71 Smith, Fighting for Ireland? in Drake, *Terrorists' Target Selection* (New York, N.Y.: St Martin's Press, 1998), p. 36.
72 Edward Said, *Orientalism* (New York, N.Y.: Random House, 1978), p. 344.
73 See 'al-Qaeda aided Istanbul bombers' at http://news.bbc.co.uk/go/pr/fr/-/1/hi/world/europe/3653744.stm; also 'Saudi Says Iran Drags Feet Returning Al Qaeda Leaders', *Washington Post*, 12 August 2003 at http://www.washingtonpost.com/ac2/wp-dyn/A46578-2003Aug11?language=printer (accessed 16 October 2003).
74 Reuven Paz, 'Middle East Islamism in the European Arena', at http://meria.idc.ac.il/journal/2002/issue3/jv6n3a6.html#Dr.%20Reuven%20Paz
75 Diane Singerman, 'The Networked World of Islamist Social Movements', in Quintan Wiktorowicz (ed.), *Islamic Social Activism* (Bloomington, IN: Indiana University Press, 2004), p. 151.
76 Quintan Wiktorowicz (ed.) *Islamic Social Activism* (Bloomington, IN: Indiana University Press, 2004).
77 See Salem Almakhi, 'Mending the Hearts of the Believers: The Link between the Campaigns in Makaleh, Fhilcha and Bali', Yoni Fighel and Yoram Kehati (trans.), in Fighel and Kehati, 'Analysis of Recent Al-Qaida Documents, Part 1', 28 November 2001, at http://www.ict.org.il/articles/articledet.cfm?articleid=453
78 Salem Almakhi, 'Mending the Hearts of the Believers: The Link between the Campaigns in Makaleh, Fhilcha and Bali', Yoni Fighel and Yoram Kehati (trans.),

in Fighel and Kehati, 'Analysis of Recent Al-Qaida Documents, Part 1', 28 November 2001, at http://www.ict.org.il/articles/articledet.cfm?articleid=453. Fighel and Kehati also note that it is far from certain that Salem Almakhi is the author's actual name.

79 Michael Taarnby, 'Recruitment of Islamist Terrorists in Europe. Trends and Perspectives,' Research Report funded by the Danish Ministry of Justice, 14 January 2005, p. 23.

80 Brian Michael Jenkins, *Countering al Qaeda: An Appreciation of the Situation and Suggestions for strategy* (Santa Monica, CA: RAND, 2002), p. 4.

81 See Boaz Ganor, 'The Changing Threat of International Terrorism', Lecture delivered August 2002 at the Sydney Institute, Australia, available at http://www.ict.org.il/articles/articledet.cfm?articleid=455

82 Boaz Ganor, 'The Changing Threat of International Terrorism', Lecture delivered August 2002 at the Sydney Institute, Australia, available at http://www.ict.org.il/articles/articledet.cfm?articleid=455, p. 18; also, see http://www.whitehouse.gov/news/releases/2003/02/counter_terrorism/counter_terrorism_strategy.pdf, p. 9.

83 Burke, *Al-Qaeda*, pp. 18 and 21.

84 One of these reasons, of course, has been the anticipated, then realized receipt of US military aid.

85 See 'Soldier Guilty of Trying to aid Al-Qaeda', *Associated Press*, 3 September 2004.

86 See 'Islamist sect linked to bombings said to be on the rise in Spain', *El Pais*, 30 December 2005; also 'Pakistanis in Spain terror charge', BBC News, 13 April 2005 at http://news.bbc.co.uk/2/hi/europe/4442059.stm

87 See the most complete coverage of jihadism in the Netherlands, including the so-called Hofstad netwok, at Dr Albert Benschop's (University of Amsterdam) site, 'Chronicle of a Political Murder Foretold', http://www.sociosite.org/jihad_nl_en.php#Internationale_connecties

88 Simon L. Garfinkel, 'Leaderless Resistance Today', 26 February 2003, at http://www.firstmonday.dk/issues/issue8_3/garfinkel/. 'Leaderless resistance' is a method of self-organisation for the conduct of terrorist activities by small cells or ideologically motivated and unaffiliated individuals, requiring no central organization.

89 Marc Sageman, *Understanding Terrorist Networks* (Pennsylvania: University of Pennsylvania Press, 2004), p. 1.

90 Rohan Gunaratna, *Inside Al-Qaeda: Global Network of Terror* (London: Hurst, 2002), p. 235.

91 For more on the role of the heroic paradigm of the principal ideologues of the GSJ, see Jeffrey Cozzens, 'Approaching al-Qaida: From Character to Combat Doctrine – Revolutionary Millennialism and Fourth Generation Warfare' (University of St Andrews: unpublished master's dissertation, 2003). Also, see Joseph Campbell, in Leonard J. Biallas, *Myths: Gods, Heroes, and Saviors* (United States: Twenty-Third Publications, 1986), p. 30; Mathieu Deflem, 'Ritual, Anti-Structure, and Religion: A Discussion of Victor Turner's Processional Symbolic Analysis', *Journal for the Scientific Study of Religion,* 30:1 (1991), pp. 1–25; Paul Tillich, *Dynamics of Faith* (New York: Harper and Row, 1957), p. 1; and Victor W. Turner, *The Ritual Process: Structure and Anti-Structure* (London: Routledge & Paul, 1969), p. 95. The revolutionary journeys of Qutb, Azzam and al-Zawahiri – principal ideologues of the GSJ – greatly resemble those of '*rites de passage*: "rites which accompany every change of place, state, [and] social position"', first classified by anthropologist Van Gennep and later expanded by Victor Turner. The '*rites de passage*' are: 'separation', 'margin' and 'aggregation'. Drawing from the anthropological literature, Joseph Campbell

wrote that the lives of heroes – those whose experiences, trials, achievements and/or messages that establish them as legendary figures – are also marked by these phases, which he re-labels "withdraw, initiation, and return". During the withdrawal, the hero is grasped by deep philosophical or religious curiosities, and drawn away from home for a period of introspection. Theologian Paul Tillich identified the drawing 'force' as one's 'ultimate concern'. One's ultimate concern, according to Tillich, demands complete subordination if one accepts the claim it makes upon one's life. The second stage of heroic development, the initiation, is where the hero exemplifies heroic qualities. Relevance and destiny become apparent to the hero in the midst of initiation trials, thereby qualifying him to perform the task that is his ultimate concern. This task is completed during the hero's return 'back into the kingdom of humanity, where the boon [of the hero's withdrawal and initiation] may redound to the renewing of the community'. By invoking Campbell's paradigm, one sees that Qutb's storied life and militant theory made him not only a charismatic leader but a hero. This perhaps explains the great influence his life and theories had on later militant Islamists who espoused the al-Qaeda worldview, albeit one that most of the dominant literature on al-Qaeda fails to note.

92 Some contemporary 'heroes' include Yusuf al-Ayyiri, former head of al-Qaeda in the Arabian Peninsula (killed by Saudi forces in 2003), and Abu Mus'ab al-Zarqawi's chief theologian, Abu Anas al-Shami (killed by the US, military in Iral-Qaeda, 2004).

93 Bin Laden said, 'I am just a poor slave of God. If I live or die, the war will continue' (see 'Bin Laden says U.S. was target', CNN, 28 December 2001, at http://archives.cnn.com/2001/WORLD/asiapcf/central/12/27/ret.bin.laden.tape/index.html)

94 This pattern was evidenced by the Madrid bombers' videotaped testament.

95 Jason Burke, Al-Qaeda: The True Story of Radical Islam (New York: Penguin Books, 2004), p. 14.

96 See Paul Tillich, Dynamics of Faith (New York: Harper and Row, 1957), p. 1.

97 Reuven Paz, 'Endless Global Jihad' Prism Series on Global Jihad, Vol. 1, No. 3 (Herzelia, Israel, 2003), pp. 3 and 4.

98 See Ayman al-Zawahiri, Knights under the Prophet Banner, serialized in Al-Sharq al Awsat, 10 December 2001, trans. Foreign Broadcast Information Service, document FBIS-NES-2001-1202, p. 74, (maintained by the Federation of American Scientists at: http://fas.org/irp/world/para/aymanh_bk.html).

99 On 'imagined communities', see Benedict Anderson, Imagined Communities (London: Verso, 1983).

100 Catherine Wessinger, in Jean E. Rosenfeld, 'The Religion of Usamah Bin Laden', at www.publiceye.org/frontpage/911/Islam/rosenfeld2001-01.htm#TopOfPage; also Wessinger (ed.), Millennialism, pp. 33–39 and 205–344.

101 B.H. Liddell Hart, Strategy: The Indirect Approach (London: Faber & Faber, 1967), p. 335.

102 Reuven Paz, 'Middle East Islamism in the European Arena', at http://meria.idc.ac.il/journal/2002/issue3/jv6n3a6.html#Dr.%20Reuven%20Paz

103 Olivier Roy, Globalized Islam (New York: Columbia University, 2004), p. 325.

104 Wessinger, in Jean E. Rosenfeld, 'The Religion of Usamah bin Laden', at www.publiceye.org/frontpage/911/Islam/rosenfeld2001-01.htm#TopOfPage.

105 Wessinger, in Jean E. Rosenfeld, 'The Religion of Usamah bin Laden', at www.publiceye.org/frontpage/911/Islam/rosenfeld2001-01.html#1TopOfPage.

106 Wessinger, in Jean E. Rosenfeld, 'The Religion of Usamah bin Laden', at www.publiceye.org/frontpage/911/Islam/rosenfeld2001-01.html#1TopOfPage.

107 Wessinger, in Jean E. Rosenfeld, 'The Religion of Usamah bin Laden', at www.publiceye.org/frontpage/911/Islam/rosenfeld2001-01.html#1TopOfPage.

108 Wessinger, in Jean E. Rosenfeld, 'The Religion of Usamah bin Laden', at www.publiceye.org/frontpage/911/Islam/rosenfeld2001-01.html#1TopOfPage.

109 See 'Translation of April 24, 2002 al-Qaeda document, A statement from *qaidat al-jihad* regarding the mandates of the heroes and the legality of the operations in New York and Washington' at http://www.mepc.org/public_asp/journal_vol10/alqaeda.html. This translation from an al-Qaeda website justifies this notion.

110 See Rohan Gunaratna, *Inside Al-Qaeda: Global Network of Terror* (London: Hurst, 2002), p. 93. Gunaratna slots al-Qaeda as an 'Apocalyptic Islamist group,' a definition which discerns some of al-Qaeda's characteristics but fails to highlight its direction.

111 One prominent example is the 'decentralization' of the doctrine of *takfir* (the act of declaring a Muslim an apostate, first legitimized by the medieval cleric Ibn Taymiyya and expanded upon by Sayyid Qutb). For some Salafists, such as al-Zarqawi's network and the GIA, this doctrine has been used to legitimize the murder of Muslim civilians belonging to the 'out group'. However, bin Laden has in the past criticized this use of *takfir*, as evidenced by his withdrawal of support from the GIA and the emergence of the GSCP; his application focuses on Arab regimes. Contrary to both interpretations, Abdullah Azzam rejected the notion of *takfi*, claiming it leads to *fitna* (internal strife).

112 Canadian Security Intelligence Service, 'Doomsday Religious Movements', pp. 53–54.

113 Canadian Security Intelligence Service, 'Doomsday Religious Movements', p. 54.

114 Canadian Security Intelligence Service, 'Doomsday Religious Movements', p. 54.

115 Rohan Gunaratna, *Inside Al-Qaeda: Global Network of Terror* (London: Hurst, 2002), p. 93.

116 See Malise Ruthven, 'War against Terrorism', *The Guardian* (30 October 2001), at http://www.guardian.co.uk/waronterror/story/0,1361,583484,00.html

117 For example, a Jaish Ansar al-Sunnah statement posted 11 November 2004 on an Islamist website read: 'If God has written for Fallujah that it fall, the Jihad will continue to Doomsday. Fallujah is no more precious than Afghanistan or Chechnya or other Muslim lands; but our enemies are certain that our fight is not for the sake of a nation or territory, but for the establishment of God's mighty shariah.' (See 'Special Reports – Through the eyes of the mujahideen,' *Jane's Islamic Affairs Analyst* (1 December 2004).

118 See David Cook, 'The Recovery of Radical Islam in the Wake of the Defeat of the Taliban', *Terrorism and Political Violence*, 15:1 (Spring 2003).

119 Author's personal interviews with former 'Afghan-Arab' mujahideen (2005–2006).

120 'Special Reports – Through the eyes of the mujahideen,' *Jane's Islamic Affairs Analyst* (1 December 2004).

121 Malise Ruthven, 'War against terrorism,' *Guardian Unlimited*, 20 October 2001, at http://www.guardian.co.uk/waronterror/story/0,,583484,00.html

122 'The Rule of Seeking Political Asylum in the Infidel World', quoted in Rueven Paz, 'Middle East Islamism in the European Arena', *Middle East Review of International Affairs*, 6:3 (September 2002).

123 See for example 'Bin Laden's Sermon for the Feast of Sacrifice', MEMRI Special Dispatch – Jihad and Terrorism Studies No. 476 (5 March 2004).

124 'Special Reports – Through the eyes of the mujahideen', *Jane's Islamic Affairs Analyst* (1 December 2004).

125 Abdullah Azzam, *The Lofty Mountain* (London: Azzam Publications, 2003), p. 6.

126 'Sheikh Abu Hamza al-Masri on martyrdom and the love of death', Middle East Media Research Institute trans. (Special Dispatch 762), 12 August 2004, at http://memri.org/bin/articles.cgi?Page=archives&Area=sd&ID=SP76204

127 See 'Al Qaeda Publication, "Sout Al Jihad" Interviews "Saleh al Oufi", New Leader of the Mujahideen in the "Al Haramain Country" [Saudi Arabia],' SITE Institute, 25 June 2004.

128 Abdullah Azzam, *The Lofty Mountain* (London: Azzam Publications, 2003).

129 See 'Commander of the Khobar terrorist squad tells the story of the operation', Middle East Media Research Institute (MEMRI) trans. (Special Dispatch Series no. 731), 15 June 2004, at http://memri.org/bin/articles.cgi?Page=archives&Area=sd&ID=SP73104

130 'Bin Laden's Sermon for the Feast of Sacrifice', MEMRI Special Dispatch No. 476, 5 March 2003, pp. 12–13.

131 Quintan Wiktorowicz, 'The new global threat: transnational Salafis and Jihad', *Middle East Policy Council*, 8:4 (1 December 2001).

132 Al-Zawahiri, *Knights Under the Prophet's Banner*, p. 72.

133 For more on European converts, see Craig S. Smith, 'Europe fears converts may aid Islamic militants', 20 July 2004, at http://www.iht.com/articles/530101.html

134 See Rueven Paz, 'Middle East Islamism in the European Arena', *Middle East Review of International Affairs*, 6:3 (September 2002).

135 Mahan Abedin, 'The Essence of Al Qaeda: An Interview with Sa'ad al-Fal-Qaidaih', *Jamestown Foundation Spotlight on Terror*, 2:2 (5 February 2004), at http://jamestown.org/publications_details.php?volume_id=402&&issue_id=2907.

136 See Jeffrey Cozzens, 'Islamist groups develop new recruiting strategies', *Jane's Intelligence Review*, 1 February 2005.

137 See Ghaith Abdul-Ahad, 'Seeking Salvation in a City of Insurgents', *The Washington Post*, 11 November 2004, p. A30.

138 Author's conversation with Dr Ranstorp, July 2003.

139 See Yvonne Y. Haddad, 'Sayyid Qutb', p. 80; also see al-Zawahiri, *Knights Under the Prophet's Banner*.

140 David Zeidan, 'The Islamic Fundamentalist View of Life as a Perennial Battle', *Middle East Review of International Affairs*, 5:4 (December 2001), at http://meria.idc.ac.il/journal/2001/issue4/jv5n4a2.htm

141 Saif al-Din al-Ansari, 'The Raid on New York and Washington – A generic description', (FBIS trans.), 1 September 2002, at http://www.why-war.com/files/qaeda_celebrate_911.txt

142 'Bin Laden's Sermon for the Feast of Sacrifice,' MEMRI Special Dispatch No. 476, 5 March 2003, p. 12.

143 Suleiman Abu Gheith, 'Why we fight America: al-Qaeda spokesman explains September 11 and declares intentions to kill 4 million Americans with weapons of mass destruction', in 'Al-Qa'ida Dispatches, December 2001 – March 2003', Middle East Media Research Institute (Spring 2003).

144 Bruce Hoffman, 'Al-Qaeda, Trends in Terrorism and Future Potentialities: An Assessment', (RAND, P-8078, 2003), at http://www.rand.org/publications/P/P8078/P8078.pdf

145 Emile Sahliyeh, 'Religious Fundamentalisms Compared', in Martin E. Marty and R. Scott Appleby (eds), *Fundamentalism and Society* (Chicago: University of Chicago Press, 1995), p. 148.

146 See 'Al Qaeda Publication, "Sout Al Jihad", Interviews "Saleh al Oufi", New Leader of the Mujahideen in the "Al Haramain Country" [Saudi Arabia]', SITE Institute, 25 June 2004.

147 See Reuven Paz, 'Middle East Islamism in the European Arena', at http://meria.idc.ac.il/journal/2002/issue3/jv6n3a6.html#Dr.%20Reuven%20Paz; and Quintan Wiktorowicz, 'The new global threat: transnational Salafis and Jihad', *Middle East Policy Council*, 8:4 (1 December 2001).

148 Abdullah Azzam, *The Lofty Mountain* (London: Azzam Publications, 2003).

149 Michael Taarnby, 'Recruitment of Islamist Terrorists in Europe. Trends and Perspectives, Research Report funded by the Danish Ministry of Justice, 14 January 2005, p. 38.

150 For instance, see 'Bin Laden's Sermon for the Feast of Sacrifice', MEMRI Special Dispatch No. 476, 5 March 2003.

151 Paul Wilkinson, 'Ethical Defences of Terrorism – Defending the Indefensible', *Terrorism and Political Violence*, 1:1 (January 1989), p. 11.

152 For example, see the contributions in Christopher Finn (ed.), *Effects Based Warfare* (London: The Stationery Office, 2003).

153 'Fourth Generation Warfare and the Relation of Military Strategy to Grand Strategy', Comment #170, http://www.d-n-i.net/fes/comments/c170.htm.

154 'Fourth Generation Warfare and the Relation of Military Strategy to Grand Strategy', Comment #170, 68; also see Ann Swidler, 'Culture in Action: Symbols and Strategies', *American Sociological Review*, Vol. 51 (April 1986), p. 280.

155 Ann Swidler, 'Culture in Action: Symbols and Strategies', *American Sociological Review*, Vol. 51 (April 1986), p. 273.

156 Donatella Della Porta, 'Introduction: On individual motivations in underground political organizations', in Della Porta (volume ed.), *Social Movements and Violence: Participation in Underground Organizations,* in Bert Klandermans (series ed.), *International Social Movement Research* (London: JAI Press, 1992), Vol. 4, p. 4.

157 Ann Swidler, 'Culture in Action: Symbols and Strategies', *American Sociological Review*, Vol. 51 (April 1986), p. 280.

158 Theo Farrell, 'Culture and Military Power', *Review of International Studies*, Vol. 24 (1998), p. 416.

159 Theo Farrell, 'Culture and Military Power', *Review of International Studies*, Vol. 24 (1998), p. 407.

160 See William S. Lind, Keith Nightengale, John F. Schmitt, Joseph W. Sutton and Gary I. Wilson, 'The Changing Face of War: Into the Fourth Generation', *Marine Corps Gazette*, 85:11 (October 1989); also see Jeffrey Cozzens, 'Approaching Al-Qaida', pp. 48–60; Cozzens, 'Al-Qaida's Combat Doctrine: Grand Strategy, Fourth Generation Warfare and the Challenges Ahead – A Strategic Perspective', Royal United Services Institute speech (London, England: June 2004). Fourth generation warfare is generally 'characterized by small agile forces focused on flexible missions, decreased dependence on centralized logistics, and a growing use of technology" (Lind *et al*, 1989). However, unlike what has been termed 'netwar' by John Arquilla and David Ronfeldt (see Abdullah Azzam, *The Lofty Mountain* (London: Azzam Publications, 2003), 4GW adversaries like the GSJ emphasize 'a new ideological asymmetry' when considered in combination with the above traits – a distinguishing quality that sets it apart from other forms of information age conflict (Cozzens, 2004).

161 Magnus Ranstorp, testimony to Select Committee on Foreign Affairs, UK House of Commons (4 May 2004), at http://www.publications.parliament.uk/pa/cm200304/cmselect/cmfaff/441/4050404.htm

162 Gilles Kepel, *The War for Muslim Minds* (London: Harvard University Press, 2004).

163 On some of the functions of al-Qaeda's narrative, see Bruce Hoffman, 'Al-Qaeda, Trends in Terrorism and Future Potentialities', at http://www.rand.org/publications/P/ P8078/P8078.pdf; also Cozzens' remarks on 'Al-Qaida's Combat Doctrine' at the Royal United Services Institute (London, June 2004).
164 Bruce Hoffman, 'Al-Qaeda, Trends in Terrorism and Future Potentialities', at http://www.rand.org/publications/P/P8078/P8078.pdf
165 Major General Greg Olson (USA), quoted in Paul Haven, 'Al-Qaida Ability Diminishing, Agents Say', Associated Press, 13 March 2005.
166 Magnus Ranstorp, testimony to Select Committee on Foreign Affairs, UK House of Commons (4 May 2004), at http://www.publications.parliament.uk/pa/cm200304/ cmselect/cmfaff/441/4050404.htm

8

UNDERSTANDING RECRUITMENT OF ISLAMIST TERRORISTS IN EUROPE

Michael Taarnby

Introduction

This study focuses on the recruitment practices in the global Jihad as they play out in Europe. While the focal point is terrorism, this study deals only with a single form of contemporary terrorism, usually referred to as the global Jihad in order to differentiate between religiously inspired conflicts of a geographically limited nature and those with a global vision. However interesting other types of terrorism might be, this study does not include secular or nationalist terrorist groups such as the IRA or ETA. Other religiously justified forms of terrorism also present within Europe have also been excluded. Examples of Islamic terrorist entities that have been excluded are the Palestinian organisations as well as Shi'a Islamic groups. They follow different trajectories and rarely interact with the internationally oriented militant Islamists. Although there are indications of some interaction, these are certainly not on a scale that would tempt anyone to label this phenomenon as a terrorist international. The various terrorist organisations do have very different agendas, and, for some of the groups, their mutual hatred surpasses that projected onto their sworn enemies. The terrorists of interest to this study are all linked to the ideology most often associated with al-Qaeda.

Europe's role in the current global Jihad is a phenomenon that was neglected by government, security services, academia and the media throughout Europe up until the attacks on the US on 11 September 2001. The lack of attention to this phenomenon will take years to remedy, but I believe the indispensability of such endeavours became quite clear with the attacks in Spain in March 2004. Previously seen as a relative backwater in the war on terrorism, Europe is now on the front line. 'It's trench warfare', in the words of a security expert. 'We keep taking them out. They keep coming at us. And every time they are coming at us harder' (Barnett 2004).

The geographical limitation imposed on this study – that of Western Europe – necessitates further elaboration. Strictly speaking, it would be impossible to consider the European dimension of the global Jihad as an isolated phenomenon. Instead it is intertwined with individuals, organisations, ideologies and situations across the world. The Jihad is truly global in nature, and it would amount to folly to ignore its close links to the Middle East, South East Asia, Central Asia and North Africa. The idea behind this study was to examine the level of recruitment activity as it unfolds in Europe, whether it has a direct impact on European affairs or affects other countries.

While some readers may be disappointed by the author's apparent lack of interest in the actual number of individuals being recruited for terrorist activity in Europe, this is not the case. However, to present reliable figures on European terrorists would require access to restricted government information across Europe. Needless to say, this was not possible to obtain, nor was it actually desirable. Several recent remarks by officials from European security services state that terrorist recruitment is on the rise. Taking these remarks into consideration, and at the same time assuming that evidence exists to verify the claims, the focus remains on the general trends exemplified by specific cases. The information used in this study comes exclusively from open sources. An obsession with numbers would probably result in a skewed and potentially misleading analysis. It is the opinion of the author that the central question that should be answered in this study concerns what future trends are to be expected in the recruitment to the Jihad in Europe. In short, will Europe experience a decline or an increase in recruitment to Islamist terrorism in the near to mid-term future? I am inclined to argue that Europe is likely to see increased participation in the global Jihad, and the following pages will serve to clarify this perspective.

The attacks on the US on 11 September 2001 by al-Qaeda were unlikely to have materialised without a significant and dedicated European component. International investigative efforts rapidly pointed out a group of Islamists residing in Germany as a critical component in the successful realisation of an ambitious operational plan. The Hamburg cell of Al Qaeda terrorists had become radicalised and later joined the global Jihad in Germany. While the attacks certainly affected the US, the operation pointed to a significant security problem emanating from Europe.

Fortunately, 11 September 2001 was contrived and organised under conditions that no longer exist. A safe haven, a training infrastructure, organisational support, and the integrity needed to prepare a complex terrorist attack have all been dismantled over the past three years (Leiken 2004). This development could lead to the assumption that Islamist terrorism has been set back irrevocably. While it is true that the terrorists have been put under considerable pressure, this perspective emphasises the organisational structure of a more or less defunct terrorist organisation and does not take the wider social context into consideration. To simplify the argument, the war on terrorism has notably been successful because al-Qaeda has suffered irretrievable losses. Yet, Islamist terrorism has simultaneously managed to metamorphose into a new threat. How did this happen, and how will it affect Europe in the future?

Among Europe's millions of Muslims, who is susceptible to recruitment? Why do they join? How does one actually join the Jihad? Those who assume that all Muslims in Europe represent a threat of some kind contribute with nothing besides a public display of ignorance. That the terrorists of concern to this study are all Muslims should be obvious, but this in itself explains nothing. Statistically speaking, militants and terrorists represent but a fraction of a minority and do not act on behalf of every European Muslim.

Something that unites a very diverse group of European militant Islamists is their decision to make a link to the Jihad. Previously, the recruitment took place in camps in Afghanistan and constituted a form of formal recruitment. While many young Muslims went to Afghanistan to train, less than thirty per cent of the trainees were invited to join a terrorist organisation (Sageman 2004). This selection process is no longer an option since the training facilities in Afghanistan have been effectively dismantled, thus depriving the militant Islamists of a place to train and interact.

Yet, the European media run stories about terrorist suspects being arrested across Europe on a weekly, if not daily, basis. It would seem that the loss of Afghanistan as a terrorist safe haven is not the victory it was claimed to be. The continuing arrests signal a new development in which Europe's role should be scrutinised closely. A new stage in the war on terrorism would be reached if Muslims raised in Western Europe were recruited, underwent their military and ideological training here, and then considered Europe as a front line. The Dutch intelligence service concluded in December 2002 that the first signs of such a development were already becoming visible (AIVD 2002). This report is inclined to argue that this is no longer a future scenario, but is already taking place.

Recruitment to Jihad in Europe before 11 September 2001

To comprehend the current situation of Islamist terrorist recruitment in Europe it is necessary to have at least a rudimentary understanding of previous cases. A very brief outline of this trend is necessary to fully appreciate the circumstances leading up to 11 September 2001 and beyond. While the members of the Hamburg cell certainly represent the most lethal of Islamists to emanate from Europe, they were by no means the first group of people to have been recruited to the Jihad. Recruitment to Jihad in Europe did not begin with the now ill-famed Hamburg cell that carried out the attacks on the US in 2001. There is no disputing the fact that there has been a clear development in the direct threat posed by Islamist groups to the West. What started as an insignificant external threat in the 1980s, almost always carried out somewhere outside Europe, has now become a threat to Europe and is emanating from within European countries. While this development has been gradual, 11 September 2001 was a turning point that marked an intensification of the recruitment process.

It should be stressed that, while a number of individuals from Europe joined various Jihads over the past decades, the vast majority did so as Mujaheddin with the intention to fight as guerrillas in irregular units. They linked up with various insurgency movements across the Muslim world, such as in Afghanistan, Bosnia, Kashmir and Chechnya, where they took part in conventional guerrilla warfare. It is important to note that very few actually became terrorists. This said, there was an overlap between the Mujaheddin and the terrorists, at times making it impossible to distinguish between them. Some who started out as Mujaheddin later turned into terrorists, and some who trained as terrorists found themselves fighting on the front lines. The various groups were to some degree intertwined through a shared ideology.

The Afghan experience

The historical significance of the Afghan war (1979–1988) must be stressed once again. The Soviet invasion of Afghanistan was a watershed in militant Islamist circles. From all over the Muslim world volunteers met, interacted and fought for an extended period, and the fact that an unknown number of the Mujaheddin originated in Europe is not surprising. Western governments were dedicated to striking a blow at the Soviet Union, preferably through the physical sacrifices of others. It appears that those willing to risk their lives fighting the Soviets were free to do so. I have not been able to detect a coherent or systematic effort to discourage European Muslims from travelling to Afghanistan during the war. The ideological impact of the Afghan war on the formation of a global Jihad cannot be overemphasised. A common enemy had united various indigenous Mujaheddin factions and foreign volunteers, and strong bonds were forged (Sageman 2004).

The end of the Afghan war and the ensuing doctrinal disputes between Mujaheddin factions shaped the later development of the Jihad. The overconfidence generated by a decisive victory against an infidel superpower led to the assumption that anything was possible and that the Mujaheddin had God on their side. However, in the late 1980s the debate centred on offensive versus defensive Jihad in a traditional way; the belief in terrorism by any means was institutionalised much later.

Within the militant Islamist circles in Europe some degree of training and indoctrination was considered indispensable, and the best place for this was Afghanistan. During the 1990s, many thousands of Islamists went to Afghanistan to train for Jihad: estimates range from 12,000 to 70,000. It is worthwhile to take a look at the experience of these volunteers because quite a few replaced their previous lifestyle with an unswerving loyalty to the Jihad. The training camps in Afghanistan provided the infrastructure for these volunteers, and handpicked instructors took care of instilling the al-Qaeda doctrine of maximum damage in the mind of the terrorist operative.

To join the Jihad prior to 11 September 2001 the only prerequisite was an acquaintance who could arrange for training in Afghanistan. A formal invitation to join a terrorist network was extended to the volunteers upon completion of their training after senior members had a chance to evaluate their dedication and usefulness. The most severe blow to terrorist recruitment is directly related to the intervention in Afghanistan in late 2001. The loss of the training facilities in Afghanistan deprived the volunteers of a place to learn the skills of a terrorist, but they also lost the opportunity to meet other volunteers from all over the world. It is possible that the loss of the training camps will gradually diminish the psychological control of the leaders over the militant Islamists, for without the intense experience of training at the centre of international terrorism in a dusty Afghan camp, the concept of a global Jihad may prove difficult to internalise.

The war in Bosnia

The civil war in the former Yugoslavia in the mid-1990s attracted many prospective Mujaheddin from the Arab world and to a lesser extent from Europe. It is difficult to define these volunteers as terrorists because the majority were involved in regular guerrilla warfare. They joined as Holy Warriors and not in order to become terrorists. They are, however, important to consider because some of the Mujaheddin were later to resurface as full-blown terrorists.

The majority of foreign Mujaheddin came from Yemen, Algeria, Egypt and Afghanistan, and many had combat experience. In addition, several hundreds of Islamists came from France, Italy, Germany and Britain. One explanation for this traffic has been provided by Abu Hamza al-Masri, who claimed to understand why young European Muslims would volunteer for the Jihad in Bosnia. In Abu Hamza's words, 'they want to struggle against something that is indisputable, which is non-Muslims raping, killing and maiming Muslims' (Kohlmann 2004).

Lessons learned and lessons ignored

The examples from Afghanistan and Bosnia illustrate that recruitment to Jihad is not a new phenomenon in Europe. A few general observations are appropriate in this respect:

- While some European Muslims expressed their sympathy with the Mujaheddin, very few actually fought.
- Not all of the Jihads have involved Europeans.
- There has been a change in modus operandi from guerrilla warfare to terrorism.

It is not surprising that, of the millions of Muslims living in Europe, some would be attracted to fighting as Mujaheddin or to becoming involved in terrorist activity. Yet, in spite of the inadequate figures available, there are indications that this group was very small indeed. While many European Muslims sympathised with one cause or another, very few actually crossed the line between vocal opposition and armed struggle. This trend clearly illustrates that it has always been a miniscule minority of European Muslims who represented a security risk, whether domestic or international. This phenomenon has not received the attention it actually merits, and further research would enlighten us on different perspectives on armed conflict within the Muslim communities.

The Islamist terrorist presence in Europe was introduced by Egyptians and Algerians in exile who continued their national struggle from European host countries. Primarily, the Egyptian Al-Gama'a Al-Islamiyya and the Algerian GIA carried their violent activities abroad, with the exception of the Algerians who set their sights on France in the mid-1990s. Compared to the support for the Afghans fighting the Soviet Union, the reach and appeal of these groups were limited because they were essentially preoccupied with political struggles in North Africa. Few Europeans fought in Asia, but this aspect was instrumental in creating a sense of spiritual commonality and global visions of Jihad, and, though it took years to develop the concept, this would later affect Europe and the rest of the world. The direct threat from Islamist terrorists to Europe was insignificant until the mid-1990s. There were few Mujaheddin in Europe, and they took no interest in targeting Europe; instead they travelled abroad to take part in Jihads in Chechnya, Kashmir, Tajikistan, Albania and Kosovo.

While the Islamist involvement in Bosnia galvanised the Mujaheddin, it never became the success they had hoped for. Their complete disregard for the local culture alienated the Mujaheddin from their only source of support. The strategy of reinforcing other Muslim communities considered oppressed was to fail again, especially in Kosovo. While al-Qaeda did recruit some members of the UCK, the Kosovo Liberation Army, and later recruited among radical Albanians in Macedonia, because of the intervention by NATO forces the influence of the Islamists was undercut, and the local Muslims of the region realised that they would be much better off if they oriented themselves towards the West and Europe in particular, in spite of the considerable availability of Islamist funds (Vermaat 2002). Foreign Mujaheddin repeated their mistakes while operating with the UCK, having forgotten the hard-learned lesson from Bosnia. Again, their propensity for mindless violence backfired, as testified in the summer of 2001 by a UCK fighter who pointed out that Albanians do not mutilate bodies, only the Mujaheddin (Taylor 2001).

Much of the picture that has been uncovered since 11 September 2001 could have been revealed earlier through studying the writings, speeches and preaching of these scholars and groups during the 1990s. There have been many arrests and investigations of suspected terrorists in Europe over the past three years; so far these activities have focused on the operational levels rather than on the cultural and social infrastructure of this phenomenon (Paz 2002). In the words of Jason Burke, the militants believe they are fighting a last-ditch battle for the survival of their society, culture, religion and way of life (Burke 2004a). Burke's perception is accurate, but exactly what culture and what form of Islam are they defending? Their actions testify to the existence of an introverted, xenophobic and extremely isolated community that tolerates no opposition whatsoever. It is from within this community that the terrorists are being recruited.

Changes affecting recruitment

As briefly illustrated in the previous section, recruitment to Jihad in Europe is not a new phenomenon. Yet significant changes have occurred, both in a long-term perspective and naturally in the wake of 11 September 2001. These changes have altered the European dimension in the global Jihad to the extent that it merits our sincere attention. One of the better analyses of the post-11 September 2001 recruitment structure in Europe comes from the Dutch security service (AIVD). Notwithstanding a little confusion about the terminology used in the report, the findings are clear and prescient. The conclusion reached by the AIVD is that recruitment to Jihad is not a new phenomenon, and that its scope and significance are becoming more important (AIVD 2002). However, in order to fully appreciate the Dutch findings it is necessary to highlight what actual changes have occurred in the recruitment environment.

From noble to savage

The most far-reaching change has largely gone unnoticed over the past two decades. The entire concept of Jihad has been exposed to a very profound transformation. In essence, what started as a noble intent some twenty years ago, intended to assist Muslims in need, has been degraded to such an extent that today Jihad is most often associated with mindless violence directed at civilians. What was previously understood as a form of self-defence against unequivocal aggression is now equated with indiscriminate bombings and beheadings. Contemporary militant Islamists who evoke a recent glorious victory against the Soviet Union in the Afghan war seem to be unaware of the severed ideological link to the very premises of the Afghan resistance. This short span of attention is noteworthy because it signals a very dynamic and ecclesiastical form of reasoning and represents a conceptual downward spiral, enthusiastically supported by a few radical clerics. The clerics who were outcasts ten years ago are now the leading proponents of armed struggle, and it is their uncompromising stance that sets the agenda. In no other respect does this subtle yet all-pervasive change affect the circumstances of the current and continued recruitment to Islamic terrorism in Europe.

The 'Real al-Qaeda'

The al-Qaeda that masterminded 11 September 2001 and created a terrorist infrastructure during the 1990s has suffered serious setbacks and heavy losses. This particular network has been significantly weakened in the global war on terror. The initiative has shifted to a new and younger generation of Islamist terrorists who are much less linked to the original core of al-Qaeda. The new generation is not affiliated with the companionship of the Afghan war, the following civil war, or the environment of the training camps. Possessing weak organisational links to the original al-Qaeda members, they have chosen instead to align themselves with the broader aims of the Global Jihad. The current networks and the associated cells are autonomous to a high degree, and the operatives do not share the organisational history of the old core, but rather display greater independence and a looser structure. There has even been speculation that the new generation sees the old al-Qaeda as an anachronism, and they are very committed to carrying the torch further (Gorka 2004).

The current and very diffuse network of al-Qaeda-inspired or related groups is extremely adaptive and dynamic. Instead of being structured and organised in a traditional organisational sense, the mutual support and coordination between members of the network is on an ad hoc basis and primarily based on a shared vision of a common enemy. Adding to the complexity is the existence of multiple, simultaneously operating networks largely independent from each other. They function like layered networks, so taking one down does not necessarily affect the others. This change in structure from a former core to a new generation of al-Qaeda operatives leads to the term the Real al-Qaeda, which implies that it is the ideological influence of Bin Laden that matters, not the actual operational control, and this corresponds exactly with the strategic vision of al-Qaeda as it was formulated years ago.

The war in Iraq

A significant factor in the transformation of the recruiting environment has been the war in Iraq. Popular opposition to the war was widespread in Europe during 2003 and this also influenced the sentiments in Muslim communities. The vast majority of European Muslims were content to express their disagreement with the invasion of Iraq by peaceful means. Active participation in anti-war demonstrations actually showed an adherence to the European ideal of expressing discontent. Some, however, perceived the invasion of Iraq as a pretext for a Western plot to subdue the Muslim world and to control natural resources in the Middle East. Even fewer people within this group responded to the call to arms to defend Muslims in Iraq.

Before the invasion of Iraq, intelligence and law enforcement officials remarked that the discussion about Iraq in Europe was being exploited by militant Islamists as a recruitment drive. 'Iraq' had become a battle cry and anti-American sermons and rhetoric increased considerably. The message clearly resonated among the young European Muslims who attended the radical talks. According to the official comments, recruitment was most visible in Britain, Germany, Spain, Italy and the Netherlands, specifically targeting a younger audience that included many converts (Natta and Butler 2003).

As observed by Rohan Gunaratna, Iraq is likely to provide a pull identical to that seen in the conflicts in Afghanistan or Bosnia in the 1990s (Gunaratna 2004). The conflict is seen in a much wider scope than that offered by Western governments. Essentially, Iraq has become a land of symbolic value which must be liberated at all costs from foreign aggression. A successful outcome to this conflict is equally important to the militant Islamists and the Western world alike. Whatever direction the situation in Iraq takes it will become a defining moment for both parties, as neither will accept a loss.

Current structure of the recruiting environment

Turning to the current trends in the recruitment environment, one historical feature should be emphasised, that of top-down versus bottom-up recruitment. The Hamburg cell is well suited for illustrating the complexities of this phenomenon. Much has been written about the Hamburg cell – perhaps too much, because the really significant feature of the cell is often obliterated by speculations on suicidal behaviour. Only a few experts have noticed one of the most striking aspects of the Hamburg cell, which is the absence of any form of top-down recruitment and alleged brainwashing of the plotters, both of which have become popular explanations for the growth of the Jihad (Sageman 2004). The Hamburg cell emerged from a convergence of nine people in an upper-middle-class expatriate student community. The terrorists-to-be were devout in their beliefs and practices, which allowed for a network of friendships to form and preceded formal introduction into the global Jihad. As a group they went through an incubation period of almost two years, during which the intensity of their beliefs and sense of brotherhood gradually transformed the members beyond recognition. The actual recruitment process of the Hamburg cell can best be described as highly unstructured in any conventional sense and therefore deserves some attention.

Based on available background information about the members of the Hamburg cell, this example of a recruitment process contained the following elements:

- individual alienation and marginalisation;
- spiritual quest;
- process of radicalisation;
- meeting and associating with likeminded people;
- gradual seclusion and cell formation;
- acceptance of violence as legitimate political means;
- connection with a gatekeeper in the know;
- going operational.

It should be remembered that the above-mentioned stages characterise the recruitment structure of the Hamburg cell and naturally occurred before 11 September 2001. This was in essence a self-generating process from below – and not structured recruitment controlled by an al-Qaeda committee. But, before we turn to the more personal reasons for joining, a cursory understanding of the recruitment structure is required.

Contrary to popular belief, there is no evidence of a top-down recruitment programme in the global Jihad (Sageman 2004). Somewhat naively, the senior leadership of al-Qaeda expected their vision to be so self-evident that recruits would eventually turn up on the doorstep of the Afghan camps, with a little guidance from their European mentors. This optimism obviously has its roots in an ideology that is only self-evident to the committed insider, but it was never rewarded on the anticipated scale. Al-Qaeda experienced internal disagreement throughout the 1990s, and the wave of future Mujaheddin never materialised. What did materialise was a small core of very dedicated individuals, so instead of a structured effort it resembled a process in which only the most radical elements joined a terrorist cell. From a conventional organisational perspective the half-hearted recruitment efforts of the past decade cannot be considered a success, yet those who actually joined were fully committed to the cause. This type of non-structured recruitment is very much in place today, and the phenomenon deserves closer scrutiny because it is a critical element in the further development of the Global Jihad.

The critical and specific element in joining is the accessibility of a link to the Global Jihad. Without the acquaintance of a gatekeeper – someone who can point out active militants to the recruits – the group of friends, students and worshippers will undergo progressive isolation. They may try to participate in the Jihad, but without know-how, resources or coordination with other terrorist cells. Although lethal, their operations do not constitute a serious threat to society. Only the Global Jihad, with its interconnectedness of resources and skills, poses such a danger (Sageman 2004). Largely drawing on Sageman's insights, the process of joining the Global Jihad follows a general pattern that entails specific elements and steps:

- The existence of a strong social affiliation between a group of Islamists. Often this affiliation is shaped by close friendships, kinship or discipleship.
- The group of Islamists embark on progressive social isolation that eventually differentiates between enlightened believers (themselves) and infidels (everybody else).
- The group of Islamists experience a progressive intensification of their beliefs, culminating in an unquestioning acceptance of Jihad, though not in the traditional sense.
- Formal acceptance and entry into the Jihad circuit are granted through acquaintance with a gatekeeper.
- After this relationship is formed they become operational.

The evidence available outlines the significance of social bonds that appear to precede the operational stage. At the mosques, small clusters form quite spontaneously out of personal friendships. Whatever the source of their social bonds, these clusters experience a prolonged period of intense social integration. The closer they become to one another, the more extreme their views. Only in this context is the number of militant Islamists residing in Europe of interest. Recruitment to the Jihad is contingent on a pool of candidates of a sufficient size in order to reconstitute itself, to recover from setbacks, and to forge new links. Without a critical mass to sustain a militant Islamist ideology the Jihad will wither to insignificance.

According to terrorism expert Magnus Ranstorp, the networks are mutating and adapting at lightning speed (USA Today 2002). The severed links to the leadership in Afghanistan are a recent development which has slowed but not stopped communication and coordination efforts. Instead, the cells within the networks are operating more autonomously than in the past. Largely self-supporting cells are now capable of planning and committing attacks relatively independently. Recruitment to the Jihad in Europe also shows that Islamist terrorism is not only a threat aimed at the Western world, but also one that is more and more professionally generated in Europe itself (Akerboom 2003).

While not directly related to Islamist terrorism in Europe, the case of the Casablanca bombings in May 2003 provided some indications of possible developments. The bombers did not go to Afghanistan for training as this was not an option at the time. The only training they received was done by themselves over weekends and cannot be considered professional in any way. Their technical ineptitude resulted in difficulties with the bomb-making process and eventually they were forced to postpone the bombings. A solution to the bomb-manufacturing problems was found on the Internet, allowing them to build explosive devices the day before the operation. Their glaring amateurishness and utter ineptitude did not discourage the bombers in their endeavours. In spite of considerable setbacks their unswerving commitment to the cause produced the desired outcome in the end. A year later this development materialised in Madrid. Again, the terrorists were relatively unsophisticated Islamists. While the inspiration from Osama Bin Laden's al-Qaeda was clear, the organisational links were less so. This development reportedly worried security services in Europe (Kepel 2004). The Madrid operation relied on home-grown Islamist militants who apparently were unconcerned by their lack of a transitional experience in Afghanistan, signifying a European presence of the Real al-Qaeda.

More recently, the Dutch security service (AIVD) noticed a worrying trend that became reality with the assassination of Theo Van Gogh. AIVD has stated that the threat of violence represented by Islamist terrorism has grown into a considerable and permanent exogenous and endogenous threat. The cases of recruitment for the Jihad with which the Netherlands has been confronted over the past few years have shown that a violent, radical Islamic movement is gradually taking root in Dutch society (Akerboom 2003). The Dutch example is representative of the general development in Europe as regards the direction of the threat. From the problem of infiltration prevalent years ago, the centre of gravity has shifted to the domestic production of Jihadists.

Robert S. Leiken from the Nixon Center concluded in his 2004 report on US immigration and national security problems that, while the terrorist threat to the US is exogenous, the European threat is endogenous. In short, while the US has to worry about foreign hit squads, Europe must contend with home-grown terrorists. Naturally, this has wide implications for counterterrorism policy on both sides of the Atlantic (Leiken 2004).

Who is being recruited?

As outlined in the introduction, the terrorists mentioned in this study are all Muslims. But what kind of Muslim is susceptible to recruitment to the Jihad? Unfortunately, this question is not easily answered; however, it is possible to make a few general assertions in order to dispel some popular myths. The most persistent of these myths concerns the role of Islam. One of the prevailing arguments in the counterterrorism debate is the trouble with Islam. But to single out a major religion as the single explanatory model for the support of terrorism reflects uninformed prejudice and a profound lack of imagination. I have vehemently and persistently argued that this assumption is dangerously misleading because it distracts attention from the multi-dimensional causes of Islamism and its offshoot, Islamist terrorism (Taarnby 2002, 2003). When terrorists readily hijack commercial airliners, public schools and relief workers, it should come as no surprise that they also hijack Islam to further their cause. Their claim to represent an Islamic truth is far too often left unchallenged. The sheer complexity involved in understanding the causes of Islamist terrorism undermines any attempt at simplifying the phenomenon, and this perspective will be clarified in this section.

Muslims in Europe

That European Muslims are the target of recruitment to Jihad is obvious, but what kind of Muslims? Although this study is about current trends instead of statistics, a few figures are relevant to place the recruitment environment in its proper context. No one knows how many Muslims are living in Europe, and for good reason. Religious belief is a personal matter and is not registered in Europe. Estimates vary considerably, from twelve to twenty million in total. The correct figure is basically irrelevant; what matters is the extent of the radicalisation process within the Islamic community – or, to be more precise, communities, because it is quite misleading to speak of a single, unified Islamic community. The existence of a single community, in Quranic terminology called the Umma, is a figment of the imagination in Islamist circles. In reality, there are hundreds, if not thousands, of Islamic communities, each defined by its religious practices and specific culture.

That the recruitment process focuses on young Muslim men is indisputable, but there are invisible yet very real divisions that are unbridgeable in Muslim Europe.

An example of the inherent limitations in recruitment is the exclusion of Shi'a Muslims. They are considered heretics by the proponents of militant Islamism, and this religious fault line prevents any form of allegiance. That a Shi'a movement such as Hezbollah has its sympathisers and fundraisers in Europe only adds to the confusion. The Shi'a Islamists inhabit a different environment separate from the Salafi or Wahabi militants. Another example would be the absence of any significant component of Turks in the terrorist networks, despite the millions of Turks residing in Europe. European radical Turks certainly exist; however, they seem to prefer other venues for expressing discontent. In short, they are not the ones who become Salafist bomb makers. From these simple but important observations it can be deduced that the global Jihad only appeals to a certain segment of European Muslims.

Mark Juergensmeyer points in the right direction when he asserts that all the groups that have advocated religiously justified terrorism have been marginal, to varying degrees, to their own religious societies (Juergensmeyer 2003). Marginality preceded the violent acts and this sequencing is of the greatest importance. Whether or not the marginality was put on public display proudly, or hidden from public view because of feelings of shame and guilt, the ensuing violence became a means of empowering the individual as well as the group. This marginality can be viewed either from the inside or the outside. The insiders are those within the Islamic communities who can identify with the experiences of those feeling marginalised, while the outsiders are those who have little understanding of the conditions facing Europe's plethora of Muslim communities. Again, drawing on Juergensmeyer's insights, the terrorists' perspectives are shaped by socio-political realities of their immediate environment, which in turn provokes a radical response in religious cloaking.

Striking among the European Islamists who have embraced terrorism is their newfound spirituality. In rejecting the superficiality and emptiness of secular modernity, where they do not fit in, they logically become attracted to a religious ideology that promises to fill the vacuum. The Islamist ideologues promise only an uphill struggle towards personal fulfilment, but this does not seem to discourage their followers: on the contrary, they are more than ready for a challenge as long as it also involves a higher meaning. In resorting to a 'traditional religion' which is anything but traditional, they have exposed their concerns not for the fate of mankind, Islamic civilization or Islamic communities, but for themselves. As Robert S. Leiken emphasises in a comparative study, the alienated Muslim communities in Europe would appear to be a much more fertile ground for recruitment for radical groups than Muslim communities in the US (Leiken 2004). Through his case studies, Leiken noticed the difference in the level of integration and assimilation between US and French Islamist sleeper cells. Leiken's analysis resulted in a distinction between two types of candidates for Muslim terrorists, the outsiders and the insiders. The outsiders are the aliens, foreign dissidents, students or asylum seekers, some of whom have sought refuge from anti-Islamic crackdowns in the Middle East or North Africa. The insiders are citizens from the downwardly mobile second-generation immigrants from Muslim countries (Leiken 2004).

I am inclined to argue that Leiken's typology could be augmented by a third type, that of the European convert. Supporting this view is the excellent study by the Dutch security service (AIVD) from 2003 on the recruitment of Islamist terrorists in the Netherlands. AIVD had identified a few dozen individuals under suspicion of being involved in a recruitment process. They were all young Muslim men between eighteen and thirty-two years old who fell into three general categories: converts, recent immigrants and second-generation immigrants. Each of these three categories deserves some attention.

Outsiders and recent immigrants

Newcomers to Europe sometimes experience confusion about their new situation. Being cut off from their community of origin and unable to understand their new country leads to social isolation and an identity crisis. While many students, migrant workers and asylum seekers are familiar with such a situation, only a few become overwhelmed by the experience. The best example is the Hamburg cell, which was largely composed of foreign students. Their individual identity crisis in an expatriate community made them look for a source of companionship, and the most accessible place to meet new friends with similar backgrounds was the mosque. Here, various types of shared, negative cross-cultural experiences formed the basis of a small circle of friends. The mosque environment became a source of stability that served to counter their poor assimilation. Some were religious before moving to Europe, but most were not and very few were militant Islamists.

The transformation necessitated a transplantation into an alien culture; it did not occur in the country of origin. The religious revival was not anchored in tradition, but instead in individuals who experienced a profound crisis of identity. Their faith is extremely emotionally oriented and disregards both theology and tradition (Roy 2003). In trying to reconstruct an identity they naturally discard their original as well as European culture and instead direct their energies toward an imagined community. This is the Umma, the all-encompassing spiritual community of believers, and this is where individuals like Mohammed Atta, Ziad Jarrah and Marwan al-Shehhi found refuge.

Second-generation immigrants

The reason why second-generation immigrants would be susceptible to recruitment is complex. Arrested terrorists have often been described as seemingly well-integrated, in itself a contradiction in terms. The terrorists were apparently only superficially integrated, and their rejection of society points to a more complex motivation, as witnessed by their deep resentment (Laquer 2004).

Studies of the French recruits have been helpful in understanding their turn-around. According to Gilles Kepel, they appear to follow a typical trajectory. These young Muslims were all born in Europe and basically tumble into the Islamist circles. The first stage is brainwashing at the hands of a Salafist imam. Later they meet an actual recruiter, who offers to quench their thirst for absolutes through a militant activism. This progression is neither systematic nor inevitable, and often there is a struggle between Salafist imams and the militant Islamists (Kepel 2004). The keyword in Kepel's analysis is tumble, because it is not possible to brainwash someone who is not susceptible. A confused mindset is the mandatory first step. Disillusioned with the society that has excluded them and tired of the empty promises of the official France, second-generation immigrants frequent the mosque to meet likeminded people. Islam becomes a way to restore their dignity. In the words of Sageman, 'People who are satisfied with life are unlikely to join a religious revivalist terrorist movement' (Sageman 2004).

According to a DST report on the recruitment of young Muslims to Jihad, Islamism represents a vehicle of protest against problems of access to employment and housing, discrimination of various kinds, and the highly negative image of Islam in public opinion (DST 2003). Zacarias Moussaoui fits this description because he rejected his parents' North African origin and did not assimilate into Western culture. He eventually found a way of expressing his discontent through what Roy has called neo-fundamentalism, a term that signifies a complete lack of allegiance to any roots (Roy 2003). A number of European Muslims who followed this trajectory have since been arrested in Europe or are imprisoned at Guantanamo.

A similar pattern has been detected in the Netherlands by the AIVD, where the second-generation terrorists are predominantly of Moroccan origin. They were either born in the Netherlands or moved there at a very young age. The majority are Dutch citizens who display little affiliation with Morocco and do not master Arabic. In the Dutch case, this group is the most active in the recruitment process. They blame Dutch society for not respecting their ethnic and religious community, to which they have very weak links. They are often guided by former Mujaheddin and, in the process, have developed a strong personal affiliation (AIVD 2004).

Converts

Individuals who have converted to Islam represent a miniscule minority in the ranks of the militant Islamists; however, they are potentially highly deployable for Jihad. While it is difficult to create a general impression of the converts' background, it would appear that they also come from the margins of society, with a few exceptions that prove there is no single profile.

The complete break with the society and culture of origin has not been examined properly and many questions remain unanswered. However, I do suspect that Olivier Roy is on the right track when he claims that the core issue is not linked to theology but to post-modernism. Those converts of interest to this study embraced Islam vigorously and proceeded to militant Islam. They entered mainstream Islam just as quickly as they deviated, thus raising some fundamental questions about their spiritual bearings. Converts who adopt Jihad as a lifestyle apparently do not possess the cultural or religious grounding necessary to assess the tenets of Islamism independently. It is considerably easier to convince a convert about the religious obligation of Jihad.

Some German converts ended up fighting with Mujaheddin against disbelievers in Chechnya and Bosnia. In the case of Germany, many converts have a special story. Often they are extremely attached to their religion and, wanting to prove themselves to their new fellow Muslims, they take their conversion very seriously and for this reason have a strong desire to demonstrate their religious commitment. As such they are an ideal target group for the terrorist organisations, who assist them in joining the Mujaheddin or send them abroad for further indoctrination – like Christian Ganzcarski and Thomas Fischer from Ulm who was killed in Chechnya in November 2003 (Rasche 2004). Some were sent to Damuscus in order to study Islam but were inserted into regular strongholds of Hamas and the Muslim Brotherhood.

The three types of young European Muslims who are susceptible to recruitment originate from a very diverse range of individual backgrounds, yet they all embraced militant Islam unconditionally. Marginalisation was present in one form or another before they accepted violent activism. The sequence of marginalisation preceding religious revival confirms the view that although Islam is an important aspect in understanding Islamist terrorism, the data available strongly suggests that social conditions serve as the foundation.

Much remains to be explored to understand why militant Islamism becomes an attractive alternative. One thing nevertheless appears certain: that motivation is a complex issue and cannot be reduced to any single factor (Nesser 2004). In cancelling their membership of society and pledging allegiance to an imaginary community, the various types of European Islamist terrorists increasingly see themselves as a part of the global Jihad.

It would appear that recruitment in Europe is somewhat structured along national and ethnic lines. For instance, in the summer of 2004 the UK intelligence service made a list of the names of 100 Islamist activists suspected of being involved in terrorist activities. The majority are British citizens and mainly of Pakistani descent (Burke 2004b), a number of whom have fought with militant Islamist groups in Kashmir. An example of the Kashmir connection is Sheikh Ahmed.

As regards national or ethnic affiliation, the Hamburg cell is perhaps the most heterogeneous example available. Quite a few of the cells that have been discovered over the past three years display some sort of similarity. An example is the Madrid cell, which was overwhelmingly North African with a few members of Middle Eastern origin. Out of the eighteen provisionally charged in connection with the March 2004 bombings in Madrid, fourteen were Moroccans.

Six out of the seven suspects who died in the blast in a Madrid apartment in April were also Moroccans. According to Spanish authorities, a prime suspect is Rabei Osman Sayed Ahmed, known as Mohammed the Egyptian, and it is presumed that Ahmed recruited Sarhane Ben Abdelmajid Fakhet at a mosque in Madrid (Haahr-Escolano 2004). Until his death in the explosion at the apartment in Leganes, Fakhet was the head of a fully operational cell that had success-fully recruited candidates within Spain. He formed his cell around North African immigrants like himself, and was able to shape the group into a well-organised and disciplined group. Fakhet was the Imam of a small mosque located in a base-ment in central Madrid. The significance of national or ethnic affiliation has not yet been explored properly and further studies would reveal if there is a pattern to the process of cell formation.

The recruitment process

A successful relationship between the recruiter and the prospective Islamist ter-rorist is highly contingent on a structure of oppositional character traits. This is not as confusing as it may seem, and a brief elaboration on a few traits makes the dual nature of this relationship quite understandable. Any recruiter who wants to attract followers into an extremist and militant ideology is of a special char-acter by any definition, exploiting his inter-personal skills in a manipulative and destructive way. The special character traits can, for obvious security reasons, rarely be displayed in public but are instead confined to one-on-one encounters, where the recruiter has an opportunity to affirm his superior position towards the candidate in a number of areas through the subtle stressing of the differences between them.

In relation to oppositional character traits I have listed seven topics, though more can no doubt be added:

- true believer/apostate;
- wise/unenlightened;
- leader/unguided;
- respected/rejected;
- brother/outsider;
- honourable/dishonourable;
- activist/powerless.

First of all, the recruiter personalises the true believer, whereas the candidate is treated as an unenlightened individual, a Muslim who has not yet realised the true meaning of Islam. This superiority of religious adherence also conveys the image of someone who holds wisdom, again testifying to the lack of religious education and grounding of the candidate. The recruiter presents himself as a leader, which draws attention to the candidate's unguided nature and confused lifestyle. This situation commands respect from someone who himself is in need of recognition and direction, and the subtly hierarchical dimension is further reinforced by an artificial form of brotherhood in which the recruiter portrays himself as a true brother whose disciple is a prospect – i.e. not yet a fully accepted member. The allusion to a sense of brotherhood introduces a sense of honour between the recruiter, who might believe his own words, and the candidate who until then had no allegiances. Having discovered The Right Way, the recruiter wants to be seen as a doer who actually acts on his revelation, which in turn appeals to someone who feels powerless to change even his own situation. The recruitment relationship is necessarily founded on inequality, although the recruiter will go to great lengths to stress the equality between two Muslims.

The process of transformation from an alienated individual to a committed activist is commonly seen in religious sects and terrorist groups and requires investment in intense and lengthy personal interactions. This implies that the fear that vulnerable young Muslims may be recruited to the Jihad through internet messages is overblown. Reading and sending messages about the Jihad on the Internet may make these individuals receptive to its appeal, but direct involvement requires interaction (Sageman 2004).

There is no doubt that the attacks on 11 September 2001 revitalised an interest in the global Jihad among European Muslims, though this interest should not be confused with sympathy. While the vast majority of Europe's Muslims were content to discuss the events and to condemn one side or the other, or even both, a parallel development occurred among a small segment of Muslim youth who became radicalised. Some expressed their views through attacks and vandalism on Jewish targets, while others openly advocated militant action and terrorism. The latter group might possibly be relatively easy prey for recruitment. Rather than a traditional Islamic trait, it is much more an explosive mixture of political realities and negative socio-cultural experiences that makes Islamist terrorism attractive for European Muslims.

Where are they being recruited?

Before 11 September 2001 European Islamists would usually operate more or less openly through certain mosques, Islamic information centres, Islamic schools and charities. Open as well as covert support was extended to the Mujaheddin in Chechnya and Afghanistan, to the apparent indifference of the authorities. Examples of radical mosques that became prominent in the process of affiliation with the Jihad are Finsbury Park Mosque in London, the Islamic Cultural Centre in Milan, the Abu Bakr Mosque in Madrid and the al-Quds Mosque in Hamburg. Throughout the 1990s these localities served as the gateway to the global Jihad and dispatched militant young Muslims to training sites in Afghanistan or to the front lines in Bosnia and Chechnya.

While there is no disputing the centrality of the above locations in the European network of militant Islamists, it is inappropriate to label these institutions as recruiting centres. They appear to have played an ambiguous role in the recruitment process, mostly serving as a radicalising agent. It is commonly assumed that the terrorists were recruited at the mosque, and this is certainly true in some cases, but most significantly it was the social environment at the mosque or religious institution that transformed young and alienated Muslims into terrorists.

Radical Islamist movements

On the transnational level there have been many speculations about the nature of the various radical Islamist movements and their role in supporting terrorism. This is indeed a complex matter and is not analysed easily; however, the radical movements are worth noticing because they appear to play a central, if indirect, role. While it is indisputable that some European Islamist terrorists have maintained very close links with, for instance, the al-Muhajiroun, the Tabligh and the Takfir wal-Hijra, many others did not.

A working hypothesis could benefit from a distinction between channels of radicalisation and actual end stations for full-blown militant Islamists in order to understand the significance of the radical movements. The above-mentioned movements certainly adhere to the most radical interpretations of Islamism, but strictly speaking they cannot be considered terrorist organisations. Then why have these movements in particular so often been associated with Islamist terrorism?

To take an example from France, the Tabligh movement illustrates the connection. The Tabligh is a pietistic movement that encourages recruitment among those who do not know their faith. Its spiritual centre is the ar-Rahma Mosque in St Denis, near Paris, and it has been active in France since 1968. The Tabligh is foremost a religious and spiritual movement, and focuses on teaching a correct understanding of Islam and what it means to be Muslim. Some of its members have gone to Pakistan for an extended stay in one of the movement's centres. It is believed that some Tabligh members later went on to training camps in Afghanistan, and onwards to Jihad, although the Tabligh does not promote violence. Instead, as Camus has pointed out, the lengthy and strict period of spiritual indoctrination has resulted in some profound personal changes in certain individuals who afterwards seem to have developed a deep interest in militant groups (Camus 2004).

While not directly linked to the global Jihad, the radical movements seem to function like a greenhouse of sorts, to use a term coined by Reuven Paz. The radical movement is the indirect framework of support created by groups that are not connected to political violence or terrorism; indeed, some of them publicly condemn such methods. These groups carry out considerable political, social, cultural and educational work in the name of Islam. As such, they preserve the Islamic atmosphere in which more extremist and violent groups thrive (Paz 2002). Adding to the complexity is the presence of a number of underground mosques that encourage support for the global Jihad. Rarely connected to any established radical movement, they are run by imams who lack credentials and qualifications. Moderate European Muslims have lashed out at what they call garage-based mosques, clearly signalling their contempt (Haahr-Escolano 2004). A group of friends who spontaneously meet in such mosques constitute one of the main venues for joining the Jihad. Their voluntary seclusion from the rest of society, European and Muslim communities as well, could be a model for future recruitment patterns and this was in essence what took place in the formation of the Madrid cell.

Conclusion

Police and intelligence operations are the visible elements in contemporary counterterrorism. These are, needless to say, indispensable, but do not address the roots of the problem. Averting the next attack obviously has priority, but this can be done only when there is a thorough understanding of the Islamist environment. The role of the security services is vital but is only the tip of the iceberg. As this study indicates, it is at the level of socially disparate groups that recruits to the global Jihad can be found, and only there. And this is outside the scope and competence of the security services.

Baltasar Garzon, the Spanish counterterrorism magistrate, aptly summed up the situation: 'There is an enormous amount of information, but much of it gets lost because of failure to cooperate. There is a lack of communication, a lack of coordination and a lack of any broad vision' (Golden 2004). The last point, which concerns the lack of a vision, is the most worrying, especially when the EU is deeply involved in a long-term asymmetrical conflict. For this broader vision to be meaningful it must be founded on a better understanding of the ideological, cultural, religious and social factors of this phenomenon in order to counter it efficiently. This is the role of the research community.

Much more research is needed to understand the complexities involved in the current process of terrorist recruitment in Europe. Andrew Silke has summed up the predicament quite well: 'Yet three decades of study on terrorism has taught one lesson with certainty, and that is that terrorism is not a simple phenomenon with easy explanations and direct solutions. On the contrary it is a highly complex subject' (Silke 2003). The modest amount of research that does exist on Islamist terrorism in Europe is highly fragmentary, often outdated and contains little data to support the conclusions. The lack of academic attention to the radicalisation process in Europe has left the field wide open to interpretations of all sorts, often founded on guesswork.

The systematic gathering of available information on individual terrorists and their respective organisations is indispensable to eliminate the current profusion of guesswork in this particular field. The information collected would serve as the basis for informed analysis of a difficult and complex topic, and, as this author speculates, would reveal a number of interesting patterns. Detailed case studies of terrorist organisations active in Europe are needed, especially with an eye to comparative studies. The radicalisation process which fuels the recruitment into the Jihad has not followed an identical trajectory across European societies. While some countries are currently faced with a serious security problem that threatens social stability, others have been spared this development. These different trajectories are little understood and it is quite possible that a closer look at the differences would reveal a number of entry points for action to counter not just terrorism but radicalisation.

The war on terrorism is no longer the same as in the aftermath of 11 September 2001. The al-Qaeda that conceived, planned and executed the strikes on the US some four years ago has largely been eliminated or driven underground to the extent where it has lost its global operational reach. Instead a number of 'al-Qaedas' have sprung up, merged or realigned, and Europe lies firmly along the various trajectories of the changing Jihad. This development has occurred at unprecedented speed and only one thing seems certain – and that is continued uncertainty. This in turn requires a new approach to understanding the ideologies and motivations that are the driving forces of the Jihad. The most discussed messages from the al-Qaeda leadership have been eclipsed by a profusion of publications, some of which are considerably more radical and vitriolic than statements not yet a decade old. Studies of the changes in contemporary militant Islamist ideology should therefore be very high on Europe's to-do list.

That recruitment into militant Islamism is intrinsically linked to the current increased interest in various forms of radical ideology among Europe's Muslims has been outlined previously. Terrorism is not an isolated phenomenon, but is closely linked to issues like marginalization, questions of identity, religious identity, political protest – just to mention a few. Efforts to identify the factors that lead to terrorism in a European context, often called the root causes, are still in their early stages and need to be expanded considerably. The search for the root causes of Islamist terrorism has led some observers to become distracted at a time when it is of singular importance to differentiate between various types of Jihad. Solving the Palestinian problem, which is unquestioningly connected to terrorism, will do nothing to alleviate a profound sense of socio-cultural alienation in a European suburb. These phenomena are basically unrelated, and solving one will not make the other go away. Problems that originate in marginalisation and alienation are currently being channelled into a global cause that insists on solidarity between Muslims. While it is important that the EU supports the development of democracy abroad, it needs to turn its attention to the home-grown threat as well; anything else would border on the irresponsible. Whether the European Union is up to the task of countering radicalisation and terrorism remains to be proven.

European Muslims have too often been lumped together and described as an entity when in fact they form numerous distinct communities. Olivier Roy has suggested that we develop and consult a new sociology which he terms 'Euro Islam', and this is a point well made (Roy 2003). Without solid and evidence-based research, counterterrorism policies lack the foundation for carrying out the right decisions. We should ask ourselves whether we are asking the right questions. Do we even know what we don't know?

References

AIVD (2002). *Recruitment for the Jihad in the Netherlands. From Incident to Trend.* General Intelligence and Security Service of the Netherlands (AIVD).

AIVD (2004). *Background of Jihad Recruits in the Netherlands.* General Intelligence and Security Service of the Netherlands (AIVD).

Akerboom, E. S. M. (2003). *Counter-Terrorism in the Netherlands.* General Intelligence and Security Service of the Netherlands (AIVD).

Barnet, A. (2004). Terror cells regroup – and new their target is Europe. *The Guardian*, 11 January.

Burke, J. (2004a). *Al Qaeda. The True Story of Radical Islam.* London: Penguin.

Burke, J. (2004b). British terrorist suspect list deeply flawed. *The Guardian*.

Camus, J.-Y. (2004). Islam in France. *ICT*.

DST (D.d.l.S.d.T.) (2003). *Processus d'Enrolement des Jeunes Musulmans dans le Jihad.* Paris: DST.

Golden, T. (2004). Terror suspects slip through Europe's jurisdictional cracks. *International Herald Tribune*, 22 March.

Gorka, S. (2004). al-Qaeda's next generation. *Terrorism Monitor* **2**(15).

Gunaratna, R. (2004). The Post-Madrid face of Al Qaeda. *Washington Quarterly* **27**(3).

Haahr-Escolano, K. (2004). Spain's 9/11: The Moroccan connection. *The Jamestown Foundation Terrorism Monitor* **2**(13).

Juergensmeyer, M. (2003). *Terror in the Mind of God. The Global Rise of Religious Violence.* Berkeley, CA: University of California Press.

Kepel, G. (2004). *The War for Muslim Minds. Islam and the West.* Cambridge, MA: Harvard University Press.

Kohlmann, E. F. (2004). *al-Qaida's Jihad in Europe. The Afghan–Bosnian Network.* Oxford: Berg.

Laquer, W. (2004). The terrorism to come. *Policy Review* **126**.

Leiken, R. S. (2004). *Bearers of Global Jihad? Immigration and National Security after 9/11.* Washington D.C. The Nixon Center.

Natta, D. V. and D. Butler (2003). Anger on Iraq seen as new Qaeda recruiting tool. *New York Times*, 16 March.

Nesser, P. (2004). *Jihad in Europe. Exploring the Sources of Motivations for Salafi–Jihadi Terrorism in Europe Post-Millenium.* Oslo: Norwegian Defense Research Establishment (FFI).

Paz, R. (2002). Global Jihad and the European arena. Presentation at the International Conference on Intelligence and Terrorism, Priverno, Italy, May 2002.

Rasche, U. (2004). From Jesus to Mohammed. *Frankfurter Allgemeine*, 27 August.

Roy, O. (2003). EuroIslam: The Jihad within? *National Interest* (71).

Sageman, M. (2004). *Understanding Terrorist Networks.* Philadelphia, PA: University of Pennsylvania Press.

Silke, A. (2003). An introduction to terrorism research. In: A. Silke (ed.), *Terrorism Research: Trends, Achievements and Failures.* London: Frank Cass.

Taarnby, M. (2002). *Motivational Parameters in Islamic Terrorism.* Aarhus: Centre for Cultural Research, University of Aarhus.

Taarnby, M. (2003). *Profiling Islamic Suicide Terrorists.* Danish Ministry of Justice.

Taylor, S. (2001). Bin Laden's Balkan connections. *Ottawa Citizen.*

USA Today (2002). Terrorists spread all over Europe. *USA Today*, 22 July.

Vermaat, E. (2002). Bin Laden's terror networks in Europe. *The Mackenzie Institute.*

Part II

UNPACKING THE COUNTERTERRORISM TOOLBOX

9

INTELLIGENCE ANALYSIS
AND COUNTERTERRORISM:
HOW LIES THE LANDSCAPE?

Martin Rudner

Recent events in the domain of intelligence have highlighted the centrality of intelligence analysis for responding appropriately and effectively to threats to national security. In the wake of the intelligence failures associated with the September 11th 2001 attacks on the United States and with Iraq's presumed Weaponry of Mass Destruction (WMD), several governments embarked on official inquiries – in the United States the 9/11 Commission[1] and Presidential Commission on US Intelligence Capabilities;[2] in Australia the Flood inquiry;[3] in Israel, the Knesset Foreign Affairs Committee [Shteinitz] enquiry;[4] in the United Kingdom, the Butler inquiry[5] – of unprecedented scale and comprehensiveness into their respective intelligence systems. The lessons learned, in all cases, emphasized the importance of intelligence analysis in national security tradecraft. A common finding was the urgent need for reliable, timely and actionable intelligence assessments for policy-makers; a common recommendation was to bolster up the analytical capacity of the intelligence services in order to avert repeated failures in future. Even Canada, which was not party to the military coalition against Iraq, saw fit nevertheless to issue its first-ever National Security Policy in April 2004, which called for an enhanced intelligence analysis capability to deal with contemporary threats from international terrorism.[6]

The present study surveys recent research into the intelligence analysis function, while also exploring the emergent role of intelligence analysis in the counterterrorism effort. The first section will address the institutional initiatives undertaken by the governments concerned in response to the findings of their respective inquiries as regards the place of intelligence analysis in national intelligence machinery. The next section will examine conceptual responses in terms of the development of new paradigms and refinement of existing paradigms for intelligence analysis. It will also survey the various approaches being introduced to validate and apply these new analytical methodologies, and the role of academic and non-governmental organizations in support of intelligence analysis capacity building. We conclude with a consideration of some of the challenges, constraints and deficiencies encountered in the process of strengthening institutional capabilities for intelligence analysis, especially as regards counterterrorism.

Institutional responses: coordination and fusion of intelligence analysis

The responses of Australia, Canada, the UK and the US to the aforementioned events and reports related to both the institutional and conceptual dimensions of intelligence analysis. On the institutional side the pertinent authorities moved to introduce more centralized direction and coordination over their intelligence machinery, on the one hand, and to promote greater fusion and all-source integration for terrorism threat assessments, on the other. In some countries, and in particular the United States, the issue of intelligence reform generated considerable controversy and sometimes contradictory proposals. Other countries, such as Israel and indeed Canada, remained somewhat more cautious and chary of embarking on institutional adjustments to the perceived threat environment. Nevertheless, the institutional initiatives that were taken by many countries tended to accentuate the central role of intelligence assessment in the workings of their intelligence machinery generally, and the fusion of all-source intelligence analysis as regards the counterterrorism effort in particular.

United States

The March 2005 report of the Presidential Commission on the Intelligence Services and Weapons of Mass Destruction (WMD) attributed the American intelligence community's failure as regards Iraqi WMD to its 'inability to collect good information about Iraq's WMD programs, serious errors in analyzing what information it could gather and a failure to make clear just how much of its analysis was based on assumptions rather than good evidence.' To remedy these deficiencies, the US Congress had legislated a reform of the American intelligence system which created a new position of Director of National Intelligence, intended to be the President's principal intelligence advisor and the head of the Intelligence Community, along with a high-level, specialized intelligence assessment unit, the National Counterterrorism Center (NCTC). The Director of National Intelligence was given responsibility and authority to manage programs, budgets and coordination among the various components of the US intelligence community.

NCTC was assigned overall responsibility within the US Government for integrating foreign and domestic intelligence related to terrorism, and to conduct strategic planning for counterterrorism operations at home and abroad. The Director of NCTC reports to the Director of National Intelligence, but also briefs the President on counterterrorism matters.

These organizational changes were intended to provide the President and Administration policy-makers with integrated, high quality and reliable intelligence products relating to threats to national security, whilst also improving the warning function of intelligence.

Although the reform legislation was designed to improve coordination and information-sharing between agencies, the Presidential Commission identified a potential "problem" at the very apex of the newly reformed intelligence system. The structure of authority postulated by the reform statute implied a potential role conflict between the Director of National Intelligence, who is to serve as the President's chief adviser on all intelligence activities, including terrorism, and the Director of the National Counterterrorism Center, who is subordinate to the Director of National Intelligence but is tasked to brief the President on counterterrorism matters. This responsibility of the NCTC Director may well undercut the authority of the Director of National Intelligence as regards the most pressing threats of the day.

United Kingdom

Following upon the report of the Butler inquiry, a high-level committee chaired by the Co-ordinator of Security and Intelligence in the Cabinet Office, Sir David Omand, recommended full acceptance of the Inquiry's criticism that key elements of intelligence – and the assumptions underpinning their interpretation – should be subject to rigorous testing and validation before being incorporated in assessments sent to ministers and government clients.[7] Toward that end, institutional changes have been introduced in order to create a more rigorous and coordinated framework for intelligence assessment, both at the Cabinet Office level and amongst the intelligence community itself.

At the Cabinet Office, the Joint Intelligence Committee (JIC) is responsible for providing ministers and senior officials with coordinated inter-departmental intelligence assessments on a wide spectrum of issues relating to foreign affairs, national security and defence.[8] The JIC is supported by an assessment staff, composed of analysts seconded from intelligence services and other pertinent government departments. The assessment staff is tasked with drafting assessments of situations and issues of security concern to the UK, and with providing early warning of threats to British interests and other international crises. Recent changes inspired by the Butler inquiry have resulted in an expansion of the assessment staff by about a third, to forty analysts. As well, a separate "B" team is being established to challenge assessments, precisely to diminish the risk of "group think" which concerned Lord Butler and to improve longer-term thinking about future prospective threats.[9]

Another innovation in the Cabinet Office was the appointment of a Reporting Officer, a so-called "R" (analogous to "C", the head of the Secret Intelligence Service MI-6), to serve as challenger-in-chief within the assessment staff to review and validate findings and exercise quality control over assessments before submission to the JIC. In keeping with the post-Butler thrust to intelligence assessment, "R" is expected to probe analytical assumptions, verify methodologies and evaluate findings.

At the level of the intelligence services, the Joint Terrorism Analysis Centre (JTAC) was set up already in June 2003, well before the Butler inquiry reported, as a multi-agency mechanism for producing and disseminating timely, robust all-source intelligence analysis products relating to international terrorism.[10] The centre is staffed by analysts seconded from the British intelligence services and other relevant government departments, and from the Police. Its remit includes the determination of threat levels and the issuance of alerts, as well as the production of detailed reports on trends in international terrorism for a wide range of government customers. While JTAC serves as a multi-agency intelligence assessment unit, its head is accountable to the Director-General of the Security Service, the domestic security intelligence agency also known as MI-5.

The reforms to intelligence assessment, while intended to promote contestation and synthesis among analytical units, can also lead to a confusion of roles, avoidance behavior and analytical gridlock as between "R" and the assessment staff, and between the assessment staff and its B team. If intelligence analysis is to avoid "group-think", as Lord Butler posited, it must likewise avert becoming embroiled with its close relation, consensual accommodation to mere "balance of probabilities" assessments. An adversarial process may produce not "truth to power", rather it could come up with competing and unaligned – and contentious – products and opinions that percolate upward for resolution at the policy level, an entirely unsatisfactory process for intelligence assessment.

The reformed British system may also be vulnerable to role confusion and discrepancy between the JIC and JTAC as regards the analysis and assessment of terrorist threats. JIC is responsible for providing Cabinet ministers and senior officials with coordinated inter-departmental intelligence assessments of national security matters, including terrorist threats. JTAC, for its part, is charged with producing all-source intelligence assessments on the activities, intentions and capabilities of international terrorists who may threaten British and allied interests worldwide.[11] JIC assessments of terrorism are expected to be more "strategic" by way of contextualizing JTAC assessments in broader "geopolitical" terms for Ministers and senior officials.[12] However, this role differentiation could become blurred and problematic in actual practice, producing non-congruent assessments that might confuse rather than impart actionable intelligence.

Australia

The Australian response to the Flood inquiry prompted a substantial building up of intelligence capacity at the core of an all-of-government approach to combating terrorism.[13] Increased analytical resources were vested in the Office of National Assessment (ONA), the central, all-source analytical and assessment unit in the Department of the Prime Minister and Cabinet. As well, a multi-agency National Threat Assessment Centre (NTAC) was established under the aegis of the Australian Security Intelligence Organization (ASIO), the domestic security intelligence agency, to engage in all-source monitoring and assessment of terrorist and other politically motivated threats to Australia and Australian interests abroad. Its staff is seconded to NTAC from ASIO, the Australian Federal Police, the Australian Secret Intelligence Service (ASIS), the Defence Intelligence Organisation (DIO), the Department of Foreign Affairs and Trade, the Department of Transport and Regional Services and the Office of National Assessments. The DIO has also acquired expanded counterterrorism analytical capabilities of its own. The wide-spectrum fusion of Australian threat assessments in a single centre is expected to enable faster production of threat assessments and greater assurance that all relevant information available to Australian agencies is taken into account in their preparation.

NTAC assessments are used in government decision-making about national security policies and operational measures, and are a factor in determining the national counterterrorism alert level. A new inter-agency mechanism, the International Counter-Terrorism Coordination Group, was created to coordinate and focus the efforts of the domestic and foreign intelligence services, police, customs, defence force, immigration, transport agencies, legal, development cooperation and financial authorities on responding to terrorist threats.

Canada

Canada's National Security Policy provided for the appointment of a National Security Advisor in the Privy Council Office, to serve as high-level coordinator of intelligence and security services and as purveyor of intelligence products to the Prime Minister and Cabinet.[14] In parallel, a renamed Intelligence Assessment Secretariat, now the International Assessment Staff (IAS), which served as the central assessment unit in the Privy Council Office, was substantially expanded. The IAS focuses on the production of "strategic" international intelligence assessments for policy makers and other government clients, based on in-depth all-source analysis.

Most components of Canada's security and intelligence community had also expanded their own integral analytical capabilities for tactical intelligence, including the Canadian Security Intelligence Service (CSIS), the Communications Security Establishment (CSE), the Financial Transactions and Reports Analysis Centre (Fintrac), the Royal Canadian Mounted Police (RCMP), and departments of National Defence, Transport, Citizenship and Immigration, Public Safety and Emergency Preparedness, and the Canadian Revenue Agency. Intelligence analysis functions are also performed by the provincial Police forces of Ontario and Québec apropos crime and terrorism. A multi-agency Integrated Threat Assessment Centre (ITAC) was set up to facilitate the sharing of information and the production of comprehensive assessments of terrorist threats to Canada.[15] Using analysts seconded from various intelligence and law enforcement services and government departments, ITAC assessments are based on intelligence and trends analysis derived from information provided by its partners in the security and intelligence community, and evaluate both the probability and potential consequences of terrorist threats. Although ITAC represents an integrated approach to intelligence assessment, participation by other components of the security and intelligence community is discretionary, and some units have been slow to partner in this initiative.[16]

In this decentralized Canadian constellation of intelligence analysis "strategic" assessments are produced by two organizations, the IAS and the Research, Analysis and Production (RAP) branch of CSIS. IAS is said to concentrate on international intelligence while the CSIS product focuses on specific threats to Canada.[17] Nevertheless, the distinction between these areas of coverage is not always clear cut, so that overlap and duplication may occur. While differing perspectives and viewpoints may well broaden the horizons of policy makers and client departments, mutually contradictory and conflicting intelligence assessments could confuse and impede effective action. ITAC is oriented more towards "tactical" intelligence assessments and warnings about imminent threats or potentially illegal acts, which are shared among security and law enforcement agencies.

Common trends

Centralized coordination of intelligence machinery, along with the creation of integrated fusion centres focusing specifically on terrorism-related intelligence analysis and assessment, have emerged as a major thrust of national security policy in the countries concerned. Especially for larger, multi-faceted intelligence and law enforcement communities, effectiveness requires that information on known or suspected terrorists and on potential threats, vulnerabilities and previous incidents, which may exist in many forms and in many places within these services, be integrated and fused into comprehensive and timely threat assessments.[18] These comprehensive assessments can then be disseminated to all pertinent national security agencies, international partners and relevant first responders. Integrated fusion assessment centres have been established by the UK (JTAC), US (NCTC), Australia (NTAC), Canada (ITAC) and New Zealand, which recently set up a Counter-Terrorism Assessment Group (CTAG). Other countries, among them the Netherlands (office of the National Coordinator for Counter-Terrorism), France, Germany and Spain, are introducing a similar, integrated architecture for counterterrorism assessments. Yet, it is questionable whether smaller countries and their intelligence services will be able to demonstrate a sustainable absorptive capacity for more numerous analysts and more extensive analyses dealing with terrorism, such as exists in the US and UK, even as they move towards these larger scale, integrated assessment units: certain countries, like Australia and the Netherlands, seem to have responded robustly, whereas others have remained somewhat more cautious and circumspect.

Conceptual responses: new paradigms, existing paradigms and their application

Along with structural reforms, the recent inquiries and ensuing policy initiatives have also given impetus to conceptual developments in the domain of intelligence analysis. Advances in conceptual approaches to intelligence analysis occurred along two distinct axes: in the development of methodologies for threat and risk analysis, and in the application of analytical approaches to intelligence assessment. From an analytical perspective, the contemporary threat environment lacks the equilibria, certitudes and predictabilities associated with the Cold War.[19] Contemporary terrorism is amorphous, elusive, random in its targeting, and unpredictable in its tactics. The challenge for intelligence assessments of terrorism is to develop new analytical methodologies that can offer a measure of comprehensiveness, prediction and strategic warning, even though the information available may be diffuse, partial and fragmented, buried in masses of data without well-defined links, and fraught with deception.[20]

Designing new paradigms for intelligence analysis

Like during the early Cold War period, when intelligence assessments by Western powers had to resort to "creative speculation" on Soviet capabilities and intentions,[21] the analytical effort to cope with a dearth of hard data from sources within the elusive and amorphous terrorist networks has generated new analytical paradigms to analyze linkages, discern trends and evaluate risks.[22] These new approaches seek to utilize complex mathematics and computer algorithms to fully exploit the nuggets of information that are available, thereby attempting to overcome constraints on source material. The thrust of the new analytical paradigms has pressed towards the provision of "strategic" warning rather than indicative warning, since indicators of terrorist capabilities and intentions may not be readily discernible. Also, the new analytical paradigms have moved away from simple analogue, or linear, assumptions in order to deal with quantum leaps in terrorist capabilities, intentions or targeting, the essence of strategic surprise.

These paradigms are also comprehensive in scope, covering all aspects of the terrorist threat (e.g. recruitment, terrorism, finance) and not just singularities, and in all its dimensions: CBRN (chemical, biological, radiological, nuclear), critical infrastructure protection, economic/financial, health, agricultural/veterinarian, science and technology.[23] Yet, along with these attributes the new paradigms also carry certain methodological risks, notably over-dependence on the fallacy of "expertise" in making judgments,[24] postulating futures based on past experience, projecting behavioral traits onto others, and mirror imaging.

Refining and existing methodologies for intelligence analysis

Existing analytical paradigms are also being rejuvenated or refined as part of the counterterrorism effort. Their principal approaches may be grouped according to methodological precept, into the following typologies:

1. search and retrieval (data mining), which enables target profiling;
2. information extraction and link analysis – Suspicion by association;
3. question answering;
4. structured argumentation;
5. imagery and video analysis;
6. GIS/visualization;
7. foreign language processing;
8. ethnographics.

Some of these approaches impart certain inherent methodological challenges for operationalizing intelligence assessments. Thus, link analysis may imply guilt by association. Data mining can edge toward target profiling. Ethnographics presume a careful, detailed knowledge of the linguistic and interdisciplinary topography of the targeted communities, without which it degenerates into stereotyping. In the last analysis intelligence assessment is an art form, crafted from knowledge and judgment, which can be enhanced but not totally captured by computer science.

The application of intelligence analysis to assessments

The actual application of these existing as well as new analytical paradigms to intelligence assessment is being similarly subjected to review and refinement. These paradigms for intelligence analysis are predicated on knowledge discovery and dissemination, on the derivation of novel intelligence from massive data, and on predictive analysis and hypothesis management.[25] It is clear that additional, actionable knowledge is required in order to assess terrorism trends and terrorist threats, and that this knowledge will have to be assembled nugget-by-nugget from large-scale databases. It is also clear that these intelligence assessments will have to have predictive power if they are to generate strategic warning. Intelligence assessments will have to demonstrate prediction analysis with particular emphasis on hypothesis management. Yet, since predictability is inherently constrained in the intelligence domain, the operationalization of these analytical paradigms will probably depend on innovative methods of risk-based planning.

To be sure, all these techniques – knowledge discovery, novel intelligence derivation, prediction analysis, hypothesis management, risk-based planning – are predicated on cooperation and information sharing amongst analysts, intelligence services and international partners. As with much else in the counterterrorism effort, the effective application of intelligence analysis paradigms to terrorism and terrorist threats hinges on networking and collaboration.

Hypothesis management plays an important role in prediction analysis for intelligence assessment. That reliable, independent, all-source ("diverse") analysis is predicated on hypothesis management was underscored by the US Presidential Commission on Intelligence Capabilities.[26] The process of hypothesis management places emphasis on validation, contestability, information assurance and the detection of deception. It furthermore addresses techniques for the effective communication of analytical findings to prospective clientele. The validation process for intelligence-related hypotheses is currently undergoing a profound methodological shift, at least in some analytic organizations, in favour of an approach rooted in scientific method. Rather than test hypotheses by assembling confirmatory evidence, as was commonly done until now, these agencies are turning instead to the testing of hypotheses by refutation. A valid hypothesis must withstand refutation. Emphasis is also being placed on contestability, whereby intelligence hypotheses are subject to contestation by intra-agency teams (e.g. A-team, B-team), or inter-agency staff (as between the British JIC assessment staff and JTAC, or US NCTC and CIA analysts), or through joint assessment initiatives (for example, through shared assessments among the so-called "Five Eyes" between ITAC, JTAC, NCTC, NTAC, and CTAG). Information assurance may be fostered through such techniques as analytic war gaming and simulation exercises. Explicit efforts must be made in the context of hypothesis management and information assurance to detect deception and protect against disinformation on the part of adversaries.

The communication of intelligence assessments to policy makers and other users commands its own analytical and presentational skill sets. It was cogently argued by the Butler inquiry, in particular, how important it is for intelligence analysis to communicate explicitly the reliability of its underlying information, and the vulnerabilities of its assumptions, so as to guide prospective users as to the dependability of the assessments. The US Presidential Commission on Intelligence Capabilities also put emphasis on the need to develop more client-friendly, user-relevant presentational technologies.[27] The presentational formatting of intelligence analysis also warrants analytical refinement. Analytic agencies are looking to the analysis of user expectations and requirements, along with the development and refinement of presentational technologies, to better communicate intelligence assessments in a user-relevant format. In that regard some US organizations are currently experimenting with creative visualization approaches to the presentation of their intelligence assessments, in a quest for relevance, cogency and impact.

An emergent role for external organizations

The intelligence systems of some countries have begun to involve outside, non-governmental organizations in certain aspects of the intelligence assessment function, to foster creativity and contestability in analysis. Thus, the Australian Strategic Policy Institute was established as a government-funded but independent policy research organization intended specifically to foster contestability of advice on strategic and defence policy issues, including intelligence analysis and reform, terrorism, and international security. Earlier on, certain other countries such as Denmark and Norway had established comparable research institutions for the assessment of international security-related issues, notably the Danish Institute for International Studies and the Norwegian Defence Research Establishment (FIS).

In Britain, the International Institute for Strategic Studies and Royal United Services Institute (RUSI) provide public fora for open-source discourse relating to analytical analysis. Israel's International Policy Institute for Counter-Terrorism at the Interdisciplinary Center, Herzliya, performs a similar role apropos that country's intelligence community. The annual CASIS conferences of the Canadian Association for Security and Intelligence Studies provide a wide-ranging program of panels and speakers on topics in intelligence and security studies, which have also had considerable appeal for practitioners from Canada and abroad. The US Presidential Commission on the Intelligence Capabilities of the United States recommended that a similar sponsored research institute be set up in the US to capitalize on outside expertise and expand the intelligence community's outreach efforts.[28]

Deficiencies and challenges: the organizational dynamics of intelligence analysis

The development of new and enhanced capabilities in intelligence analysis for counterterrorism is confronted by certain knowledge resource deficiencies, intelligence systemic constraints, and institutional challenges. The deficits in available knowledge and skills, and the impediments to effective intelligence cooperation and networking, militate against implementation of the new fusion role for intelligence assessment in counterterrorism. Moreover, the governments concerned will need to address the twin challenges of human resource development and knowledge and skills development in order to equip their intelligence analysis systems with the high-level competencies upon which the recent institutional reforms were predicated.

Knowledge resource deficiencies

The intelligence communities of most Western countries suffer from an acute scarcity of knowledge resources pertaining to the cultures, social systems and languages of societies and groups of interest to counterterrorism. Universities across Europe and North America experienced decades of under-investment in cross-cultural or area study programs on Islam, the Middle East and North Africa, and South and Central Asia. As a result, these countries have been left with a diminished human resource capacity to relate to the languages, cultures, religions and societal systems of Arab and Muslim societies and attendant groups.[29] Comparatively few graduates with language proficiency and cross-cultural knowledge of these areas and groups are even available, whether for recruitment to government service or for research and analysis positions in nongovernmental organizations, including universities. Intelligence agencies admit to possessing very few staff having access to these language skills and cross-cultural knowledge, except through secondary sources, even in their analytical units.[30]

To overcome this knowledge deficit, the US launched in 2004 the Pat Roberts Intelligence Scholars Program (PRISP), a three-year pilot program designed to provide scholarship support for American university students interested in careers as analysts with the US intelligence community. The PRISP scholarship program focuses on building knowledge in "critical regional studies" and other relevant analytical skills. Each component of the US intelligence community is allocated a number of PRISC scholarship awards in proportion to the size of its analytical element. The Central Intelligence Agency utilized its awards to support studies of the Middle East, Central Asia and China, and also studies relating to counterterrorism, sciences and engineering; the National Security Agency allocated its awards to language training in Arabic, Farsi, Urdu, Mandarin and Korean; the Defense Intelligence Agency awards emphasized training in these same languages; while the National Geospatial Intelligence Agency prioritized its requirements for imagery and orbital analysts, geostatisticians, geodists, and Arabic and Turkic linguists. Building on the PRISP precedent, the 2004 Intelligence Reform and Terrorism Prevention Act foreshadowed the introduction of a new and expanded scholarship program, to be known as the Intelligence Community Scholars Program (ICSP), to further accelerate the development of language and other skills and disciplinary proficiencies of relevance to the US intelligence community.[31]

In the meantime, the US set up a National Virtual Translation Center that brought together translators of relevant languages from across the American intelligence community to try and patch the linguistic gap in the struggle against terrorism.[32]

The new counterterrorism paradigms being developed for "strategic" warning presumes a capability for prediction which seems to exceed the knowledge potential of contemporary analytical methodologies. British reforms charged analysts with discerning "the thin wisps of tomorrow" so as to alert decision-makers about future "challenges".[33] Yet, whereas the social and behavioral sciences, the mainstays of intelligence analysis, can contribute considerable explanatory capacity to counterterrorism paradigms, they are nevertheless relatively deficient in predictive powers. This remains the case even when these methodologies are enhanced by elegant mathematical modeling and computerized projections of future trends. In the words of the late General Yehoshafat Harkabi, a former head of Israeli military intelligence (Aman):

> Any assessment of future developments must take into consideration humanity's generally poor track record in predicting the future. Frequently what actually happens was unanticipated, and the new developments significantly change conditions and problems. Nor do developments frequently correspond to what ostensibly follows from rational analysis of the present. Our analyses are not identical with the logic of history. Rational analysis may ignore a factor that influences the future course of events ... Despite reservations about the human capacity for prophecy, if we want to formulate policies we have no alternative but to try to understand the current situation and anticipate future developments to the best of our ability.[34]

The predictive capabilities of the social and behavioral sciences are constrained, in effect, to considerations of "probabilities". Evaluations of probability may indeed be of value for certain operational requirements, but fall short of the predictive standard on which strategic warning paradigms seem to postulate.

Other methodological deficiencies may constrain the applicability of risk-management techniques to counterterrorism paradigms. Risk management in the national security context takes account of threat assessments, vulnerability and criticality, the latter being defined in terms of consequential effects of damage to the physical asset(s) under consideration. While actuarial risks (e.g. accidents, criminal acts, fire) can be assessed quite conventionally through insurance-type risk-assignment and risk-sharing principles, the evaluation of terrorism risks presents significantly more problematic challenges to the techniques of risk management. While actuarial risk analysis usually allows for strictly limited consequential liabilities, considerations of criticality for terrorism risk management can involve consequential damages and knock-on effects that are far reaching and long lasting.

Certainly, large-scale terrorism can wreak havoc on a modern industrial economy and society above and beyond the damage to a particular target. Terrorist attacks have inflicted massive and cascading financial and economic dislocation on Western economies through physical destruction, capital losses, market upheaval, business disruption and the high recurrent costs of protection.[35] Thus, the material damage caused by the September 11th attacks on the World Trade Center and the Pentagon was estimated at $30 billion; however, the knock-on effects on the global economy have been estimated at an additional $800–$900 billion.[36] To deal with threats of such magnitude, risk management will have to reach beyond the insurable-risk paradigm to a materiality-risk paradigm, which assumes actuarial risks to be low but any damage as potentially catastrophic; or even to an asymmetric warfare-risk paradigm, which regards actuarial risk irrelevant but assesses probabilities of damage to be high and the consequences potentially catastrophic.[37] Unless and until risk management techniques acquire the knowledge and techniques capable of dealing with cascading and catastrophic criticality of such magnitudes, their applicability and relevance to the new paradigms of intelligence analysis may not meet operational expectations.

Systemic constraints

The emergent role of intelligence analysis in the counterterrorism effort is predicated on cooperation and information sharing both within intelligence agencies and amongst partners. New analytical paradigms based on knowledge discovery, the derivation of novel intelligence from massive data, prediction analysis, risk-based planning and hypothesis management all presume a high degree of networking and collaboration. Whereas, traditionally, intelligence agencies operated within a framework of secrecy, governed by a "need to know" principle, recent intelligence reforms emphasizing coordination and fusion are grounded in a "need to share" principle.

The circle of secrecy that bound intelligence agencies tended to inhibit professional collaboration, networking and information sharing amongst various components of national intelligence communities and their analysts.[38] The reports of the United States' 9/11 Commission and the British Butler inquiry were critical of impediments to inter-agency information sharing and restrictions on cooperation, even while accepting that these derived from current law and policy. Lessons learned are being incorporated into the systemic reforms that were implemented in response to past failures. The creation of the integrated fusion centres, ITAC, JTAC, NCTC, NTAC and CTAG, was designed explicitly to promote and expedite cooperation and networking in national efforts at intelligence analysis and assessment.

The magnitude of the threat posed by international Jihadist terrorism has prompted an unprecedented dynamic of international cooperation amongst hitherto secretive and generally autarkic national security agencies.[39] The scale and complexity of the counterterrorist effort impelled even the preeminent superpower, the United States, to seek international cooperation with other countries in an intelligence coalition against terrorism. This emergent coalition has been characterized by different modes of cooperation, different degrees of information sharing, and different operational specializations involving the various partners. Indeed, shared participation in assessment processes, and exchanges of assessment products and comments, have been taking place among the "Five Eyes" for some time.[40] The new fusion centres are expected to continue and build on this practice. Nevertheless, international cooperation in the domain of intelligence, and in the international sharing of intelligence products, is fraught with ambiguities. Intelligence services have a propensity to monitor even friendly countries, which can render international cooperation somewhat awkward.[41]

There is also a risk that agencies engage in intelligence sharing not merely to inform partners, but to enable the shared intelligence to be manipulated and tailored to shape and influence the direction of others' policies.[42] As it is said: "There are no friendly secret services, only the secret services of friendly states."

The risk of politicization of intelligence analysis constitutes an intrinsic systemic hazard, as is highlighted by the controversy surrounding the flawed pre-Iraq war assessments of Iraqi WMD capability. Proximity to government and decision-makers may tend to induce cooption and shared mind sets, if not direct influence on analytical outcomes. Although the subsequent inquiries in the UK, US and Australia explicitly exonerated their respective analytical bodies from suspicions of politicization,[43] their ensuing recommendations emphasized the importance of ensuring the independence of assessment.

A close kin to politicization is ideological bias. Indeed, ideological predilections may represent a far more profound and problematic systemic constraint for intelligence analysis to have to deal with. Ideology represents a cognitive lens through which empirical realities are perceived and understood. In becomes part of the analyst's mind-set, and creates a predisposition towards certain findings and outcomes.[44] In the 1980s, Australia's Office of National Assessments was wracked by accusations of ideological bias in its analytical treatment of the Soviet Union. Australian intelligence assessments allegedly tended to be excessively apologetic for Soviet misdeeds.[45] Another form of ideological bias, a prevailing preconception, marked the "conseptsia" that distorted Israeli intelligence assessments of Egyptian and Syrian intentions at the outbreak of the 1973 Yom Kippur war.[46] The result was a near-catastrophe for the Israel defence forces. The Agranat Commission, having investigated the intelligence failure of Yom Kippur, urged the creation of a contestation mechanism within the intelligence analysis system in order to militate against preconceptions and other forms of ideological bias.[47] To the extent that it is possible to offset institutionalized biases in intelligence analysis, the solution points clearly in the direction of systems of contestation, networking and cooperation, that effectively pluralize the testing of the "truths" that intelligence assessments seek to transmit to "power".

Human resource development challenges for intelligence analysis

Tradecraft in intelligence analysis is a product of the quality of the human resources deployed in this key function, as analysts and as managers of analysts. The innovative analytical paradigms that accompany the current reforms and institutional developments in the architecture of intelligence will generate new and higher-level requirements for advanced knowledge in specific areas of intelligence interest, specialized skills and sophisticated techniques.[48] Intelligence communities have a direct stake in building up the education and training systems, the professional development programs and the attendant research and development (R&D) capacity to meet these emergent human resource development requirements.

Education and training for intelligence analysis

Intelligence analysts in the counterterrorism domain are expected not just to demonstrate competence about terrorism, but also to acquire interdisciplinary knowledge about related political, economic, sociological and cultural-religious issues, about chemical, nuclear and biological weapons of mass destruction, about science and technology, about information assurance, and other attendant concerns.

The United States' intelligence community is endowed with by far the most developed and resourceful educational and training infrastructure for its analytical elements. The major services each maintain institutionally dedicated facilities for higher education, professional training and research in intelligence analysis, among other intelligence-related disciplines. Thus, the CIA maintains the CIA University, which incorporates the Sherman Kent Center for Analytic Tradecraft, a professional school and research center dedicated specifically to intelligence analysis. Similarly, the US Department of Defense and Defense Intelligence Agency support the Joint Military Intelligence College (JMIC), which offers academic and professional programs in the various intelligence disciplines.[49] JMIC recently established a new Center for Strategic Intelligence Research. At the West Point Military Academy, the Combating Terrorism Center promotes studies and research on terrorist threats and counterterrorism. The 2005 report of the Presidential Commission on the Intelligence Services furthermore recommended the creation of a new community-wide 'National Intelligence University' to meet the anticipated human resource requirements for a reformed US intelligence system.[50]

Until recently, American colleges and universities were not especially active in intelligence studies, neither have they been engaged in training and research relating to intelligence analysis. Singular exceptions stand out. Mercyhurst College, in Erie, Pennsylvania, offers undergraduate and graduate degree programs in intelligence studies, and has been actively involved in professional-quality training for the Federal Bureau of Investigation and other intelligence services, and for the Department of Homeland Security. Recently, additional universities and colleges, among them Georgetown University's School of Foreign Service, embarked on course offerings in Intelligence Studies. By way of providing further incentive, the Department of Homeland Security recently announced a "Centers of Excellence" initiative of financial support to consortia of universities in conducting research on issues within the departmental remit.

In a significant new initiative, the Southeast Asia Regional Center for Counterterrorism (SEARCCT) was set up in Kuala Lumpur at the behest of the Malaysian government, with backing from the US and Australia. Having commenced operations in 2003, SEARCCT is intended to serve as a regional training center for professional development and upgrading of counterterrorism analysts and practitioners from all ten ASEAN member countries, and from other countries as well.

Other countries have adopted rather less formal and much less systematic approaches to the training and professional development of their intelligence analysts. Most intelligence services do not recruit specifically or directly for analyst positions. Rather, intelligence officers from the general intake may be seconded to analyst positions for portions of their career. Any training they get is typically given on-the-job, supplemented – if at all – by occasional in-house training courses. In some countries analysts may be able to access more formal professional training within the framework of their national defence colleges or police academies. However, such training opportunities do not usually embrace all analysts and are seldom comprehensive in scope, given the generally limited commitment of these institutions to intelligence analysis as such.

Higher educational institutions in countries apart from the United States also offer academic programs in disciplines of interest to the intelligence community, but these are rarely, if ever, tied to professional training requirements or actual tradecraft. Great Britain and Israel seem to have the most extensive array of university offerings in these areas. In the UK, Brunel, Cambridge and Wales/Aberystwyth universities offer degree programs in Intelligence Studies; the University of St Andrews Centre for the Study of Terrorism and Political Violence, King's College London's Department of War Studies, and Cranfield University/Royal Military College of Science (RMCS) conduct specialized academic and also training programs in their respective domains; while Middle East, Islamic and Arabic languages studies are available at Cambridge, Durham, Exeter, Oxford, and the School of Oriental and African Studies, University of London. Several Israeli universities, among them the Hebrew University of Jerusalem, Bar-Ilan University, the universities of Tel Aviv and Haifa, and the Interdisciplinary Center, Herzliya, provide teaching and research on international security, terrorism, Middle Eastern and Islamic Studies, and Strategic Studies.

Elsewhere in Europe, the Middle East and Asia, the academic coverage of these disciplines is sparse. Even without engaging in actual tradecraft, the mere availability of academic programs can generate a flow of relatively knowledgeable graduates who may be interested in careers in intelligence analysis, whilst also offering analysts opportunities for further education and professional upgrading.

Professional development in intelligence analysis

Intelligence analysis is a dynamic craft, geared to advances in knowledge and analytic tradecraft. To keep abreast of developments in both the substantive disciplinary areas of knowledge and in methodological approaches and techniques, intelligence analysts need to have periodic exposure to professional development opportunities. By the same token, attention has to be directed towards the building of research capacity in intelligence analysis. Research is warranted both to evaluate and refine current analytical methods and to pursue the creation of new analytical paradigms, especially in relation to evolving threats of terrorism.

Most intelligence agencies provide some periodic, intra-institutional programs for the professional development of their analysts. Mostly these consist of *ad hoc*, sporadic, stand-alone courses or seminars that are rarely integrated into a coherent curriculum for professional progress. To be sure, more specialized training may occasionally be put in place at service academies, such as the Sherman Kent Center, West Point or JMIC in the US, or by arrangement with external institutions like the University of St Andrews in the UK. Nevertheless, the intelligence analysis communities seem to be on the whole less well served in terms of professional development opportunities as compared to the more robust and well-structured professional training available to military officers through national defence and service colleges. The US Presidential Commission on Intelligence Capabilities placed considerable emphasis on the development of community-wide career-long training programs for analysts and managers of analysts.[51]

In a bid to remedy this deficiency and to offer a more systematic form of training for analysts, the Canadian Centre of Intelligence and Security Studies at Carleton University, Ottawa, designed and delivered a series of advanced training conferences on Intelligence Analysis for the Canadian security and intelligence analysis community. Other universities in the United States and Europe are said to be contemplating similar initiatives.

In May 2005, the Mitre Corporation, a US not-for-profit organization working on national projects in, *inter alia*, information technology and operational concepts convened the "First International Conference on Intelligence Analysis" in cooperation with the CIA Office for Analysis and Production. The conference facilitated an unprecedented international and interdisciplinary discourse on advances in the craft of intelligence analysis. It also served as a forum for knowledge sharing about intelligence analysis theories, methodologies and tools.

The future of intelligence analysis calls for substantial, sustained and systematic efforts on the part of governments to promote R&D at the frontiers of information technology, knowledge management and analytic tradecraft. Academic and private research organizations will need to be enlisted in these efforts, given the scope and scale of the tasks. In the United States, research-oriented institutions such as RAND, Scania Laboratories and the Center for Strategic and International Studies (CSIS) have been commissioned to undertake research on intelligence analysis methodologies as well as on open-source analytical studies of terrorism, homeland security, and other international threats.[52] The US Department of Homeland Security has embarked on a major "Centers of Excellence" program to create university networks for research on issues pertaining to critical infrastructure protection and emergency management. Analytic tools developers and information technology specialists in the US and, to perhaps a lesser extent, the UK, will likely lead in endeavors to create the hardware and software capable of analyzing massive volumes, velocities and varieties of multilingual and multimedia data.

Research on the formulation and development of new analytical paradigms will likely be concentrated in specialist institutions such as the Sherman Kent Center for Analytic Tradecraft, JMIC, and the newly proposed National Intelligence University. However, these internal R&D efforts may be augmented by research mounted by universities and think-tanks on issues related to intelligence analysis, promoted by programs such as the US Department of Homeland Security's "Centers of Excellence" initiative.

Intelligence research and development: building a robust analytic function

Intelligence reforms that emphasize the analytic function, the creation of integrated fusion centres for counterterrorism analysis, the development of new paradigms, the refinement of existing methodologies, and efforts to bolster up education, training and R&D pertaining to intelligence analysis, all point to the emergence of intelligence analysis as a distinct epistemological community within the intelligence system. Considerable store is placed, in the context of contemporary reforms, on incubating and fostering a sense of professional community among intelligence analysts.[53] Like all professions, this epistemological community is evolving its own professional standards, norms, precepts and outlook. Except in the US intelligence community, however, this epistemological community does not enjoy professional career status in the intelligence services. In those other countries it is not uncommon for intelligence operatives to be seconded to analytical roles for part of their careers, and afterwards revert to field operations. This can be the case in some US intelligence services as well. While this approach to staffing may serve to emphasize the centrality of operations, in particular in smaller agencies, it implicitly diminishes the role of analysts and explicitly marginalizes the analytical function within the services concerned.

As intelligence analysis takes on the attributes of an epistemological community, the absence of professional status and career potential will become increasingly dysfunctional. Even in smaller services, intelligence analysts will be expected to have the same high standards of competence, the same caliber of skill sets, the same qualities of knowledge, if not better, as their counterparts in other governmental, academic and research communities. Educational and training opportunities can contribute. However, the fullest realization of the human resource potential of analysts will probably necessitate a transformation of staffing principles in intelligence analysis. The recruitment of intelligence analysts should emphasize specific knowledge and skills. Analysts should be able to pursue a career path in intelligence analysis with progressive opportunities for professional development and promotion. If analysts are to perform as envisaged by current reforms, and as warranted by counterterrorism strategy, then intelligence analysis must come to be treated as a core function of the intelligence system.

Notes

1 The National Commission on Terrorist Attacks upon the United States, *The 9/11 Report* (New York: St Martin's, 2004).

2 *Report of the Commission on the Intelligence Capabilities of the United States Regarding Weapons of Mass Destruction* (March 2005).

3 Philip Flood, AO, *Report on the Inquiry into Australian Intelligence Agencies* (Canberra: Commonwealth of Australia, 2004). http://www.pmc.gov.au/publications/intelligence_inquiry/.

4 Israel Knesset Foreign Affairs and Defense Committee, *Report on the Committee of Enquiry into the Intelligence System in Light of the War in Iraq* (March 2004). URL: http://www.knesset.gov.il/committees/eng/docs/intelligence.htm.

5 Report of a Committee of Privy Councillors, Chairman: The Rt. Hon. The Lord Butler of Brockwell, *Review of Intelligence on Weapons of Mass Destruction*, HC.898 (London: The Stationery Office, 2004).

6 Canada Privy Council, *Securing an Open Society: Canada's National Security Policy* (Ottawa: Government of Canada, 2004), p. 6; see also Martin Rudner, "Canada's Intelligence Community and the War on Terrorism", *Canadian Foreign Policy*, Vol. 11, No. 2 (Winter 2004), esp. pp. 17–22.

7 "Cats' Eyes in the Dark," *The Economist*, 17 March 2005.

8 United Kingdom, *National Intelligence Machinery* (London: The Sationery Office, 2005), p. 20.

9 "Cats' Eyes in the Dark," *The Economist*, 17 March 2005.

10 United Kingdom, *National Intelligence Machinery* (London: The Stationary Office, 2005), p. 13.

11 United Kingdom, *National Intelligence Machinery* (London: The Sationery Office, 2005), p. 13.

12 United Kingdom, *National Intelligence Machinery* (London: The Sationery Office, 2005), p. 23.

13 Australia, *Transnational Terrorism: The Threat to Australia* (15 July 2004).

14 Martin Rudner, "Challenge and Response: Canada's Intelligence Community and the War on Terrorism", *Canadian Foreign Policy*, Vol. 11, No. 2 (Winter 2004).

15 Canadian Security Intelligence Service, "The Integrated Threat Assessment Centre (ITAC)," *Backgrounder Series* No. 13 (November 2004). ITAC partners include the Canadian Security Intelligence Service, the Communications Security Establishment, the Canada Border Service Agency, the Royal Canadian Mounted Police and the departments of Public Safety and Emergency Preparedness, National Defence, Foreign Affairs Canada, Transport Canada, Privy Council Office and the Ontario Provincial Police.

16 *Report of the Auditor-General of Canada, Chapter 3: National Security in Canada – The 2001Anti-Terrorrism Initiative* (March 2004), para. 3.64.

17 *Report of the Auditor-General of Canada, Chapter 3: National Security in Canada – The 2001Anti-Terrorrism Initiative* (March 2004), para. 3.54–55.

18 *Report of the Auditor-General of Canada, Chapter 3: National Security in Canada – The 2001Anti-Terrorrism Initiative* (March 2004), para. 3.60.

19 Stéphane Lefebvre, "A Look at Intelligence Analysis," *International Journal of Intelligence and Counter-Intelligence*, Vol. 17, No. 2 (Summer 2004), esp. pp. 244–246.

20 Jeffrey Isaacson and Kevin O'Connell, "Beyond Sharing Intelligence, We Must Generate Knowledge", *Rand Review*, Vol. 26, No. 2 (Summer 2002), p. 49.

21 Lawrence Aronsen, "Seeing Red: US Air Force Assessments of the Soviet Union, 1945–1949", *Intelligence and National Security*, Vol. 16, No. 2 (Summer 2001), p. 111.

22 Frederick Hitz and Brian Weiss, "Helping the CIA and FBI Connect the Dots in the War on Terror", *International Journal of Intelligence and Counter-Intelligence*, Vol. 17, No. 1 (Spring 2004).

23 *Report of the Commission on the Intelligence Capabilities of the United States Regarding Weapons of Mass Destruction* (March 2005), p. 402.

24 Steven Rieber, "Intelligence Analysis and Judgmental Calibration", *International Journal of Intelligence and Counter-Intelligence*, Vol. 17, No. 1 (Spring 2004), esp. pp. 98–102.

25 See *Report of the Commission on the Intelligence Capabilities of the United States Regarding Weapons of Mass Destruction*, pp. 405–406.

26 *Report of the Commission on the Intelligence Capabilities of the United States Regarding Weapons of Mass Destruction*, pp. 405–407.

27 *Report of the Commission on the Intelligence Capabilities of the United States Regarding Weapons of Mass Destruction*, pp. 417–418.

28 *Report of the Commission on the Intelligence Capabilities of the United States Regarding Weapons of Mass Destruction*, pp. 399–400.

29 Frank Davies, "In Fight vs. Terrorism, Linguists Gain Clout. The Nation's intelligence agencies have beefed up their translation efforts with part-timers, many with academic backgrounds", *Miami Herald*, 2 May 2005.

30 See Lindsay Moran, "More Spies, Worse Intelligence?", *New York Times*, 12 April 2005.

31 "Secret Students Major in Spying", *Kansas City Star*, 5 June 2005. Some academics, including Britain's Association of Social Anthropologists, expressed opposition to the scholarship program, which they termed ethically "dangerous" and divisive: "Fears over CIA 'university spies'", BBC News, 2 June 2005: http://news.bbc.co.uk/go/pr/fr/-/2/hi/uk_news/education/4603271.stm

32 "Word Warriors: Translators fill Gap in War on Terrorism", *Billings Gazette* (Montana), 8 May 2005.

33 "Cat's Eyes in the Dark," *The Economist* [London], 19 March 2005, p. 33.

34 Yehoshafat Harkabi, trans. Lenn Schramm, *Israel's Fateful Hour* (New York: Harper & Row, 1986), p. 65.

35 Martin Rudner, "Challenge and Response: Canada's Intelligence Community and the War on Terrorism", *Canadian Foreign Policy*, Vol. 11, No. 2 (Winter 2004), pp. 20–21.

36 Rohan Gunaratna, *Inside al Qaeda: Global Network of Terror* (New York: Columbia University Press, 2002), pp. 300–301; see also Kurt Campbell and Michéle Flournoy, *To Prevail: An American Strategy for the Campaign Against Terrorism* (Washington, DC: Centre for Strategic and International Studies, 2001), Chap. 10, pp. 125–129.

37 Martin Rudner, "Hunters and Gatherers: The Intelligence Coalition Against Islamic Terrorism", *International Journal of Intelligence and Counter-Intelligence*, Vol. 17, No. 2 (Summer 2004), p. 223.

38 On the risks of secrecy for intelligence analysis see William Kennedy, David Baker, Richard Friedman and David Miller, *The Intelligence War. Penetrating the Secret World of Today's Advanced Technology Conflict* (London: Salamander Books, 1983), esp. pp. 194 *et passim*.

39 Martin Rudner, "Hunters and Gatherers: The Intelligence Coalition Against Islamic Terrorism", *International Journal of Intelligence and Counter-Intelligence*, Vol. 17, No. 2 (Summer 2004), pp. 193–223.

40 Martin Rudner, "Contemporary Threats, Future Tasks: Canadian Intelligence and the Challenges of Global Security", in Norman Hillmer and Maureen Appel Molot (eds), *Canada Among Nations 2002. A Fading Power?* (Don Mills, ON: Oxford University Press, 2002), p. 159; Martin Rudner, "Hunters and Gatherers: The Intelligence Coalition Against Islamic Terrorism", *International Journal of Intelligence and Counter-Intelligence*, Vol. 17, No. 2 (Summer 2004), p. 213.

41 Richard Aldrich, *The Hidden Hand. Britain, America and Cold War Secret Intelligence* (London: John Murray, 2001).

42 Martin Rudner, "Hunters and Gatherers: The Intelligence Coalition Against Islamic Terrorism", *International Journal of Intelligence and Counter-Intelligence*, Vol. 17, No. 2 (Summer 2004), p. 213.

43 Report of a Committee of Privy Councillors, Chairman: The Rt. Hon. The Lord Butler of Brockwell, *Review of Intelligence on Weapons of Mass Destruction*, HC.898 (London: The Stationery Office, 2004), esp. paras. 446, 449, 450; *Commission on the Intelligence Capabilities of the United States Regarding Weapons of Mass Destruction*, p. 11; Philip Flood, AO, *Report on the Inquiry into Australian Intelligence Agencies* (Canberra: Commonwealth of Australia, 2004). URL: http://www.pmc.gov.au/publications/intelligence_inquiry/, p. 28.

44 Yehoshafat Harkabi, trans. Lenn Schramm, *Israel's Fateful Hour* (New York: Harper & Row, 1986), p. 78.

45 William Kennedy, David Baker, Richard Friedman and David Miller, *The Intelligence War. Penetrating the Secret World of Today's Advanced Technology Conflict* (London: Salamander Books, 1983), p. 194.

46 Uri Bar-Joseph, *The Watchman Fell Asleep. The Surprise of Yom Kippur and its Sources* (Lod: Zmora-Bitan, 2001) [in Hebrew]; see also William Kennedy, David Baker, Richard Friedman and David Miller, *The Intelligence War. Penetrating the Secret World of Today's Advanced Technology Conflict* (London: Salamander Books, 1983), p. 194.

47 Judge Moshe Agranat, *Report of the Agranat Commission, Commission of Inquiry into the Yom Kippur War* (Tel Aviv: Am Oved, 1975) [in Hebrew].

48 See David Moore, Lisa Krizan and Elizabeth Moore, "Evaluating Intelligence: A Competency-Based Model", *International Journal of Intelligence and Counter-Intelligence*, Vol. 18, No. 2 (Summer 2005), pp. 204–220.

49 Dr Max Gross, Dean "Joint Military Intelligence College: A Brief History", in Joint Military Intelligence College, *Preparing America's Leaders* (2002), pp. 12–30.

50 *Report of the Commission on the Intelligence Capabilities of the United States Regarding Weapons of Mass Destruction*, pp. 325–326.

51 *Report of the Commission on the Intelligence Capabilities of the United States Regarding Weapons of Mass Destruction*, pp. 409–411.

52 Michael Rich, "How U.S. Think Tanks Interact with the military" (22 November 2002). Michael D. Rich is Executive Vice-President of RAND. http://usinfo.state.gov/journals/itps/1102/ijpe/ijpe1102.htm.

53 *Report of the Commission on the Intelligence Capabilities of the United States Regarding Weapons of Mass Destruction*, esp. pp. 390–391.

10

COUNTERTERRORISM AS GLOBAL GOVERNANCE: A RESEARCH INVENTORY

Ronald D. Crelinsten

Introduction

Plus ça change, plus c'est la même chose
(The more things change, the more they stay the same)

Almost 30 years ago, I wrote a paper about the problems that terrorism poses for research (Crelinsten 1978). I argued that terrorism was what Jerome Ravetz (1971) calls a 'practical' problem as opposed to a 'scientific' or a 'technical' one. For Ravetz, a scientific problem is one 'where the goal of the work is the establishment of new properties of the objects of inquiry and its ultimate function is the achievement of knowledge in its field' (p. 317). A technical problem, by contrast, is one 'where the function to be performed specifies the problem itself. The goal of the task is fulfilled, and the problem is "solved", if and only if that function can be adequately performed' (p. 318). A practical problem is one where 'the goal of the task, in principle, is the serving or achievement of some human purpose. The problem is brought into being by the recognition of a problem-situation, that some aspect of human welfare should be improved' (p. 319). I also argued that 'undue emphasis on origins and causes tends to treat terrorism as if it were primarily a scientific problem, while undue emphasis on strategies and tactics of prevention and control tends to treat terrorism as if it were primarily a technical problem' (pp. 108–109). The trick was to treat terrorism as a practical problem, with scientific and technical aspects.

Practical problems, argues Ravetz, cannot be reduced to single parameters or simple solutions. As such, too rigorous applications of the scientific method, in a misguided attempt to emulate the physical sciences (a common tendency in the social sciences), can distort the true nature of the problem under study. 'The inherent complexity of a practical problem, both in its objects and in the cycle of its solution, calls for a diversity of operations, skills, and approaches even greater than in the case of technical projects' (Ravetz 1971: 356). This is why, for example, prediction cannot be the primary goal of terrorism research. The nature of the problem does not easily lend itself to the kind of scientific research that allows – or promises – accurate prediction. Terrorism, and its control, is too messy a phenomenon to accommodate the mathematical elegance of the scientific method with its observations, measurements, hypotheses and testable conclusions. Ravetz, writing over 30 years ago, felt that researchers who deal with practical problems were overly influenced by the tradition of scholarship and research and too little by the engineering notion of doing the best one can with available knowledge. Of course, he was writing in a time before the emergence of chaos theory, catastrophe theory, network theory, and the development of computer-based analytic tools that can describe and quantify the complex relations inherent in objects of study such as terrorism and counterterrorism. Nevertheless, his point remains valid to this day.

Echoing Ravetz, it is common nowadays, and particularly after the attacks of 11 September 2001, to hear calls for a 'comprehensive approach' to countering terrorism. Even before that fateful date, the complex impact of globalization on a variety of policy domains and issues was making decision-makers and researchers more and more aware of the need to take a broader, more multidisciplinary, cross-sectoral, interdepartmental and cross-jurisdictional look at policy-relevant problems and issues. It is striking that Ravetz addressed this problem in the early 1970s and it is sobering to realize that the problem he identified then has only become more complex and its solution more pressing. *Plus ça change, plus c'est la même chose.*

Terrorism and counterterrorism (the responses to it and the efforts to prevent it) are intimately related and are best studied and analysed together, not in isolation from each other. As terrorism and the efforts to control or prevent it acquire a more and more global scale, the framework used to study and understand these interrelated phenomena must become commensurately broad in scope and complexity. The context in which terrorism and counterterrorism interact and co-evolve is a crucial variable in understanding how individuals and groups choose to resort to terrorism, to abandon it, or to refrain from using it in the first place in favour of other means of protest, advocacy and dissent. Context also helps us to understand how states choose to use coercive means to control terrorism, such as criminal justice or counterinsurgency, to abandon their use, or to refrain from using these means in the first place in favour of other methods of control. Context is also critically important for understanding how groups can use a variety of activities simultaneously and in concert – social, cultural, economic, political, criminal and revolutionary – to pursue their goals, while governments in turn do the same in the area of control. In view of these complexities, it is difficult and increasingly undesirable to confine research on terrorism and counterterrorism within one or two academic disciplines. Multidisciplinary research that combines the methods and theoretical traditions of several disciplines, or what might be called 'transdisciplinary' research that moves across disciplinary boundaries, becomes imperative. Similarly, counterterrorism policy can no longer remain compartmentalized in one or two areas but must be coordinated across a wide array of policy domains, while the traditional separation between domestic and foreign policy can no longer be strictly maintained. In sum, the study of terrorism and counterterrorism has to reach across disciplinary boundaries, to bridge pure and applied research, to be policy-neutral as well as policy-relevant, to transcend national borders and jurisdictional boundaries, combining domestic (national), international and transnational forms of terrorism and counterterrorism within its object of inquiry, to move beyond a purely state-centric focus to include non-state actors and institutions and, finally, to avoid truncating the field of study to suit political or ideological agendas.

In this chapter, I shall first describe the geopolitical context in which terrorism and counterterrorism interact. This will involve a description of what James Rosenau (1990, 1997) calls a 'multicentric world', as well as the complex security architecture that has emerged along with it. In describing this context, I shall address the issue of whether things are really that new since the September 11 attacks or whether it is more a question of continuity than radical change. I shall then introduce the concept of global governance and its application to the study of counterterrorism. Once I explain the concept of counterterrorism as global governance, I shall turn to the challenges posed by today's complex environment on the achievement of global governance in the area of counterterrorism. In doing so, I shall identify ways in which research might contribute to understanding and perhaps even meeting these challenges. I shall then conclude by summarizing the kinds of knowledge required for a comprehensive approach to counterterrorism, contrasting what I call the easy way to fight terrorism with what I call the hard way to fight terrorism.

What is a multicentric world?

A multicentric world is one in which entities other than states interact and play an increasingly important role in international politics. According to Rosenau (1990), this world of non-state, sovereignty-free actors exists alongside the more traditional state-centric world of sovereignty-bound actors. The result is a world with eroding boundaries and increasingly porous borders. It is a world with de-territorialized threats that come from far away, not just from neighboring states, such as pollution or transnational terrorism. It is a world in which non-state actors, many of whom are transnational, acting across borders, are becoming increasingly important and influential players. They include:

- multinational enterprises/corporations (MNEs/MNCs);
- non-governmental organizations (NGOs), both domestic and international;
- international organizations (IGOs) or supranational organizations;
- the international media, particularly electronic media such as radio, television and especially the Internet and the World Wide Web (WWW), with its web blogs and alternative websites;

- international and transnational terrorist groups;
- drug traffickers, smugglers, pirates and other transnational criminal organizations;
- mercenaries, demobilized fighters, private security companies, private armies and a whole conglomeration of privatized entities that perform what have traditionally been state-run security operations including VIP protection, target-hardening, surveillance, policing, imprisonment and war.

Underlying all these elements is the impact of globalization, both technological and cultural. With the rapidly expanding reach and speed of global communications technologies and jet travel, areas such as trade, finance and migration have been transformed. On the cultural front, areas such as immigration, welfare, development, human rights, education and tolerance of diversity and difference within societies and between states have all been greatly affected. This has resulted in severe challenges to state sovereignty and authority and increasing limits to state control over a wide variety of policy problems, including terrorism and its control. While those who argue that the state is disappearing, weakening or eroding probably go too far, it is fair to say that the state is transforming under the pressures of globalization. It must now interact with all these non-state actors and deal with these transnational threats and vulnerabilities – not alone, but within a framework of international and regional cooperation and global governance. This is the wider geopolitical context in which terrorism and counterterrorism co-evolve. And it is in this complex environment that security, in particular, needs to be addressed.

The security architecture in a multicentric world before and after September 11

In a multicentric world, where state actors coexist with non-state ones, there are multiple referent objects when one asks the question: security for whom? No longer is it just the state that needs to be secured, but it is now societies and individuals who must be protected. Alongside international security – the traditional purview of realist theory in international relations – there is now societal security, where issues of culture and identity are paramount, and human security, where issues of poverty, disease, environment and resources become central. Since the attacks of September 11, a new term, 'homeland security', has entered the lexicon, and its main tenet is that we must work on many fronts at once to ensure security of the state, its societies and its people.

In the area of security threats, the current security environment is characterized by the coexistence of old and new threats. Traditional threats, such as nuclear proliferation, remain, as India and Pakistan remind us; but they are also transformed, as the threat of nuclear material falling into the hands of terrorists becomes an increasing concern, particularly after the collapse of the Soviet Union. Non-traditional threats, such as pandemics (SARS or avian flu) or CBRN (chemical, biological, radiological, nuclear) terrorism, compete with traditional ones for the attention of the policy-maker. The dangers of environmental degradation, economic collapse, mass migration, or failed or collapsed states have all entered the security domain, even before the September 11 attacks. Central to this security architecture is the challenge of responding to uncertain threats and certain vulnerabilities. The current fixation with WMD (weapons of mass destruction) and CBRN terrorism is a perfect illustration of this. While the vulnerability to such attacks is certain, the threat itself is far from certain. How do we apportion scarce resources – money, time, personnel, political will – when faced with such uncertain threats at the same time that other, more certain threats, but with less devastating impact, continue to pose a serious problem?

This dilemma posed by the disjunction between threats and vulnerabilities is compounded by a technology gap between the world's only superpower – some would say 'hegemon' – and the rest of the world, including the European Union. In the United States, the revolution in military affairs has led to increasing financial and research commitment to new technologies and new ways of conducting wars. This has led to the possibility of an economic security dilemma, whereby states must remain competitive in the global market while maintaining control over new technologies (Crawford 1995). The decision of the US Defense Department that 'vastly expanding the amount spent on unmanned aerial technologies, space-based intelligence and communications systems and efficient sensor-to-shooter data management systems – while maintaining existing weapon systems – was more important than introducing new generations of artillery and fighter aircraft' (STRATFOR 2002) suggests that a generational shift in weapons systems has begun in the United States that will put it several generations ahead of other major powers. This change could very well trigger new security dilemmas in those states and could greatly affect their economic, as well as military, policies as a result of what Barry Buzan (1991) has called 'the technological imperative'. Buzan and Segal (1998: 100–101), for example, describe the arms build-up in East Asia after the end of the Cold War. China's recently announced intention to sharply increase its military spending, as well as the recent confirmation that North Korea has indeed produced a nuclear weapon, may both be related to this dimension of the current security architecture. Every state is now faced with the challenge of updating military technology within budgetary limits, although Buzan and Segal (1998: 100) argue that states experiencing rapid economic growth can afford the expensive advanced technology of modern warfare. They also point out that these increases in defence spending are not as apparent, since they are not expanding as a percentage of GDP.

Another technological challenge is that of dual-use technology. Examples include US concerns, especially post-9/11, over satellite imagery aiding terrorist planning. This led to the removal of many satellite imaging maps from Internet websites. In the case of nuclear technology, the problem of dual-use technology has been a central part of American and European concerns over Iran's nuclear ambitions. Of course, this problem is not a new one. In the 1950s and '60s, Canada had a nuclear technology-transfer program with India, having been given assurances that the technology was for peaceful purposes only. *Plus ça change, plus c'est la même chose.*

A fourth characteristic of today's security environment is the global securitization of terrorism and WMD. 'Securitization', a term coined by Ole Waever (see, for example, Waever 1995), means that a public issue is 'presented as an existential threat, requiring emergency measures and justifying actions outside the normal bounds of political procedure' (Buzan *et al.* 1998: 23–24). Issues as wide ranging as migration, environmental degradation, organized crime and drug trafficking have all been absorbed into the mandate of security services seeking to find new enemies in the wake of the Cold War. After September 11, and particularly after the spread of anthrax in the US postal system, public health, local emergency preparedness and environmental safety have all been securitized, becoming important elements in US counterterrorism policy. But the most striking example of securitization has been the post-9/11, pre-Iraq-War rhetoric conflating rogue or pariah states with the increasing risk of WMD terrorism. Part of this was driven by opportunism and a desire to demonize Saddam Hussein. But part of it was related to the need to justify a new doctrine of pre-emptive defence to replace the longstanding one of deterrence and containment. The ideological work underlying this securitization of terrorism and WMD is, again, related to the challenge of maintaining balance and perspective in the face of terrifying threats and vulnerabilities. The prospect of a rogue or failed state helping a terrorist group to acquire WMD is indeed a terrifying one, but does it justify a whole new approach to security that undermines existing strategic doctrines and international legal regimes?

A fifth characteristic of the current security context relates to the kinds of states that coexist in today's world. One distinction is between the trading state and the garrison state and involves the complex interrelationships among market liberalization, democratization and state-building. There is a common belief that trading states do not wage war, that democratization reduces the risk of violence and terrorism, and that state-building in post-conflict situations should strengthen state capacity in the judicial, policing and security areas. All of these assumptions are more problematic than they appear at first glance (see, for example, Rapoport and Weinberg 2000; Stepanova 2003) and they highlight the difficulties that we are faced with in attempting to establish good governance in a rapidly globalizing world. How do we reconcile interdependence with sovereignty, or national security with regional or international security?

Related to the question of state type is the structure of the international system itself. Barry Buzan's notion (2002) of '1+4' – the US plus the EU, China, Russia and Japan – highlights the uneven distribution of power and influence in the current structure, even of the most powerful states. The issue of pivotal states, such as India, Brazil, South Africa and Mexico, highlights the fact that other states are beginning to assert their own claims to power and influence within the international system. UN Secretary-General Kofi Annan's recent proposal for Security

Council reform and the discussion over which states should become permanent members underscores this issue. After the September 11th attacks, other states became important as the US attempted to establish and maintain a global coalition in its 'war on terror'. The Sudan, Colombia, the Philippines, Indonesia, Georgia and Uzbekistan all received special attention. Buzan's description of the international system as one involving the interleaving of two worlds, the core and the periphery, is also pertinent here. The core is characterized by liberal thinking and interdependence, while the periphery is characterized by realist thinking and balance-of-power politics. This bifurcation is not only an international one but also an intra-national one, since the poor and dispossessed within the core constitute a periphery within the core, while the elites in the periphery constitute a core within the periphery. This bifurcated, nested structure highlights the challenge of interdependence and the danger of creating regional 'gated communities' instead of addressing the root causes of terrorism, namely the grievances that are used by charismatic leaders to mobilize resentment, hatred and the adoption of terrorist violence.

One final aspect of the security architecture of today is the distinction between rogue states and failed states. Both terms are as much rhetorical devices as empirical phenomena. If a rogue state is one that ignores international law and rejects international cooperation, then the consistent rejection of international treaties by the current US administration, including the application of the Geneva Conventions to prisoners captured in Afghanistan and Iraq, makes the United States look like a rogue superpower. If a failed state is one that cannot provide security for people, groups and cultures that live within its borders, then Russia begins to look more and more like a failed state, not to mention post-war Iraq. And in many Western countries where neoliberal policies prevail, government services have become commodities that are marketed as products to be consumed not by citizens but by clients or customers (Crelinsten 2001). Coupled with downsizing and offloading of government services to the private sector and civil society, the result has been that many states in Buzan's 'core' have abdicated their responsibility for the welfare of their citizens, even in the area of security. Whether this is a new form of failed state – by refusing to act like a state – is an open question. One result has been the increasing importance of the private sector in conducting much of what used to be state business, including many functions related to security, such as policing, prisons, surveillance, peacekeeping, foreign aid, and even war.

Counterterrorism as global governance

'Governance' refers to the sets of rules, decision-making procedures and programmatic activity that serve to define social practice and to guide the interactions of those participating in these practices. 'Global governance' refers to the global rules, procedures and programs that typically are institutionalized as legal regimes within international organizations such as the WTO, the EU, the OSCE and the United Nations and its agencies. Examples include:

- refugee determination;
- immigration rules;
- border and passport controls;
- sustainable development;
- environmental protection;
- control of international trade, investment and foreign aid;
- human rights and minority rights (individual and collective rights);
- rule of law;
- rules of war;
- peacekeeping/making;
- conflict resolution.

When we apply this concept to the area of counterterrorism, the most obvious example of an attempt to achieve global governance is the set of international conventions that have emerged over the past several decades to compel all states to adopt national legislation reflecting the contents of these treaties. Taken together, they can be viewed as an emerging legal regime in the area of counterterrorism (Dartnell 2000). There are currently fourteen in force and they deal with the following subjects, presented in chronological order:

- acts committed onboard aircraft (Tokyo, 1963);
- unlawful seizure of aircraft (The Hague, 1970);
- acts against the safety of civil aviation (Montreal, 1971);
- biological weapons (1972);
- crimes against internationally protected persons (New York, 1973);
- taking of hostages (New York, 1979);
- nuclear materials (New York/Vienna, 1980);
- acts against the safety of fixed platforms on the continental shelf (Rome, 1988);
- maritime navigation (Rome, 1988);
- violence at airports (Montreal, 1988);
- plastic explosives identification (Montreal, 1991);
- chemical weapons (1994);
- terrorist bombings (New York, 1997);
- terrorist financing (New York, 1999).

Looking at the list, it is clear that the conventions focus primarily on terrorist tactics: hijacking, kidnapping and hostage-taking, bombings, and unconventional weaponry (biological, nuclear, chemical). The last one represents a shift that already preceded the September 11 attacks: terrorist financing. The dates of the conventions are also revealing in that they show us which tactics were the focus of attention and when. The 1960s and '70s were the era of airline hijackings and hostage-taking; the 1980s saw more armed assaults on infrastructure; and the 1990s saw increasing sophistication in explosives and bombing and a concern with terrorist financing.

There are other areas in which the international community or, at the very least, regional allies have attempted to systematize, institutionalize and coordinate their rules and procedures in an effort to improve the efficiency and efficacy of counterterrorism efforts. It has long been recognized, even before the intelligence failures surrounding the September 11 attacks and the war in Iraq, that intelligence sharing is a crucial element of good counterterrorism policy. Similarly, police cooperation – both within states (intra-national, cross-jurisdictional) and between states – is a critical part of effective anti-terrorist law enforcement. With the increasingly transnational nature of terrorism and other security-related threats, the need to harmonize border, customs, refugee and immigration policy has become more evident. In the area of extradition, it has long been recognized that states refusing to extradite terrorist suspects to requesting states because they do not feel that the suspects will receive a fair trial in that country are obliged to prosecute these suspects themselves. This principle of *aut dedere aut iudicare* – either extradite or prosecute – has more often been honored in the breach than in the observance. In the area of counterterrorism, many international and regional conventions, such as the European Convention for the Suppression of Terrorism, even except terrorist offences from the political offence exception that allows states to refuse extradition in the first place (the exception to the exception). Also in the area of international law, some have argued that war crimes tribunals and especially the International Criminal Court (ICC) can be useful in combating terrorism, especially in post-conflict situations and the context of rebuilding states shattered by civil conflict and internal war. Alex Schmid (1993: 11–13) has argued that terrorism should be considered the peacetime equivalent of war crimes, opening the way to prosecuting transnational and international terrorists before such courts.

Another area in which efforts have been made to achieve a more coordinated response to terrorism is that of military cooperation. There has been a long tradition of joint military exercises and the use of war games and simulations to test the level of integration of different forces. Since the end of the Cold War there has been an increasing tendency to blur the boundaries between police and military functions, as well as those between internal and external security. This has been reflected in the expansion of cooperation amongst police, military, customs, immigration and border control agencies (Crelinsten 1998). This tendency has only been amplified since September 11, 2001. With the US 'war on terror' there have been increasing efforts to go beyond traditional alliances, such as NATO, to include the militaries of other states seen as pivotal in the fight against terrorism. In the area of arms control and anti-proliferation regimes, there have been increased efforts to incorporate such regimes into the counterterrorism toolbox, especially in the context – previously discussed – of WMD and the spread of unconventional weapons to terrorist groups.

The economic realm has seen increasing attention paid to money laundering, capital flows and fund-raising by charitable organizations. With the 1999 UN Convention for the Suppression of Terrorist Financing, the idea that terrorism can be countered by attacking the source of terrorist funding gained international consensus. Since September 11, terrorist financing and the role of charitable organizations in raising funds for groups that engage in terrorism has become a central concern for counterterrorism efforts. As such, banks and other financial institutions, as well as religious and charitable organizations, have become partners – if often reluctant ones – in the global efforts to counter terrorism. Increased attention has also been paid to the importance of development and foreign aid in addressing the 'root causes' believed to underlie resort to terrorism in the first place. While poverty, in and of itself, does not cause terrorism, the widening disparities between rich and poor within the developed world (Buzan's core) and between rich and poor countries (core vs periphery) are seen by many to lie at the root of the genesis of conflict and the resort to terrorism. The concern about failed states becoming terrorist havens or conduits for terrorist acquisition of WMD, or generating spillover of terrorism and violent conflict into neighbouring states or into the integrated network of international trade, commerce, tourism, and travel, has led many to call for integrating development and foreign aid into the counterterrorism toolbox. The G8 summit in Kananaskis, Canada in June 2002, for example, pledged to reduce debt for the most heavily indebted poor countries (HIPC), though to a much lesser extent than those countries had requested, and focused in particular on development in Africa. The next G8 summit in France also focused on Africa. In March 2002, US President Bush announced a US $5 billion increase in foreign aid to poor countries. That the President made this increased aid conditional on recipient countries 'improving their governance, rule of law, social safety nets, investment climates and anticorruption practices' (Friedman 2002) highlights both the comprehensive nature of current approaches and the complex interrelatedness of issues and policy areas.

On the cultural and social front, there have also been increasing efforts to harmonize and coordinate social and cultural policy on a whole range of dimensions, from integration of immigrants and refugees to education. Efforts to cultivate tolerance of social, religious and cultural diversity and to stem the rise of racism and hate-mongering are increasingly seen as an integral part of the counterterrorism toolbox. When a new Japanese textbook can trigger collective violence in China (albeit government-tolerated), it is not surprising that many people feel that the revision of textbooks – whether in the Middle East or elsewhere – and the promotion of mutual understanding and appreciation between different societies and cultures can help to reduce the sea in which the terrorist fish swim. Post-September 11, the most common manifestation of this has been the widespread call for the reform, if not the outright elimination, of the religious schools or madrassahs that so often are accused of fomenting anti-Western, anti-American and anti-Semitic hatred in their young devotees. Another area, which I shall turn to later, is the promotion of women's education.

Challenges to global governance: a research inventory

Even in a world said to be forever changed by terrorism, demands for better security are, just four months after the attacks, hitting an old reality of competing interests, entrenched lobbies and reluctance to make financial or practical sacrifices.

(Zernike and Drew 2002)

It is all well and good to call for a comprehensive approach to counterterrorism, but how can this be achieved in practice and what obstacles come in the way of successful implementation? How might research help to understand the nature of these obstacles, to point the way to possible solutions and to avoid unexpected consequences? It is beyond the scope of this chapter to fully map out the answers to these questions. What follows is an attempt to highlight the most pressing challenges and to indicate research strategies that might help to address them and possibly point to policy initiatives that could resolve or mitigate them.

1. The problem of definition

The definition of terrorism has always posed a problem for international cooperation and the creation of a regime of global governance in the area of counterterrorism. One man's terrorist is another man's freedom fighter, so the saying goes. A common approach in legal conventions has been to avoid defining terrorism altogether and focus on terrorist tactics alone. We have seen this, for example, in the area of extradition. Some define terrorism very narrowly; others very broadly. UN Secretary-General Kofi Annan has recently proposed a definition that confines terrorism to acts against civilians and non-combatants (Annan 2005). The problem here is that this merely shifts the debate from what constitutes terrorism to what constitutes innocent civilians and non-combatants. Elsewhere, I have argued that terrorism cannot be defined in terms of its motive or purpose or by who does it. Instead, it should be defined in terms of what it tries to do – what I call a behavioral definition (Crelinsten 2002: 83). If terrorism is seen as a particular form of violent, coercive communication, then one can escape the ideological trap surrounding its definition. If freedom fighters use terrorism as part of their strategy, then they are terrorists; if counterterrorists use terrorism as part of theirs, then they are terrorists as well. Then we have to ask why different actors, non-state or state, use terrorism and this leads to a consideration of root causes and context. Here is where research comes in. Case studies that focus on group decision-making, internal dynamics, and the cycle of action and reaction between terrorists and counterterrorists may allow us to identify those circumstances under which the resort to terrorism is most likely. Conversely, such research may also reveal those circumstances under which terrorism is likely to be abandoned or rejected in the first place. This can have policy implications in terms of how counterterrorism strategy can promote the latter circumstances and impede the former.

2. International cooperation and the primacy of national interests

It is viewed as almost axiomatic that the only way to combat terrorism is to promote international cooperation, not only among traditional allies but among all nations. After all, terrorism – particularly post-September 11 – is generally considered a worldwide threat that can strike anywhere. The regime of 14 international conventions, as well as a bevy of regional anti-terrorism conventions, have all struggled to achieve consensus on the means to combat terrorism in its various forms. Yet the main stumbling block has always been the primacy of national interests. Take the area of extradition and the principle of *aut dedere aut iudicare*. In 1977 the Palestinian terrorist, Abu Daoud, was arrested in France. Widely believed to have masterminded the 1972 Munich Olympics attack on Israeli athletes, Daoud entered France on 7 January 1977 from Beirut, using a false name and a false Iraqi passport, to attend the funeral of a PLO representative who had been murdered. Tipped off by Israel, the French police arrested him. Both Israel and (then) West Germany applied for his extradition. The French government refused both requests on flimsy technical grounds and within four days he was flown to Algiers. It was widely believed that France acted in its own national interest, not wishing to antagonize Arab states with which it wanted to maintain good relations (Clutterbuck 1993). Twenty-two years later, when PKK leader Abdullah Öcalan was apprehended in Italy in1999, Italy refused an extradition request from Turkey, while Germany, which had an international arrest warrant out for the Kurdish leader, rescinded the warrant and did not request extradition. Italy eventually refused to grant Öcalan refugee status in Italy but allowed him to leave the country. When the Turks finally seized him in Nairobi, Kenya, Öcalan was carrying a fake Greek Cypriot passport with a false name and had been a 'guest' of the Greek government which had secretly flown him to its embassy there (Crelinsten 2000: 171–172). Again, national interest prevailed in both Italy and Germany for not following the principle of extradite or prosecute. A longstanding enmity towards Turkey and the principle of 'the enemy of my enemy is my friend' explained Greece's behavior.

Research on foreign policy decision-making, as well as on the relationship between foreign and domestic policy, could reveal how heads of states and governments balance the needs of maintaining alliances or regional influence with the need to adhere to international norms and legal regimes. The disparity between state behavior and state obligations under international rules of governance is apparent in a whole range of policy domains, including human rights, trade and commerce, and environmental protection. Some regimes do succeed, while others fail or are undermined by states with an interest in doing so. The study of regime formation and maintenance, and case studies of success and failure, form another potentially fruitful avenue of research (Crelinsten 2001; Thomson 1992). Realists argue that the success of regime formation is dependent on the interests of powerful, hegemonic states. Neo-liberals, on the other hand, argue that mutual interests are more important. In the case of piracy, Chambliss (1989) shows how it was only when powerful states were seriously harmed by piracy that they agreed to do something about it. Until then, piracy was a useful alternative to war. The parallel with contemporary state-sponsored terrorism and transnational organized crime is striking. States can still condemn international terrorism, transnational organized crime, drug trafficking, arms trafficking or the dumping of toxic waste as threats to peace and security, since their laws usually proscribe such activities or they are signatories to international conventions proscribing such activities. Yet, when such acts are seen to be a less risky alternative to more direct confrontation, such as war, or a boon to economic development or the maintenance of competitiveness in international markets, then many states choose to provide all kinds of assistance to transnational groups. This is consistent with the realist view on international regimes; national interest will usually be the sticking point upon which such regimes will falter or fail. Whether at the international, national, sub-national or institutional level, the conflicting goals of states, jurisdictions, organizations, governmental departments and agencies will often be a key variable in determining the extent to which cooperation and regimes succeed or not.

3. Policy harmonization and different traditions

Another common theme in counterterrorism is the need to harmonize policies between countries across a wide range of policy domains. The challenge here is to achieve harmonization when states possess widely differing traditions in particular policy domains. For example, some EU countries have refused to extradite arrested terrorist suspects to the United States because of the latter's policy on capital punishment. This example is one involving traditional allies. When one moves into the area of widely different cultures and political traditions, the problem is compounded. When does the push for policy harmonization transform into cultural imperialism? While most Western states and their citizens firmly believe that human rights are universal, many in the developing world argue that they are not, or that they must be secondary to economic development. Comparative research on different state traditions, on the local context within which international norms and regulations are implemented, and the interaction between the global and the local could help us to understand such tensions and to formulate policy harmonization mechanisms that can be acceptable to all parties and achieve the common goals we all desire. Research on values that do enjoy widespread consensus is another objective (Bok 2002).

4. Intelligence gathering and sharing

Another central tenet of good counterterrorism strategy is the importance of intelligence and the need to share intelligence between states and across jurisdictions within states. Related to this is the often-touted need for police and military cooperation. In a world where internal and external security are merging and threats can come from a wide variety of agents, the range of agencies required to share intelligence expands enormously. This can include border officials, customs officials, health officials, and regulatory agencies involved in critical infrastructure protection. As such, truly comprehensive intelligence sharing could include non-state actors, the private sector and civil society. The central challenge here is the question of trust. Too often, different agencies within the same country distrust each other: the rivalry between the CIA and the FBI in the US is legendary. The same can be said for intelligence agencies from allied nations.

Another intelligence-related problem is the inevitable tension between the needs of intelligence gathering and the requirements of law enforcement (Crelinsten 1989, 2002). Arrest can prevent further intelligence gathering, whereas protection of intelligence sources can impede successful prosecution. Both criminal and security intelligence have become extremely important in the counterterrorism effort following September 11, especially since it is now generally agreed that the attacks revealed a massive intelligence failure. Precisely because much was known before the attacks – security experts were predicting a major attack on the US mainland within the span of five years – the importance of human intelligence (HUMINT) has also been underscored (McGeary 2001). Bureaucratic inertia, turf battles, careerism in upper management and a reluctance to share information between different branches of government have all emerged as additional factors underlying the intelligence failure before September 11. The massive effort to block terrorist funding, for example, has run into obstacles related to infighting between agencies, most notably the US Treasury Department and the FBI, as well as skepticism from allies such as Switzerland about the credibility of the evidence against organizations whose assets are to be frozen (Meyer and Lichtblau 2002). Refusal to share intelligence within the banking sector, as well as between even friendly governments, has therefore proven to be a major obstacle to effective tracking of terrorist money and financing.

Research in this area might begin with an overview of who gathers intelligence, who uses it, and how to coordinate all the different intelligence products in order to best serve a global counterterrorist effort. Research could also focus on the consequences, expected or unexpected, of increased intelligence sharing and cooperation across a wide range of agencies concerned with security in its expanded post-September 11 form. In the 'war on terror', who is responsible for intelligence gathering and with whom do you share what intelligence is gathered and analyzed? When there are political disagreements among allies, sensitive information can be leaked to the wrong places. During the 1999 bombing of Serbia, for example, a French officer in the NATO command apparently leaked targeting information to the Serbs, enabling them to prepare for air strikes in advance. In the EU, Didier Bigo has shown how increased police cooperation has led to informal and semi-official networks that are highly flexible and outside the control of citizens and even governments – a kind of bureaucracy beyond the state, 'i.e. a body whose professional aims go beyond the state. The interests of this bureaucracy may no longer correspond to those of the nation, nor may it see any advantage in a supranational political accountability' (Bigo 1994: 169). In the wake of September 11 and calls for increased intelligence sharing among security services and cooperation among police of various countries, it remains to be seen whether a more global version of what Bigo describes for the EU will develop. The handing over of captured al-Qaeda fighters by British troops in Afghanistan to US troops, or the kidnapping of al-Qaeda suspects in various countries and their transfer to countries where they are wanted for terrorist offences without their going through formal extradition proceedings, may be examples where military and police cooperation is proceeding at a non-institutionalized level more or less outside of political control. Whether the same is true in the area of intelligence is a question for research, though accusations that the US is allowing states with no concern for human rights to interrogate suspects suggests that a perverse kind of intelligence sharing is going on that circumvents the strictures of due process.

5. The role of bureaucracies in a networked world

Over and above the bureaucratic infighting and turf battles that were mentioned in the previous section, there is the problem of bureaucratic inertia. Slow and ponderous bureaucracies are charged with fighting terrorist networks that are flexible and adaptable. Witness the transformation of al-Qaeda since 11 September 2001. The US war in Afghanistan destroyed its command and control centre and led to its decentralization and dispersion. This, in turn, led to the outsourcing of terror attacks to sympathetic or like-minded affiliates in countries throughout southeast Asia, North Africa, the Middle East and even the EU, including Indonesia (Bali), Morocco, Saudi Arabia, Turkey and Spain. While research has begun to focus on how these networks emerge, operate and transform (see chapters by Cozzens and Hayden in this volume), similar research should be done on what kinds of counterterrorism networks would best meet the challenge they pose. This research problem is further compounded by the necessity of embedding any counterterrorist network in a legal framework of accountability and oversight (see below and the chapter by Pollard in this volume, as well as Held 2003).

One of the primary challenges faced by any counterterrorism effort is the problem of information overload in an electronic age. With the proliferation of ways that terrorists can communicate with one another, from websites and blogs to e-mail and cellphone text messaging, information overload and the need to sort out the 'wheat' from the 'chaff' is a constant problem. This glut of information can be a boon and a curse at the same time – increasing the availability of information not hitherto readily accessible, but also increasing the chances of information overload and/or red herrings and false leads. Accusations that important messages collected before September 11 were not translated and analyzed in time highlight the enormous challenge faced by both data collectors and analysts in the area of counterterrorism. It is one thing to pass legislation and allow police access to, for example, e-mail accounts of suspected terrorists. It is another to find the time and resources to properly handle this potential deluge of information. There is an urgent need for good and timely analysis and HUMINT agents with the requisite linguistic and cultural knowledge to deal with the complex networks that exist today. In addition, ordinary citizens are more aware of global politics, yet, because of the mass of information available from a myriad of sources, they are also often misinformed about or simply ignorant of the details and complexities. This makes the policy process much more complex and has led to an increasing sophistication in governments' use of the electronic media, especially in time of crisis (Crelinsten 1994, 1997).

6. Issues of transparency, accountability and legitimacy

With the increasing involvement of the media, NGOs and civil society in international politics, including the current war on terror, issues of transparency, accountability and legitimacy have become more salient than ever before. In democratic societies, governments are expected to be open and accountable about what they do. That is what gives them legitimacy in the eyes of those whose interests they are supposed to protect. In a multicentric world, claims on the state multiply exponentially and demands for accountability in a wide variety of policy arenas proliferate. As these demands have increased, governments have become less willing and less able to deal with all kinds of problems (Crelinsten 2001). In response, they have increased partnering with the private sector and civil society to develop and implement policy initiatives and these new partners are beginning to develop skills usually restricted to the political elite. As airline companies, private security firms and other private-sector actors develop skills and expertise to help governments deal with a variety of issues, they will also have to develop procedures and structures more consistent with democratic governance than with the closed world of private profit and competition. The same can be said for interest groups, aid agencies and not-for-profit organizations. Many of these groups possess expertise that governments find invaluable in developing their policies. Public consultation has become the new mantra in public management as governments have reached out to civil society for help in dealing with public problems (Pal 1997: 217–221). Such groups will find that the more they are involved, the more they will be subjected to the type of scrutiny usually reserved for government. As a result, they will have to pay more attention to accountability and openness, as well as ensuring the reliability of their information sources.

Research in this area should focus on the different agencies that have been incorporated into the counterterrorism effort and examine how they have adapted to working in an environment with conflicting and competing demands for secrecy, openness, impunity and accountability. Eric Lipton (2005), for example, describes an ongoing lawsuit involving the head of the US Federal Air Marshal Service's employee union and the Department of Homeland Security, which includes the Federal Air Marshal Service, over the right of air marshals to speak publicly about their work. The suit argues that current restrictions fail to protect whistleblowers. 'The case may end up serving as a test of restrictions imposed on workers throughout the Department of Homeland Security, whose rights to speak out publicly are often compromised, employee leaders say, because of excessive concern about the possibility that their comments might compromise public safety' (Lipton 2005). In the Abu Ghraib abuse case in Iraq, military personnel, including some higher ranks, were prosecuted and though the recent acquittal of the higher ranking officers remains controversial, there was some semblance of accountability. The same cannot be said of some of the private contractors involved in Iraqi prisons. Research on the role of the private sector in the counterterrorism effort is essential (see Holmqvist 2005; Bailes and Frommelt 2004).

One example, in the area of development and foreign aid, shows how implementation of global governance has proven much more complex, with surprising, unintended consequences. Even before September 11, Mark Duffield (2001) identified what he calls the 'new wars', which involve increasingly privatized networks of state and non-state actors who operate outside the purview of sovereign states with the aid of black or shadow economies that thrive under market deregulation. These 'political complexes of network wars' have led to the merging of security and development and the emergence of 'strategic complexes of global governance', consisting of state and non-state actors, including donor governments, military establishments, IGOs, NGOs and the private sector. These strategic complexes interact with, and regulate, the political complexes of network wars by linking aid and development to conflict resolution and the reconstruction of societies. The ironic result is that global governance of the new wars often leads to complicity with and accommodation to various warring parties in these conflicts. This outcome demonstrates how legitimacy can be ultimately compromised despite the best of intentions.

7. Delicate balances

The problem of countering terrorism in a way that does not existentially threaten a democratic way of life or a free market economy leads to a host of research questions concerning what I call 'delicate balances'. The most commonly discussed one is the need to balance security and freedom. This is the problem of liberal democracies under existential threat and the issue of democratic acceptability of counterterrorist strategies and tactics. Whether or not the use of torture is acceptable in any rules-based counterterrorism effort is a hotly debated example at present (Cohen [ed.] 2005). Another related challenge is to balance necessity and proportionality: the dual problems of overreacting and underreacting to uncertain threats and certain vulnerabilities. Here, the most hotly contested issue is what to do about WMD and, in particular, CBRN weapons. A third challenge, referred to already, is that of balancing the need for operational secrecy with political openness and accountability: the issue of judicial and political oversight. Former UK Home Secretary David Blunkett, for example, has argued that any expanded powers should be coupled with expanded oversight (Blunkett 2002).

A fourth challenge in liberal democracies is the problem of anti-democratic political movements and whether there are acceptable limits to the right to free expression, assembly and participation in political life: the balance between freedom of expression and freedom from expression. Violent rhetoric, such as sedition or hate propaganda, or violent imagery such as some pornography, create special policy problems. Freedom of expression collides with freedom from threat and intimidation. While most civil liberties organizations are loathe to criminalize such activities in the interests of protecting free speech, many realize that there are limits to the free expression of hateful, demagogic speech and the outright promotion of violence. Clearly, the links between propaganda, the promotion of hate and violence, and the mobilization and recruitment of terrorists and their supporters and sympathizers is a vast area for research in a variety of disciplines (see, for example, Taarnby's chapter).

A fifth challenge relates to terrorist financing, banking and charitable organizations: how to balance the needs of security with legitimate activities of fundraising and banking (see also von Hippel's chapter). In the 'war on terror', some charitable and religious organizations, particularly those with links to countries where it is known that al-Qaeda operates, have become suspect and are considered either as fronts for terrorist planning and organization or as engaged in illegal activity as well as more legitimate charitable work. It is well known, for example, that Hamas engages not only in suicide bombings but also in important charity and social work. The US government seized the assets of the Holy Land Foundation for Relief and Development, the largest Muslim charity organization working in the United States, accusing it of funnelling money to Islamic charity committees in the West Bank and Gaza that were controlled by Hamas. The money was spent primarily on families of Hamas suicide bombers and on social services designed to gain popular support (Firestone 2001). Differentiating between legitimate charitable organizations and fronts for terrorist financing is made all the more difficult by the fact that many organizations perform multiple functions that can range from legal to illegal. In some cases, those who give money to such organizations do not even know of this duplicity, yet they can be charged for supporting terrorist activity, have their assets seized or become targets for continuing surveillance. In Somalia, 'money transfers from abroad remain the main source of income for an estimated 70–80 per cent of the Somali population and amount to US $500 million annually, as compared with just $60 million in international humanitarian aid for 2000' (Stepanova 2003: 32). When the US government froze the assets of Somalia's main banking, telecommunications and construction group, al-Baracaat, in November 2001, the move aggravated Somalia's already critical economic situation drastically. Research here could focus on how effective counterterrorist efforts have actually been in this area, as well as what is the wider socioeconomic impact of such efforts beyond its impact on terrorist financing *per se*.

A sixth challenge, also in the economic area, is the tension between the need for stringent customs and border control and the promotion of free trade and free movement of goods and services across borders. Canada and the US are each other's largest trading partners and they are part of a North American Free Trade Agreement with Mexico. On 11 September 2001, the long US–Canadian border was shut down to all cross-border traffic. The impact on the Canadian trucking industry was devastating. One unexpected consequence of this is that the Canadian Truckers' Union is now one of the most avid supporters of biometric identification cards for cross-border traffic. In the debate over balancing security with privacy, the truckers have come down on the security side because it will allow them to continue their economic activity despite stringent border security. Some, such as Friedman (2002), have argued that the promotion of free trade could serve as a means of countering the inequities and resentments that fuel sympathy, if not outright support, for al-Qaeda's terrorist activities, particularly in the Muslim and Arab world. This highlights the thesis that trading states do not tend to go to war with each other and again underscores how a global response to terrorism can be effective only if it embraces a wide spectrum of policy domains and includes both short-term and longer-term initiatives. It also highlights why inconsistency in trade policy, such as the US imposition of steel tariffs and increasing farm subsidies in 2002, can have a negative effect on international cooperation in the fight against terrorism. If a trade war were ever to break out between the EU and the US (*The Economist* 2002), cooperation in other areas, including counterterrorism, could also be affected.

The final 'delicate balance' concerns the area of arms control and the problem of dual-use technology already referred to in discussing today's security architecture. It is embedded in larger questions about how to maintain a balance between promoting international trade and the economic development and self-sufficiency of developing countries on the one hand, and the control of conventional arms and WMD proliferation on the other. Many Western nations sell arms and military technology, only to have them used against them in unconventional 'new' wars. Similarly, many developing countries desire nuclear technology in order to boost their economic development and self-sufficiency, yet the fear is that they are also building up nuclear weapons programs in an effort to deter Western threats to their security. Such security dilemmas are crucial areas for continuing research on the interrelatedness of security and economic issues such as trade, foreign aid and international development.

Specific challenges for transitional states

For post-conflict states, or states that are undergoing a transition from a non-democratic past and are in the process of democratization, market liberalization and state-building, there are a whole series of challenges that can have a serious impact on efforts to create a globally coordinated and integrated counterterrorism regime, especially since many such states constitute actual or potential allies in the current 'war on terror'. Many of these states have an authoritarian/totalitarian or an imperial/colonial past. State institutions are weak and there is endemic corruption. Their state-run economies are also weak and often compete with or are completely supplanted by black or underground economies that involve organized crime, mafia, drug trafficking or narcoterrorism. Civil society is weak and there is limited democratization, if any. In such transitional states, which comes first: market liberalization or democratization? Collective security or individual freedom? As discussed previously, the promotion of Western values of democracy, human rights and open and transparent government can often appear to such states as a form of cultural imperialism. Efforts at policy harmonization can be (or be seen to be) a disguised form of subordination. Research can be conducted on how Western values are perceived in other societies and cultures and how homologous concepts in those societies, perhaps in different form, can create points of contact for harmonization efforts. Post-war Iraq would serve as an excellent case study.

One area that is too often neglected in security studies, in general, and counterterrorism research in particular, is the issue of gender. More specifically, gender inequality – 'that is, the subordinate status or inferior treatment of females in political, legal, social, or economic matters' (Hudson and den Boer 2004: 4) – can have direct, if too often unrecognized, implications for developing an effective counterterrorism strategy, especially in the long term. This is even more so today, post September 11, when many scholars and practitioners are focusing on Asia as a major hub of al-Qaeda activity, and on the emergence of China and India as major world powers. One of the most compelling measures of gender inequality is what Hudson and den Boer call 'offspring sex selection'. Two examples of this practice are female infanticide and sex-selective abortion, where female fetuses are aborted while male fetuses are allowed to come to term. The latter practice, ironically, is possible due to ultrasound technology, which is widely perceived to be a major medical advance. The result of extreme forms of offspring sex selection, particularly in China – where a one-child policy has been in effect for some time – and India, but throughout Asia as well, is a drastic increase in the male/female sex ratio. This surfeit of males means that many young men in these countries will never have a hope of ever finding a mate, marrying or raising a family. These 'bare branches', as the Chinese call them, are perfect fodder for terrorist recruitment. Imagine a young man who can never have sexual relations with a woman, who is forever shut out of the institutions of marriage, family, school (other than religious) and job. As militaries around the world have known for centuries, teenage males are extremely susceptible to indoctrination, to bonding rituals and to organized channeling towards sanctioned and condoned violence supported by appropriate appeals to God, country or fraternity (Crelinsten 1995). Add to this the sexual and social frustrations of a 'bare branch', and you have a perfect candidate for the commission of indiscriminate violence, including suicide bombing.

Studies by the United Nations Development Program have shown a significant inverse correlation between the level of a woman's education and the number of children she bears. In the long term, the best antidote to the bare branch problem would be the promotion of education and empowerment of women throughout the world and particularly in those regions where the sex ratio significantly favours males. Research on how this might be achieved, and the possible obstacles – social, cultural, economic, political – that might impede its progress should be an important component of any serious research program on counterterrorism.

Conclusion

September 11 has resulted in a global alliance against terrorism. What we now need is not just an alliance *against* evil, but an alliance *for* something positive ... (Stiglitz 2002).

He who fights with monsters might take care lest he thereby become a monster.

Friedrich Nietzsche: *Beyond Good and Evil* (1886)

The kinds of knowledge that are necessary for analyzing and understanding such complex relationships as discussed in this chapter can be identified in terms of a series of polarities that typically divide counterterrorism and security professionals when they consider the question of what we should know and how we should go about gaining this knowledge.

- *Certain vulnerabilities vs uncertain threats*: do we focus on those vulnerabilities that we know, without question, would lead to catastrophic consequences were we to ignore them? Here, we are talking primarily about the threat of WMD terrorism and, in particular, CBRN threats. The problem here is that the probability of terrorists carrying out such attacks is extremely low, the persistence of supposedly well-informed doomsday predictions notwithstanding. As the Bali bombing, the Moscow theatre siege and the Madrid train bombings demonstrate, terrorists can wreak havoc using the traditional tactics of bombing and hostage-taking that have long been the favored weapons of the weak. The key is that these tactics can be used in new contexts (Bali) or in frighteningly new variants (Moscow; Madrid). As such, they constitute uncertain threats as opposed to certain vulnerabilities. Should research be focused on the former – a task fraught with difficulties relating to understanding terrorist target selection and motivation – or the latter – a task that usually requires worst-case thinking that deliberately ignores what we know about terrorist motivation and is more focused on emergency preparedness and damage limitation, both infrastructural and sociopolitical?

- *Short term vs long term*: do we focus on the short term, which means that we primarily look at current groups, their motivations, preferred targets and tactics, and their organizational structure, or do we focus on the long term, which necessitates not only that we consider the larger picture – the social and political context in which known groups operate – but also that we try and consider how such groups might transform themselves in response to counterterrorist measures and which new issues might trigger new (or old) groups to consider terrorism or a non-violent alternative?

- *Hard power vs soft power*: what kind of knowledge is necessary for supporting and rendering more effective those counterterrorist measures that rely on the state's monopoly on the use of violence, namely police, courts and military, and what kind of knowledge is necessary for supporting more persuasive forms of control, such as economic sanctions, public education and diplomatic initiatives? If a criminal justice or military model of counterterrorism prevails, then certain kinds of knowledge about terrorist constituencies or terrorist financing may not be necessary. But if the exercise of soft as opposed to hard power is to be seriously entertained as an essential component of a comprehensive counterterrorism strategy, then other kinds of knowledge become important.

- *Unilateralism vs multilateralism*: similarly, a unilateralist approach to counterterrorism may have knowledge requirements that differ significantly from those of a multilateralist one – the latter requiring a detailed knowledge of different policy approaches, different political cultures and different levels of training and competency of those charged with counterterrorism that the former may not need to consider.

- *Tactical vs strategic*: many of the distinctions outlined above boil down to the difference between tactical and strategic analysis, whereby the former tends to be more short term, more oriented towards supporting the exercise of hard power, more easily done unilaterally, and more generally reactive in that the primary concern is to protect certain vulnerabilities exposed by a small sample of past attacks and the worst-case scenario projections that derive therefrom. Strategic analysis, on the other hand, tends to be longer term, and lends itself more easily to supporting the exercise of soft power which must consider a much broader range of issues than tactical analysis and is better done on a multilateral basis since it can allow for the kinds of analysis, such as comparative and historical analysis (see Duyvesteyn's chapter), that take longer to do. As such, strategic analysis is better suited to dealing with uncertain threats – who will do what when and how – in a complex environment of ever-evolving threats and vulnerabilities.

While I have polarized the kinds of knowledge into two different and opposing 'schools of thought', the ultimate challenge is not to decide which is better ('either/or') but to figure out a way to do both ('both/and'). Only by combining different types of knowledge and different modes of thought and methods of analysis, can we hope to achieve a comprehensive research plan commensurate to the challenges posed by countering terrorism in a multi-centric world.

As for the policy implications of such a comprehensive research plan, I again present these in the form of a dichotomy. There is an easy way to fight terrorism and a hard way. The easy way to fight terrorism is as follows:

- seal off borders (both to insiders and outsiders);
- repress all political and social opposition;
- offer social and economic incentives for informing on neighbours and dissidents;
- create a secret police to control all aspects of social and political life;
- centralize the economy and create an autarky;
- control the media and deny the public alternative visions, viewpoints and vistas.

In sum, create a totalitarian regime and resist or disrupt global governance. The result: homeland security via unilateralism and isolationism. The Soviet Union had no significant terrorism until, ironically, the period of *glasnost* and *perestroika*.

The hard way to fight terrorism is as follows:

- respect the rule of law;
- sign, ratify and adhere to all international conventions against terrorism and related acts;
- extradite or prosecute suspected terrorists;
- participate in international regimes that control trade, aid, finance, arms control, WMD proliferation;
- complement police, military and legal control of terrorism (the exercise of 'hard power') with economic, social, cultural and environmental measures that address the root causes of political, social and religious grievances (the exercise of 'soft power');
- work both domestically and internationally to reduce the gap between rich and poor peoples and nations and to create a better world for all human beings.

In sum, create and strengthen democratic regimes and encourage or support global governance. The result: homeland security via multilateralism and international cooperation.

If we choose the easy path to counterterrorism, then we simply confirm the beliefs of those fanatics, zealots and ideologues who claim that their terrorism and violence are legitimate responses to tyranny, oppression and state terror. If we choose the difficult path to counterterrorism, we shall ultimately succeed in undermining those beliefs among the vast majority of people, isolating the fanatics, zealots and ideologues and facilitating their being brought to justice. But the key word is 'ultimately'. Short-term solutions and 'quick fixes' may work for a while – until the next terrorist attack or the next terrorist movement. Coupled with long-term efforts, their impact will be much more long lasting.

References

Annan, Kofi (2005). 'A Global Strategy for Fighting Terrorism', Keynote Address to the Closing Plenary of the International Summit on Democracy, Terrorism and Security, Madrid, March 10. Available at <http://english.safe-democracy.org/keynotes/a-global-strategy-for-fighting-terrorism.html>.

Bailes, Alyson J.K. and Isabel Frommelt (eds) (2004). *Business and Security: Public–Private Sector Relationships in a New Security Environment* (Oxford: Oxford University Press).

Bigo, Didier (1994). 'The European Internal Security Field: Stakes and Rivalries in a Newly Developing Area of Police Intervention', in Malcolm Anderson and Monica den Boer (eds), *Policing across National Boundaries* (London: Pinter Publishers), pp. 161–173.

Blunkett, David (2002). 'Civic rights: Freedom and security are two essentials that citizens look to the government to provide. Whatever balance is struck, someone will be unhappy. But negative attitudes to the state simply distort the debate', *The Guardian*, 14 September.

Bok, Sissela (2002). *Common Values* (Columbia, MO: University of Missouri Press).

Buzan, Barry (1991). *People, States and Fear: An Agenda for International Security Studies in the Post-Cold War Era,* 2nd edition (Boulder, CO: Lynne Rienner).

Buzan, Barry (2002). Remarks at ASAM Conference, 'Globalization, Security, and the Nation State,' 15–16 June, Ankara, Turkey.

Buzan, Barry and Gerald Segal (1998). 'Rethinking East Asian Security', in Michael T. Klare (ed.), *World Security: Challenges for a New Century.* 3rd edition (New York: St Martin's Press), pp. 96–112.

Buzan, Barry, Ole Waever and Jaap de Wilde (1998). *Security: A New Framework for Analysis.* (Boulder, CO: Lynne Rienner).

Chambliss, William J. (1989). 'State-Organized Crime – The American Society of Criminology, 1988 Presidential Address', *Criminology*, 27(2): 183–208.

Clutterbuck, Richard (1993). 'Negotiating with Terrorists', in Alex P. Schmid and Ronald D. Crelinsten (eds), *Western Responses to Terrorism* (London: Frank Cass), pp. 261–287.

Cohen, Stanley (ed.) (2005). 'Torture: A User's Manual', *Index on Censorship* 34(1): 24–81.

Crawford, Beverly (1995). 'Hawks, Doves, but no Owls: International Economic Inter-dependence and Construction of the New Security Dilemma', in Ronnie D. Lipschutz (ed.), *On Security* (New York: Columbia University Press), pp. 149–186.

Crelinsten, Ronald D. (1978). 'International Political Terrorism: A Challenge for Comparative Research', *International Journal of Comparative and Applied Criminal Justice*, 2(2): 107–126. Reprinted in Rosemary H.T. O'Kane (ed.), *Terrorism*, 2 volumes (Cheltenham, UK: Edward Elgar Publishing, 2004).

Crelinsten, Ronald D. (1989). 'Terrorism, Counter-Terrorism and Democracy: The Assessment of National Security Threats', *Terrorism and Political Violence*, 1(2): 242–269.

Crelinsten, Ronald D. (1994). 'The Impact of Television on Terrorism and Crisis Situations: Implications for Public Policy', *Journal of Contingencies and Crisis Management*, 2(2): 61–72.

Crelinsten, Ronald D. (1995). 'In Their Own Words: The World of the Torturer', in R.D. Crelinsten and A.P. Schmid (eds), *The Politics of Pain: Torturers and their Masters* (Boulder, CO: Westview Press), pp. 35–64.

Crelinsten, Ronald D. (1997). 'Television and Terrorism: Implications for Crisis Management and Policy-Making', *Terrorism and Political Violence* 9(4): 8–32.

Crelinsten, Ronald D. (1998). 'The Discourse and Practice of Counterterrorism in Liberal Democracies', *Australian Journal of Politics & History*, 44/3 (September): 389–413. Reprinted in Alan O'Day (ed.), *The War on Terrorism* (Aldershot, UK: Ashgate, 2004).

Crelinsten, Ronald D. (2000). 'Terrorism and Counter-Terrorism in a Multi-Centric World: Challenges and Opportunities', in Max. Taylor and John Horgan (eds), *The Future of Terrorism* (London: Frank Cass), pp. 170–196.

Crelinsten, Ronald (2001). 'Policy Making in a Multicentric World: The Impact of Globalization, Privatization and Decentralization on Democratic Governance', in Gordon S. Smith and Daniel Wolfish (eds), *Who is Afraid of the State? Canada in a World of Multiple Centres of Power* (Toronto: University of Toronto Press), pp. 89–130.

Crelinsten, Ronald (2002). 'Analysing Terrorism and Counter-Terrorism: A Communication Model', *Terrorism and Political Violence*, 14(2): 77–122. Reprinted in Alan O'Day (ed.), *Dimensions of Terrorism* (Aldershot, UK: Ashgate, 2004).

Dartnell, Michael (2000). 'A Legal Inter-Network for Terrorism: Issues of Globalization, Fragmentation and Legitimacy', in Max. Taylor and John Horgan (eds), *The Future of Terrorism* (London: Frank Cass), pp. 197–208.

Duffield, Mark (2001). *Global Governance and the New Wars: The Merging of Development and Security* (London: Zed Books).

Firestone, David (2001). 'F.B.I. Traces Hamas's Plan to Finance Attacks to '93: Eight years ago, electronic eavesdropping provided the first clear indication that the group planned to raise money in the United States for terrorism in Israel', *The New York Times*, 6 December.

Friedman, Thomas L. (2002). 'Better Late Than . . .: President Bush's speech on Thursday announcing a big increase in foreign aid for poor countries is a breakthrough for this administration', *The New York Times*, 17 March.

Held, David (2003). 'Bringing International Law to Bear on the Control of the New Terrorism in the Global Age', in Charles Kegley, Jr (ed.), *The New Global Terrorism: Characteristics, Causes, Controls* (Upper Saddle River, NJ: Prentice Hall), pp. 253–266.

Holmqvist, Caroline (2005). 'Private Security Companies: The Case for Regulation', SIPRI Policy Paper No. 9 (Stockholm: SIPRI).

Hudson, Valerie M. and Andrea M. den Boer (2004). *Bare Branches: The Security Implications of Asia's Surplus Male Population* (Boston, MA: MIT Press).

Lipton, Eric (2005). 'Some U.S. Security Agents Chafe under Speech Limits', *The New York Times*, 26 April.

McGeary, Johanna (2001). 'Ears to the Ground: The hunt for bin Laden is going to take what the U.S. does least well: dirty, diligent human spying', *Time*, 15 October, pp. 56–57.

Meyer, Josh and Eric Lichtblau (2002). 'Crackdown on Terror Funding is Questioned – Finance: U.S. officials say a lack of evidence and fighting among agencies have hampered the drive', *Los Angeles Times*, 7 April.

Pal, Leslie (1997). *Beyond Policy Analysis: Public Issue Management in Turbulent Times* (Scarborough, ON: ITP Nelson).

Rapoport, David C. and Leonard Weinberg (eds) (2000). *The Democratic Experience and Political Violence* (London: Frank Cass).

Ravetz, Jerome R. (1971). *Scientific Knowledge and its Social Problems* (London: Oxford University Press).

Rosenau, James N. (1990). *Turbulence in World Politics: A Theory of Change and Continuity* (Princeton, NJ: Princeton University Press).

Rosenau, James N. (1997). *Along the Domestic–Foreign Frontier: Exploring Governance in a Turbulent World* (Cambridge: Cambridge University Press).

Schmid, Alex P. (1993). 'The Response Problem as a Definition Problem', in Alex P. Schmid and Ronald D. Crelinsten (eds), *Western Responses to Terrorism* (London: Frank Cass), pp. 7–13.

Stepanova, Ekaterina (2003).*Anti-terrorism and Peace-building During and After Conflict* (Stockholm, SIPRI).

Stiglitz, Joseph E. (2002). 'Globalism's Discontents', *The American Prospect Online*, 1 January.

STRATFOR (Strategic Forecasting LLC) (2002). 'U.S. Undertaking Generational Weapons Shift', 3 May.

The Economist (2002). 'Bush the anti-globaliser: America's monstrous new farm bill could wreck any chance of further trade liberalisation', in 'How sick is Europe?,' 11–17 May print edition, pp. 14, 16.

Thomson, Janice (1992). 'Explaining the Regulation of Transnational Practices: A State-Building Approach', in James N. Rosenau and Ernst-Otto Czempiel (eds), *Governance Without Government* (Cambridge: Cambridge University Press), pp. 195–218.

Waever, Ole (1995). 'Securitization and Desecuritization', in Ronnie D. Lipschutz (ed.), *On Security* (New York: Columbia University Press), pp. 46–86.

Zernike, Kate and Christopher Drew (2002). 'Efforts to Track Foreign Students are Said to Lag', *The New York Times*, 28 January.

11

COMPETING WITH TERRORISTS IN CYBERSPACE: OPPORTUNITIES AND HURDLES

Neal A. Pollard[1]

It is "obvious and unarguable" that no government interest is more compelling than the security of the Nation.

US Supreme Court, *Haig v. Agee* (1981)

Introduction

Cyberspace is a front in the global war on terrorism. Terrorist use of information technology extends beyond legions of hackers and doomsday scenarios of "electronic Pearl Harbor." Rather, the US and her allies are engaged in a strategic competition with terrorism in cyberspace, over the effective use of information technology (IT) and other engines of globalization, as tools, weapons, and targets.

Terrorists exploit the engines of globalization to wield disruptive power. Certainly they exploit cheap transportation and open commerce, free travel and trade, and they bury their finances in the global financial system. They especially exploit, hide in, surveil, and even target our information systems and critical infrastructures. They use the internet and the World Wide Web for critical processes such as recruiting, training, propaganda, planning, surveillance, and coordination and communication. They use electronic infrastructures to travel, trade, and transact. And there is significant concern that they will someday target and attack the very infrastructures and information systems that they rely on today. The competition with terrorists in cyberspace is the effort to deny terrorists these exploitative abilities, while using the same technology and infrastructure to find and counter terrorist activities.

Many technological opportunities exist to compete more effectively with terrorists in cyberspace. However, the United States is limited in exploiting these opportunities. This limitation is not technical, nor is it measured by numbers of computers, bandwidth capacity, or internet connectivity. This limitation is an inability to integrate the co-development of technology, law, and policy, and it will persist until we can successfully integrate law and policy into the foundation of technological development.

To be sure, the US wields information and technology daily, to counter terrorism successfully across a number of areas. However, we have strategic opportunities in three domains of information technology (IT) where we must first establish clear policies and resolve legal uncertainties and tensions, before we will be able to make most effective use of these tools to compete with terrorism in the information space. These three domains of strategic IT include intelligence and knowledge, critical infrastructure protection, and cyber conflict and defense.

Globalization's bastards

Modern terrorism was born on July 22, 1968.[2] On that date, terrorists from the Popular Front for the Liberation of Palestine (PFLP) hijacked an El Al flight from Rome to Tel Aviv, and demanded the release of comrades-in-arms. It certainly was not the first hijacking, but it was unprecedented for a number of reasons: its purpose of trading hostages for prisoners, the specific targeting of an Israeli-flagged airliner, forcing Israel to communicate with a *persona non grata* terrorist group, and the specific aim of creating an international media event. Zehdi Labib Terzi, the Palestine Liberation Organization's chief observer at the UN, said in a 1976 interview, "The first several hijackings aroused the consciousness of the world and awakened the media and world opinion much more – and more effectively – than 20 years of pleading at the United Nations."[3] Terrorists found a powerful means of expressing themselves globally at the convergence of two recent technological developments: cheap intercontinental travel using airplanes, and a pervasive global media using international communications technology. Not coincidentally, cheap intercontinental transportation and global information communication are the two main engines of globalization.

Modern globalization resulted in modern terrorism. Some have argued that the terrorism of September 11, 2001 was the death knell for globalization. Others have argued that terrorists have hijacked globalization, as though it were a force external to globalization. Neither argument is totally accurate: terrorism *is* globalization, or at least, its illegitimate, rebellious, highly agitated offspring. The strategic use of information technology continues to be a key field of competition between liberal democracies and extremist groups, as both benefit from globalization.

Crisis trends

This competition in cyberspace emanates from the convergence of four trends of globalization, driven by IT. If a crisis represents both opportunity and danger, then these are truly four crisis trends.

The first trend is the removal of political, economic, and technological divisions (e.g., borders, geography, industrialization) as a hindrance to commerce, communication, and movement, creating worldwide networks of interdependence. This is the essence of globalization, and many definitions of globalization include this characterization.[4]

The second trend is the connectivity to cyberspace of virtually every private or business actor. It is near impossible to function as an individual in modern industrial society without connecting to the internet at some point in daily life. Even if an individual avoids information technology of all forms, those from whom he receives products or services certainly rely on the internet for efficiency and productivity. Certainly not everyone is connected to cyberspace. But the trend is not one of decreasing connectivity.

The third trend is the availability and multiplicity of data and databases of public information on individuals and entities. When a private or business actor connects to cyberspace, often that connection leaves data that is collected and stored for later usage by a variety of public and private actors, from government agencies to statisticians to insurance and credit companies to marketing professionals. Much of this information is provided knowingly and voluntarily, but what then happens to the data is somewhat more opaque, as illustrated by recent fraud cases involving commercial data aggregators ChoicePoint and LexisNexis.

The fourth trend is the increasing power of information technology to access disparate databases, mine and aggregate data, and identify and analyze patterns. ChoicePoint alone collects almost 4,000 data sources per month and houses over 100 terabytes of data.[5]

These trends present opportunity, in that they are enablers of globalization and its benefits to liberty, productivity, and progress. The engines of globalization – the information revolution, cheap and open intercontinental transportation, global 24-hour media, electronic finance infrastructure, increasing participation in international organizations, and liberalized trade and investment – increase productivity, business and trade efficiency, cost-effectiveness of human and capital migration, scientific collaboration and development, and the ability of the media and individual communications to overcome government oppression, abuse, and corruption. These are arguably boons to humanity, and they benefit the US.

These trends present two dimensions of danger, however. The first dimension is the danger that, as illustrated before, globalization can be exploited by both good guys and bad guys. The second danger is that there are significant non-technological hurdles that prevent the US and allies from exploiting IT as effectively as terrorists and criminals.

The state does not enjoy an absolute monopoly on the ability to influence international relations and security, or to affect the global distribution of effective power. Non-state actors – both profit- and ideologically driven – also wield influence on the international plane. Legitimate international actors – states, multinational corporations, and non-governmental organizations – have exploited globalization and its technological nexus for legitimate ends.

Table 11.1 International actors in the globalization age

Type of actor	Legal actor	Illegal actor
State	United Nations member	"Rogue state"
Profit	Multinational corporation	Transnational organized crime syndicate
Policy	Non-governmental organization	Transnational terrorist group
Technology/ globalization nexus	• Information revolution • Global media • Scientific collaboration and development • Electronic finance • Increased foreign investment • Cheap intercontinental travel and transportation of goods • Greater productivity	• Cyber-terror/crime • Propaganda, al Jazeera • Proliferation • Money laundering • Terror sponsorship and fundraising • Smuggling • September 11, 2001, Russian organized crime

However, every legitimate international actor has an illegitimate counterpart: "rogue" states, transnational organized criminal syndicates, and terrorist networks. These illegitimate actors have also exploited globalization and technology. Table 11.1 illustrates this continuum of international actors, and the technological nexus with globalization that enables them to influence the international system.

Technologically, the US is capable of maximizing the opportunities arising from globalization trends. The challenge is to exploit these opportunities, and deny terrorists the effective use of information technology and cyberspace, without eroding the civil libertarian, social, cultural, and economic advantages of IT and globalization.

Technology opportunities

There are three areas of opportunity in IT to compete more effectively with terrorists: intelligence and knowledge, critical infrastructure operations and protection, and cyber conflict and defense. However, the US is limited from exploiting these opportunities by an inability to integrate effectively the co-development of technology, law, and policy.

In intelligence and knowledge, there are significant opportunities in technology for data mining and aggregation, pattern analysis and "non-obvious link awareness," and structured hypothesis generation and competition. The potential of these opportunities arises from a provocative hypothesis: if one can track terrorists' transactions and processes, one can track, anticipate, and interdict terrorists.

Terrorists transact, and these transactions create records and leave footprints in cyberspace. When terrorists decide to exploit an opportunity, they are consumers. They buy products and services, they travel, they communicate, they send or receive money, they apply for and present passports, they drive cars, they rent hotel rooms, and they conduct surveillance on their targets. In virtually all cases, terrorists have left detectable clues in transactions, generally found after the attack. The hypothesis underlying the use of data mining, aggregation, and pattern recognition is that these transactional patterns, indicative of terrorist activity, can be identified and interdicted before an attack.

Technology for intelligence and knowledge also offers the opportunity to resolve deficiencies in intelligence analysis – a subject of much attention in recent commissions such as the 9/11 and Silberman–Robb commissions. Data mining and pattern analysis offer opportunities to aid counterterrorism intelligence officers and policymakers in processing, analyzing, and disseminating masses of disparate data and critical information about terrorist groups, and identifying patterns of terrorist activity.

For example. the Silberman–Robb commission recently identified the need for "alternative hypothesis generation" and "structures and practices and increased competitive analysis." IT offers tools to meet these requirements. Data mining, visualization, and reasoning tools allow analysts and decision-makers to explore different implications of data and trends, to understand the extent to which hypotheses are supported or refuted by available data, and to identify critical gaps in data that might better support alternative hypotheses. To be sure, these functions are performed now by analysts, but this is an inefficient use of analysts' time. Some tasks within these functions can be performed more efficiently and effectively by IT. The role of IT is to reduce analysts' time spent researching and compiling data from myriad databases as well as generating hypotheses implicated by the data. If these tasks are effectively accomplished by IT, then more analyst time can be spent focusing on those tasks only a human can perform: tasks involving judgment, intuition, experience, and imagination. This holds the potential for a dramatic increase in the effectiveness of intelligence analysis.

Figure 11.1 illustrates this point. One might consider analytical tasks grouped among three categories: research, analysis, and presentation. Research – gathering, sorting, and cross-checking data – and production – structuring, presenting, and completing hypotheses – are tasks that can be machine assisted. Pure analysis – application of reason, judgment, experience, intuition, and imagination – is where humans have the greatest opportunity to add value that machines cannot. Figure 11.1 displays the results of an experiment, using tools described above, where traditional analytical processes (i.e., human-intensive)

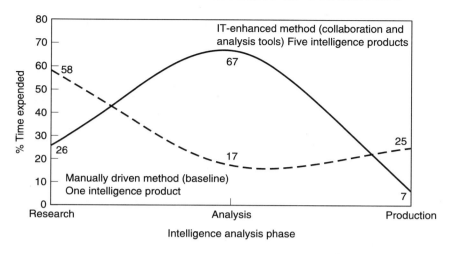

Figure 11.1 IT-enhanced v. manually-driven intelligence analysis.[6]

were used to produce one intelligence product, versus IT-enhanced analysis to produce five intelligence products. In the latter trial, IT increased by 50% the amount of human analyst time devoted to those tasks humans can best perform.

IT offers opportunities in critical infrastructure protection. As described above, terrorists move through global infrastructures, using them for transactions, communications, surveillance, propaganda and recruitment, and perhaps as targets. In the US, 80 to 90 percent of critical infrastructure is owned and operated by the private sector. The opportunities lie in marshalling the resources of the private sector toward national goals of protecting infrastructures from attacks that wreak national failures, and tracking and denying terrorist use of infrastructure to communicate, transact, and move about. The strategic use of IT in protecting our critical infrastructures requires the government to strike a public/private partnership that brings to bear the full resources of corporate information technology to secure the infrastructure without eroding its social or economic viability.

Finally, the US has technological opportunities in cyber conflict and defense. The strategic use of IT in cyber conflict is, simply put, waging war in cyberspace – using IT in support of computer network attacks (CNA) on terrorist infrastructure or processes in cyberspace, while defending against terrorist electronic attack on our physical or electronic systems. Technology opportunities for cyber-conflict extend well beyond hacking, viruses, and corporate espionage, to include analytical tools, and models to predict the effects of alternative approaches to network disruption. They include technologies that provide the ability to target, access, and sustain disruption of critical electronic systems, enabling the US to track, intercept, or shut down communications on terrorist-affiliated websites and internet accounts, divert terrorist funding, shut down regional electronic infrastructures on which terrorists rely, and even wreak havoc on the infrastructures of terrorist sponsors. Furthermore, these technologies can also be used to defend against enemy cyber-attack. A recent article in *Wired* characterizes the technological potential of the US military underlying these capabilities, operated by US Strategic Command's Joint Functional Component Command for Network Warfare.[7] However, as the article points out, despite a 2002 Presidential directive to develop guidelines for offensive cyber-warfare, the rules of engagement and supporting legal and policy structures are emerging more slowly than the technological capabilities.

Transferring risk

Security is about risk management. Once risk is assessed, it can either be borne, reduced, or transferred from one actor to another. Assessing risk usually involves three measurements: probability of failure (e.g., terrorist attack), severity of failure (e.g., consequences), and effectiveness of mitigation to reduce the probability or severity of failure (e.g., threat reduction or consequence management).

Effectiveness of mitigation itself has two underlying variables: the likelihood that mitigation will actually work according to plan, and the costs that mitigation imposes upon other important considerations. For example, consider the threat of smuggling a chemical weapon across the Mexican–American border to attack Los Angeles. Shutting down and hermetically sealing the southern border of the US will drastically reduce the probability of threat, and will likely work, but the costs to commerce, trade, free movement of people, etc., are too burdensome to balance the equation, and reasonable people may question whether it would even work. Similarly, requiring the citizens of Los Angeles to wear protective suits against chemicals, 24 hours a day and seven days a week, would significantly reduce the consequences of a chemical attack, with high likelihood of successful mitigation, but at an unreasonable burden to many other public policy interests.

In terms of national or homeland security, risk transference usually focuses on effectiveness of mitigation. Risk and cost are transferred among competing public policy objectives: security, civil liberty, economic viability, commerce, scientific progress, infrastructure development, and other objectives that governments pursue to benefit the polity. Risk is also transferred among actors that generate or bear risk: different levels of government, the corporate sector, private citizens, and even among different nations.

Technology, policy and law are all tools that can be used to reduce or transfer risk. As argued above, information technology holds great opportunity to reduce or transfer risk by providing capabilities in intelligence and knowledge, critical infrastructure protection, and cyber conflict and defense. However, law and policy are not adequate to support exploitation of these opportunities. That is, these technologies are not used as effectively as they could be because of unresolved legal uncertainties and unnecessary or outdated policy restrictions. These legal and policy hurdles to technology exploitation will persist until the

US resolves substantive legal and policy uncertainties, updates or refines policy restrictions, and implements an effective process to integrate the co-development of technology with policy and law. This is a challenge of both substance and process.

Substantive hurdles: intelligence, knowledge, and privacy

Technology opportunities in intelligence and knowledge require trading risks among public policy objectives, especially security and privacy. "Connecting the dots" of intelligence information is critical to homeland security. Technologies show potential to enhance intelligence capabilities. In well-publicized cases, the government has halted development or implementation of these technologies out of privacy concerns: in their calculation, the benefits to security did not outweigh the costs to privacy interests.

Substantively, the US has not adequately defined public policy objectives on privacy with respect to the modern trends described above. It is difficult to measure costs to an interest that has been poorly defined. Most of the basic principles of privacy law, *vis-à-vis* government surveillance and Fourth Amendment protections, were articulated during the 1960s and 1970s, codified into such statutes as the Omnibus Crime Control and Safe Streets Act of 1968 (specifying the procedure for criminal investigation wiretaps), the Privacy Act of 1974, and the Foreign Intelligence Surveillance Act of 1978.

These statutes, and their underlying principles, come from a profoundly different time in US history. The US faced a different threat. Technology was profoundly different, and the crisis trends described above had not yet revolutionized society. Even the government abuses were different, giving rise to such bodies as the Church Commission. During that period, the concern was that the FBI or CIA would gain surreptitious access to information to which they had no right. Today, the risk of abuse is not so much illegal government access to information, but the uncertainty of what the government ought to do with information to which it has legal access.

The change in threats, technologies, and government authorities demands a reexamination of fundamental principles of public policy, in light of technological advances and market demand for those technologies. Justice Brandeis' maxim still holds true, that the right to privacy is the "right to be left alone." But this is not the same thing as a right to anonymity, which the Supreme Court is not prepared to recognize. The court has articulated that privacy is guaranteed around those personal areas where one has a reasonable expectation that society is prepared to accept. But what is a reasonable expectation of privacy with respect to information that people freely give to third parties (websites, rental car companies, airlines, etc.)? If technology can potentially frustrate privacy interests, can it also be used to protect privacy interests, simultaneously contributing to privacy and security? If a surveillance technology gives 'false positives', what are the consequences or harm of false positives, and what rate is unacceptable? Do data mining and aggregation really pose a qualitatively different level of intrusion? How much data must be aggregated before privacy is violated? Can the potentially intrusive effect of data mining and aggregation be mitigated by data anonymization? If so, what level of 'anonymization' is sufficient, and what is the best way to guarantee and oversee it? What constitutes personally identifiable information, how much of it should be available to government, and under what circumstances? What kinds of duties and liabilities do we want to place on those private-sector entities that collect and maintain data (e.g. ChoicePoint)? What are the long-term effects on public policy of data aggregation by both government and private entities? Technology opportunities have been missed because these substantive questions remain unanswered.

Substantive hurdles: critical infrastructure protection and private responsibility

Critical infrastructure protection is about trading risks between the government and the private sector. Homeland security is the ultimate responsibility of the government. The problem is, critical infrastructures are about 90 percent owned by private sector providers, and their interconnectivity and efficiencies are driven by information technology. The threshold between homeland security and corporate responsibilities has not been well defined, and thus there is a substantive policy gap between homeland security interests and shareholder interests.

This creates a hurdle to efficient, reasonable, or even practical assignment of appropriate risks to be borne respectively by the government and shareholders. How then to enlist the private sector for public goals? How do we secure these infrastructures without degrading their efficiency? How do we deny terrorists the use of these infrastructures without hindering social and economic commerce? What tools can the government use to reconcile private commercial objectives with public policy objectives? What national responsibilities and obligations can be reasonably and efficiently borne by shareholders? Can these responsibilities overlap, rather than fall victim to a gap?

As far back as 1997, the US government has systematically tried to answer these questions. The most promising opportunities to protect our infrastructures are oriented around the strategic use of corporate IT, but this use will be limited to local patches in system vulnerabilities until key balances are struck that will enable the strategic use of IT to protect critical infrastructures while maximizing their efficiencies. This will come about only after the private sector infrastructure providers are full partners with the government and international community, marshalling the full extent of corporate resources and technologies in securing infrastructures. This partnership will not come about until the government develops imaginative tools and incentives, in law and policy, that reconcile the interests of the private sector and public safety. This reconciliation would go beyond simply creating a business case for security – it would demonstrate how corporate goals and homeland security objectives are consistent and mutually supportive, by identifying and matching the intersections where corporate and public interests are complementary or mutually supportive, and resolving with tools and incentives those discrete areas where interests diverge.

The need for this reconciliation is evident. The private sector still does not take critical infrastructure seriously beyond its own corporate objectives. The August 16, 2004 issue of the *New York Times* reported that almost half of roughly 100 companies surveyed had not increased annual spending on security after 9/11. Furthermore, nearly 40% of the corporate executives surveyed said security was an expense that should be minimized. A quarter of the companies surveyed said their chief executives had not met in the last year with their security chiefs. Experts say the reasons for the faltering revolution are varied, ranging from a concern about costs to simply a lack of sustained focus and vigilance. "There were even some companies that buried their heads in the sand," said William Daly, a former FBI counterintelligence investigator who directs the New York office of Control Risks Group. "Security is kind of incident-driven, and continues to be that way."[8]

Incident-driven security is not strategic, it is reactive, and it continues to provide terrorists with opportunities. Homeland security strategy is different in substance from corporate strategy. Certainly protection against low-level insider threats such as proprietary information theft is a corporate responsibility. On the other end of the protection spectrum, defending against the North Korean air force bombarding our industrial infrastructure is clearly the responsibility of the Defense Department. But in between, the threshold is very fuzzy and undefined where corporate responsibility ends and government responsibility begins, and, against threats in the middle of this spectrum, one partner may assume it is the responsibility of the other partner to defend, leaving a seam of vulnerability and an opportunity for terrorists.

Certainly, defining this responsibility threshold is important to reconciling corporate and public interests. However, the government must conceive more imaginative tools in law and policy, considering each infrastructure sector on its own terms and interests, thus reflecting a more detailed understanding of where public and private interests converge and diverge. To date, regulation has been one of the most popular tools the government has used in the interest of public welfare. As any corporate manager will tell you, regulation usually costs shareholders money. But not always, and even when regulation does cost shareholders money, it is not in the same manner across all infrastructures.

Regulation is an unwieldy tool to use evenly across all infrastructure sectors because different infrastructure sectors respond differently (in economic and operational terms) to regulatory measures. For example, the nuclear power infrastructure was heavily regulated from its inception. Corporate burdens imposed on nuclear power providers are neither unexpected nor disruptive to commerce. On the other hand, information and telecommunications systems – especially the internet – are notoriously hard to regulate, and ham-handed regulation frequently imposes great corporate costs, without necessarily resolving the public safety issue the regulation was crafted to solve. This has been apparent from anti-trust regulation to Internet taxation regimes to regulations supporting subpoena powers against internet service providers.

Regulation has in the past had unintended consequences contrary to national security interests, despite successful fulfillment of regulatory goals. Both anti-trust policy and homeland security policy have at their heart the economic interests of the United States – one through prevention of predatory competitive practices, the other through assurance of the economic viability of critical infrastructures. The tools wielded in pursuit of these policies are not always as complementary. The 1984 break-up of AT&T was a victory for anti-trust policy, but many national security officials at the time, including Defense Secretary Caspar Weinberger in court testimony, opposed the break-up on grounds of national security policy. Weinberger and others argued that a dominant and robust telecommunications provider like AT&T, and its support of the national security telecommunications system developed in response to the Cuban Missile Crisis, was critical to national security. The main concern was that several telecommunications providers, in competition, would result in lack of interoperability and thus jeopardize critical communications in times of emergency, whereas a single, national provider would have the resources and system redundancies to maintain communications even if America were under attack. Thus, there were potentially bad unintended consequences for homeland security goals, even though equally valid anti-trust goals of public policy were achieved.

Even when crafting regulation with harmless unintended consequences, one cannot assume that the divergence between corporate and public interests is the same across infrastructures. For example, in the banking and finance sector, the corporate imperatives for security include protection against theft, fraud, and money laundering, to secure against financial loss, liability, and erosion of consumer confidence. The corporate use of IT in pursuing these objectives is going to result in achieving many public policy objectives, i.e. protection of the banking and finance infrastructure against disruption and loss, preventing its use by criminals and terrorists to transfer and launder money, and sustaining the confidence in the infrastructure of industry and international trading partners. Thus, the corporate interests of using IT readily support the strategic use of IT in homeland security.

In contrast, there is a significant divergence between corporate and public interests in the public health infrastructure. The imperatives of homeland security call for great redundancy in hospital and health care capacity, so that catastrophes – especially involving bio-terrorism – do not overwhelm our public health infrastructure. On the other hand, hospitals are largely owned by corporations, and empty beds and excess capacity equate to inefficiency, which shareholders do not appreciate. Reconciling the corporate and public interests of the health care system thus appears to be more challenging than for banking and finance. IT can be used to monitor capacity, direct patients, provide insight into capacity and resources at local and national levels, protect privacy, provide epidemiological surveillance information to law enforcement, etc., fulfilling a variety of corporate and/or public policy goals, if they are not mutually exclusive. The strategic use of IT by corporations to protect infrastructure is hindered not by technology barriers, but by these divergences.

These divergences are discovered and mitigated at the beginning of infrastructure protection strategy as one considers how infrastructures are interconnected and interdependent at the most fundamental levels. Once infrastructure protection is aggregated at the highest national policy levels, it is much more difficult to grasp the complexity of their interconnectivities and the various convergences and divergences of interests. This requires the development of legal and policy tools at the beginning of strategy development, where the interconnectivities among infrastructures are discovered. Law and policy at the end of strategy development, when infrastructures are considered "top-down," will misunderstand how interdependencies and interconnectivities operate to contribute to, or undermine, homeland security interests.

Governments must develop tools in law and policy that are more imaginative than regulation, to bring the corporate sector into the homeland security mission. These tools might include liability limitation and "safe harbors," subsidies or tax breaks to cover the gap between corporate and homeland security, perhaps even quasi-socialization of specific components or processes of infrastructure as "public goods," or a combination of one or more of these tailored to specific infrastructure sectors, their respective needs and interests, and gaps or overlaps between their specific interests and broader national interests. Different sectors and different countries have had different experiences and lessons in all of these approaches. Furthermore, America's vulnerability in cyberspace does not stop at her shores, but rather is enmeshed in the interconnectivity with other nations' critical infrastructures, the cyber-fabric of globalization. Thus, international conventions and agreements should also be considered as useful tools to balance international commerce, domestic economics, and homeland security.

Innovative tools and approaches must reconcile, and seek common ground between, business interests and homeland security interests, and balances must be tailored to specific sectors and industries. For example, *Business Week* recently described some innovative tools:

> ... a bill now pending, sponsored by Senators John D. Rockefeller IV (D-W.Va.) and Olympia J. Snowe (R-Me.), [will] let companies [recover] expense equipment costs when they build networks of at least 20 megabits a second. A U.S.-backed bond program would encourage municipalities to build their own fiber networks and then lease them to upstarts. And government can attract broadband to sparsely populated regions without tax dollars by creating pools of local buyers – a measure Canada has adopted to reach its vast rural expanses.[9]

These tools speak to corporate interests of tax incentives and market interests of greater broadband. Greater broadband also benefits homeland security, in that it provides more graceful degradation if parts of the national network fail. Such commonalities of interest will vary from sector to sector, and will require different mixes of tools to reach common ground. It is up to the government to investigate into best practices and lessons learned in developing these tools, and derive either new policy or legal tools or innovative ways to combine and apply existing tools, define the varying and dynamic thresholds between corporate and government responsibility, reconcile interests, and deploy these tools to protect our infrastructures without degrading them.

Substantive hurdles: cyber conflict, defense, and international law

Cyber conflict is about trading risks between the government and the private sector, as many cyber battles will be fought across systems that are privately owned. Defining the role of the private sector in cyber conflict is a sensitive element of critical infrastructure protection (but it is probably unreasonable, and possibly illegal, to envision an offensive role for the private sector in cyber conflict). In addition, systems that host cyber conflict will criss-cross through other nations' public and private infrastructures, but with no recognition of national borders. Thus, conducting offensive (and even defensive) acts in cyberspace will implicate international law and risks and relations among states.

Cyber conflict and computer network attack (CNA) are poorly understood in the context of war: both in terms of their usage, and in responding to them with conventional military force. What kind of a cyber attack would be considered an act of war? Can we use CNA to disrupt al-Qaeda's presence in cyberspace without due process or covertly, if it means trampling on infrastructures of other Western economies which are interconnected with our own? Would such a tactic be an act of war? During wartime, what is a legal use of cyber weaponry? Are there any "civilian" targets that would be prohibited by the law of armed conflict? How does one restrict the effects of a cyber attack to a specific enemy or region, and prevent the effects from cascading throughout the global information infrastructure?

Most problematic are questions of how to respond to cyber attacks. It is not clear what magnitude of cyber attack would rise to the threshold of an act of war (and thus justifying a conventional military response in self-defense). One may argue there are at least three general types of cyber attack that might justify some kind of military response.

First, a cyber-attacker might pursue strategic societal disruption. This would include many of the popular doomsday scenarios of "bringing down" the national banking and finance system through electronic weapons, or even electronic weapons coordinated with physical attacks such as truck bombs on Wall Street. Second, an attacker might seek to disrupt regional infrastructures that are critical to local national security functions. An example of this would be a regional attack that affects a major military base and prevents deployment or otherwise disrupts a strategically vital military activity. Third, an attacker might seek to exploit a strategic dependence on information technology. An adversary could conceivably install a "back door" or other vulnerability in software that has been outsourced to a front organization for development and incorporated into strategically vital infrastructure systems without appropriate quality control.[10] Aum Shinrikyo perpetrated this approach on the government of Japan.[11]

Assuming international consensus (and clear definitions) that these three modes of attack justify military response, there remain significant legal questions that require answers before we can respond to cyber attacks. Confidence in attribution will challenge the rationale and type of response. How confident must a defending state be before it responds, and does that confidence vary depending on the severity of either attack or response? International law requires that actions taken in self-defense must be necessary and proportionate. How does one measure necessity and proportionality, especially if one is responding to a cyber attack with conventional military force, with varying levels of confidence about who the enemy is?

Process for integrating technology, policy, and law

The substantive hurdles and questions of law and policy discussed above need to be reconciled before we can effectively exploit IT to compete with terrorists. Before that can happen, there must exist an adequate process to answer these questions and modernize policy and law in these substantive areas. Missed technology opportunities indicate that technology development can no longer flourish in a policy vacuum. Similarly, law and policy development is ineffective unless it recognizes the possibilities, policy implications, and market demands for technology. Resolving this dual dilemma requires a process that integrates development of technology with development of policy and law.

Technology developers must, at the onset of development, consider the policy ramifications of their technology. This is especially true for IT, where the pace of development and rush to implementation are so quick. Policy and legal objectives and options ought to be included alongside technical objectives in program plans. For example, if a technology program focuses on data mining and aggregation, it ought to identify potential policy ramifications (for example, on privacy policy) and identify options – in policy and technology development – for addressing any potential negative ramifications. If a data mining program identifies privacy as a possible policy concern, it ought to take steps to articulate policy objectives as well as technical objectives to mitigate this concern, and provide possible policy and technology options, such as anonymization technology and policy processes that prevent unwarranted de-anonymization. A tool to facilitate this might be a "legal impact statement," analogous to an environmental impact statement required by the Environmental Protection Agency.

An effective process to integrate co-development of technology, policy, and law will bridge the expertise gap between the technological world and the policy/legal world. Of course, technology experts are not lawyers, and cannot be expected to have the expertise needed to identify all potential policy ramifications or formulate effective but nuanced policy options. This process must bridge the technology–policy gap so that technology developments are informed from a policy perspective. Similarly, this process must inform policymakers and lawmakers of opportunities and implications of emerging technology. Policymakers and legislators need not understand the programmatic details of every technology program. But they need to understand when general technology trends, or 'technology push', challenges current policy or law, or even suggests the need for change in policy or law.

With such information, policymakers and legislators can provide technology developers with law and policy requirements, analogous to how technology users generate technical requirements. These law and policy requirements will focus on how technology should be used to trade risks and reconcile competing policy interests, where additional technology opportunities lie to reconcile policy problems, and what policies ought to be implemented into technology systems, and where (e.g., what policy requirements, standards of proof, or oversight and review mechanisms might accompany technologies for anonymization to protect privacy in data mining, at what stage in the system these policies ought to be implemented, etc.).

Summary and conclusion

This paper has outlined some of the substantive legal and policy hurdles that must be overcome before the US and her allies can effectively exploit information technology to compete with terrorists. This paper also has outlined the elements of a policy process to overcome these substantive hurdles.

Like globalization and the information infrastructure, these issues do not recognize borders. Competing with terrorists in cyberspace will require international cooperation and mutual understanding of varying corporate interests, privacy law, and expectations of security. The substantive answers to the policy issues described above will differ from country to country. Yet all countries are interconnected, creating seams in infrastructure for terrorists to exploit when IT is used as the terrorist's tool, and allowing cascading effects when IT is the terrorist's target.

Competing with terrorists requires cooperation from allies. This means engaging international organizations, and perhaps constructing international agreements or other diplomatic and commercial instruments, setting international standards for data access, sharing or pooling, reconciling and finding common ground among different countries' privacy laws and policies and their respective use of commercial data providers, formulating common expectations of corporate responsibility in securing and protecting infrastructure, identifying opportunities and lessons learned in implementing policy and legal tools for infrastructure protection, and forging partnerships to track terrorist activity in cyberspace, deny terrorists cyber-safe havens, and respond quickly to cyber attack as its effects and perpetrators emerge.

International law governing competition in cyberspace will emerge either normatively – from international instruments and organizations, or perhaps from resolutions and agreements within the United Nations framework – or as a positivist expression of the actual behavior of states. A normative expression of common expectations and limitations is more desirable, because of the need for common ground – among states as well as corporate actors – on the issues described above. Otherwise, standards will emerge ad hoc from event-driven responses, at best undermining common efforts to counter terrorism while securing cyberspace, at worst wreaking economic and social havoc in cyberspace with unintended consequences of unilateral action cascading throughout the global information infrastructure.

The US and her allies – particularly the Council of Europe – have the opportunity for leadership in the United Nations and other bodies such as the World Trade Organization, for developing a foundation that would aim to craft common standards, expectations, and limitations for competing with terrorists in cyberspace. This is an opportunity that democratic nations ought to seize upon, while we have the luxury to modernize privacy expectations and corporate obligations, and before the threat of cyber conflict truly manifests as a destructive mode of warfare. Democratic nations have two significant advantages over terrorism: the capabilities and resources of advanced technology, and the values and resiliency of liberal democracy. One advantage need not erode the other.

Notes

1 The author is Vice President of Hicks & Associates, Inc., General Counsel of the Terrorism Research Center, Inc., Adjunct Professor at Georgetown University, and is admitted to the Virginia Bar. The opinions expressed herein are solely those of the author, and do not reflect the policies of any affiliated institutions.

2 Bruce Hoffman, *Inside Terrorism* (London: Victor Gollancz, 1998), p. 67.

3 Bruce Hoffman, *Inside Terrorism* (London: Victor Gollancz, 1998), p. 68.

4 See, e.g., Joseph Nye, *The Paradox of American Power* (Oxford: Oxford University Press, 2002), p. 81; Defense Science Board, *Final Report of the Defense Science Board Task Force on Globalization and Security* (Washington, DC: US Defense Department, 1999), p. 5; A.T. Kearney, "Measuring Globalization: Economic Reversals, Forward Momentum," *Foreign Policy*, Vol. 54 (March/April 2004), p. 141.

5 Mary DeRosa, *Data Mining and Data Analysis for Counterterrorism* (Washington, DC: Center for Strategic and International Studies, March 2004), p. 11.

6 These results were derived from data produced in the Defense Advanced Research Projects Agency's Total Information Awareness program. Figure provided by Dr John Poindexter, former Director of DARPA Information Awareness Office.

7 "U.S. Military's Elite Hacker Crew," *Wired*, http://wired-vig.wired.com/news/privacy/0,1848,67223,00.html?tw=wn_tophead_1 (accessed April 21, 2005).

8 Benjamin Weiser and Claudia H. Deustch, "Many Offices Holding the Line on Post-9/11 Security Outlays," *The New York Times* (August 16, 2004). Internet source: <http://www.nytimes.com/2004/08/16/nyregion/16security.html> (accessed August 17, 2004).

9 Catherine Yang *et al.*, "Behind in Broadband," *Business Week* (September 6, 2004), http://www.businessweek.com/magazine/content/04_36/b3898111_mz063.htm (accessed April 22, 2005).

10 *See* Hicks & Associates, Inc., "Defense Against Information Attack," *Selected Papers, Volume II* (McLean, VA: Hicks & Associates, Inc., 1999), pp. 10–12.

11 Lars Nicander and Magnus Ranstorp (eds), *Terrorism in the Information Age – New Frontiers?* (Stockholm: Swedish National Defence College Press, 2004), p. 16.

Part III

FUTURE DIRECTIONS IN TERRORISM RESEARCH

12

RESEARCH DESIDERATA IN THE FIELD OF TERRORISM

Berto Jongman

More than twenty-five years ago I missed the first terrorism conference in the Netherlands because I was studying in Stockholm. The step to organize a conference on this topic in 1979 was very controversial and the organizing professor, Hylke Tromp, had to defend himself in the university newspaper. He convincingly argued that terrorism was an important topic that could be studied in an academic way. He considered terrorism as a form of irregular warfare. The idea for the conference was triggered by developments in the Netherlands. The country was faced for the first time with terrorism on its territory by the Moluccan community. Moluccans came to the Netherlands in the 1950s. The second generation became more militant and was involved in several terrorist attacks, including an occupation of an embassy, a train hijacking and a hostaging of a school. For the first time the Dutch government had to decide to use military force (3 for and 2 against) to end a hostaging situation. Later it was revealed that the Moluccan militants had also planned an attack on the Royal Palace which was disrupted by our police and domestic intelligence service.

These were exceptional incidents at the time for a stable society which would again be shocked by terror several decades later in the form of political assassinations. The first was the killing of one of my professors at Groningen University who went into politics. Pim Fortyn was the leading figure of a new political movement which suddenly became popular. Opinion polls indicated he would do very well in an upcoming election and it was speculated that he could be a candidate for prime minister. He was shot a few days before the election by an environmental activist. The perpetrator was immediately captured, and is now serving a prison sentence.

The most recent assassination was on 2 November 2005. A Dutch national of Moroccan origin shot and stabbed Theo van Gogh, a well-known writer, journalist, documentary and film maker. The killing was triggered by a documentary he produced in cooperation with Dutch MP Ayaan Hirsi Ali, a Somali immigrant, who studied political science in Leiden. She made the termination of the repression of women within Islam one of her political missions. The documentary was meant to shock and showed the dilemmas for Muslim women. Besides these domestic developments, the 9/11 attacks in New York and the 11M attack in Madrid have had a tremendous impact on the terrorism debate in the Netherlands. In the last year there have been several terror alerts that caused great concern.

Dutch society is still trying to recover from the two political assassinations, which polarized society. Tensions are still high and a new controversial MP, Geert Wilders, is trying to tap into the dissatisfied section of society and establish a new political centre right movement. As a result of the current situation, both MPs, Geert Wilders and Ayaan Hirsi Ali, are under protection and stay in safehouses. Both were temporarily kept in military barracks during the night; Geert Wilders even had to sleep in a prison cell at Camp Zeist. The government is currently seeking homes that are well protected where they can lead a normal life. Never before in Dutch history have these kinds of measures had to be taken to guarantee the life of acting MPs. The Dutch 'no' vote in a referendum on the EU constitution is partly due to the way the government handled these two incidents.

After 9/11 I had the opportunity to switch from academia to government. For more than a decade I had worked together with Alex Schmid who coordinated a small research institute at the University of Leiden, focusing on human rights research. Schmid started his career as a terrorism researcher at the end of the 1970s when Dutch society experienced its first serious terrorist attacks.

The developments described above illustrate why it was interesting to make the switch to government and to have a view into the kitchen of counterterrorism in order to see how a government is coping with a threatening situation and constant public pressure to prove that it can protect its people from terrorism. It was, however, quite a culture shock. I had to adapt to another working environment. The academic research cycle is completely different from what is called the intelligence cycle. I gained access to other sources of information and I had to write different products. I had to adapt to standard formats and regular frequencies and had to develop a different writing style from what I was used to at university. In my current job there is a stronger focus on current affairs, and pieces have to be produced under time pressure. Usually we get no more time than a few hours or a few days to write an answer to a specific question. There is a stronger urgency. Sometimes lives can depend on whether some piece of information gets in time on the desk of the right agency to deal with it. In my current job there is very often no time to get into academic debates about methodology or theory. That is why I still like to attend academic conferences. I have also had to cope with government bureaucracy, meaning getting used to compartmentalization, turf battles between different agencies and departments, competence struggles and political correctness.

I had hoped that I could build on my academic work. One of the products at university was the well-known 'World Conflict and Human Rights Map', an overview of the current situation in the world where political conflict was shown according to three levels of violence. In almost all of these conflicts parties make use of terrorist tactics, and numerous organizations indicated on the map are involved in protracted terror campaigns. The map can be used as a tool to initiate debates on conflict prevention, military action or counterterrorism measures. When I arrived at my new job everybody wanted to have a copy and it is still hanging on the walls of the offices of many of my colleagues. As of today I have not been able to persuade my superiors to make the map one of their ongoing projects. It did not suit their priorities. In my view it would be an excellent tool to use in the process of drafting the annual information collection plan. This is an agreed-upon document that is used to set priorities for the production of intelligence products and is the result of negotiations between those on the demand side and those on the production side. Annual editions of a world map provide clues on conflict dynamics and can be used as an early warning tool.

I mention the world map because in my view it illustrates that almost all terrorism is related to political and armed conflict. Doing research on terrorism, one cannot ignore these conflicts and their dynamics. A good overview of ongoing conflict is an absolute necessity for research. Overviews of conflicts, groups and terrorists involved in them and the violent incidents they cause are basic tools for a terrorism researcher. Unfortunately, in all four categories we still have a long way to go. When it comes to counterterrorism it will be almost impossible to measure the effects of the measures taken if we don't have access to these basic tools. This is one of the main reasons for the recent controversy about the Country Reports on Terrorism published by the US State Department.

When working with Alex Schmid at Leiden University I always admired him for his ability to inspire students to pick topics for research that could add something to our existing knowledge, and to force them to include at least a few conclusions in which they try to translate their findings into policy. He always kept lists of interesting topics. A few years ago, during a terrorism conference in Italy, he made one of these lists public for the whole research community. Since then we have gradually expanded the list. Currently it contains 444 topics in 25 different categories. Most of the topics were picked from the recent terrorism literature. For those who are interested a detailed bibliography is available. For reasons of space it is impossible to go into much detail. In the following paragraphs I can only highlight some of the main issues and questions that we need to answer if we want to come to a better understanding of this highly complicated research topic.

1. Types of terrorism

This category deals mostly with motivations for terrorism and its different forms. Currently most terrorist incidents are inspired by a fundamentalist interpretation of Islam. There are, however, also fundamentalist Christians, Hindus and Jews who have been responsible for terrorism. This category also deals with new forms of terrorism like agro-terrorism, maritime terrorism and cyber terrorism.

Although we have not seen many examples, experts have been warning of the dangers and the consequences when terrorists move in these directions. An interesting question is also whether the Tokyo metro attack and the 9/11 attacks were outliers or whether they fit a historical pattern. Recent research has indicated that they do fit a historical pattern and are not outliers. One outcome of a recent investigation was that the probability of this kind of attack is quite high for the coming years.

2. Linkages

This category deals with phenomena that are closely linked to the phenomenon of terrorism, like the arms trade and drug trafficking. It deals with the linkages with armed conflict, conventional politics and migration. Finally, there are questions related to contacts between terrorist organizations and the command and control issues within terrorist networks. To keep a conflict going, war economies usually develop on the basis of all kinds of illicit financing. It is estimated that there are at least 30 ongoing conflicts that are fuelled by drug trafficking. A better understanding of war economies is a necessary condition for finding ways to terminate conflicts.

3. Kidnapping/hostage-taking

Kidnapping and hostage-taking are not only done for political but also for criminal reasons. In some countries wholesale kidnapping industries have developed. More knowledge about the motives and modus operandi and the determinants for the safe release of hostages could contribute to the activities of hostage negotiation teams. Recent cases in Iraq illustrate that differences in approach may be decisive for the safe release of hostages. Why did Kenneth Bigley have to die whereas French and Italian journalists were released?

4. International cooperation

Many regional organizations have been actively involved in developing counterterrorism policies and implementing them. Countries in these regions very often have common characteristics. Within regional organizations international measures can be fine-tuned and they are sometimes better able to encourage cooperation. Most regions have developed their own anti-terrorism agreements. Terrorism can only be dealt with in a multilateral way. Over the years a comprehensive UN strategy to fight terrorism has evolved.

5. State responses

Since 9/11 there has been a focus on the use of hard power instead of soft power in dealing with terrorists. There has also been a shift to pre-emptive measures by states. A whole debate has emerged over what the right balance should be between the different tools a government has at its disposal to fight terrorism. New weapon technologies are being developed. What is the effectiveness of these weapons in the ongoing battle? In certain regions there is a tendency to fuse the war on drugs and the war on terror. Is this a good development or not? There are tools a government can use that are questionable and can have averse effects on the dynamics of an ongoing conflict. In 1999 the Chinese government decided to prohibit the activities of the Falun Gong movement. It is considered a threat to national security and since then it has been repressed severely. Already more than 800 members have died in detention. One could debate whether this is the right approach in dealing with this movement. Another important issue is the compatibility of counterterrorism measures with human rights laws. The tough debate on new anti-terrorist legislation in Britain illustrated the sensitivities that exist in many countries. In 2005 UN secretary-general Kofi Annan announced in Madrid that he would appoint a special UN rapporteur on this issue. The UN, however, depends on the cooperation of the member states. Progress reports on the effectiveness of sanctions against al-Qaeda and the Taliban indicate that these sanctions have had only limited effects on the activities of these two organizations. At the recent Madrid conference Kofi Annan had the opportunity to present a comprehensive UN strategy. Time will tell whether the member states are willing to implement the various measures announced by Annan. An increasing number of terrorist organizations consider the UN to be a partial actor or an instrument of the US and some even consider it to be a legitimate target for terrorism. The UN has to work hard to improve its image in a substantial part of the world.

6. 'Best practices' and 'lessons learned': UN member state experiences

This section deals with experiences in implementing different counterterrorism measures. What works and what doesn't? Different countries very often have different experiences. What works in one situation does not necessarily work in another. Hopefully we can learn from each other. Also, questions are asked about target selection. While many expected a mass-casualty attack on a soft target, Dutch society was suddenly faced with an assassination of a well-known person. Is this a one-time incident or is it going to be a pattern that we will see in other countries? A terrorist strategy document with the title 'Savagery management' that was put on the Internet in March 2005 indicates that the killing of persons is part of the first stage of a total of three stages that had to be followed by jihadist organisations in different theatres.

7. Psychological and sociological factors

In this section psychological and sociological issues are important. Questions are asked about mindset, psychological effects of the use of violence, not only on the perpetrators but also on the victims. Why have we seen this sudden exponential growth in suicide terrorism? Why are people willing to sacrifice their own lives for the benefit of the group? Another important question is: why do people join or leave terrorist groups? The attack in Madrid has raised the issue of the effect of attacks in election periods. South Africa kept information secret when it arrested terrorists who were planning attacks during the election period. British authorities were concerned about one of the masterminds of the Madrid attacks, who reportedly was planning an attack during the last election period in the UK. Fortunately it did not materialize, although, at the time of writing, the man is still active and is said to be based in Iraq.

There are several reports about training of child slaves and orphans as terrorists. This is a disturbing development. During recent violence in Thailand there were a number of unclaimed dead bodies without personal documentation. According to one hypothesis these were orphans hired as mercenaries. The other hypothesis was that they were international terrorists.

Mass casualty attacks can have severe effects on society. The lessons learned from large-scale natural disasters like earthquakes or the recent tsunami in Southeast Asia may give us clues about the effects of future terrorist attacks with weapons of mass destruction.

8. Security

A great number of issues are related to security and protection. As preparations are made for bigger terrorist attacks our response possibilities have to improve. This raises questions of streamlining, coordination and legislation on different levels of administration. New organizational structures are emerging. In the Netherlands, the National Coordinator for Counterterrorism has become operational since the beginning of this year. It is widely seen as a step towards the introduction of a whole new Ministry of Security in the near future. We have to see whether this is the right path to follow. In March 2005, the director of the Homeland Security Department announced a whole range of new measures because things were not working as they should. Since then more information has become available on the Muslim Outreach Program and a new approach to counterterrorism. It is expected that the new policy will probably be formulated in a new presidential directive.

Also, within the framework of the EU and NATO, there are efforts to improve response capabilities. A major issue for many countries is the introduction of so-called alert systems for the general public. The US colour system is not very useful. The question is by what system it should be replaced. In the Netherlands we are experimenting with sector-wise alert systems. The first system has already been introduced for the Dutch railway system. Similar systems will be gradually introduced for other sectors of society.

Technological developments in biology will create a whole new range of challenges for authorities if they are exploited by terrorists. In many countries there has been an proliferation of private security companies. This development raises the question of the right balance between private and public security. A major policy issue is how the foreign policy of countries can be aligned with the objectives of private military companies (PMCs).

9. Legal efforts

In the legal fields a lot of work has to be done in order to be able to face new terrorist threats that are not yet covered by existing laws and agreements. In order to be effective, countries have to harmonize existing laws, otherwise terrorists will exploit the loopholes. New rules have to be written to be able to face situations that have never happened before. The development of a new regime for the so-called PMCs will be a major policy issue in the coming years. We will also have to see whether the new International Criminal Court (ICC) is up to its tasks. In March 2005, ICC judges in The Hague came together for the first time to debate the first case related to war crimes in the Congo.

We will see new ways of transnational cooperation. France and Spain already are experimenting with joint investigative teams. Very little use has been made of legal dossiers for social science purposes. These dossiers, however, contain a lot of useful information that can be better exploited by terrorism researchers.

10. Training

Since 9/11, training courses and manuals in counterterrorism have expanded exponentially. There are many products on the market provided by various agencies and organizations. Also, all kinds of new research tools and software have become available and have revolutionized research on terrorism. Overviews and assessments could be helpful in making choices easier.

11. The evolution of terrorism

This section deals mainly with conflict dynamics. Why are certain tactics characteristic of certain historical periods? Why do organizations dissolve? Is it possible for a terrorist organization to develop into a political party? The cases of Hamas and Hezbollah are very interesting from this perspective. Rapoport introduced his wave theory of terrorism. According to his theory we are currently experiencing the fourth wave of international terrorism in history (the three previous ones being the anarchist wave, the anti-colonial wave and the new left wave). What does this mean for the future and will there be a fifth wave? According to Rapoport, researchers focus too much on current developments and don't realize that life cycles of terrorist waves usually last a whole generation (40 years). That would mean that the current wave could last until 2025, to be replaced by another. Some organizations (PLO and IRA) have been able to survive during two successive waves. Each wave generates its own organizations with certain preferences for a specific tactic. Terrorist waves have been facilitated by transformations in communication and transport patterns. As the energy of a wave no longer inspires new organizations it will gradually disappear. Organizations may disappear before the wave is ended. Currently, the ideology of the jihad still attracts many new recruits, with Iraq being an important magnet where recruits can gain fighting experience. Radical Islam is also spreading to new territories.

12. War and terrorism

Since 9/11 the Global War on Terrorism (GWOT) has become a commonplace concept. What are the implications of this strategy? In this respect the term Fourth Generation Warfare (4GW) has been introduced. A victory in 4GW can be gained by destroying the moral bonds of the enemy that allow the organic whole to exist. The cohesion of the enemy can be destroyed by menace, mistrust and uncertainty. This requires a specific way of operating that is different from the operations of conventional armies. That is why special forces have become important again. In the battle against terrorism they have to be able to operate in different regions. Some authors have pointed at the evolution of global guerrilla warfare as a method that will be exported around the world and will be focused on infrastructure sabotage, market disruption, state failure and de-legitimization. As a result of current developments the distinctions between conventional warfare, non-conventional warfare and terrorism have been blurred.

13. Terrorism and the criminal justice system

In this section questions are raised about the prosecution of terrorists. What happens to them in court and in prison? What kinds of evidence and which witnesses can be used against them in court? In the Netherlands legislation has been changed. Official reports of the domestic intelligence agency can be used as evidence and employees of the domestic intelligence agency can be heard as witnesses in trials of terrorist suspects. Existing rules in one country can be circumvented by transporting suspects to other countries. The current debate about the US rendition policy is an interesting topic. Prisons have become avenues for recruitment and in some countries prisons have become terrorist headquarters from which operations can be coordinated.

14. Media

The current generation of terrorists is better educated and knows how to use a computer. This means that they are better capable of exploiting modern communication technologies to spread their propaganda and to maintain contact with each other. According to the latest assessments there are about 5000 terrorist-related websites on the Internet. Monitoring the content and the characteristics of these websites has become quite a challenge. By using the latest technologies terrorist organizations will become even better at persuading audiences to support their cause. They may also become more lethal in developing new attack methods. The way terrorism is presented in the media varies according to region and culture. This has important consequences for how the general public perceives and experiences terrorism and how it affects their personal lives.

15. Terrorism and the public

The impact of terrorism on various segments of the population varies. We don't know what the determinants of popular support for terrorist organizations are and how people react to blackmail, intimidation and propaganda. The news menu has become more varied. With satellite TV people are able to watch the channels they prefer. With this greater variety the possibility of governments to influence audiences has been reduced. The public diplomacy campaign of the US in the Islamic world has become a failure because it was not realized that visual images had less impact in the Islamic world, which is more orally oriented. This may be one reason why the latest technology of podcasts (locally produced radio programs that can be downloaded on ipods) may have a totally different impact on a population. The way the murder of Theo van Gogh was covered in the media has been criticized by several observers. The way the case was covered has contributed to the polarization of the society and led to feelings of insecurity by segments of the population. Never in my life have I seen such broad coverage by the world media of a single incident in the Netherlands.

16. Counterterrorist measures and responses

This category is one of the biggest and contains general and specific questions on the effectiveness of a wide range of countermeasures. Governments, regional organizations and international organizations have all developed so-called action plans on counterterrorism which are currently being implemented. As a result of the enormous investments in security a whole new range of investigative techniques and new security technologies is being developed and introduced. We shall have to see whether they will be effective in stopping or preventing terrorism. One of the critical questions is: how can success be measured? The wide variety of measures that can be taken raises many questions about balance, efficiency and coordination. In several countries measures are taken to merge domestic and foreign intelligence. Also, many new investigative methods and technologies have been introduced. Terrorism is a form of communication. Thus far I have seen too much focus on hard power and technology. A major question is whether more emphasis on soft power would result in more success.

17. Trends and statistics

After all these years we still have not developed the right databases for our research community. The IMPT database is currently one of the best and most user-friendly. Everyone with access to the Internet can now make graphs for certain countries or regions or certain groups. The statistics we have on terrorism are still very incomplete. The databases of governments are not much better. Every year I am shocked by the bias of the annual US Report on Global Terrorism, which is a total misrepresentation of reality. It was only at the appearance of 2004's edition that a sincere debate was held on its reliability. In 2005 the controversy about the report was even more heated as the State Department decided to leave out the statistics. It argued that the National Counterterrorism Center (NCTC) was responsible for the statistics. It had found that the number of incidents had tripled during the year 2004. A special hearing in Congress was organized at which government officials had to explain why the number of incidents had increased, why the statistics were not reliable and comprehensive and why they could not be seen as a score card for the current counterterrorism policy. A number of suggestions have been made to improve the situation.

It is ironic that some of the private initiatives seem to have more credibility than government initiatives. Those who have been doing research on armed conflicts will all admit how difficult it is to get reliable data on casualty statistics.

As the University of Maryland has launched a new initiative to integrate the Pinkerton database I again have my doubts. When I was a correspondent for Pinkerton I sent much information on terrorist incidents in Kashmir. When I asked why my incidents were never included in their reports they said that they were not interested in that region. When the NCTC increased research capacity from three half-time analysts to ten full-time analysts it suddenly registered a sharp increase in incidents for Kashmir. For those knowledgeable with the region, it was no surprise.

Joshua Sinai of the Department of Homeland Security has indicated that there are six important components of terrorist activity that should be investigated: organizing among radical communities, plots and blueprints, information campaigns on the Internet, aborted operations, thwarted operations and successful operations. The two interesting categories of aborted and thwarted operations do not form part of the chronologies we use for our research. Sinai is developing an interesting model using 31 indicators that can be used to predict whether a terrorist group will focus on conventional low or high impact terrorism or CBRN terrorism. He hopes that his research could be helpful in categorizing terrorist groups in different tiers according to the high probability of using high-impact terrorism or CBRN terrorism. One of the major questions is predictability. A major test would be whether his model works and whether the available data on terrorism of the last 20 years would predict the developments of the last five years.

18. Consequences of terrorism

This section deals mainly with the economic consequences of terrorism. We still don't know enough about the economic costs of large-scale attacks. Economic costs will become more important and are part of the calculations of terrorist organizations. In a recent message of Osama bin Laden he argued that future attacks would be directed against the oil industry. He argued that the current price was not a reflection of the market. He considered a price of $100 per gallon a reasonable price. He assumed that by attacks on the oil industry he could create a situation that would result in price increase that would disrupt the American economy. This illustrates how international terrorism in one country can have severe consequences for other countries.

19. Terrorist groups: organizations and characteristics

This section deals mainly with group, cell and network characteristics. What is the optimal cell size? What is the optimal size of a terrorist network to maintain a resilient organization? In this area, also, our databases are quite poor. The 1988 Schmid/Jongman volume on political terrorism contained for the first time a comprehensive survey of organizations and groups. In the last decade there has been a proliferation of new organizations and the disappearance of many others. I've not seen a comprehensive new survey yet that could be used to make a comparison with the 1988 volume. Also, the data in the existing surveys is very often incomplete and outdated. Again there is the dominance of the Global Patterns of Terrorism, which is widely used. It only contains information on a few dozen organizations that are officially designated as terrorist by the US. My private list, which I maintained when working on the world conflict map, contains names of more than 1000 organizations. In 2007 Schmid plans to update his 1988 volume. We hope that we can also update the section on organizations. It will probably point at several interesting trends and developments. One of them would be related to the increasing role of women in terrorist organizations. An interesting role is currently played by so-called proselytizing organizations that are considered portals for terrorism. They have come under the scrutiny of law enforcement agencies. Another interesting issue is the role of children. Some organizations deliberately recruit children. The United Nations launched a special campaign to persuade states and guerrilla organizations not to recruit them.

20. Victims

Becoming a victim of terrorism can be a very disturbing experience that can have an impact for life. Also, the loss of relatives has a great impact on the lives of many people. Care for the victims is becoming an important issue. Sometimes victims organize themselves, which is also a way of coping with the problems. In many cases they are left in the cold by their governments. Two weeks ago the families of the victims of 11M in Madrid did not participate in the official commemorative ceremonies. They organized their own activities to underline the fact that the parliamentary investigative commission was used for party politics and did not reveal the truth.

21. Terrorist demands and tactics

Terrorists can chose from a wide variety of attack methods and technologies. They are also faced with questions of what works and what doesn't. Over time they have gained more expertise and have become more lethal. They have been able to integrate new technologies in their attack methods. A lot of research is being done on how these technologies are developed and spread among organizations. New technologies have to be tested. This means that they have to have safe havens where these tests can be done. Special attention is deserved for the organizations that have shown an interest in CBRN weapons. So far the number of incidents has been limited but many intelligence reports indicate that it is just a question of time before something nasty will be used. There is no consensus which category of weapons would be used first, but the order of the letters CBRN is also considered to be an order of probability, where chemical and biological weapons are seen as more likely than radiological or nuclear weapons. Another interesting issue is how military knowledge is transferred to terrorist organizations. Some countries have had special training programs for terrorists. The more lethal organizations that exist today can rely on the expertise of former military personnel.

22. Theoretical/conceptual/definitional considerations

The literature on terrorism is very much dominated by the US with its government agencies, think tanks and universities specializing in terrorism. There could be more sensitivity for alternative views. Another important issue in this category is how to understand the practices and relationships between research producers and users.

23. Risk assessment

Future terrorist attacks will be focused more on the economic effects, striking at the vulnerable spots in our societies with the aim of creating cascading effects. Threat and risk assessments could be helpful in identifying these weak spots and suggesting ways to mitigate the effects. The strong focus on terrorist dangers may result in a situation where other dangers are ignored or neglected. Also in this area we have to find the right balance. The focus on terrorism should not be at the expense of other important hazards. The change in climate and rise of the sea level has led to a strong debate in the Netherlands on measures to improve the dikes. This will cost billions of Euros. With limited financial means, important choices have to be made which can have important consequences for the future.

24. Dynamics of terrorism

This section deals mainly with issues related to how organizations are kept alive. What skills are required to survive and be successful? It also raises a number of questions related to decision-making within terrorist organizations. What kinds of strategies are they following and how do these affect their target selection? As al-Qaeda has lost its training camps in Afghanistan where does it currently train its recruits? A new development is the so-called 'virtual training' on the Internet. How does this effect a terrorist organization? What are the main trends in attack methods and what determines the differences between organizations?

25. General background factors facilitating international terrorism

Recent research has found interesting relationships between terrorism, democracy and globalization. Why is it that most terrorist events take place in the least, globalized and least democratic countries? Terrorism also seems to concentrate in the least well connected and democratized part and the most connected and democratized parts of the world. The current wave of Islamist terror is fuelled by the continuation of a number of protracted conflicts and extremist ideology. Why is it that no solutions for these protracted conflicts can be developed, and why is the current extremist ideology so popular among certain segments of Islam and still gaining more support? When I talk with colleagues or friends about my work they very often come up with ideas for frightening terrorist scenarios which would not be very difficult to execute. I have always been puzzled by this question: why has there have not been a far larger series of terrorist-related disasters?

Final remarks

The research desiderata below are meant to stimulate research. In the Netherlands there is no specialized research institute on terrorism. Students have to be creative and adapt their study programs to their own wishes. They can pick topics for their papers and study projects within their own discipline, be it history, sociology, psychology, administration, politics or international relations. As the long list illustrates, the field of terrorism research is quickly expanding as the result of a range of new developments. By improving our research tools end research methods we may be able to get a better understanding of the current and future threats and find the right balance in our counterterrorism policies.

RESEARCH DESIDERATA: AN UPDATE OF A LIST ORIGINALLY PREPARED BY THE UNITED NATIONS' TERRORISM PREVENTION BRANCH[1]

A.P. Schmid and A.J. Jongman

Categories

1. Types of terrorism
2. Linkages
3. Kidnapping/hostage-taking
4. International cooperation
5. State responses
6. 'Best practices' and 'lessons learned': UN member state experiences
7. Psychological and sociological factors
8. Security
9. Legal efforts
10. Training
11. The evolution of terrorism
12. War and terrorism
13. Terrorism and the criminal justice system
14. Media
15. Terrorism and the public
16. Counterterrorist measures and responses
17. Trends and statistics
18. Consequences of terrorism
19. Terrorist groups: organizations and characteristics
20. Victims
21. Terrorist demands and tactics
22. Theoretical/conceptual/definitional considerations
23. Risk assessment
24. Dynamics of terrorism
25. General background factors facilitating international terrorism

1. Types of terrorism

1 Religious/fundamentalist terrorism: comparisons of Christian, Hindu, Jewish, Islamist and other groups, including apocalyptic sects and suicidal cults.

2 Right-wing and racist terrorist groups: dynamics of entrance and exit of members.
3 Separatism and terrorism: comparative case studies.
4 Terrorists and chemical, biological, radiological and nuclear weapons: motives and capabilities of major terrorist movements most likely to acquire such weapons.
5 Nuclear proliferation: patterns of stealing, smuggling and selling of radioactive substances.
6 Cyberterrorism and cybercrime: typology of computer and Internet offences, with examples.
7 Case studies on single-issue terrorist groups (e.g. animal liberation and anti-abortion groups).
8 State terrorism: selected comparative case studies.
9 State-sponsored terrorism: selected comparative case studies.
10 Vigilante and death squad terrorism.
11 Unclaimed terrorist attacks and multiple-claim terrorist attacks: problems of identification of real perpetrators.
12 Catastrophic terrorism: is it a new type of terrorism?
13 New types of terrorism.
14 Is there a shift to maritime terrorism?
15 What are the determinants for the use or non-use of suicide terrorism?
16 Is 'Islamofascism' a useful label for describing the current Islamist threat – dark historic links.
17 Are the lessons learned during the Cold War in the containment of communism applicable today in the containment of Islamist terror?
18 Diaspora terrorism (groups or agents from third countries carrying out attacks on fellow nationals on the territory of established democracies. Perpetrators and victims come from non-democracies).
19 Is terrorism stratified in the sense that international acts of terrorism are more likely to be carried out among those countries which are most like each other, and less likely among countries and people who are less alike?
20 Some-time, part-time, one-time terrorism.
21 Agro-terrorism: how vulnerable is the food supply to terrorism?
22 The concept of threat: a revision.
23 Terrorism: the outcome of the rule of treating one as one has been treated.

2. Linkages

24 The nexus between arms trade, drugs production and terrorism.
25 Narco-terrorism: uses of terrorist tactics to defend drug cartels; uses of drug sales to finance terrorist strategies.
26 Organized crime and the financing of terrorism.
27 Drugs and conflict: how illicit narcotics fuel 30 ongoing armed conflicts.

28 Backstage terrorist organizations and front-stage political parties: division of labour-case studies.
29 NGOs, charities and refugee organizations as terrorist front organizations: selected case studies.
30 Links between terrorist groups across borders.
31 Varieties of terrorist financing.
32 Collaboration between domestic and international terrorist organizations.
33 The interface between violent crime and armed conflict.
34 The tracing and penetration of transnational terrorist networks.
35 Command and control within and between terrorist networks: the (dis)advantages of high-tech and low-tech means of communication.
36 Israel: frontier of Russian organized crime (1 million Russian immigrants): the threat of the transfer of crime tactics to Palestinian terror groups.
37 Cutting-edge platforms for analysing and managing threat networks: examples (e.g. www.trackingthethreat).

3. Kidnapping/hostage-taking

38 The kidnapping industry in various countries (e.g. Colombia, Mexico, Brazil, Guatemala, Iraq, Chechnya and the Philippines).
39 The factor of time in kidnap and siege situations: statistical explorations.
40 Terrorist deliberations for selectively killing and releasing hostages.
41 Determinants of the size of ransoms in commercial and political kidnappings.
42 Kidnappers: analysis of motives and modus operandi.
43 Kidnapping negotiations and hostage situations: commonalities and differences.

4. International cooperation

44 Analyses of cooperative counterterrorist efforts: multilateral, regional and bilateral.
45 The European Union and terrorism: before and after the creation of Interpol.
46 Interpol and terrorism.
47 Europol and terrorism.
48 NATO and terrorism.
49 The United Nations and terrorism: the effectiveness of the conventions and protocols, 1963–2005: problems of measuring effectiveness.
50 The debates on terrorism in the General Assembly and the 6^e Committee.
51 The effects of the UN sanctions committee (SC1267) with respect to al-Qaeda and the Taliban.
52 The achievements and further potential of the Nunn–Lugar anti-proliferation regime.

53 The UN Security Council's Counterterrorism Committee: the implementation of UNSC resolution 1373 (2001): the record so far.

54 The evolution of a comprehensive UN strategy to fight terrorism, and its implementation taskforce.

55 What could be the role of a new world anti-terrorism center as proposed in February 2005 in Riyadh?

56 Regional organizations (African Union, Arab League, ASEAN, OAS, Islamic Conference) and terrorism: a comparison of measures taken.

57 EU–US cooperation: implementation of the Dromeland Castle declaration (26 June 2004).

58 EU mutual evaluations of national systems to combat terrorism: the record so far.

59 The EU Action Plan to combat terrorism: assessment of its implementation.

60 The European Council: implementation of the Hague programme: an assessment.

61 Impact of the establishment of an EU Risk Analysis Center in Helsinki on strengthening of the EU's common external border.

62 The evolution of a European strategy against radicalization and recruitment.

63 The accession of new member states to the EU: consequences for crime and terrorism.

64 The rising number of attacks against NGOs and relief workers: the need for better security.

65 The handling of terrorism and related issues throughout the UN system: progress report on the newly established implementation task force.

5. State responses

66 Comparisons of state practices in combating terrorism as related to the seriousness of the terrorist threat (longitudinal analyses).

67 State responses to terrorism: liberal democracies vs non-liberal democracies.

68 Questionable state responses to terror campaigns: case studies of cases where the cure was worse than the disease.

69 The instruments of anti-terrorism and counterterrorism: a review of the tools available to governments, with a discussion of the conditions for their effectiveness.

70 Rules of engagement and standard operating procedures in combating terrorism: terrorism and weak democracies and countries in transition.

71 Terrorism and legitimate resistance against foreign occupation.

72 Terrorism and resistance against non-democratic governments.

73 Centralization and coordination of anti-terrorism measures across ministries.

74 Stimulation of alertness on different administrative levels to anti-terrorism aspects and crisis management consequences.

75 The role of paramilitary organizations in counterterrorism (institutionalized corruption, human rights abuses, long-term instability): comparative case studies.

76 Parliamentary investigations: truth commissions or whitewash operations?

77 State support of drug trafficking: comparative case studies.

78 Intergovernmental poaching: a growing problem.

79 The development of new cruise missiles (to be launched from submarines – launchable within 15 minutes and able to hit targets at a distance of 1500 miles): new means to strike rogue states and terrorist organizations: the usefulness of standoff weapons against terrorists?

80 Is a failed state better than a rogue state?

81 Fusing the 'war on terror' and the 'war on drugs': a misleading intellectual roadmap.

82 National anti-terrorism databases online: first experiences (e.g. www.frstrategie.org, www.interieur.gouv.fr)

83 The special UN rapporteur on the compatibility of counterterrorism measures with international human rights laws: first experiences.

84 The development of a European Union Intelligence Service (EUIS) and its position within the EU framework.

6. 'Best practices' and 'lessons learned': UN member state experiences

85 Preventing and combating terrorism in general: an inventory of proposals since 9/11.

86 Hostage negotiations and rescue operations: their interplay in kidnapping and hostage situations.

87 Hijacking rescue operations: comparisons of fortunate and unfortunate outcomes.

88 'Best practices' identified in the general terrorism- and crime-prevention literature.

89 Deterrence tested: an empirical study of claims of successful deterrence of terrorist attacks.

90 Protecting executives against terrorist attacks: lessons from the open literature.

91 The use of military force in countering terrorism: lessons learned.

92 Secret negotiations with terrorist movements: determinants of failure and success.

93 The Cold War counterinsurgency literature: what can it teach us on countering contemporary terrorism?

94 Failures of VIP protection: determinants of successful assassinations.

95 Land- and sea-based hostage rescue missions which went wrong: lessons learned.

96 Terrorist target selection: extrapolations from the past.

97 Crisis management in terrorist incidents: best/promising practices and lessons learned.

98 How past terrorist campaigns were successfully brought to a halt: negotiated and other settlements: comparative case studies.

99 Strategies of counterterrorism that failed or were counterproductive: comparative case studies.

7. Psychological and sociological factors

100 The mindset of terrorist perpetrators: how terrorists defend their activities.

101 The justification and morality of terrorist violence, according to the terrorists' own writings and speeches.

102 Analysis of terrorist pamphlets and claim letters.

103 Terrorist atrocities: the psychology behind them.

104 Before they turned terrorist: the antecedents of terrorist movements.

105 The sociology and psychology of human undergrounds: resistance and terrorist organizations compared.

106 Do terrorists also suffer from post-traumatic stress disorders (PTSD)?

107 Post-traumatic stress disorders of victims of terrorism and victims of natural disasters compared.

108 The victim–terrorist nexus: under what circumstances do ex-victims turn into terrorists?

109 Long-term refugee camps as breeding grounds for terrorists: comparative case studies.

110 The role of the media in terrorism and in countering terrorism.

111 What can the literature on psychological operations teach us on countering terrorism?

112 Impact of terrorism on public behaviour at election times: comparative case studies.

113 Sabotaging peace talks through acts of terrorism: successful and unsuccessful attempts compared.

114 Improving coping and healing strategies for victims of terrorism: promising practices.

115 Determinants of identification processes with victims or perpetrators during and after incidents of terrorism.

116 Suicide terrorists: the psychology of kamikaze terrorism.

117 The rise and fall of terrorist profiling.

118 Probable consequences for society of large numbers of victims in case of attacks with weapons of mass destruction: what lessons can be learned from the effects of large-scale natural disasters?

119 Determinants of radicalization of individuals or groups in society.

120 The healing of nations: promises and limits of political forgiveness.

121 Psychiatric and socio-psychological profiles of terrorists and the alienated: distinctions between the pathological loner, criminals and those with a cause.
122 Terrorism: the ultimate breakdown of communication.
123 The enforced training of children (orphans and slaves) for terrorist purposes: the terrorists of the next decennium.
124 Former terrorists turning into regular police or military: comparative case studies.

8. Security

125 Comparative airport security.
126 Comparative port security.
127 Terrorism and major events: securing big sports events (Olympic Games) and VIP summits (e.g. World Economic Forum): lessons learned since München 1972.
128 Embassy security; lessons learned.
129 The role of intelligence services in the prevention of terrorism.
130 Decision-making criteria for the transfer of authority to the Ministry of Defence in case of catastrophic terrorism: emergency/crisis planning.
131 Simulation exercises (on national, provincial, local levels) for crisis management: an inventory of training materials.
132 Necessity to adapt existing legislation to cope with the terrorist threat to use new weapons of mass destruction.
133 Streamlining of organization/authority structures in the field of anti-terrorism/counterterrorism: an inventory of measures taken in selected countries.
134 The establishment of a unified command structure in which all capabilities of the fight against catastrophic terrorism are integrated (from national to EU/NATO/world level).
135 Review of anti-terrorism policy/budgeting.
136 Problems encountered when an area has to be put under quarantine.
137 Problems encountered with the introduction of forced inoculation.
138 Research and development desiderata of counterterrorist technologies.
139 Improvement of security standards for the production, storage and transport of dangerous agents or substances in research laboratories and other facilities as protection against theft and interdiction.
140 Development of an international monitoring programme that can serve as a warning system for the outbreak of infectious diseases and possible terrorist experiments with biological substances: Real-time Outbreak and Disease Surveillance system (RODS) as an extension of the Epidemic Intelligence Service (EIS).
141 Early warning: closing the gap between warning and decision-making (fear of erring, poor planning, complacency).

142 How can negative effects of incorrect decisions be limited? (Type I error: say no where the correct answer is yes; Type II error: say yes when the correct answer is no.)

143 Is there any use in so-called Security Impact Statements (SIS) as an analogy to Environmental Impact Statements (EIS)?

144 Establishing safe houses for high-value potential targets of terrorism (international judges, politicians, opinion leaders, ambassadors): national experiences and lessons learned.

145 The rise and proliferation of private security companies: what is the right balance between private and public security?

146 The introduction of general alert systems: the shift from general national colour systems to sector-wise systems (e.g. drinking water system, electricity system, air travel system, banking system, railway system, computer infrastructure).

147 Do more advanced travel documents (introduction of biometrics) have an effect on terrorist operations?

148 Nuclear plants: adapting safety measures to new realities.

149 Strange and unexplained accidents: early warning indicator for terrorism (e.g. suspicious incidents under investigation: http://unitedstatesaction. com).

150 The shift towards military entrepreneurship.

151 Iraq as the turning point for the use of private military companies (PMCs): a unique combination of drivers.

152 Aligning the contrasting desires of US foreign policy and the objectives of PMC industries: a policy issue to be solved.

9. Legal efforts

153 Extradition requests and successful extraditions in cases of terrorism.

154 The (mis-)use of the political offence exemption in extradition requests and denials.

155 Comparing national anti-terrorism legislations and regulations.

156 The sentencing of terrorists: national varieties.

157 The working of the various international conventions and protocols on terrorism – comparing the records of ratifiers and non-ratifiers.

158 International treaty to improve cooperation in the field of preventing cyber-attacks, and the response to them – the state of the discussion.

159 The effects of the expansion of investigative powers on civil liberties: how much freedom are we willing to give up?

160 Legal dossiers of terrorist suspects: connecting case files: a terra incognita for social science.

161 What to do if a significant part of the parliament or cabinet is wiped out as a result of a terrorist attack (US: Sensenbrenner Law): comparison of national legislation.

162 The International Criminal Court (ICC): experiences with preparing the first cases (Congo, Uganda, Sudan).

163 The United Nations as the most suitable oversight body for a regulatory regime to regulate PMCs (standards of conduct and quality, rules for the treatment of PMC employees if captured, rules on when PMCs may be employed).

164 Potential problems if such a regime does not emerge–trial and execution of PMC employees for war crimes (they are not protected by the Geneva conventions); gross misconduct by untrained, unqualified PMC personnel in war zones; the establishment and operation of PMCs that operate against the international community of nations.

165 Lawfare: tactic whereby lawyers are called in to try and gain some military advantage via court proceedings: case studies.

166 The evolution of a super EURO-Just with increased transnational investigative and juridical powers.

167 The (ab)use of lawyers by terrorists in prisons: case studies.

10. Training

168 Training manuals and courses in counterterrorism: an inventory of public and private sector products.

169 Bomb threat assessments: operating procedures in national capitals compared.

170 Explosives and bomb detection and disposal techniques.

171 Teaching anti-terrorism to foreign states: a comparative study of the programmes of the US, Israel, France, Russia, China and the UK.

172 The improvement of counterterrorism training methods: lessons learned.

173 The application of new software tools (Analyst Notebook) in investigative research: a revolution in determining timelines and links within and between networks.

11. The evolution of terrorism

174 Case studies on the rise and decline of selected terrorist groups.

175 How terrorist organizations dissolve.

176 Unilateral armistice offers of terrorist organizations: how seriously should they be taken? An analysis of various offers and their outcomes.

177 Successful transformations of terrorist organizations to political mass movements or parties: comparative case studies.

178 Selective terrorist careers: from criminal to statesman – from statesman to terrorist.

179 'Old' and 'new' terrorism: has terrorism really changed since the 1970s and 1980s?

180 Recent shifts in assuming and denying responsibility by terrorist groups.

181 Determinants of change in terrorist tactics and strategies.
182 Historical successes and failures of terrorist organizations and their determinants: comparative case studies.
183 Terrorist weaponry: shifts in arms and levels of violence?
184 Ethnic Russian Muslims: the new 'jannisaries' (reference to fanatical forces of the Ottoman empire who were forced converts from Christian communities).

12. War and terrorism

185 Uses of terrorism in interstate warfare.
186 Uses of terrorism in civil war.
187 Exploding a bomb in the marketplace and bombing a marketplace from the air: exploring the morality of the use of force by state- and non-state actors.
188 War crimes and acts of terrorism: similarities and dissimilarities.
189 The status of domestic belligerents: freedom fighters, guerrillas, terrorists, lawful belligerents – how to differentiate?
190 The return of the Iraqi veterans: the transfer of terrorist expertise to other regions.
191 Damaged war veterans: the propensity of traumatized veterans to engage in terrorist and other violence.
192 Did military involvement in Iraq harm rather than benefit the war on terrorism?
193 Does the establishment of military bases drive insurgent groups into the camps of al-Qaeda and Jemaah Islamiya?
194 The inclusion of counter-narcotics operations in military operations: time for a reappraisal?
195 Military operations in the Global War on Terrorism (GWOT): comparative case studies (Africa, Afghanistan, Philippines, Colombia) – implications for the overall GWOT strategy?
196 The Pan-Sahel initiative: an assessment?
197 US military operations in the Horn of Africa: template for future GWOT operations?
198 Merging peacekeeping and counterterrorism operations under NATO command: advantages and disadvantages.
199 'War on terrorism' is wrong: terrorism is a tactic, not an enemy.
200 Reorganizing the armed forces for long-term stability tasks (more lethal, rapidly deployable, for a broader spectrum of threats): national experiences.
201 The use of police terror against drug gangs: comparative case studies (e.g. Brazil and Thailand).
202 The development of A-teams for covert operations abroad: national experiences.

203 Black budgets for intelligence: are we getting value for our money?

204 The use of special task forces (e.g. Task Force 121) for the hunt of so-called high-value targets: successes and failures.

205 The use of military exercises as cover for counterterrorism operations: comparative case studies.

206 Hearts-and-minds campaigns combined with intelligence collection efforts: comparative case studies.

207 Grand strategy: isolating the enemy across three essential vectors: physical, mental and moral.

208 Fourth Generation Warfare (4GW) tactics (rear area operations, psychological operations, ad hoc innovation): contemporary applications.

209 Victory in 4GW: destroying the moral bonds that allows the organic whole to exist (cohesion) by reinforcing menace, mistrust and uncertainty: successes and failures.

210 The implications of the replacement of terrorism as a method of warfare by global guerrilla warfare (infrastructure sabotage, market disruption, state failure and de-legitimitization).

211 The evolution of global guerrilla warfare: a method of warfare that will be exported around the world.

212 The blurring of the distinctions between conventional war, non-conventional war and terrorism: the need for a reconsideration of the missions of conventional armed forces, police forces and surveillance agencies.

213 WWIII: the biologist's war.

214 Applications of system theory to terrorism (e.g. if 25% of the components of a system are lost the probability of systemic failure is more than 80%): case studies.

13. Terrorism and the criminal justice system

215 Terrorists in prison: comparative case studies.

216 Terrorists in court: comparative case studies.

217 The penitent terrorist as crown witness: problems of credibility and equality before the law.

218 Arrest and punishment of terrorists: how many are caught after how much time?

219 Prisons as terrorist headquarters: problems with putting terrorist inmates together.

220 Prisons: viable venue for Islamic radicalization and recruitment.

221 Witness protection programmes for terrorist trials: the record so far.

222 Special courts for terrorist crimes: comparisons between states using this instrument.

223 Effectiveness of the International Convention for the Suppression of the Financing of Terrorism.

224 Cybercrime: the desirability and effectiveness of an international treaty focused on the harmonization of national legislation, the sharing of information, the provision of early warnings, and the formulation of acceptable procedures for the execution of international investigations of cybercrime.

225 The refusal to let important terrorist suspects appear as witnesses in trials of other terrorist suspects: debates about accessibility of certain types of evidence and the hearing of certain witnesses.

226 The UN special rapporteur on the compatibility of counterterrorism measures with international human rights law: first experiences.

14. Media

227 Media guidelines on dealing with terrorist stories: useful in practice?
228 Terrorist propaganda: if publicity is the (only) goal, should one give in?
229 The portrayal of terrorists in contemporary fiction.
230 The portrayal of terrorists in contemporary videos/movies.
231 Silencing the press: journalists as terrorist targets.
232 Copycat crime: televised terrorist acts repeated: a review of the evidence.
233 Dealing with the media: comparing police practices.
234 Terrorism and the Internet: the dark web portal: uses and abuses.
235 Terrrorist perpetrators: media images and realities.
236 Hollywood as re-enactor and proliferator of terrorist scenarios: a reality check.
237 Live broadcasts of crisis games/simulations with government officials as a way to sensitize the public on crisis decision-making problems and dangers in society.
238 Monitoring terrorist websites: future directions (advent of weblogs, RSS and other forms of social software, direct clues about impending attacks, a closer alignment between the stated goals on the websites of the terrorist networks and their actions).
239 The digital cat-and-mouse game with cyber terrorists.

15. Terrorism and the public

240 The impact of terrorism on various segments of the population.
241 Determinants of popular support for terrorist organizations.
242 Public opinion and terrorism: reactive patterns in cases of terrorist blackmail, terrorist intimidation and terrorist propaganda.
243 Educating the public about terrorism: national experiences.
244 The desirability and use of personal preparedness guides: national experiences.
245 The desirability and progress made with a global campaign against terrorism (modelled on the landmine and child soldier campaigns).

16. Counterterrorist measures and responses

246 State security services and terrorist groups: varieties of relationships.
247 National counterterrorist special units: a comparison of doctrine, organization, tactics and weaponry.
248 Unilateral and bilateral armistices with terrorists: comparative case studies.
249 Interrogating terrorists: licit and illicit practices.
250 Torturing terrorists for purposes of intelligence gathering: how widespread is the practice?
251 Effectiveness in counterterrorism: methodologies of measurement.
252 Terrorist safe havens: why some countries do not extradite terrorists.
253 Military responses to insurgent terrorism: comparative case studies.
254 Judicial responses to various types of terrorism.
255 Choosing appropriate strategies: law enforcement vs military responses to terrorism.
256 Police strategies and tactics against terrorism.
257 Target hardening by prospective victims: does it lead to displacement of the locus of victimization?
258 The effect of amnesty on terrorist organizations.
259 Possibilities and limitations of technical solutions in countering terrorism.
260 The possibilities of limiting the freedom of terrorists to recruit and train.
261 The effectiveness of blacklisting countries that are non-cooperative in fighting terrorism.
262 The effectiveness of placing terrorist individuals and organizations on terror lists.
263 The effectiveness of blocking terrorist fundraising.
264 The desirability and effectiveness of the monitoring of foreign students.
265 Boomerang effect: miscalculations of intelligence services in their interaction with terrorists.
266 The effectiveness of a policy of 'pre-emptive assassination' ('permissive termination', 'calculated elimination').
267 The effectiveness of digital investigations in tracing and prosecuting terrorists.
268 The 'export' of terrorist suspects to regimes known for torture practices.
269 Intelligence and morality: explorations of ethical dilemmas in dealing with terrorist groups.
270 The justification and effectiveness of a policy of 'terrorizing the terrorists' (do to the terrorists what they do to innocents).
271 Dilemma of national governments: how can the effectiveness of anti-terrorist policies be measured and expressed to the general public (in other words can they justify the increase in budget for security)?
272 The fusion of government information (customs, immigration service, police, intelligence, economic control, tax office): determinants of success?

273 Threat analysis by intelligence agencies: successes and failures in identifying threats.

274 Counterterrorism: from law enforcement to war fighting: national experiences of transition.

275 Post 9/11 reorganization of special forces: new tasks and responsibilities: national experiences.

276 The fusion of domestic and foreign intelligence: national experiences.

277 The establishment of Ministries of Security: national experiences.

278 Deep access data mining techniques to track terrorists: new developments and national experiences.

·279 Attempts to create so-called 'total information awareness' (horizontal integration of information from all sources at all levels of classification): national experiences.

280 Working with so-called 'red teams': national experiences.

281 Experiences with linchpin analysis (identifying the role of key factors in the analytic calculus).

282 Experiences with alternative forms of analysis (devil's advocacy, risk–benefit analysis, high-impact low-probability analysis, quality of information check).

283 A consolidated score card against al-Qaeda: www.angelfire.com/terrorismscorecard

284 Thinking beyond the traditional practitioner's tool kit: the need for a new breed of conflict management practitioners to draw in and sustain a dialogue between the politically marginalized groups and government elites.

285 Replacing 'hard' power with 'soft' power: a formula for success?

286 Investigative committees into the functioning of intelligence services: national experiences.

287 The desirability of a moratorium on the development and sale of synthetic nanoscale materials in organisms.

288 Measuring feelings of insecurity: the use of opinion polls in debates on security.

289 Vaccines needed to counter bioterrorist threats: factors determining sufficiency.

290 WMD civil support teams (first response teams in case of CRBN attacks): national experiences.

291 Nuclear emergency support teams (NEST): national experiences.

292 Recalling the 33 000 pounds of highly enriched uranium that was distributed to 43 countries in the last two decades: progress made.

293 The establishment of radio and TV stations to counter terrorist and rogue state propaganda: recent experiences in the Middle East, Central Asia and Asia.

294 The desirability of a biological research security system (a system on the basis of peer review for the permission of dangerous experiments and the issuing of licences to scientists and facilities).

295 Standards for nuclear detectors and personal protection equipment against CBRN attacks: an assessment.

296 The use of controversial satellite tracking technologies (with help of bio-implants) for anti-terrorist purposes: first experiences.

297 The symbiosis between intelligence and business (e.g. the Joint Intelligence Committee sends a weekly assessment of the economic and trade situation in the world to the Bank of England).

298 The integration of former terrorists in police forces and/or armed forces: national experiences.

299 The use of psyops: spreading rumours about the capture or death of important terrorists.

300 Monitoring charities: national experiences.

301 Improving control over the nuclear arsenals of states of concern: case studies.

302 The disentangling of the Khan network (with involvement of the US, Netherlands, Israel, South Africa, Germany, Japan, Singapore, Spain, UK, Malaysia and Dubai): a case study.

303 Public education campaigns with the aim to increase security awareness of civilians: national experiences.

304 Keeping information on key infrastructures secret: national experiences.

305 The use of low-tech technologies (e.g. global systems for mobile communications, GSMs) to collect intelligence and prevent terrorist attacks: examples.

306 The Global Outbreak Alert and Response Network (GOARN) of the World Health Organization: the need for more research into 'zones of emergence': implications for bioterrorism.

307 The spread of the West Nile virus in the US: implications for bioterrorism.

308 The negative impact of a stricter control of Hawala/Hundi money transfer systems: an assessment.

309 The establishment of serious organized crime agencies: national experiences.

310 Persuading terrorist organisations to enter peace talks with a promise to remove them from terrorist blacklists: successes and failures.

311 The construction of walls or electric fences: impact on levels of violence and societies involved: comparative case studies (e.g. Israel/Palestine, Malaysia/Thailand, South Africa/Mozambique).

312 The use of hiring creative thinkers who can imagine the impossible.

313 Unearthing potential members of operational cells well prior to the 'h-hour of the op': case studies.

314 Analysing connections of connections to identify emerging network 'leadership': case studies.

315 Signals of impending attacks (increased activity on the network, reversal of money flows, face-to-face meetings of key members): case studies.

316 Designing a system that can keep up with the manufacture of new toxic substances: the challenge of avoiding Big Brother and deadly bureaucracy.

317 Dealing with state sponsors of terrorism: small carrots for small gestures, large sticks for large infractions.

318 Use of the insurance industry as a vehicle to drive chemical facilities, food companies, utilities and other businesses to take greater precautions against terrorist attacks without heavy-handed new regulations: first experiences.

319 Introduction of new sensor technologies: e.g. muon cosmic ray screening device developed by Los Alamos: first experiences with use for screening vehicles at border crossings or ship cargo at major ports.

320 Denying terrorists the support of constituents: case studies.

321 From joint regional to a world counterterrorism centre.

322 The new hows and whys of global eavesdropping.

323 The Interpol resource centre on bioterrorism: sharing information between police, health officials and scientists, and informing member countries about current threats and best practices.

324 Terrorism as a consequence of past government policies.

325 The removal and retraining of extremist clerics and teachers: national experiences.

326 The full facts about the detention, interrogation and rendition authority and practices of American government agencies.

327 Pakistani and Saudi support for proselytizing organizations: the incompatibility with their claims to be key allies in the war on terror.

328 The Trans-Sahara Counter Terrorism Initiative: an assessment.

329 The introduction of enhanced maritime safety and security teams (EMSST): first experiences.

330 The feasibility of the development of a global nuclear detection architecture (task of the newly established Domestic Nuclear Detection Office (DNDO) in the US.

17. Trends and statistics

331 Cross-national and longitudinal trends of various types of terrorism (single issue, left-wing, right-wing, nationalist, irredentist, separatist, racist, revolutionary, religious, vigilante, state-sponsored, criminal, pathological, etc.).

332 Longitudinal and cross national analyses of datasets on international terrorism (e.g. US State Department, NCTC, RAND, Mickolus, Engene, IMPT, Terrorism Knowledge Base).

333 Statistics on domestic and international terrorism: how good are the data?

334 Comparative international apprehension rates of terrorists.

335 Frequency and consequences of terrorist hoaxes.

336 Dataset on prevented attacks: successful intelligence or failures in preparation.

337 Ron Motley's database on Islamist terrorism: 1 million pages waiting for analysis.
338 The difficulty of collecting detailed, reliable casualty statistics in war zones: what does this mean for databases on terrorism?

18. Consequences of terrorism

339 The consequences of terrorism (for various actors such as family, media, state, former hostages, etc.).
340 Terrorism and the tourism industry: damage assessments.
341 Accountability of terrorist groups for the consequences of their crimes.
342 Accountability of terrorist leaders for the consequences of their crimes.
343 What are the secondary effects of catastrophic terrorism? (economic recession, disruption of travel and transport, disruption tourism industry, loss of innocence).

19. Terrorist groups: organizations and characteristics

344 Organizational characteristics of contemporary terrorist organizations.
345 Activities (other than terrorist) of terrorist movements.
346 Infiltrators and informers in terrorist organizations: successes and failures.
347 The terrorist cell/network: varieties of organizational structures.
348 How do terrorist organizations react to leadership loss?
349 Terrorist arms procurement: what do we know?
350 The role of women in terrorist organizations.
351 Criminal activities of political terrorists.
352 Trademarks of explosive experts.
353 Development of 'exit' strategies that would encourage desertion.
354 Recruitment of a new generation of terrorists: impact on the level of sophistication?
355 Media departments of terrorist organizations: comparative case studies (e.g. the Global Islamic Media group).
356 The role of Councils of Guardians of Islamic terrorist organizations (e.g. Hamas, Muslim Brotherhood): case studies.
357 The use of music/video clips to spread propaganda (e.g. Dirty Kuffar clip of the Soul Salah Crew).
358 The rise of a new generation of terrorist leaders: comparative case studies.
359 Mapping terrorist networks: e.g. al-Qaeda: requirements for a resilient organization (expect operation networks to be run by relative unknowns, assassination of a single network leader will not work, strategic attacks are possible with a network of less than 70 people).
360 Unraveling the entire network of al-Qaeda: analysing the people who received training in Afghanistan.

361 The rise of terrorist social services: replicating the social responsibilities of nation-states: is there a generalized ('business') model that can be derived for fully developed terrorist organizations operating in failed states?

362 The resilience of terrorist networks against decapitation (redundant design, meta-matrix design, dynamic design): case studies.

363 When is a liberation movement dangerous and wicked, and when is it part of the progress toward a democratic society?

364 Monitoring Deobandi and Wahhabi proselytizing organizations: jihad's stealthy legions (e.g. Tabliqhi Jamaat, Hezb ut Tahrir, Tanzim e-Islami, Islamic Circle of North America).

365 The recruitment of children by terrorist or guerrilla organizations: comparative case studies.

366 Terrorists' other target audience: the aggrieved populations that they purport to represent.

367 Proposals for establishing a common database on terrorist organizations and their accomplices: feasibility and obstacles.

20. Victims

368 Victim and target selection processes by different types of terrorist groups.

369 UN and ICRC officials as victims of terrorism: the record so far.

370 Victims' treatment: comparison of country programmes for victims (e.g. USA, France, Israel, Spain, Colombia, Russia).

371 Post-traumatic stress disorders: short-, medium- and long-term effects on victims, onlookers and perpetrators compared.

372 The psychology of fear in victims of violent crime and victims of terrorism.

373 Hostage and kidnapping experiences: a survey of the literature on survival and mental strength.

374 Coping with anxiety, fear and terror: theories of emotional control.

375 Varieties of victim responses to terrorism.

376 The impact of terrorist death threats on the lives of prospective victims.

377 Comparing victimization patterns across time and space: class, occupation and role of victims.

378 The utility of mutual self-help among former victims of terrorism compared to professional counselling.

379 Debriefing released hostages: what can be learned?

380 The Stockholm syndrome: beyond the original case.

381 Female prisoners marrying military officers they met in torture centres: Stockholm syndrome taken to an extreme (e.g. Argentina).

382 The financial and non-monetary costs of terrorism.

383 The establishment of an international fund to compensate victims and their families, to be financed in part from assets seized from terrorist organizations: a progress report.

21. Terrorist demands and tactics

384 Nature and variety of terrorist demands.

385 Terrorist blackmail: comparative case studies of demand fulfilment and demand denial.

386 The use of terrorist tactics by liberation movements.

387 Aborted terrorist attacks: why they failed.

388 Successful terrorist blackmail: analysis of factors leading to the release of imprisoned terrorists in exchange for hostages.

389 Scenarios of chemical, biological, radiological and nuclear blackmail.

390 Terrorist intimidation: determinants of mass panic, based on examples from recent history.

391 Terrorist uses of the Internet.

392 Anarchist cook books: a review of the do-it-yourself manuals for creating mayhem.

393 Target analysis: preferred targets in longitudinal and cross-national comparison.

394 Terrorist rhetoric and strategy: analysis of their documents: reading between the lines.

395 Terrorist threats and warnings: how to deal with them?

396 Guerrilla uses of terrorist tactics, terrorist uses of guerrilla tactics, terrorist uses of organized crime tactics: the nature of crossovers.

397 Identity card fraud and illegal immigration: their role in terrorist use of organized crime and in countering terrorism.

398 'Pockets of anarchy' as safe havens for terror organizations.

399 The dirty dozen: the terrorist groups that have expressed an interest to acquire, develop and use CBRN weapons: how far have they progressed?

400 The threat of nuclear suitcase bombs: a continuing story.

401 The application of 'smart mobbing' by terrorist organizations: case studies.

402 The danger of an electronic Pearl Harbor (the danger of a large-scale attack via the Internet to disrupt banking traffic and ruin the economy?): an assessment.

403 The 419 scam: application of similar methods to raise funds for terrorism.

404 Secret torture camps where youths are trained in torture and killing: comparative case studies.

405 Iraq: the establishment of satellite cells around the country that facilitate the supply of volunteers for suicide operations: disentangling the network of financiers and facilitators.

406 The rise in kidnappings for ransom of upper-class children: national experiences.

407 The 400 000 missing passports: unhindered travel opportunities for terrorists.

408 Trade marks of terrorist bomb makers (e.g. Terrorist Explosive Device Analytical Center (TEDAC), Quantica, Virginia).

409 The global system for the construction of bombs for terrorist purposes: the proliferation of more advanced bomb blueprints and techniques.

410 The development of a 'white' or 'blue-eyed' al-Qaeda: myth or reality?

411 The development of new types of IEDs that are capable of circumventing existing security measures: case studies.

412 The application of swarming tactics by terrorist organizations (an attack from multiple directions by autonomous units on a single target or unit): case studies.

413 How terrorist organizations use prior knowledge of attacks to generate revenue from global financial markets: case studies (attacks on individual corporations, attacks on oil infrastructure, taking states hostage).

414 Nation states targeted or threatened with infrastructure disruption unless they make a large ransom payment: case studies.

415 Homemade directed energy weapons (HERFs) the weapon of choice for terrorist organizations intent on infrastructure destruction: developments and examples.

416 Was 9/11 a black swan (an unpredictable event that defies prediction)?

417 Understanding the stigmergic signalling between global guerrillas: requirement for the development of ways to disrupt their activity (stigmergy: method of understanding underlying patterns of swarming activity).

418 Temporary autonomous zones (TAZs) (geographic zones that are free of state control – an organic byproduct of a failed or weak state) and their exploitation by terrorist organizations (basic shelter, freedom of movement, open commerce): comparative case studies.

419 Global guerrillas operating from geographical dispersed locations: e.g. failed and collapsed states, zones of chaotic organic disorder, the Internet: comparative case studies.

420 The complex problem of eliminating TAZs (taking into consideration the rapidly shifting locations, locations that resist interdiction and diversity): case studies.

421 The economics of defence against CRBN attacks.

422 Amateurish attempts to produce CBRN weapons (e.g. botulism, ricin, sarin, bubonic plague bacteria, typhoid bacteria, hydrogen cyanide, VX): changes in frequency and progress made.

423 Analysis of accidents that have already taken place involving contagion and death while testing a nuclear device or a man-made disease transmission device.

424 The exponential change in the technology of killing devices and in logistics and communications: what casualties can be inflicted by a small organized group of dedicated individuals in a single action? – an assessment.

425 An export model to overthrow dictators peacefully: comparative case studies, e.g. Serbia, Ukraine (Orange revolution), Georgia (Revolution of the

Roses), Lebanon (Cedar revolution); Kyrguzstan (Tulip revolution) and the next candidates.

426 Terrorist manifests/manuals with instructions/guidelines to finance terrorism via cyber fraud: an assessment of Internet vulnerabilities and constantly developing policies (e.g. Imam Samudra, JI).

427 Cyberspace: where the bad guys are going.

428 Crossing thresholds: the compulsion of norm breakers to offer *ex post facto* justifications of their actions.

429 Terrorism: adopting the global business model.

430 Terrorism: utilizing 'brown zones' in Western societies (specific neighbourhoods or particular types of organizations where state governments are reluctant to intervene).

431 The rise of so-called 'tiger kidnappings' (taking hostage relatives of an employee to get his or her cooperation in robbing a company): case studies and national comparisons.

432 Urban terrorism: key innovations of militant organizations.

433 Cell phone technology: an explosive tool for insurgents.

434 The transfer of bomb technology from states to terrorists (e.g. the Al-Ghafiqi project (R&D for all types of IEDs) of the M-21 directorate of the Mukhabarat): case studies.

435 Radicals in sheep's clothing: silencing people with the accusation of xenophobia.

436 The ongoing battle between criminals/terrorists and corporate security experts: new types of Internet scams.

437 The emergence of hotspots of cybercrime (e.g. Romania): determining factors?

438 Seizing laptops of top-level terrorists: what can be learned from them?

22. Theoretical/conceptual/definitional considerations

439 The literature on terrorism: mainstream and alternative interpretations of terrorism.

440 The causes of terrorism as reflected in terrorist writings and the literature on terrorism.

441 The concept of political crime or political offence in national and international law.

442 Theorists of terrorism: analysis of their writings.

443 Political violence other than terrorism: conceptual issues.

444 Attacks on military forces – terrorist or not? A discussion based on case studies from Lebanon, Saudi Arabia and Russia.

445 The conduct and process of research: how to understand practices and relationships between research producers and users.

23. Risk analysis

446 Threat and risk assessments: evaluating intelligence on possible terrorist attacks.

447 Early warning indicators of terrorist escalation.

448 Political risk analysis: the state of the art.

449 Cascading system failures: case studies.

450 The vulnerability of complex infrastructures to non-planned events: how terrorists exploit the assumptions of designers to create major disruptions in complex networks; the concept of highly optimized tolerance (HOT).

451 Intergovernmental relations/federalism/governance issues: the arrival of the Department of Homeland Security (DHS): the need for definition and description of the changes to federalism: positive and negative effects and unintended consequences.

452 Reconsidering the all-hazards vs specific hazards approach: are we actually moving towards or emphasizing one type of hazard (terrorism) at the expense of others (natural hazards)?

453 Cultural differences between the 'old' and emerging organizations responsible for emergency management in the DHS.

24. Dynamics of terrorism

454 Training camps for terrorists: what do we know about them?

455 From physical training in camps to do-it-yourself training by Internet or CD-ROM.

456 Interviews with terrorists: what do they tell us?

457 Countering terrorist propaganda rather than countering terrorist violence: outline of an alternative strategy.

458 The self-image of the terrorist and how to weaken it.

459 Terrorist decision-making: what do we know?

460 What do terrorists hope to gain? Their motives and strategies.

461 Keeping a terrorist organization alive: skill-sets for facilitators (recruitment, false documentation, travel and transit, safe houses, finance, families, media, knowledge transfer, couriers).

462 Executing a successful terrorist operation: skill sets for terrorist operators (surveillance, counter-surveillance, communication, constructing cells, target selection, reconnaissance, operational planning, operational security, device construction).

463 Changes in the repertoire of current terrorist organisations (ambush, siege, stand-off attack, kidnapping, close-quarter assassination (CQA), man-portable air defence systems (MANPADS), improvised explosive devices (IEDs), vehicle-borne improvised explosive devices (VBIEDs), personal-borne improvised explosive devices (PBIEDs) and water-borne improvised explosive devices (WBIEDs)).

464 The role of former military officials in terrorist organisations: key assets in the transfer of essential knowledge needed for setting up underground organizations.

465 The possibility of developing a transferable template for attacking any target country: an assessment.

466 Determinants of prevention (e.g. public vigilance, unprecedented security, intelligence, law enforcement, military cooperation, proactive targeting of cells, planning and preparing attacks): is the threat diminishing?

467 Strategy meetings of terrorists: basic indicator of future threats.

468 The rising threshold of violence caused by the porosity of borders between terrorist organizations and the exchange of technical and human expertise between terrorist groups: case studies.

469 Are terrorism and drug-trafficking rooted in the same environment?

25. General background factors facilitating international terrorism

470 What is the relationship between terrorism, democracy and globalization?

471 Do most terrorist events take place in the least globalized and least democratic countries?

472 Terror in the least well connected and democratized part and the most connected and democratized parts of the world?

473 How is the process of democratization linked to different levels of political violence? – comparative case studies.

474 Fuelling the Muslim rage: the continuation of catalyst conflicts (e.g. Palestine, Iraq, Chechnya, Kashmir, Mindanao (Philippines), Maluku (Indonesia), Sulawesi (Indonesia), Algeria, Afghanistan).

475 Extremist ideology: the principal driver of contemporary violence.

476 Islam: a blessing for humanity.

477 Occidentalism: the West in the eyes of its enemies.

478 New oil/gas contracts as early warning indicators of armed conflict: case studies.

479 Addiction to the jihad: an explanation.

480 The Saudi paradox: the power of the principle and doctrine of Tawhid (monotheism) and the doctrine of Taqqarub (peaceful co-existence with unbelievers).

481 Sheikh Muhammed ibn Abdul Wahhab: driving force and source of inspiration for the jihad.

482 The duty of Tawhid (Islamic monotheism).

483 Ijtihad: reinterpreting Islamic principles.

484 Are there inhibiting factors that mitigate against a species self-destructing?

485 The puzzle: why has there not been a far larger series of terrorist-created disasters?

486 Ethnic cleansing in reverse: state population policies with the aim to change the ethnic distribution: unintended consequences (e.g. Malaysia).

487 The exploitation of Islam to create a national identity: negative impact (e.g. Malaysia).

488 Rejectionist movements: the attraction of new spirituality.

489 Identifying factors making a nation 'hospitable' to transnational crime and terrorism.

490 The convergence of global terror and international migration.

Note

1 The original list was published as Appendix C in Alex P. Schmid (ed.) *Countering Terrorism through International Cooperation*. Proceedings of an International Conference held 22–24 September 2000 in Courmayeur, Italy (Milan: ISPAC, 2001), pp. 378–385. The categories have remained unchanged but the number of entries has been expanded and in some cases modified.

13

THE COMPLEXITY OF TERRORISM: SOCIAL AND BEHAVIORAL UNDERSTANDING

Trends for the future

Nancy K. Hayden[1]

Some problems are so complex that you have to be highly intelligent and well informed just to be undecided about them.

Laurence J. Peter

Blessed are the curious for they shall have adventures.

Lovelle Drachman

I haven't a clue as to how my story will end. But that's all right. When you set out on a journey and night covers the road, that's when you discover the stars.

Nancy Willard

Life is not a problem to be solved, but a mystery to be lived.

Thomas Merton

Introduction

Terrorism can be viewed as an emergent phenomenon of complex, dynamically interacting social, technological and institutional systems. Considering terrorism through this lens has significant implications for social and behavioral research and analysis, made possible by advances in understanding complex systems over the past twenty years. First, the universal principles that govern the behavior of complex systems provide a much needed, *common framework* that transcends traditional academic boundaries and allows synergistic consideration of knowl-edge from diverse conceptual domains, multiple cultural perspectives, and a wide range of behavioral scales. Second, technical advances in *analytic methods* derived from complexity science – such as multi-scale dynamic network analysis, evolutionary computing algorithms, agent-based modeling and simulation and multi-dimensional pattern analysis – provide means for data analysis and hypothesis generation and testing that have been computationally intractable in the past. Third, new *paradigms for sense-making* in situations of high complexity and ambiguity provide intelligence and policy analysts the means to explicitly consider complex social and behavioral phenomena such as emergence, innovation, adaptation, self-organization and surprise in developing counterterrorism strategies. This chapter provides an analytic framework based on the principles of complex systems analysis and describes how key analytic methods fit into that framework thereby providing new paradigms for sense-making.

Naming the problem: wicked complexity

Forty years of research have shown terrorism to be an emergent phenomenon characterized by a strong coupling between the evolutionary dynamics of the groups that engage in terrorist activities; their strategies and tactics; the social, cultural, and political systems within which they are embedded; and the infrastructures available to these groups for sustaining their operations. A complete literature review in each of the relevant subject domains is beyond the scope of this paper. However, key social and behavioral principles that can be drawn from the corpus of terrorism research are that:

- Terrorism is predominantly a group phenomenon of normal psychology,[2] functioning at the apex of a pyramid of a larger, diverse social system of sympathizers and supporters that exert multiple influences on individual beliefs and behaviors.[3]
- The path to terrorism is shaped by multiple and diverse motivational factors with no single root cause.[4]
- Terrorist groups and their supporting social systems are embedded within institutional and geopolitical structures that co-evolve within specific historical contexts[5] and complex religious belief systems.[6] The associated cultural norms that justify killing are typically mirrored in the legitimizing ideology of the group; the evolutionary development of this perversion provides an observable pattern of radicalization within a subculture.[7]
- Terrorist actions are targeted towards multiple audiences and co-evolve with public, state and media responses to those actions.[8] While this phenomenon is well known, the dynamics are not well understood or explained by current research, especially with respect to the advent of the Internet as an instantaneous, unregulated, self-organizing communication channel.
- Changes in security environments (whether as counterterrorism measures or as the natural course of exogenous events) are met with innovation and adaptation in targets, operations, and strategies.[9] A prime example is the

continual adaptation of improvised explosive devices (IEDs) by Iraqi insurgents against targets that have evolved from US military forces to foreign
civilians to Iraqi security officers to segments of the Iraqi civilian population.
Another is the changed operational nature of al-Qaeda from an organization with a centralized strategic planning staff, prior to the US invasion of
Afghanistan, to a self-organizing network characterized more by 'leaderless
resistance' strategies after the invasion.

- Self-organizing terrorist groups form primarily through social networks; the
  structure and dynamics of these networks are determined to a large degree by
  the strength and nature of social ties and transactions that take place through
  them.[10]
- The emergence of the "small world" phenomenon through decentralized
  terrorist networks facilitates resiliency in operations, diffusion of ideology
  and innovation, and distribution of resources and information.[11] The post
  9/11 attacks in London, Madrid and Bali are examples of this emergence,
  predicted by Sageman as he monitored the dissolution of al-Qaeda's "central
  staff."[12] So too is the evidence of increasing association of terrorist financing
  with organized crime networks, as the accessibility of legitimate financial
  institutions to distribution of funds by terrorist organizations was shut down
  worldwide after 9/11.

As a whole, these characteristics describe dynamically interacting systems of
social, technological and institutional entities. Understanding the nature of these
systems, their interdependencies, and how they co-evolve is critical for future
terrorism analysis. In a prescient article – written prior to 9/11, the Madrid
bombings of March 2004, the insurgency in Iraq, or the London bombings of
July 2005 – Walter Lacquer described this analytic challenge:[13]

Scanning the contemporary scene, one encounters a bewildering multiplicity of terrorist and potentially terrorist groups and sects. An
individual may possess the technical competence to steal, buy, or manufacture the weapons he or she needs for a terrorist purpose; he or she
may or may not require help from one or two others in delivering these
weapons to the designated target. The ideologies such individuals and
mini-groups espouse are likely to be even more aberrant than those of
larger groups. And terrorists working alone or in very small groups will
be more difficult to detect unless they make a major mistake or are discovered by accident. ... Society has also become vulnerable to a new
kind of terrorism, in which the destructive power of both the individual
terrorist and terrorism as a tactic are infinitely greater. New definitions
and new terms may have to be developed for new realities, and intelligence services and policymakers must learn to discern the significant
differences among terrorists' motivations, approaches, and aims.

Discernment of differentiating behavioral characteristics amidst ambiguity and complexity is a critical problem for terrorism analysts. The 9/11 Commission report recognized this, and attributed the lack of this discernment to a "failure of imagination" in the analytic process. Where analysts were found to have information, they did not know that they had it or did not know the collective significance of it. What they did know and use, they used in old models.[14] Correcting this situation requires "an alternative analysis approach that is more aimed at promoting 'mindfulness' – continuous wariness of analytic failure – than a set of tools to employ."[15]

What kind of analysis frameworks can provide this "mindfulness"? Since 9/11, intense introspection on the part of intelligence, research, and policymaking communities alike has pointed to the need for collection, synthesis, and sense-making of information from multiple (and often contradictory) sources and perspectives. This information must be interpreted, hypothesized about, and responded to in the context of diverse social, behavioral, technical, political and institutional models to support a spectrum of counterterrorism decision-making policies and actions (see Figure 13.1).

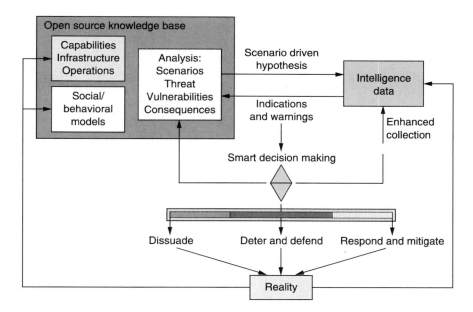

Figure 13.1 Within the spectrum of decisions to be considered, each has a potential impact on others that are rarely analyzed holistically. Present analytic stovepipes based on classification of information, information domains, cultural mindset of analysts, and analytic methods present significant barriers to a holistic understanding. This figure was developed by the Advanced Concepts Group at Sandia National Laboratories, under the leadership of Dr Gerry Yonas.

Specific characteristics of "wicked" problems were delineated by Horst Rittel in the context of civic planning.[16] Today's scholars, analysts, and policy makers will recognize all of the following with respect to understanding and responding to terrorism:

1. There is no definitive formulation of the problem.
2. There is no end to the problem.
3. Solutions are not true-or-false, but good-or-bad.
4. There is no immediate and no ultimate test of a solution to the problem.
5. Every solution to the problem is a "one-shot operation"; because there is no opportunity to learn by trial-and-error, every attempt counts significantly.
6. There is not an enumerable (or an exhaustively describable) set of potential solutions, nor is there a well-described set of permissible operations that may be incorporated into a plan.
7. Every instantiation of the problem is essentially unique.
8. The problem is actually a symptom of another problem.
9. The existence of discrepancies when representing the problem can be explained in numerous ways. The choice of explanation determines the nature of the problem's resolution.
10. The planner has no right to be wrong.

In Rittel's view, the multiplicity of factors and conditions that impinge on wicked problems – all embedded in a dynamic social context – ensure that that no two wicked problems are alike, and that the solutions to them will always be custom designed and fitted. The framing will determine the problem's resolution. In the case of terrorism, the social science literature falls into political, social, religious, and historical frames. These need to be considered synergistically to avoid the disastrous consequences that can result from acting on singular frameworks that do not accommodate the full complexity of the problem. The development of the insurgency in Iraq is a case in point, which supports Rittel's claim that it is the *social complexity* of these problems that overwhelms most problem solving and management approaches. Thus, understanding terrorism is a problem that is wicked. It is also, as we shall see, formally complex.

Before going further then, one must ask, just what does it mean to be complex, and, for that matter, just what *is* a complexity?

Varying definitions of complexity and associated measures have been proposed by the research community from a diversity of perspectives. Probabilistic, computational, and algorithmic definitions of complexity were some of the first proposed, and involve measuring how much information (or information processing) is required to completely describe a system and reduce uncertainty.[17] The units of measure in these formulations, typically originating from computational experiments, are in terms of the length of information strings (schema) or other measures of information content.

Crutchfield has shown that these formulations, which describe deterministic complexity in terms of randomness, are insufficient for describing the structural complexity present in natural systems.[18] He resolved this by the introduction of a statistical metric of complexity based on stochastic processes and entropy that are correlates to a relative measure of structure. In his formulation, relative measures of both randomness and structure are necessary for determining a system's complexity, as shown in the "complexity–entropy" curve in Figure 13.2.

At the extremes of randomness, the system is structurally simple. Statistical complexity – which is correlated to structure – is greatest in the intermediate regime. In complexity literature, this intermediate regime is referred to as the "edge of chaos" and is where some of the most interesting system behaviors occur – such. as surprise, innovation, and phase transitions. It is at phase transitions, for example, that the forces leading to order and disorder compete, producing unique critical states, more complex than those away from the transition.[19]

Crutchfield's complexity–entropy formulation has significant implications about the *predictability* of complex systems. At the extremes of randomness, where statistical (stochastic) complexity is lowest, predictability is greatest. This is true even in deterministic chaotic systems in the short term, although long-term predictability of such systems is impossible.[20] However, these predictions are of limited value as they represent average behaviors, whereas the more significant behaviors are those of the outliers. An example is the case of the perpetrators of the London subway attacks in July 2005.

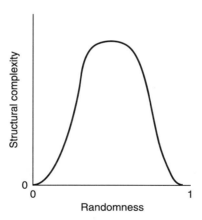

Figure 13.2 Statistical complexity is based on the notion that randomness is statistically simple: an ideal random process has zero statistical complexity. At the other end of the spectrum, simple periodic processes have low statistical complexity. Complex processes arise between these extremes and are an amalgam of predictable and stochastic mechanisms. Reprinted with permission.

The implications for terrorism analysis are profound. It means that we must cease to ask questions about *explicitly predicting* future events (e.g., How likely is it for an event of type x to occur over time period y perpetrated by group z at location a?), and instead ask questions that seek to *explore possibilities* of future behaviors and the key indicators for those behaviors in terms of dynamic patterns of interactions and the underlying structures upon which those transactions take place (e.g., Given that we see certain types of relationships forming and interactions taking place in certain contexts, what are the risks of a terrorist event?). Fortunately, since Rittel first proposed the notion of wicked problems, advances in understanding the nature of complex systems – in particular self-organizing complex systems – have provided grounding principles that enable actionable discernment into differentiating patterns of behaviors as we follow these lines of questioning.

Principles of complex systems

The power of using complexity as a paradigm for terrorism analysis is that the fundamental principles that govern the behaviors of self-organizing, purposeful, complex systems transcend the boundaries of academic disciplines and bring about a convergence among them. The following principles are derived from research across a diverse spectrum of scientific fields – e.g., nonlinear systems dynamics, organizational dynamics, computer science, statistical mechanics, physics, biology, zoology, sociology, economics, and cultural anthropology.[21]

I. *Complex systems are wholes with irreducible properties that emerge from the interaction and interdependence among its parts.*

II. *Complex systems that are purposeful are capable of maintaining themselves and initiating action to achieve goals in a changing environment.*

III. *Purposeful complex systems create themselves in response to self-creativity in other systems.*

IV. *Complex systems are coordinating interfaces in Nature's holarchy.*[22]

These principles result in universal characteristic properties, structures, and dynamics of purposeful complex systems, as discussed below.

I. Complex systems are wholes with irreducible properties that emerge from the interaction and interdependence among its parts

This first principle introduces the key concept of *emergence*. In common parlance, it says that "the whole is greater than the sum of the parts". Some of the consequences are that system properties cannot be predicted *a priori*; cause and effect are almost always only evident in retrospect, and understanding of the latent potential state of the system is best obtained through selectively probing the system and assessing the responses. The central concepts of emergence trace back to statistical mechanics and the laws of thermodynamics, when it was recognized that by dealing with ensembles of particles or ensembles of states, macroscopic observables – such as pressure and temperature – could be described in terms of microscopic states. In the context of social sciences, this first principle explains why groups can exhibit fundamentally different behavioral properties than those of the individuals who comprise the group. In the case of terrorism, an example introduced previously is the emergence of a "normalized" ideology for legitimizing killing that is in harmony with prevailing cultural norms.

The dynamics of emergence, and how emergent properties depend on the system state and structure, are an active area of research in complexity science. In the words of John Holland,[23]

> Despite its ubiquity and importance, emergence is an enigmatic, recondite topic, more wondered at than analyzed.

Indeed, the very concept and definition of emergence itself is a field of ongoing research, as is the means by which to detect it. Crutchfield defines emergence in terms of structure and pattern formation at the intuitive, operational, and intrinsic systems levels, providing a useful construct for social and behavioral analysis. Intuitively, one knows there is emergence when something new appears that was not part of the initial and boundary conditions; it was created by the underlying system. Operationally, one identifies emergence when new types of organized patterns are observed in a dynamical system. There is intrinsic emergence when the system itself capitalizes on the patterns that appear, and more powerful levels of interaction appear that were not present in earlier conditions.[24]

II. Complex systems that are purposeful are capable of maintaining themselves and initiating action to achieve goals in a changing environment

This second principle tells us what it is about complex systems that makes intrinsic emergence possible. It says that the *purposeful* nature of complex systems results in *dynamic, self-organizing* processes required for the system to achieve a balance between the natural tendencies to degrade and the input of energy required for self-maintaining in a steady state of equilibrium.[25] The principle is expressed through the *interactions* between entities in the system and the resulting *structures* formed. The nature of those interactions – e.g., *cooperative, collaborative*, or *competitive* – create the forces of tension that give rise to structural complexity, and are paramount in determining the emergent properties of the system. To quote John Holland again,

You have to look at the way the various pieces support each other . . .
It's the interaction of the pieces from which the strength emerges. It's
the same in all complex adaptive systems. Interaction is the key.

Axelrod, a pioneer in the study of cooperation in complex systems, first examined the evolution of cooperative interactions during the Cold War, using the
iterated Prisoner's Dilemma as a frame of reference, with the intention of promoting cooperation between two sides in a bipolar world.[26] Since that time, he
has led the expansion of research on purposeful complex system interactions
to include collaboration within a multiplicity of forms – such as building and
enforcing norms, winning a "war", building up an organization, or constructing
a shared culture. His work shows that as potential forms of collaboration and
cooperation expand, so do potential forms of competitive interactions. Examples
are: conflict between violators and enforcers of norms, contests among organizations for resources and members, or competing pulls of social influence for
cultural change.[27] Again, Iraq provides an excellent example, where the cooperative forces between the US military and various segments of Iraqi society turned
to forces of conflict as the US was increasingly perceived in the role of enforcer
of new norms in the process of cultural change, and as the various factions of
resistance to that change competed for resources and social influence. This is also
seen in the splitting and splintering that happens within terrorist organizations,
such as that described by Drummond in his account of the white separatist and
Christian identity movements in the US and by Wickham in her account of the
Muslim Brotherhood's mobilization efforts in Egypt.

III. Purposeful complex systems create themselves in response to self-creativity within themselves and in other systems

This third principle is about change, brought about through *evolution* and *innovation*. The dynamics of evolution and the many mechanisms through which it
occurs – e.g., *selection, variation, learning, adaptation* – explain the diversity
of structure, function, and behavior in complex systems. It also explains why
complex systems that stay complex are not in a steady state of equilibrium – as
would be implied by the second principle alone – but instead exist in dynamic,
quasi-stable non-equilibrium states. Two fundamentally different types of evolutionary processes drive change: those that occur as a result of differentiation
between individual entities in the system, and those that occur as a result of
all entities simultaneously undergoing a similar, generalized transformational
process.[28] Any or all of these processes may be operative in a complex system, depending on both intrinsic properties and external conditions, as described
below.

Evolution at the (macro) systems level that comes about as a result of differentiated changes at the (micro) level of individuals within the system is known
as *organic* or *variational* evolution, and embodies the neo-Darwinian concept.

Changes in system properties result from expression of the differential enrichment of individuals. This diversity is brought about through mechanisms such as *genetic variation* and *mutation*. Gradual adaptation, expressed as a series of small changes over time, leads to locally optimized behaviors and the emergence of new form and function. This type of evolution can be viewed as an optimization process where the environment provides constraints and the ensemble of individuals is able to incrementally change in ways that take advantage of or mitigate the constraints. In this view, evolution is a reactionary process; the environment is the source of novelty and the instigator of change.[29] A particularly interesting (and topically relevant) example of this type of evolution in social systems is the adoption of innovative technological change, which has been shown to occur through a universally applicable process of diffusion and adaptation.[30] Rogers showed that the enabling mechanism for evolution through innovation diffusion is the *communication* among potential adopters, and the social learning that occurs, based on perceived advantage of the innovation. The evolution of methods used for creating IEDs in Iraq is an example of this type of process.

In contrast to variational evolution, *transformational* evolution is associated with collective system responses to immutable external factors in the environment or larger ecological system. Consider the evolution of stars in a galaxy. In this case, the evolutionary process is expressed through the same generalized transformational processes for each star.[31] An example is the transformative evolution of global social communication norms among youth with the simultaneous advent of the Internet and wireless technologies.

In general, variational and transformational evolutions have relatively long time periods associated with change. However, in the former case, the timeframe is determined by the rate of diffusion of innovation, whereas in the latter case it is the rate at which the exogenous forces effect the global system change.

Evolution in complex systems need not be gradual, as in the above processes, but can be *episodic*, characterized by sudden *adaptive innovation* that arises through the series of *discovery, adaptation, phase transition,* and subsequent *stabilization*. Evolutionary mechanisms proposed to explain these phenomena include *adaptive fitness landscapes* and *punctuated equilibria*.[32] These mechanisms explain evolutionary dynamics when the external environment is the source of innovation; they do not explain the origin of the innovation when it comes from within the system itself. The concept of *epochal evolution* synthesizes all of the preceding notions of evolution – organic, transformational, and episodic. It allows for intrinsic emergence of innovation and subsequent selection and diffusion at a microscopic (individual) level within a defined space/time state (epoch), to be combined with population and survival dynamics at a mesoscopic (system) level in a larger ecological space of functionality.[33] An example of this type of process is the worldwide response of the Muslim community to the publication of Danish cartoons of Mohammed. In this case, Islamic clerics in the Netherlands with a local grievance evolved their strategies organically as their efforts to engage the regional political structures failed. At the same time, a latent grievance with the West was building globally in the Muslim community through a transformational process, as evidenced by surveys worldwide. These two processes came together when the Islamic clerics deliberately exploited the global sentiments to further their local cause, resulting in an unanticipated global outrage.

As system behaviors change, so too do the underlying structures of the systems themselves. Evolutionary models account for the self-stabilizing feedback in structural complexity on the one hand, and the creation and transmission of innovation through a network of interacting systems on the other. Applied to social systems, the epochal evolutionary model in particular encompasses the phenomenon of the "strength of weak ties" in social networks discovered by Granovetter,[34] the resulting structural complexity in the form of scale-free networks,[35] and the dynamics associated with these networks,[36]

IV. Complex systems are coordinating interfaces in Nature's holarchy

The fourth principle is about the *organizational dynamics* between systems that are embedded within "systems of systems". Systems of systems are multi-level, flexibly coordinated structures that act as wholes despite their complexity. There are many levels, and yet there is integration. Each of the individual systems is an autonomous whole in regard to its parts. However, in as much as each is also a part with respect to higher-level wholes, none can be fully explained by a study of its parts.

It is this final principle that makes the paradigm of complex systems so powerful, as it provides a means by which to incorporate in a single, unified analysis behavior mechanisms that operate on different scales in response to different mechanisms. Complicated analytic problems can be simplified by focusing on (1) the *self-similar patterns* that exist within different systems in the holarchy, and (2) the *interface dynamics* at the boundaries.

Communication and *associations* across interfaces are dominant mechanisms in shaping the structures and behaviors that evolve out of the whole. Communication – the means by which it occurs and the speed at which it occurs – establishes what information is "known" by each system in the whole. In some cases, increasing speed of communication may set up "future shock" because adaptive capacities may be exceeded. At the same time, associations between the parts of the system establish a network of interactions: parts of wholes might associate with parts of other wholes, thereby creating new wholes that can again be split into parts, and so forth *ad infinitum*. Together, the amount of communication and association among systems partially determines the behavior of the whole system. On one extreme, systems with little interaction or communication fall into static patterns, while on the other extreme, "overactive" systems "boil with chaos."[37]

Framing the problem

In the previous sections, we established that understanding terrorism can be characterized as both a wicked and a complex problem, examined the nature of wickedness and complexity, and postulated the principles of purposeful complex systems that provide an analytic foundation for discerning differential social and behavioral factors that lead to the emergence of terrorism. In the following sections we examine what the resulting analysis framework might look like and the analytic methods that are useful within that framework.

Systems theorist Gharajedaghi attributes the wickedness associated with social complexity to the "multi-mindedness" of purposeful systems. In as much as choice is at the heart of all systems involving humans, he argues that one must understand the rational, emotional and cultural dimensions of choice holistically within a systems context, and base decisions on the multiplicity of choices possible among an ensemble of systems and the spectrum of potential future end states to which those choices can lead.[38] In complex, self-organizing, adaptive systems, there can be many such possible end states originating from the same beginning point. Similarly, a final end state may be arrived at from a multiplicity of beginning points, along a variety of pathways. These two notions have fundamental implications for how we frame our analysis.[39]

An integrated analysis framework requires grounding in terms of three critical dimensions: the epistemology of the analysis (e.g., what knowledge does the analysis purport to achieve and how is it to be used?), the degree of complexity to be considered (in terms of both vertical and horizontal dimensions of the system), and the timescale necessary to capture the system dynamics (Figure 13.3).

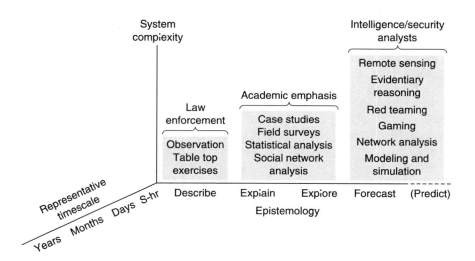

Figure 13.3 Integrated analysis framework.

Epistemological characterization of an analysis is essential for choosing the appropriate level of system complexity and dynamic timescale, but is often overlooked. Analytic inquiry can range from seeking to understand *what is*, to understanding *why something is*, to seeking *what is possible*, or predicting *what will be*. Representative (but neither prescriptive nor comprehensive) epistemological regimes are shown in Figure 13.3, along with typical analytic methods used within those regimes and the communities of analysts who employ them.

On one extreme, where the epistemology seeks to answer the question of what is, the dynamic, iterative and interactive nature of complex systems requires that analysis be grounded within an appropriate, finite timeframe and a specific context. Law enforcement and front-line military (expeditionary) forces provide examples of communities with a primary focus on answering questions about what has just happened or is currently happening. These communities require frameworks and analytic methods that facilitate understanding of direct observations in relatively short timeframes.

On the other extreme, some analytic epistemologies seek to predict what will be. However, we have shown that a characteristic of complex systems is their unpredictability. Therefore, attempts to quantitatively and explicitly predict complex system behaviors will fail. If the hypothesis of this paper is correct – namely, that terrorism is an emergent phenomenon of complex systems – then attempts to predict its specific instantiation in time and place will also fail. Unfortunately, the culture within which much of terrorism analysis occurs fosters an approach of attempting to achieve such "point" predictions.

The most appropriate analytic framework for complex systems has an epistemology intermediate between these two extremes. The academic community tends to focus on this regime – asking questions about what explanations there are for the things that have happened or are happening, and questions about what these explanations might mean for what could happen in the future. There is a need to bring the academic, intelligence, military, policy, and security analysis communities together to build frameworks that can holistically generate understanding of what is happening and why, and to use that understanding to explore potential future states under a variety of policy options.

In addition to the need for analytic frameworks that can provide such holistic understanding, there is a need to map analytic methods to epistemological regimes, and to understand the interfaces between these analytic methods. The barriers to achieving this are numerous – such as the differential level of system complexity that different methods have been developed to represent, the access to distributed data and differentiated classification of information that is required, the different cultures of the analytic communities, and different ontological representation of concepts that are "named" differently in different problem-solving domains.

These latter points bring us directly to the second and third dimensions that must be addressed in building an analytic framework: identifying the level of system complexity and specifying the timeframe of relevance. Let us consider system complexity first. On the surface, this may seem problematic, as we have seen that there is no one consistent definition and measure of complexity. However, the common element across all measures of complexity is that they are analogous characterizations of systems on a spectrum between order and chaos (or randomness).

Most relevant to the social and behavioral sciences is the structural measure proposed by Crutchfield, which he arrived at through an argument using statistical mechanics. In Crutchfield's formulation, complexity is correlated to[40]

varying degrees of organization – or structure, regularity, symmetry and intricacy – in a system's behavior or its architecture.

In analysis of terrorism, individual entities can be at the level of the individual, group, organization, state, or culture within which they are embedded. The structural architecture between those entities, the dynamic nature of those structures and interactions between them can all be defined in terms of complexity.

The third dimension required of a framework relates to the periodicity of the timeframe of the analysis, and the corresponding rate of information transmission through the system. Some of the main questions to ask when analyzing a complex system through the framework of structural complexity are about the timeframe for when and how the system stores, transmits and transforms information; as well as the nature of that information, who the agents are for its transmission, and how receiving agents react to it. The third critical dimension for constructing the analytic framework is therefore to identify the relevant timeframe that encompasses both the rate of information transmission and the periodicity associated with system behavior in response to that information. In doing so, one must account for the nature of information in dynamic systems – its periodicity is measured not by the clock but by characteristic rhythms and iterations,[41] and long periods of stasis can be interrupted by sudden change.[42]

Together, the epistemology of the emergent behavior of interest, the degree of system complexity, and the timeframe and dynamic nature of the information transmission within the system prescribe the framework of the evolutionary model appropriate for the analysis. This framework must be flexible and adaptable, as we have seen that every attempt to solve a wickedly complex problem will, in fact, change our understanding of the problem. Moreover, in acting on the problem, we will find that "success is the devil" as every successful solution will lead to imitation, inertia, and sub-optimization characterized by increasing vestedness in singular "right answers" aligned with a prevailing culture, discouraging alternative views.[43] This cycle is a potential trap for analysts and researchers alike, demanding openness to paradigm shifts and a keen "intellectual wariness".

As a final, practical note, the analyst must also consider the timeframe available for the analysis in choosing the analytic method!

Taming the problem: complex systems analysis

The previous discussion introduced a conceptual foundation for a holistic analytic approach to understanding the social and behavioral dimensions of terrorism through the complex systems paradigm. This analytic framework is integrative, looking at structure (networks), the dynamics of those structures, emergent behavior, and the resulting patterns that form. This framework allows a synthesis of mechanisms studied in a diversity of fields: e.g., physics; statistical mechanics; biology; information theory; sociology and social movement theory. As summarized by Bar-Yam,[44]

> The conceptual shift from reductionist strategies of inquiry to integrative, transdisciplinary and unified descriptions afforded by the science of complex systems has a profound impact on our ability to discern the composite significance of environmental, social, political, economic, biological, and physical aspects of the world. Where the real world teaches us that events and actions have multiple causes and consequences, the concepts and methods of complexity science can be used to address questions which cannot be answered by focusing on individual forces or parts, thus building our understanding of the functional and coincidental relationships in and between systems. These concepts provide a unity and simplification of the otherwise bewildering properties of diverse complex systems into a common framework that allows for both horizontal and vertical integration.

Complex systems analysis allows the analyst to integrate both vertically and horizontally, using the principles of self-similarity and finding common features in terms of shared aspects of organization and repeating patterns. Through this integration, a system in one perspective is treated as a subsystem in another, while maintaining a perspective of integrated wholeness, never as a mechanistic aggregate of parts in isolable causal relations. Dynamics at interfaces are examined through the intrinsic properties of the complex system at those interfaces.

So it seems that the complexity paradigm provides a potential path forward for investigating wicked problems in a number of dimensions. Yet a key challenge remains in "taming" the problem so as to render the results germane to real-world decision-making, using information that is consistent with the epistemology of both the analysis and the basis for decision-making. In part, this can be done with analysis methods that employ inductive reasoning algorithms over large ensembles of computational experiments, to discover the conditions under which emergent behaviors occur through the dynamics of learning, adaptation, and innovation. This makes it possible to systematically compare alternative policy options in the context of wicked problem-solving. These methods can study emergence under conditions typical of wicked problems – such as those in which cause and effect might be separated in space and time; in which one event can have multiple effects; and in which a set of variables that initially played a key role in producing an effect may be replaced by a different set of variables at a different time, in which case removing the initial cause will not necessarily remove the effect.

These abstracted models of complex systems can be brought to bear on problems in sociological research that are key to understanding the emergence of terrorism. An example is the analysis of data relating to the structural topology of social networks and their underlying dynamics. Previously intractable problems, such as the relationship between emergent behavior in the small world problem – based on the strength of weak ties as formulated by Granovetter[45] – and the dynamical and structural nature of the system, can be examined. The effect of feedback mechanisms and co-evolution as other parts of the system respond to that emergence can also be studied.

In the computational methods developed for complex systems analysis, both structure and emergent behaviors are typically based on agent behaviors in characteristic structures of organized entities and the dynamic pattern of transactions that take place across those structures. The modeling emphasis is on both organization and interactions: how entities (or agents) and sets of events involving these entities are structured, how those structures evolve, and how the entities function in relation to each other and to their environment – other sets of things, likewise structured in space and time.[46] When simulating the type and form of interactions that exist among the parts of a complex system, the types of global behaviors can be varied such that the complex system as a whole can be globally goal-seeking while only local information is passed around by the parts. This means that a collective form of computation can take place without an explicit global algorithm.[47] The results are examined in terms of Crutchfield's intuitive definition of emergence (i.e., when "something new appears"); the patterns that are formed and the organization that is observed; and the intrinsic emergence that occurs when the system itself capitalizes on patterns that appear.[48] An example introduced previously is the phenomenon of deviant legitimation, whereby leaders of terrorist groups employ methods to "normalize" killing as a means to achieve their ends through the creation of messages that mirror, and are in harmony with, prevailing cultural norms. Occurring in the context of the broader culture within which this phenomenon is embedded, patterns of its evolution as evidenced in rhetoric and activism may be correlated to the group's relationship to its broader base of support; these patterns may provide key indicators of intrinsic emergent behavior prior to its expression in action.

The most common method for this type of analysis is agent-based modeling (ABM). In ABM, emergent properties are constantly produced in real time. If the processes that generate them cease to exist, the phenomena may cease to exist as well. They cannot even be stored for future use. As emergent properties cannot be measured directly but are realized through their manifestations, the analyst infers emergence on the basis of observations of the agent's responses, which are in co-relation with its environment and can be based on memories of the past.

As noted above, one of the analytic challenges is to know how to recognize this emergence as something truly new if it is intrinsic to the system.

ABM has been pioneered in such diverse fields as cellular automata, economics, sociology, epidemiology, political science, and biology to study emergent behaviors such as swarming, flocking, adaptation, cooperation, competition, to name but a few.[49] Learning, adaptation, and communication between agents are modeled through a variety of mathematical formulations such as neural networks, genetic algorithms, epidemiological contagion rates, Markhov chains, etc. In applying ABM to the study of emergent behaviors, it is critical to choose the underlying mathematical model within an appropriate framework (e.g., Figure 13.3).

Just as the development of agent-based modeling has provided advanced computational methods to study emergent behavior within complex systems, so too has the development of methods to study the network structures upon which those interactions occur. Building on the original random graph theory developed by Paul Erdos and Alfred Renyi,[50] today's mathematical models of complex networks provide means to study the evolution of network topologies (e.g., random, scale-free, hub-and-spoke, etc.), the mechanisms that shape that evolution (e.g., preferential attachment, phase transitions, etc.), the correlation between the resulting network topology and its properties (e.g., robustness, connectivity, betweenness, centrality, etc.), and characteristic rates and path lengths of interactions that occur upon it. These methods, based in large part on a marriage between statistical mechanics and sociology, have been widely applied to diverse problems in sociology, economics, communications, engineering, physics, biology, epidemiology, organizational dynamics, and computer science.[51]

Application of both ABM and network analysis are underutilized in the field of terrorism research. While these methods are commonly used within government research institutions and analytic communities, and are the subject of many weblogs, with the exception of a few[52] there is little application to terrorism that appears in the refereed social science literature. One must wonder why, as the methods are grounded in, and derived from, social science theory.

It could be that much of terrorism research to date has focused on the actions of terrorist groups, especially international terrorist groups (seen as a more significant threat to developed countries). This amounts to selecting the dependent variable of interest such that the origins of terrorism are obscured, and in particular its emergent character.[53] Innovative research and analysis frameworks that combine a small world, social network analysis approach – such as that pioneered by Sageman in his study of al-Qaeda – with the social movement approach – such as that pioneered by Della Porta in her study of the Italian Red Brigades – are needed. These conceptual models are well suited to the methods of complex systems analysis. An opportunity and challenge for future terrorism research and analysis is to build more academically diverse teams that can appropriately frame analyses to better exploit these methods, thereby providing better understanding of the social and behavioral factors that lead to terrorism.

Making sense of it all

At the end of the day, terrorism analysis should inform better decision-making. But this is "wicked hard". Terrorism analysis will produce no silver bullets; there will be no clear and unambiguous answers to questions posed. Making sense of the corpus of terrorism research and analysis demands collective intelligence, collaboration, and an openness to learning to see different perspectives in the course of problem-solving. The natural course of sense-making on wicked problems is driven by opportunity, and occurs more in the realm of learning among all of the stakeholders, rather than on individual – or even collective – knowledge. Experts cannot guide this process down a linear, logical path from observation to conclusion. The more novel the problem, the more the problem-solving process involves a spiral learning process about the problem domain.[54]

> The feeling that we are "wandering all over" is not a mark of stupidity or lack of training. This non-linear process is not a defect, but rather the mark of an intelligent and creative learning process.

As terrorism research has matured and progressed, so too has research into the nature and behavior of systems – specifically, open systems of purposeful, interacting entities, the ensemble of which exhibit nonlinear, adaptive behaviors within self-organizing, continuously evolving structures. Approaching terrorism analysis through the paradigm of purposeful, complex adaptive systems provides a research framework capable of integrating across traditional academic boundaries and allowing synergistic consideration of knowledge from diverse conceptual domains, multiple cultural perspectives, and a wide range of behavioral scales. This framework should address the specific context and epistemology of the community of stakeholders, and incorporate sense-making insights from literature that will explain sources of order in loosely coupled, under-structured organizations.[55]

We have shown that complex system behaviors are characterized and shaped by the structures that exist within and between the components in the system, the dynamic transactions that occur across those structures, and the dynamics of how those structures evolve over time. To exploit this paradigm to its fullest potential for terrorism analysis, the social science research community can work collaboratively with the complexity-science community to develop better structural understanding of the complex relationships linking individuals, groups, organizations, and social and political institutions. Doing so will advance understanding in both fields.

Acknowledgements

The thoughts contained in this paper were inspired by my colleagues in the Advanced Concepts Group at Sandia National Laboratories – Judy Moore,

John Whitely, Jessica Glicken, Laura McNamara, Wendell Jones and Gerry Yonas, and at the Santa Fe Institute – Jim Crutchfield, John Miller, Eric Bonnabeau, Gary Horne, Merle Lefkoff and Murray Gell-Mann. These individuals tackled with me the intellectual challenges of applying complexity "science" to terrorism and intelligence analysis. I thank Dave Hamon at DTRA for his inspiration and support, and my colleagues in the social science community who have been my mentors and collaborators – especially Marc Sageman, Clark McCauley, Ariel Merari, Scott Atran, Gary Ackerman and Jonathan Drummond. I owe special thanks to Michael McDonald for his painstaking review. Most of all, I thank Magnus Ranstorp for his patient and persistent encouragement. All errors are my own.

Notes

1 Sandia is a multiprogram laboratory operated by Sandia Corporation, a Lockheed Martin Company, for the United States Department of Energy under contract DE-AC04-94AL85000. The views and opinions expressed herein do not necessarily state or reflect those of Sandia Corporation, the United States Government or any agency thereof.

2 A persistent perception in the mass public and among policy decision-makers is orthogonal to this characterization of the psychology of terrorism. Primary research findings that indicate the construct of psychological normality need to be better understood as a point of departure and framing for analysis done in support of good sense-making. See: Drummond, J. (2002) *From the Northwest Perspective to Global Jihad: Social Psychological Aspects of Construction of the Enemy, Political Violence, and Terror* (Westport, CN: Praeger); Horgan, J. (2003) 'The Search for the Terrorists Personality' in A. Silke (ed.) *Terrorists, Victims, and Society: Psychological Perspectives on Terrorism and its Consequences* (West Sussex, UK: Wiley & Sons; McCauley, C., and M. Segal (1987) 'Social Psychology of Terrorist Groups' in C. Hendrick (ed.) *Review of Personality and Social Psychology*, Vol. 9, 231–256. (Beverly Hills, CA: Sage); McCauley, C., and M. Segal (1989) 'Terrorist Individuals and Terrorist Groups: The Normal Psychology of Extreme Behaviors', in J. Groebel and J.H. Goldstein (eds) *Terrorism: Psychological Perspectives*, 36–64 (Seville, Spain: Publicaciones de La Universidad de Seville); McCauley, C. (2002) 'Psychological Issues in Understanding Terrorism and the Response to Terrorism', in C. Stout (ed.) *The Psychology of Terrorism, Volume III: Theoretical Understandings and Perspectives* 3–30 (Westport, CN: Praeger); Silke, A. (1998) 'Cheshire-Cat Logic: The Recurring Theme of Terrorist Abnormality in Psychological Research; *Psychology, Crime and Law* 4: 51–59; Silke, A. (2003) 'Becoming a Terrorist' in A. Silke (ed.) *Terrorists, Victims and Society: Psychological Perspectives on Terrorism and its Consequences*, (West Sussex, UK: Wiley & Sons).

3 The importance of the base is described in literature in political/social movement frames. The connectedness between the elements of this pyramid and its shape – e.g., "sharpness" – is a factor in determining the behavior of group members and the ability of the group to sustain itself. In the case of smaller and more resource-constrained opposition groups, such as radical racist right-wing groups in the United States, Drummond has found that individuals at the apex take on greater numbers of roles in efforts to mobilize popular support. When these individuals are removed, the group has difficulty sustaining itself, such as occurred with The Order upon the incarceration

of David Lane. Drummond also found that the degree of political activism exhibited by group members to generate support for their cause within democratic political structures in the US made them visible to authorities prior to their engagement in terrorist actions. In contrast, Wickham (Wickham, C. (2002) *Mobilizing Islam: Religion, Activism and Political Change in Egypt*, (New York, NY: Columbia University Press)) found that in the case of the Egyptian Muslim Brotherhood, where political opportunity structures were not available to the activist groups under the authoritarian regime of Nasser, their efforts to generate this base of support migrated to social institutions, making them harder to detect at the time; the success of these efforts in building a base of support were not apparent for several decades, until Sadat relaxed the government's repressive measures. See also: Crenshaw, M. (ed.) (1995) *Terrorism in Context* (University Park, PA: Pennsylvania State University Press); Della Porta, D. (1995) 'Left-Wing Terrorism in Italy' in Crenshaw, M. (ed.) *Terrorism in Context* (University Park, PA: Pennsylvania State University Press); Della Porta, D. (1995) *Social Movements, Political Violence, and the State* (Cambridge, UK: Cambridge University Press); McAdam, D., J. D. McCarthy and M. N. Zald (eds) (1996) *Comparative Perspectives on Social Movements: Political Opportunities, Mobilizing Structures, and Cultural Framings* (New York, NY: Cambridge University Press).

4 See, for example, Reich, W. (1998) Introduction to W. Reich (ed.) *Origins of Terrorism: Psychologies, Ideologies, Theologies, States of Mind* (Washington, DC: Woodrow Wilson Center Press).

5 Crenshaw, M. (ed) (1995) *Terrorism in Context* (University Park, PA: Pennsylvania State University Press) Della Porta, D. (1995) *Social Movements, Political Violence, and the State* (Cambridge, UK: Cambridge University Press); Kaplan, J., and L. Weinberg (1998) *The Emergence of a Euro-American Radical Right* (Piscataway, NJ: Rutgers University Press); Merari, A. (1993) 'Terrorism as a Strategy of Insurgency', *Terrorism and Political Violence* 5: 213–251; Rapoport, D. (2002) 'The Four Waves of Rebel Terror and September 11', *Anthropoetics – The Journal of Generative Anthropology* 8; Schmid, A., and B. Jongman (1988) *Political Terrorism: A New Guide to Actors, Authors, Concepts, Data Bases, Theories, and Literature* (Amsterdam: North-Holland); Sprinzak, E. (1977) 'Extreme Politics in Israel', *Jerusalem Quarterly* 5; McCormick, G.H. (2003) 'Terrorist Decision-making', *Annual Review of Political Science* 6: 473–507.

6 This context can be critical to analysis. Drummond shows that the evolutionary development of an ideology of violent solutions to perceived threats or grievances is justified as a morally required defensive action that is an altered or perverted version of what the parent culture socializes as justifiable killing. The evolutionary pattern of rhetoric can be a useful "footprint" that can be observed; the stage of maturity in these arguments and the advancement process by which the violence is made acceptable can be an indicator of how close to violent action an individual or small group might be. This sets up a complex dynamic between religion as justification and as motivation for action. See, for example: Atran, S., and A. Norenzayan (2004) 'Religion's Evolutionary Landscape: Counter-intuition, Commitment, Compassion, Communion', *Behavioral and Brain Sciences* 27: 1–58; Atran, S. (2005) 'The "Virtual Hand" of Jihad', *Terrorism Monitor* 3: 8–11; Ayoob, M. (2004) 'Political Islam: Image and Reality', *World Policy Journal* 21: 14; Ranstorp, M. (1996) 'Terrorism in the Name of Religion', in R. Howard and R. Sawyer (eds) *Terrorism and Counterterrorism* (Guilford, CT: McGraw-Hill); Sookhdeo, P. (2004) *Understanding Islamic Terrorism* (Wiltshire, UK: Isaac Publishing); Wickham, C. (2002), *Mobilizing Islam: Religion, Activism and Political Change in Egypt* (New York, NY: Columbia University Press).

7 This concept has been developed by Drummond and Darly as the deviant legitimizing construct.

8 This is an area needing more research to understand unintended consequences, and to formulate more effective responses to terrorism. See: Hoffman, B. (1998) *Inside Terrorism*. (New York, NY: Columbia University Press); Kern, M., M. Just, and P. Norris (2003) 'The Lessons of Framing Terrorism', in Norris, P. (ed.) *Framing Terrorism: The News Media, the Government, and the Public* (New York, NY: Routledge); Nacos, B. (1994) *Terrorism and the Media* (New York, NY: Columbia University Press); Silke, A. (2003) 'Retaliating Against Terrorism', in Silke, A. (ed.) *Terrorists, Victims and Society: Psychological Perspectives on Terrorism and its Consequences* (West Sussex, UK: Wiley & Sons); Wiemann, G. (1993) *The Theater of Terror: Mass Media and International Terrorism* (UK: Longman Group) Wilkinson, P. (1997) 'The Media and Terrorism: A Reassessment', *Terrorism and Political Violence* 9: 51–64.

9 Blomberg, S.B., G.D. Hess, and A. Weerapana (2004) 'Economic conditions and terrorism', *European Journal of Political Economy* 20: 478; Cragin, K. and S. A. Daly (2004) *The Dynamic Terrorist Threat: An Assessment of Group Motivations and Capabilities in a Changing World* (Santa Monica, CA: RAND Corporation) 61–81; Hoffman, B. (1998) *Inside Terrorism* (New York, NY: Columbia University Press); Horgan, J. (2003) 'Leaving terrorism behind: An Individual Perspective. Terrorists, Victims and Society', in *Psychological Perspectives on Terrorism and its Consequences* (West Sussex, UK: Wiley & Sons); Lacquer, W. (1996) 'Postmodern Terrorism', *Foreign Affairs* 75: 24–36.

10 Recent studies show that there is a group-dependent, differentiating nature to the types of links through which this social integration takes place. For example, Drummond found that members of racist right wing extremist groups in the US were socially integrated into the group through friendship and even romantic relationships, whereas Sageman (Sageman, M. (2004) *Understanding Terror Networks*, (Philadelphia, PA: University of Pennsylvania Press)) found that kinship relationships are more prevalent for social integration into the Global Salafi Jihad. See also: Della Porta, D. (1988) 'Recruitment Processes in Clandestine Political Organizations: Italian Left-Wing Terrorism', *International Social Movement Research* 1: 155–169; Della Porta, D. (1995) 'Left-Wing Terrorism in Italy', in Crenshaw, M. (ed.) *Terrorism in Context* (University Park, PA: Pennsylvania State University Press).

11 While we are beginning to build an understanding of the transmitting and operational power of these networks, we still need research to understand the limits of their formation, disruption and healing mechanisms, and their causal factors that result in the collapse, sustained presence or growth of these networks. See: Barabasi, A.-L., and R. Albert (1999) 'Emergence of Scaling in Random Networks', *Science* 286: 509–512; Watts, D. (2003) *Six Degrees – The Science of A Connected Age* (New York, NY: W. W. Norton.

12 Sageman, M., personal communication, summer 2003.

13 Lacquer, W. (1996) 'Postmodern Terrorism', *Foreign Affairs* 75: 24–36.

14 Kean, T. K. (chair) (2004) *The 9/11 Commission Report; Final Report of the National Commission on Terrorist Attacks upon the United States*, US Government Printing Office.

15 Fishbein, W., and G. Treverton (2004) 'Rethinking "Alternative Analysis" to Address Transnational Threats', *Sherman Kent Occasional Papers* 3.

16 Rittel, H., and M. Weber (1973) 'Dilemmas in a General Theory of Planning', *Policy Sciences* 4: 155–169.

17 Gell-Mann, M. (1994) *The Quark and the Jaguar – Adventures in the Simple and the Complex* (New York, NY: W. H. Freeman); Holland, J. (1998) *Emergence: From Chaos to Order* (Cambridge, MA: Perseus Books); Suh, N. (2005) *Complexity:Theory and Applications* (New York, NY: Oxford University Press).

18 Crutchfield, J. (2003) 'When Evolution is Revolution: Origins of Innovation' in Crutchfield J. P and P. Schuster (eds) *Evolutionary Dynamics: Exploring the Interplay of Selection, Neutrality, Accident, and Function* (New York, NY: Oxford University Press).

19 Holland, J. (1998) *Emergence: From Chaos to Order* (Cambridge, MA: Perseus Books).

20 Flake, G. W. (1998) *The Computational Beauty of Nature: Computer Explorations of Fractals, Chaos, Complex Systems, and Adaptation* (Cambridge, MA: MIT Press).

21 Waldrop, M.M. (1992) *Complexity: The Emerging Science at the Edge of Order and Chaos* (New York, NY: Simon and Schuster); Gell-Mann, M. (1994) *The Quark and the Jaguar – Adventures in the Simple and the Complex* (New York, NY: W. H. Freeman); Strogatz, S. (1994) *Nonlinear Dynamics and Chaos: Applications to Physics, Biology, Chemistry, and Engineering* (Cambridge, MA: Perseus Books); Crutchfield, J.P. (1994) 'Is Anything Ever New? Considering Emergence', in Cowan, G., D. Pines, and D. Melzner (eds) *Santa Fe Institute Studies in the Sciences of Complexity: Complexity – Metaphors, Models, and Reality* (Reading, MA: Addison-Wesley); Arthur, B. (1997) 'The Economy as an Evolving Complex System II', in Durlauf, S., and D. Lane (eds) *Series in the Sciences of Complexity* (Reading, MA: Addison-Wesley); Holland, J. (1998) *Emergence: From Chaos to Order* (Cambridge, MA: Perseus Books); Cronk, L. (1999) *That Complex Whole: Culture and the Evolution of Human Behavior* (Boulder, CO: Westview Press); Gharajedaghi, J. (1999) *Systems Thinking: Managing Chaos and Complexity* (Woburn, MA: Butterworth-Heinemann); Bar-Yam, Y. (2000) 'Significant Points in the Study of Complex Systems', in Bar-Yam (ed.) *Unifying Themes in Complex Systems (I)* (Boulder, CO: Westview Press); Wolfram, S. (2002) *A New Kind of Science* (Champaign, IL: Wolfram Media); Morowitz, H. (2002) *The Emergence of Everything* (New York, NY: Oxford University Press).

22 Koestler, A. (1967) *The Ghost in the Machine* (Harmondsworth: penguin Press). Holarchy is a word coined by Koestler. It is a combination of the Greek word 'holos' meaning whole and the word 'hierarchy', and is defined as hierarchically organized structure of units or entities that are called 'Holons'. A holon can be regarded as either a whole or a part depending on how one looks at it. A holon will look as a whole to those parts beneath it in the hierarchy, but it will look as a part to the wholes above it. So, a holarchy is then a whole that is also a structure of parts that are in themselves wholes. http://www.worldtrans.org/essay/holarchies.html

23 Holland, J. (1998) *Emergence: From Chaos to Order* (Cambridge, MA: Perseus Books).

24 Crutchfield, J.P. (1994) 'Is Anything Ever New? Considering Emergence', in Cowan, G., D. Pines, and D. Melzner (eds) *Santa Fe Institute Studies in the Sciences of Complexity: Complexity – Metaphors, Models, and Reality* (Reading, MA: Addison-Wesley).

25 Laszlo, E. (1996) The Systems View of the World: A Holistic Vision for Our Time in Mortuori. A (ed.) *Advances in Systems Theory, Complexity, and the Human Sciences* (Cresskill, NJ: Hampton Press).

26 Axelrod, R. (1986) *The Evolution of Cooperation* (New York, NY: Basic Books).

27 Axelrod, R. (1997) *The Complexity of Cooperation* (Princeton, NJ: Princeton University Press).

28 Lewontin, R. (2000) 'Evolution', in Bar-Yam, Y (ed.) *Unifying Themes in Complex Systems (I)* (Boulder, CO: Westview Press).

29 Crutchfield, J. (2003) 'When Evolution is Revolution: Origins of Innovation', in Crutchfield J.P. and P. Schuster (eds) *Evolutionary Dynamics: Exploring the Interplay*

of Selection, Neutrality, Accident, and Function (New York, NY: Oxford University Press).

30 Rogers, E. (1995) *The Diffusion of Innovation* (New York, NY: The Free Press).

31 Lewontin, R. (2000) 'Evolution', in Bar-Yam, Y (ed.) *Unifying Themes in Complex Systems (I)* (Boulder, CO: Westview Press).

32 Gould, S.J. (2002) *The Structure of Evolutionary Theory* (Cambridge, MA: Belknap Press).

33 Crutchfield, J. (2003) 'When Evolution is Revolution: Origins of Innovation', in Crutchfield, J. P. and P. Schuster (eds) *Evolutionary Dynamics: Exploring the Interplay of Selection, Neutrality, Accident, and Function* (New York, NY: Oxford University Press).

34 Granovetter, M.S. (1973) 'The Strength of Weak Ties', *American Journal of Sociology* **78**: 1360–1380.

35 Watts, D. (2003) *Six Degrees – The Science of A Connected Age* (New York, NY: W. W. Norton).

36 Albert, R., and A.L. Barabasi (2002) 'Statistical Mechanics of Complex Networks', *Review of Modern Physics* **74**: 47–97; Barabasi, A.-L., and R. Albert (1999) 'Emergence of Scaling in Random Networks', *Science* **286**: 509–512; Barabasi, A.-L. (2002) *Linked: The New Science of Networks* (Cambridge, MA: Perseus Publishing).

37 Flake, G. W. (1998) *The Computational Beauty of Nature: Computer Explorations of Fractals, Chaos, Complex Systems, and Adaptation* (Cambridge, MA: MIT Press).

38 Gharajedaghi, J. (1999) *Systems Thinking: Managing Chaos and Complexity* (Woburn, MA: Butterworth-Heinemann).

39 The three dimensions of Gharajedaghi's decision-making model parallel the concept of decision-making based on "satisficing" first espoused by Herb Simon. See: Simon, H.A., M. Egidi, R. Marris, and R. Viale (1992) in Egidi, M., and R. Marris (eds) *Economics, Bounded Rationality, and Cognitive Revolution* (Brookfield, VT: Edward Elgar).

40 Crutchfield, J. (1994) *The Calculi of Emergence: Computation, Dynamics, and Induction*, Santa Fe Institute Working Paper 94-03-016.

41 Gleick, J. (1987) *Chaos: Making a New Science* (New York, NY: Viking Penguin).

42 Crutchfield, J.P. (1994) 'Is Anything Ever New? Considering Emergence' in Cowan, G., D. Pines, and D. Melzner (eds) *Santa Fe Institute Studies in the Sciences of Complexity: Complexity – Metaphors, Models, and Reality* (Reading, MA: Addison-Wesley).

43 Gharajedaghi, J. (1999) *Systems Thinking: Managing Chaos and Complexity* (Woburn, MA: Butterworth-Heinemann).

44 Bar-Yam, Y. (2000) 'Significant Points in the Study of Complex Systems'. in Bar-Yam (ed.) *Unifying Themes in Complex Systems (I)* (Boulder, CO. Westview Press).

45 Granovetter, M.S. (1983) 'The Strength of Weak Ties: A Network Theory Revisited', *Sociological Theory* **1**: 201–233.

46 Laszlo, E. (1996) 'The Systems View of the World: A Holistic Vision for Our Time' in Mortuori, A. (ed.) *Advances in Systems Theory, Complexity, and the Human Sciences* (Cresskill, NJ: Hampton Press).

47 Flake, G. W. (1998) *The Computational Beauty of Nature: Computer Explorations of Fractals, Chaos, Complex Systems, and Adaptation* (Cambridge, MA: MIT Press).

48 Crutchfield, J.P. (1994) 'Is Anything Ever New? Considering Emergence', in Cowan, G., D. Pines, and D. Melzner (eds) *Santa Fe Institute Studies in the Sciences of Complexity: Complexity – Metaphors, Models, and Reality* (Reading, MA: Addison-Wesley).

49 Schelling, T. (1978) *Micromotives and Macrobehavior* (New York, NY: Norton); Holland, J. (1995) *Hidden Order: How Adaptation Builds Complexity* (Cambridge,

MA: Perseus Books); Axelrod, R. (1997) *The Complexity of Cooperation* (Princeton, NJ: Princeton University Press); Arthur, B. (1997) 'The Economy as an Evolving Complex System II', in Durlauf, S., and D. Lane (eds) *Series in the Sciences of Complexity* (Reading, MA: Addison-Wesley); Bonabeau, E., M. Dorigo, and G. Theraulaz (1999) *Swarm Intelligence: From Natural to Artificial Systems (Santa Fe Institute Studies in the Sciences of Complexity)* (New York, NY: Oxford University Press); Epstein, J. M., and R. Axtell (1996) *Growing Artificial Societies: Social Science from the Bottom Up* (Washington, DC: Brookings Institution); Farmer, J. D., A. S. Lapedes, N. Packard, and B. Wendroff (eds) (1986) *Evolution, Games, and Learning: Models for Adaptation in Machines and Nature* (Amsterdam: North Holland Physics Publishing).

50 Erdos, P., and A. Renyi (1959) 'On Random Graphs', *Publicationes Mathematicae,* **6**: (290–297); Erdos, P., and A. Renyi. (1960) 'On the Evolution of Random Graphs', *Publications of the Mathematical Institute of Hungarian Academy of Sciences* **5**: (17–61); Erdos, P., and A. Renyi. (1961) 'On the Strength and Connectedness of a Random Graph, *Acta Mathematica Scientia Hungary* **12**: 261–267.

51 Barabasi, A.-L., and R. Albert (1999) 'Emergence of Scaling in Random Networks', *Science* **286**: 509–512; Barabasi, A.-L. (2002) *Linked: The New Science of Networks* (Cambridge, MA: Perseus Publishing); Albert, R., and A.L. Barabasi (2002) 'Statistical Mechanics of Complex Networks', *Review of Modern Physics* **74**: 47–97; Kleinberg, M. (2000) 'Navigation in a Small World', *Nature* **406**: 845; Newman, M.E.J., and M. Girvan (2003) 'Mixing Patterns and Community Structure in Networks' in R. Pastor-Satorras, R.J., Rubi, and A. Diaz-Guilera (eds) *Statistical Mechanics of Complex Networks* (Berlin: Springer); Newman, M. E. J. (2004) 'Who is the Best Connected Scientist? A study of scientific coauthorship networks', in Ben-Naim. E., H. Frauenfelder, and Z. Toroczkai (eds), *Complex Networks* (Berlin: Springer) 337–370, M. E. J. Newman (2005) 'A Measure of Betweeness Centrality Based on Random Walks', *Social Networks* **27**: 39–54; Balthrop, J., S. Forrest, M. E. J. Newman, and M. M. Williamson (2004) 'Technological networks and the spread of computer viruses', *Science* **304**: 527–529; Watts, D. (2003) *Six Degrees – The Science of A Connected Age* (New York, NY: W. W. Norton).

52 Such as: Carley, K. (2002) 'Smart Agents and Organizations of the Future', in Lievrouw, L., and S. Livingstone (eds) *The Handbook of New Media* (Thousand Oaks, CA: Sage); Krebs, V. (2001) 'Mapping of Terrorist Network Cells', *Connections* **24**: 43–52. International Network for Social Network Analysis, reprinted at http://firstmonday.org/issues/issue7_4/krebs/

53 I thank Clark McCauley for this thought.

54 Conklin, J. (2003) *Wicked Problems and Social Complexity*, CogNexus Institute White Paper, http://cognexus.org/wpf/wickedproblems.pdf

55 See, for example, Weick Karl, (2001) *Making Sense of the Organizations* (Malden, MA: Blackwell Publishing); Kurtz, C. F., and D. Snowden (2003) 'The New Dynamics of Strategy: Sense-Making in a Complex and Complicated World', *IBM Systems Journal* **42**: 462–483.

14

RESEARCH INTO TERRORISM STUDIES: ACHIEVEMENTS AND FAILURES

Paul Wilkinson

Readers may be interested in the early stages in the development of the academic study of terrorism. A valuable pioneering essay by J.B.S. Hardman, offering a social scientific analysis of the subject, appeared in the 1934 edition of the *Encyclopaedia of the Social Sciences*.[1] Important contributions were made by two scholars working on different aspects of terror in Eastern Europe: Feliks Gross on political violence and terror in 19th and 20th century Russia and Eastern Europe,[2] and J.S. Roucek's essay 'Sociological Elements of a Theory of Terror and Violence', published in 1962.[3] Two years later came two significant efforts at developing conceptual and taxonomic tools for the further exploration of the field: T.P. Thornton's seminal essay on 'Terror as a Weapon of Political Agitation',[4] and Eugene V. Walter's classic work on regimes of terror, *Terror and Resistance: A Study of Political Violence with Case Studies of some African Communities*.[5]

From its earliest stages the study of terror and terrorism has been, of necessity, a multidisciplinary endeavour. Not surprisingly, political scientists and international relations scholars have been particularly active in the field, but historians, sociologists, psychologists, anthropologists, lawyers, philosophers, criminologists and even economists have made significant contributions to the literature.

To give one striking illustration of this, the Norwegian Institute of International Affairs organized a meeting of international experts in June 2003 to discuss the root causes of terrorism. The Chairman was Dr Tore Bjorgo, who is a social anthropologist by training and has edited one of the most valuable symposia on the violent far-right movement ever published, *Terror from the Extreme Right* (1995). The experts at the Root Causes conference came from universities and institutes in 17 different countries and included political scientists, lawyers, psychologists, criminologists, historians, a psychiatrist, international relations scholars, a professor Emeritus in sociology and a professor in communications studies. Their meetings addressed some key issues:

- Will influencing root causes have an effect in reducing terrorism?
- What factors can provide preconditions for emergence of various kinds of terrorism?
- What are the typical precipitants for outbreak of terrorist acts?
- Since we know terrorism sometimes continues for other reasons, will the root causes approach be useful at all?

I hope the fascinating papers at the meeting will be published soon.[6]

The academic study of terrorism has also inevitably been a particularly multi-national effort. It is well known that some of the world's leading scholars are based in the United States – for example, Professor Walter Laqueur of CSIS,[7] Brian Jenkins, a consultant to RAND,[8] Dr Bruce Hoffman, also of RAND,[9] Professor Martha Crenshaw[10] of Wesleyan University, Connecticut, Dr David Rapoport of UCLA,[11] my colleague, friend and co-editor of the academic journal *Terrorism and Political Violence*, and the late Dr J. Bowyer Bell[12] of Columbia University.

However, it is very important to bear in mind that almost every major democracy has, in its academic institutions, specialist researchers and analysts in this field. It would be invidious to list them all, but a random list of leading figures would include Dr Alex Schmid[13] and Dr Albert Jongman,[14] Professor Ariel Merari,[15] Professor Fernando Reinares,[16] Dr David Charters,[17] the late Dr Ehud Sprinzak, Dr Tore Bjorgo[18] and Dr Magnus Ranstorp[19] – both risen stars and rising stars.

It would also be unfair to overlook the substantial contribution made by British researchers and writers in this field. Some, like Professor Leonard Schapiro[20] and Robert Conquest,[21] produced masterly studies of the Soviet use of the weapon of terror as a weapon of state control, repression of dissent and foreign policy. Others, notably the late Dr Richard Clutterbuck[22] who made a second career as an academic at Exeter University after retiring from the Army as a Major-General, focused on the threats posed by sub-state terrorist groups to the liberal democratic state and the search for responses that were both effective and fully compatible with democracy and the rule of law.

Again, not surprisingly, some of the finest work amongst British scholars has focused on the violence in Northern Ireland. See, for example, the work of Professor Steve Bruce,[23] Professor George Boyce[24] and Dr M.L.R. Smith,[25] and Professor Caroline Kennedy-Pipe.[26] It is worth noting that by no means all the best work on Northern Ireland terrorism has come from within Northern Ireland's universities. There may be something in the theory that a degree of distance can lend greater objectivity and perspective. Nor should we forget the blockbusting works by gifted freelancers and journalists, such as David McKittrick,[27] the *Independent's* Ireland correspondent, and Robert Kee's[28] magisterial historical overview of Irish nationalism. And, on Britain's anti-terrorism legislation, I must mention the superb Blackstone Guide to the subject by Professor Clive Walker[29] of the Institute of Criminal Justice Studies at Leeds University, and Paul Rogers'[30] important work on international response at Bradford University.

It is good to be able to pay tribute to the work of these and other academic specialists from the United Kingdom who have added to our knowledge and understanding of the complex phenomenon of terrorism. But the most striking feature of the British case is the astonishingly small number of academic specialists in the field. When one considers the long UK experience of terrorism emanating from the latest Northern Ireland conflict, Britain's earlier experience of anti-colonial struggles by insurgents using terrorism, and our special relationship with the USA, the country most frequently targeted by international terrorists, it is truly astonishing to find that only a small number of individuals, dispersed around relatively few of our universities, have had a major or even a secondary interest in terrorism.

St Andrews University's Centre for the Study of Terrorism and Political Violence (CSTPV)[31] is one of the very few research institutes dedicated primarily to research in this area. Prior to the events of 9/11 the International Institute of Strategic Studies almost completely ignored the subject. Chatham House occasionally covered the subject in articles in its journals and in its conferences. The only British institute, which regularly published briefings and reports on terrorism in the 1970s and 1980s, was the Institute for the Study of Conflict, later reorganized at the end of the Cold War to become the Research Institute for the Study of Conflict and Terrorism. The first academic journal on the subject, *Terrorism and Political Violence*,[32] founded and co-edited by David Rapoport and myself, did not emerge until 1989. It is a pleasure to see a rival academic journal, *Studies in Conflict and Terrorism*.[33] a rather newer title, edited by Dr Bruce Hoffman, providing us with stiff competition with bimonthly issues as compared to our quarterly publication process.

How can one explain the long delay in the emergence of terrorism studies as a viable branch of multi-disciplinary research in international studies, political science and other branches of learning? No doubt one factor was the hostility of many established university departments to multi-disciplinary studies of any kind. Some may have been deterred by the widespread confusion about the concept; even now some use terrorism as a synonym for guerrilla warfare or even for politically motivated violence in general.

But without doubt the decisive factor causing the deliberate neglect of the subject throughout the Cold War was the preoccupation of powerful governments, think tanks and research institutes with other matters far more pressing at the time: the nuclear arms race, arms control, détente, Kremlinology, containment etc. During the Cold War all democratic governments, with the conspicuous exception of Israel, did not see terrorism as a strategic issue. It was, as Hedley Bull[34] shrewdly observed, a relatively minor issue of law and order or internal security for most states.

If it had been higher on the policymakers' agenda, terrorism would undoubtedly have been able to obtain research funding for major projects. It is a sad fact that the first really significant funding of terrorism research by the UK research councils did not occur until after the 9/11 attacks.[35] This funding is to be warmly welcomed, but it must be admitted that it is yet another example of closing the stable door after the horse has bolted.

The scale of mass killing and destruction caused by the 9/11 attacks caused a sea change in the attitudes of governments and inter-governmental organizations, such as the UN, towards terrorism. It is now seen as a strategic threat, a serious threat not only to national security but also to international peace and security. 9/11 has had a radical impact on almost every major institution from cabinets and parliaments to the boards of multinationals, and on powerful bodies such as the armed forces, the media, the emergency services and the police, and even the universities and research institutes. In regard to Academia, it is now widely recognized that there is a real need for independent objective research of high quality into the phenomena of terrorist activity – and the discovery of better means of preventing it and protecting the public.

At a recent meeting of the UK research councils to discuss possible research projects in terrorism, it was striking that the overwhelming majority of the projects outlined were being put forward by scientists and technologists interested in such problems as identifying explosives more reliably and accurately, biometric techniques of identifying personnel, access control and the physical protection of potential targets.

I fully agree that some of the developing security technologies could be of considerable practical assistance,[36] but I put in a heartfelt plea for ensuring that the proposal from the research councils included a good proportion of social science research. What on earth is the good of developing more and more expensive gizmos for security companies and business and governmental organizations if you do not understand the belief systems, motivations, intent and combat doctrines of the major terrorist groups we confront today? How can we learn more about the leaders of terrorist groups, their personalities and relationships with their closest henchmen and their followers? How can we learn more about the way terrorist networks obtain and manage their finances and how they have learned to avoid the controls initiated by the UN, the Finance Ministers' Action Task Force, and national governments? Can we improve our knowledge of how terrorist networks manage to secure their covert communications so effectively? And how they succeed at the same time in using the mass media to convey their propaganda? Just how effective or ineffective are al-Qaeda and their affiliates in winning (a) recruits and (b) wider public support amongst Muslim communities? To what extent, and by what means, do terrorist groups/networks and their leaders learn by their mistakes and succeed in adapting to new challenges and opportunities in their political environment? And to what extent do the requirements of sustaining the organization – e.g. Using crime to raise funds – take over from the longer-term primary concern? Despite the significant decline in the role of state sponsorship of terrorism we know a number of states do still lend support, safe haven and logistic backup to terrorist groups. What exactly are the connections between terrorist movements and state sponsors? What exactly are the linkages between major terrorist groups? It hardly needs saying that al-Qaeda's shifting relations with other terrorist groups and movements are of special interest.[37]

My own major research preoccupation for many years has been the study of responses to terrorism on the part of the democracies and the international community.[38] What works? What doesn't? Under what circumstances and by what means can we adapt conflict resolution techniques to address some of the most deeply entrenched and bitter ethno-nationalist conflicts, which so frequently spawn terrorism? Drawing on the experience of some relatively successful peace processes, what lessons can we learn about the prerequisites for success? What can be done to prevent terrorists and extremists opposed to the peace process from derailing it? And if we are confronting an incorrigible terrorist movement such as al-Qaeda, the archetype of the 'New Terrorism', with which any deals or compromises are clearly totally unthinkable, how do we deal with the situation?

In my recent book *Terrorism versus Democracy: The Liberal State Response*, the response I propose is to maximize multilateral cooperation against terrorism at all levels and to deploy a multi-pronged strategy led by high-quality counterterrorism intelligence, the best possible intelligence sharing, police and judicial cooperation, measures to crack down on terrorist finances, and counter-proliferation measures to adapt the counter-proliferation regime to non-state actors. Last, but by no means least, I urge that we start making far more serious efforts to win the battle of ideas with the terrorist groups and the extremists who support them. In the context of combating al-Qaeda and its affiliates this means enlisting moderate religious and community leaders in Muslim countries and in the Muslim diaspora to campaign as strongly as they can within their communities against extremism and the terrorism spawned by religious extremists.

In the field of international response to terrorism there are all too many problems for research to address. In the study of international legal responses, for example, how can the inadequacies of extradition as a method for recovering fugitive terrorists to justice be reduced if not overcome? To what extent have the UN measures taken after 9/11 made an effective contribution to combating terrorism? By what means, if any, could the UN measures be enhanced? And how can they be more effectively enforced? What assessment can be made of the contribution of the UN Counter-Terrorism Committee's work?[39] What are the prospects of strengthening or supplementing the existing UN Conventions against terrorism? How can basic civil liberties be protected adequately under the conditions of terrorist emergencies, particularly in the possible circumstances of a CBRN attack by terrorists?[40]

My research colleagues in CSTPV, St Andrews University and in the Mountbatten Institute, Southampton University have worked together in a major Economic and Social Research Council project on 'Domestic Preparedness for Terrorist Attacks against the UK'. Kings College London and Lancaster

University are engaged in closely related research under the ESRC's auspices. We should bear in mind that there is a pressing need for similar research projects on the preparedness of other countries both within and outside the EU. I could go on, and on posing key research issues and problems for political scientists and other social scientists to investigate. I hope I have said enough to indicate the rich variety of research work needed in the terrorism studies field. I should add that, when I was writing this section, I recalled arguing the case for many of these research tasks to be undertaken when I wrote my introduction to *Contemporary Research on Terrorism* (1987).[41] It is a sad comment on the chronic under-resourcing and understaffing of terrorism studies that so little of my suggested 1987 agenda for terrorism research has actually been accomplished.

A key problem in the development of a liberal democratic response to terrorism is how to find a proper balance between pursuing the policies and measures needed to protect the public against terrorist attack and at the same time safeguarding democracy, civil liberties and the rule of law. The dilemmas involved have been thrown into sharp relief in the conduct of the War on Terrorism declared by President Bush after the 9/11 attacks.

Can it ever be justifiable, for example, for a democratic state to imprison indefinitely without trial those who are merely suspected of involvement in terrorism? Should those suspected of terrorist activity be denied access to the normal criminal courts where they could establish their innocence? Should they be handed over to military courts where they will not be free to select their own lawyers, where the standards of evidence required for conviction will be less than in a criminal court, and where proceedings can be held in camera? And what of the cases of those suspected or alleged terrorists who may be subjected to torture and other human rights violations while in the hands of other countries belonging to the coalition against terrorism? Should 'confessions' obtained by the use of such methods be used as evidence in the proceedings of democratic states' legal systems? Surely not!!

The Guantanamo Bay incarceration of terrorist suspects without trial and without any right of appeal or redress to the US justice system, and without access to lawyers, is surely an extraordinary and morally unacceptable departure from the norms of the US criminal justice system. It is difficult to see why the US Federal courts are not being trusted by the Executive branch of government to handle judicial proceedings against those detainees against whom the authorities have genuine evidence of involvement in terrorism. Did the Federal courts fail to provide effective trials for Ramzi Youssef, for example, or for the four al-Qaeda terrorists convicted for their part in the US Embassy bombings in East Africa?

I think not! Federal criminal trials would not only ensure basic rights to the defendants, they would also show to the US public and world opinion that justice was seen to be done. If the world's leading democracy begins to abandon basic democratic values, such as respect for the rule of law, it has in a real sense already begun to allow the terrorist groups to undermine democracy and it has provided the terrorist ringmasters with a gratuitous propaganda boost and aid to recruitment. Let's face it – is the Guantanamo Bay situation likely to contribute to a lessening of hatred of the US in the Muslim world?

Nor can the United Kingdom claim a clean record on the right to a fair trial for those merely suspected of terrorist activity. I am one of many who opposed Section 4 of the Anti-terrorism, Crime and Security Act of 2001, which reintroduced detention without trial into British anti-terrorism legislation, and required the UK to abrogate from Article 5 of the European Convention on Human Rights. The UK government was correct in saying that it involved a very small number being interned, and that technically, as the Home Secretary reminded us, the detainees have the right to go abroad either to their state of origin or to another country that will have them. However, there would be a real danger to the detainees if they were forced to return to their own countries, and it is very difficult to find a third country that would be prepared to grant asylum, given that fact the person has been interned on suspicion of involvement in terrorism. It is true that the detainees do have the right to appeal to an independent tribunal, and access to lawyers, but they are not allowed to see the evidence against them. Surely, a far better solution would be to give the police and security services the resources to monitor the activities of the small number of suspects involved and to use intercepts as evidence in Court. If they then gather sufficient evidence to prove terrorist involvement, they should be afforded the right to a trial under the relevant section of the Terrorism Act 2000 so that they have the opportunity to prove their innocence. This would render the UK's abrogation under Article 5 if the ECHR unnecessary. Similar objections can be raised against the Prevention of Terrorism Act rushed through the UK parliament in 2005: house arrest is, after all, only another form of detention without trial.[42]

Still more challenging for liberal democratic values and institutions are the dilemmas posed by pursuing a political pathway out of terrorism[43] through a peace process. As we have seen in Northern Ireland, this is likely to involve the release of terrorists imprisoned for major crimes, including murder, programmes for the general release of prisoners belonging to the terrorist groups that are party to the Peace Process, and admitting former terrorist leaders into government posts, including ministerial positions. Should any group or party be allowed to benefit from rehabilitation while it is still maintaining its secret army and terrorist weaponry and capability?

It is hardly surprising that these issues are already arising in the Sri Lankan peace process. Peace processes in terrorist conflicts can save hundreds of lives but they require patient diplomacy and careful attention to the security issues and the nurturing of mutual confidence and trust between the leaders and communities previously engaged in violent conflict.

Democratic governments and IGOs clearly need to work together to promote and assist efforts to resolve the bitter, deep-seated conflicts, which have spawned so much violence and terrorism. The Israeli–Palestinian conflict, the Kashmir conflict and the Chechen conflict are all potentially corrigible by political and diplomatic means because they are based on ethno-nationalist disputes about territory and national autonomy.

However, even if some of these long-standing conflicts could be resolved this would not address the New Terrorism of al-Qaeda and its affiliates, which is politically incorrigible because of the nature of the al-Qaeda network's ideology and aims. Al-Qaeda wants nothing less than the reordering of the international system,[44] the expulsion of any Western presence in the Muslim world, the toppling of the current Muslim governments it accuses of collaborating with the US and its allies, and, ultimately the creation of a pan-Islamist caliphate to unite all Muslims.

This 'New Terrorism' undoubtedly constitutes a strategic threat not only to the national security of the US, the UK and other states in the coalition against terrorism, but against the peace and security of the whole international community.[45] Al-Qaeda has shown that it is prepared to kill thousands of civilians without any compunction.[46] Bin Laden's movement has developed a complex network of local and regional affiliates as vehicles for its self-proclaimed holy war. Despite the severe setbacks it has suffered during the War on Terrorism, it is still capable of posing a real threat of terrorist attack against the US and UK homelands and other Western countries. And, as demonstrated in recent attacks in Saudi Arabia, Afghanistan, Pakistan, Morocco, Iraq and Turkey, al-Qaeda is also a major threat to fellow Muslims, many of whom have lost their lives in these outrages. This is a major strategic blunder by al-Qaeda, as Muslim governments and their populations are becoming increasingly aware of this threat and are supporting harder-line policies and measures against the 'New Terrorism'. This is clearly demonstrated in recent responses to terrorism in Indonesia, Morocco, Saudi Arabia and Turkey.

I have deliberately avoided re-entering the debate about the case for and against the invasion of Iraq. I suspect this debate will be a major focus of other contributors. However, I am on record in my testimony to the House of Commons Select Committee on Foreign Affairs (3 June 2003)[47] in warning that the war in Iraq would seriously hamper the campaign against al-Qaeda and deflect attention from the urgent security needs of Mr Karzai's interim government in Afghanistan, where Taliban and al-Qaeda are still trying to regain a foothold in provinces in the East and South of the country.

However, in conclusion, I do wish to emphasise that one of the US government's responses to 9/11, the new National Security Doctrine of Pre-emptive Attack, has not been accorded sufficient critical scrutiny either within the US or internationally. There is a real long-term risk that not only will this doctrine be used by the US to justify future invasions of 'axis of evil' states, but also that the doctrine will be used by other states as a convenient pretext for invading another state. India has already indicated it could apply to its confrontation with Pakistan. China could use it as an excuse for an invasion of Taiwan. What is sauce for the goose can be sauce for the gander.

When the new doctrine was launched in Washington, Henry Kissinger dryly remarked that he did not believe it was in the long-term security interests of the US. It would be a true irony if the War on Terrorism opened that door to much bloodier inter-state wars in which not thousands but hundreds of thousands of civilians and troops could be killed. Let us not forget that, even though Iraq turned out not to have had WMD, some of the possible belligerents in future pre-emptive wars (e.g. North Korea?) do already have nuclear weapons.

Once again terrorism may have become the trigger for escalation to far deadlier mass killing and destruction than has ever been perpetrated by terrorists. We need to strengthen multilateral cooperation to manage major conflicts rather than provoke new wars in order to deal effectively with transnational terrorist threats but also, and most important, to ensure that our responses to terrorism do not destroy the chances of a managed peace.[48]

Notes

1 J.B.S. Hardman, 'Terrorism', in *Encyclopaedia of the Social Sciences*, ed. E.R. Seligman, Vol. 14 (New York: Macmillan, 1934), pp 575–9.
2 Feliks Gross, *The Seizure of Political Power* (New York: Philosophical Library, 1957), and Feliks Gross, 'Political Violence and Terror in 19th and 20th Century Russia and Eastern Europe', in *Assassination and Political Violence*, Vol. 8 of *A Report to the National Commission on the Causes and Prevention of Violence*, ed. J.F. Kirham, S.G. Levy and W.J. Crotty (Washington, DC: US Government Printing Office, 1969), pp. 421–476.
3 J.S. Roucek, 'Sociological Elements of a Theory of Terror and Violence', *American Journal of Economics and Sociology*, 21:2 (April 1962), pp. 165–72. See also J.S. Roucek's interesting entry on IMRO, *Slavonic Encyclopaedia* (New York: Philosophical Library, 1943), pp. 531–532.
4 Thomas P. Thornton, 'Terror as a Weapon of Political Agitation', in *Internal War,* ed. Harry Eckstein (New York: Free Press, 1964), pp. 71–99.
5 Eugene V. Walter, *Terror and Resistance: A Study of Political Violence with Case Studies of some Primitive African Communities* (New York: Oxford University Press, 1969).
6 Tore Bjorgo, *Root Causes of Terrorism* (London: Routledge, 2005). Tore Bjorgo also edited another valuable major contribution by Ehud Sprinzhak, 'Right Wing Terrorism in Comparative Perspective', in *Terror from the Extreme Right* (London: Frank Cass, 1995) pp. 17–43.
7 Professor Laqueur's publications on terrorism include: *Terrorism* (London: Weidenfeld and Nicolson, 1977); Walter Laqueur (ed.), *The Terrorism Reader: A historical anthology* (New York: New American Library, 1978); and *The New Terrorism: Fanaticism and the Arms of Mass Destruction* (New York: Oxford University Press, 1999).
8 Early publications include: Brian M. Jenkins, 'International Terrorism: A New Mode of Conflict', in *International Terrorism and World Security* ed. D. Carlton and C. Schaerf (London: Croon Helm, 1975), pp. 13–49; Brian M. Jenkins, *International Terrorism: Trends and Potentialities*; *A Summary* (Santa Monica, CA: RAND, 1978); and Brian M. Jenkins, *Terrorism in the 1980's* (Santa Monica, CA: RAND, 1980). His recent works include: *Aviation Terrorism and Security* (with Paul Wilkinson) (London: Frank Cass, 1999); *Countering Al Qaeda* (Santa Monica, CA: RAND); and *Deterrence*

and Influence in Counterterrorism (with Paul Davis) (Santa Monica, CA: RAND, 2002).

9 Bruce Hoffman's publications include: Bruce Hoffman, 'Right Wing Terrorism in Europe', *Conflict*, 5:3 (1984), pp. 185–210; Bruce Hoffman, *Recent Trends in Palestinian Terrorism* (Santa Monica, CA: RAND, 1985); Bruce Hoffman *et al.*, *A Reassessment of Potential Adversaries to US Nuclear Programs* (Santa Monica, CA: RAND, 1986); Bruce Hoffman, *Terrorism in the US and the Potential Threat to Nuclear Facilities* (Santa Monica, CA: RAND, 1986); and Bruce Hoffman, *Inside Terrorism* (London, Victor Gollancz, 1998).

10 Martha Crenshaw (formerly Crenshaw Hutchinson) has made a number of major contributions to the terrorism studies literature; for example: 'The Concept of Revolutionary Terrorism', *The Journal of Conflict Resolution*, 16:3 (September 1972), pp. 383–396; Martha Crenshaw, *Revolutionary Terrorism: The FLN in Algeria, 1954–62* (Stanford: Hoover Institution Press, 1978); Martha Crenshaw, 'The Psychology of Political Terrorism', in *Handbook of Political Psychology*, (ed.) M. Hermann (San Francisco: Jossey Bass, 1985); Martha Crenshaw (with M.I. Yildarsky and F. Yoshida), 'Why violence spreads: the contagion of international terrorism', *International Studies Quarterly*, 24:2 (June 1980), pp. 262–298; and Martha Crenshaw (ed.), *Terrorism in Context* (Philadelphia, PA: Pennsylvania State University Press, 1995).

11 David C. Rapoport, *Assassination and Terrorism* (Toronto: Canadian Broadcasting System, 1971); David C. Rapoport and Yonah Alexander (eds), *The Morality of Terrorism: Religious and Secular Justifications* (New York: Pergamon Press, 1982); David C. Rapoport and Yonah Alexander (eds), *The Rationalization of Terrorism* (Frederick, MD: University Publications of America, 1982); and David C. Rapoport, 'Fear and Trembling', *American Political Science Review*, 78 (Sept. 1984), pp. 658–677.

12 Among J. Bowyer Bell's seminal works the best known are: *The Secret Army: The IRA 1916–1970* (Cambridge, MA: MIT Press, 1970, second ed. 1974); *Terror Out of Zion* (New York: St Martin's Press, 1977); 'Trends on Terror: the Analysis of Political Violence', *World Politics*, 29:3 (April 1977), pp. 476–488; and *A Time of Terror: How Democratic Societies Respond to Revolutionary Violence* (New York: Basic Books, 1978).

13 Alex P. Schmid and Albert J Jongman *et al.* produced the most comprehensive and useful guide to terrorism studies: *Political Terrorism: A New Guide to Actors, Authors, Concepts, Data Bases, Theories and Literature* (Amsterdam: North Holland Publishing Co., 1988). The author is pleased to report that a new updated and revised edition of this invaluable reference work will be published soon. Other publications by Alex P. Schmid include: 'Terrorism and the Media: The Ethics of Publicity',*Terrorism and Political Violence*, 1:4 (Autumn 1989); (with Janny deGraaf) *Violence as Communication, Insurgent Terrorism and the Western News Media* (London: Sage, 1992).

14 See Note 13 above.

15 Ariel Merari's published work includes: Ariel Merari (ed.), *On Terrorism and Combating Terrorism* (Fredrick, MD, University Publications of America, 1985); (with A. Kurz) Ariel Merari, *ASALA: Irrational Terror or Political Instrument?* (Boulder, CO: Westview Press, 1985); and Ariel Merari and S. Elad, *The International Dimension of Palestinian Terrorism* (Boulder, CO: Westview Press, 1987).

16 Fernando Reinares (ed.), *Terrorismo y Sociedad Democratia* (Madrid, Akal, 1982); Fernando Reinares, 'The Political Conditioning of Collective Violence: Regime Change and Insurgent Terrorism in Spain', *Research on Democracy and Society*, 3 (1996), JAI Press, pp. 297–326.

17 David Charters (ed.), *Democratic Reponses to International Terrorism* (New York: Transaction Publications, 1990).

18 Tore Bjorgo (ed.), *Terror from the Extreme Right* (London: Frank Cass, 1995); Tore Bjorgo (with R. Witte) (eds), *Racist Violence in Europe* (Basingstoke: Macmillan, 1993). Ehud Sprinzak's classic article 'Right-Wing Terrorism in Comparative Perspective' appeared in Tore Bjorgo (ed.), *Terror from the Extreme Right* (see above). Sprinzak also produced a renowned study on *The Ascendance of Israel's Radical Right* (New York: Oxford University Press, 1991); and a provocative article which caused many terrorism studies specialists to revisit the WMD issue: 'The Great Superterrorism Scare', *Foreign Policy,* 112 (Autumn 1998), pp. 110–124.

19 One of the major contributions made by a small group of social scientists and historians over recent years is to deepen our knowledge and understanding of groups that claim to commit extreme violence and terror in the name of religion. My colleague, Magnus Ranstorp, carried out some pioneering work in this field in his study of *Hizb'allah in Lebanon: the Politics of the Western Hostage Crisis* (Basingstoke: Macmillan, 1997). See also his 'Terrorism in the Name of Religion', *Journal of International Affairs,* 50 (Summer 1996), pp. 41–62; Mark Juergesmeyer, *Terror in the Mind of God: The Global Rise of Religious Violence* (Berkeley and Los Angeles: University of California Press, 2000); and Olivier Roy, *Globalised Islam* (London: Hurst and Co., 2004), first published in 2002 as *L'islam Mondialisé* (Paris: Editions de Seuil).

20 See Leonard Shapiro, (*Totalitarianism* (London, Pall Mall Press, 1972).

21 Robert Conquest, *The Great Terror: Stalin's Purge of the Thirties* (London: Macmillan, 1968).

22 Richard Clutterbuck, *Kidnap and Ransom: The Response* (London: Faber, 1978); Richard Clutterbuck, *The Media and Political Violence* (London: Mamillan, 1981); Richard Clutterbuck, *Terrorism, Drugs and Crime in Europe after 1992* (London: Routledge, 1990); and Richard Clutterbuck, *Terrorism and Guerrilla Warfare* (London: Routledge, 1990).

23 Steve Bruce, *The Red Hand: Protestant Paramilitaries in Northern Ireland* (Oxford: Oxford University Press, 1992); and 'The State and Pro-State Terrorism in Northern Ireland', in *The State*, ed. R. English and C. Townshend (London: Routledge, 1999).

24 D.G.Boyce, *Nationalism in Ireland* (London: Routledge, 1991).

25 M.L.R. Smith, *Fighting for Ireland: The Military Strategy of the Irish Republican Movement* (London: Routledge, 1995).

26 Caroline Kennedy-Pipe, *The Origins of the Present Troubles in Northern Ireland* (Harlow: Longman, 1997).

27 David McKittrick, Seamus Kelters, Brian Feeney and Chris Thornton, *Lost Lives: The stories of the men and women and children who died as a result of the Northern Ireland troubles* (Edinburgh: Mainstream Publishing, 1999). This is an essential reference work for all students of the Northern Ireland conflict.

28 Robert McKee, *The Green Flag* (London, Melbourne and New York: Quartet Books, 1976).

29 Clive Walker, *The Blackstone Guide to the Anti-Terrorism Legislation* (Oxford: Oxford University Press, 2002).

30 Paul Rogers, *A War on Terror: Afghanistan and After* (London: Pluto Press, 2004).

31 For further information see CSTPV's website at http://www.st-andrews.ac.uk/intrel/research/cstpv

32 *Terrorism and Political Violence* is now published quarterly by Routledge. From its foundation in 1989 until 2004 it was published by Frank Cass.

33 *Studies in Conflict and Terrorism* is published by Taylor and Francis and is bimonthly.

34 Hedley Bull, 'Civil Violence and International Order', *Adelphi Papers* No. 83, Part II (London: International Institute for Strategic Studies, 1971), pp. 27–36.

35 Grants for research on terrorism were awarded by the UK's Economic and Social Research Council to a combined St Andrews, CSTPV and Southampton University, Mountbatten Institute team, to Kings College, London, and to Lancaster University.

36 For discussions of the roles of technology in preventing, deterring and combating terrorism see the contributions to Paul Wilkinson (ed.), *Technology and Terrorism* (London: Frank Cass, 1993). However, we should also be giving close attention to the major technological vulnerabilities that currently exist in our national civil infrastructures, for example, in our energy sectors. See, for example, US–Canada Power Station Outrage Task Force, *Interim Report: Cause of the August 14th Blackout in the United States and Canada* (Washington, DC: Government Printing Office, November 2003).

37 For an interesting analysis of some of the key linkages see Mariam Abou Zahab and Olivier Roy, *Islamic Networks: The Pakistan–Afghan Connection* (London: Hurst, 2004); and Marc Sageman, *Understanding Terror Networks* (Philadelphia: University of Pennsylvania Press, 2004).

38 See, for example, Paul Wilkinson, *Terrorism and the Liberal State* (revised and enlarged edition) (Basingstoke: Macmillan and New York: New York University Press, 1985); Paul Wilkinson (ed.), *Technology and Terrorism* (London: Frank Cass, 1993); Paul Wilkinson and Brian Jenkins (eds), *Aviation Terrorism and Security* (London: Frank Cass, 1999); Paul Wilkinson, *Inquiry into Legislation Against Terrorism*, Vol. 2 of the Report by Lord Lloyd of Berwick (London: Stationery Office, Oct. 1996, cmd 3420); and Paul Wilkinson, *Terrorism Versus Democracy: The Liberal State Response* (London: Frank Cass, 2000).

39 Report of the Counter-Terrorism Committee (CTC) on its revitalization S/2004/124), http://www.un.org/Docs/sc/committees/1373/cted.html

40 This key issue is discussed in Michael Ignatieff's lucid and courageous *The Lesser Evil: Political Ethics in an Age of Terror* (Edinburgh: Edinburgh University Press, 2004), especially in Chapters 2 and 6.

41 Paul Wilkinson and A.M. Stewart (eds), *Contemporary Research on Terrorism* (Aberdeen: Aberdeen University Press, 1987) pp. XVII–XX.

42 A Council of Europe draft report by its Commissioner for Human Rights, Alvaro Gil-Robles, in Summer 2005, expressed serious concerns about the terrorism control orders, introduced by the UK government in its Prevention of Terrorism Act immediately prior to the 2005 British general election. The report claimed that the control orders violated the right to liberty and the right to fair trial.

43 I discuss some of the problems and issues involved in my *Terrorism Versus Democracy* (London: Frank class, 2000) Chapter 4.

44 See Olivier Roy, *Globalised Islam* (London: Hurst, 2004) for an analysis of al-Qaeda's aims and ideology.

45 As UN Security Council Resolution 1368 passed on September 12, 2001 stated in its opening paragraph: "[The Council] unequivocally condemns in the strongest terms the horrifying terrorist attacks which took place on September 11, 2001 in New York, Washington (DC) and Pennsylvania and regards such acts, like any act of international terrorism, as a threat to international peace and security".

46 In their notorious Fatwa urging fellow Muslims to join a world jihad, Bin Laden and his co-signatories explicitly call upon all Muslims to kill Americans and their allies, including civilians, whenever and wherever possible. Al-Qaeda is thus committed to mass killing of its professed 'enemies'.

47 See House of Commons Foreign Affairs Committee, *Foreign Policy Aspects of the War Against Terrorism* (London: The Stationery Office Ltd, 2003, HC405), pp. Ev.96–Ev.111.

48 For those readers who are interested in a detailed and comprehensive account of
more recent research trends in terrorism studies, including the social psychological
and criminological aspects, I strongly commend Andrew Silke's recent edited volume
Research on Terrorism: Trends, Achievements and Failures (London: Frank Cass,
2004). Chapter 10, by Andrew Silke, is entitled 'The Road Less Travelled ...' (the
line is from Robert Frost's famous poem 'The Road Not Taken') and is particularly
valuable in identifying areas of the subject that have been almost entirely neglected
by scholars, and the themes that have received disproportionate attention. Let us
encourage our colleagues and the research funding bodies to take the roads 'less
travelled'. For the reflections of the most distinguished historian of terrorism on the
state of knowledge of the subject and the prospects of future terrorism in the twenty-
first century, see: Walter Laqueur, *No End to War: Terrorism in the Twenty-First
Century* (New York/London: Continuum, 2004).

INDEX

xenophobia 39, 41, 170

Yemen bombings (1992) 84
Yom Kippur war 202
Yonas, Gerry 295
Youssef, Ramzi 321

al-Zarqawi, Abu Musab 140, 144
al-Zawahiri, Ayman 99, 129, 133, 136,
    139–44
al-Zayyat, Montasser 9
Zeidan, David 145
Zeitgeist 66
Zernike, Kate 220